The New Global Frontier

The New Global Frontier

Urbanization, Poverty and Environment in the 21st Century

Edited by
George Martine,
Gordon McGranahan,
Mark Montgomery and
Rogelio Fernández-Castilla

earthscan
publishing for a sustainable future

London • Sterling, VA

First published by Earthscan in the UK and USA in 2008

ISBN: 978-1-84407-559-1   hardback
         978-1-84407-560-7   paperback

Typeset by JS Typesetting Ltd, Porthcawl, Mid Glamorgan
Printed and bound in the UK by MPG Books, Bodmin
Cover design by Susanne Harris

For a full list of publications please contact:

Earthscan
Dunstan House
14a St Cross Street
London EC1N 8XA, UK
Tel:+44 (0)20 7841 1930
Fax: +44 (0)20 7242 1474
Email: earthinfo@earthscan.co.uk
Web: **www.earthscan.co.uk**

22883 Quicksilver Drive, Sterling, VA 20166-2012, USA

Earthscan publishes in association with the International Institute
for Environment and Development

A catalogue record for this book is available from the British Library

Library of Congress Cataloging-in-Publication Data

The new global frontier : urbanization, poverty and environment in the 21st century /
edited by George Martine ... [et al.].
     p. cm.
   Includes bibliographical references.
   ISBN 978-1-84407-559-1 (hardback) – ISBN 978-1-84407-560-7 (pbk.) 1.
Urbanization–Economic aspects. 2. Urbanization–History–21st century. 3. Cities
and towns–Growth–History–21st century. 4. Urban economics–History–21st
century. 5. Poverty–History–21 century. I. Martine, George.
   HT371.N475 2008
   307.7609172'401--dc22
                              2008016058

The paper used for this book is FSC-certified.
FSC (the Forest Stewardship Council) is an
international network to promote responsible
management of the world's forests.

Mixed Sources

Product group from well-managed
forests and other controlled sources
www.fsc.org Cert no. SA-COC-1565
© 1996 Forest Stewardship Council

Contents

PART V – REGIONAL PATTERNS OF URBANIZATION AND LINKAGES TO DEVELOPMENT

List of Boxes, Figures and Tables

BOXES

FIGURES

TABLES

Acronyms and abbreviations

APHRC	African Population and Health Research Center
AUWSP	Accelerated Urban Water Supply Programme (India)
BNH	Banco Nacional de Habitacao
BSUP	Basic Services to Urban Poor (JNNURM, India)
CEP	Centre for Economic Performance (LSE)
CIAT	International Center for Tropical Agriculture
CIESIN	Center for International Earth Science Information Network
CODI	Community Organizations Development Institute (Thailand)
COHRE	Centre for Housing Rights and Evictions
CSH	Centre de Sciences Humaines (India)
DHS	Demographic and Health Survey
DSS	demographic surveillance systems
ECLAC	Economic Commission for Latin America and the Caribbean
ESCAP	Economic and Social Commission for Asia and the Pacific
EPZ	export processing zone
FAO	Food and Agricultural Organization of the United Nation
FDI	foreign development investment
GDP	gross domestic product
GEC	global environmental change
GIS	geographic information system
GRUMP	Global Rural–Urban Mapping Project
GTZ	German Technical Cooperation
IDSMT	Integrated Development of Small and Medium Towns (India)
IFPRI	International Food Policy Research Institute
IIED	International Institute for Environment and Development
ILO	International Labour Organization
INEC	Instituto Nacional de Estadística y Censos (Ecuador)
IPPF	International Planned Parenthood Federation
IT	information technology
JNNURM	Jawaharlal Nehru National Urban Renewal Mission (India)
LAC	Latin America and the Caribbean

LDC	least developed country
LDR	less developed region
LECZ	low elevation coastal zone
LSE	London School of Economics
MDG	Millennium Development Goal
MDR	more developed region
MICS	Multiple Indicator Cluster Survey
MIDUVI	Ministerio de Desarrollo Urbano y Vivienda (Ecuador)
MIPAA	Madrid International Plan of Action on Ageing
MPCE	monthly per capita expenditure
MSF	Médecins san Frontières
NGO	non-governmental organization
NOAA	National Oceanic Atmospheric Administration
NIUA	National Institute of Urban Affairs (India)
NRCIM	National Research Council and Institute of Medicine
NSSO	National Sample Survey Organization (Government of India)
OAF	Fraternal Assistance Organization
OECD	Organisation for Economic Co-operation and Development
OUP	organization of the urban poor
PEVODE	People's Voice for Development (Tanzania)
SDI	socioeconomic and demographic information
SDI	Shack/Slum Dwellers International
SEDAC	Socioeconomic Data and Applications Center (GRUMP)
SERFHAU	Servico Federal de Habitacao e Urbanismo
SEWA	Self-Employed Women's Association (India)
SRTM	Shuttle Radar Topography Mission
SSA	sub-Saharan Africa
SUDENE	Superintendencia do Desenvolvimento do Nordeste
TSP	total suspended particulates
TVE	township and village enterprise
UHI	urban heat island
UN	United Nations
UNDP	United Nations Development Programme
UNFPA	United Nations Population Fund
UN-Habitat	United Nations Human Settlements Programme
UNRISD	United Nations Research Institute for Social Development
WCRC	Wattville Concerned Residents Committee (South Africa)
WFS	World Fertility Survey
WIDER	World Institute for Development Economics Research
WIEGO	Women in Informal Employment: Globalizing and Organizing
WPR	workforce participation rate

Introduction

The New Global Frontier: Cities, Poverty and Environment in the 21st Century

THE EMERGING PROFILE OF THE NEW FRONTIER

The cities and towns[1] of Africa, Asia and Latin America are central to the demographic, economic and environmental challenges of the 21st century. The urban centres of low- and middle-income countries represent the new global frontier. Virtually all of the world's population growth is projected to occur in these cities and towns, and it is likely that they will account for most of the economic growth as well. Currently, more than 3.3 billion people live in towns and cities; the number is expected to rise to some 5 billion by 2030. Over 80 per cent of this growth will accrue to Asia and Africa, with most of the rest to Latin America.[2]

The urban transformation can be viewed as a set of momentous demographic and economic developments that present policymakers with opportunities as well as challenges. Cities are the locus of most economic expansion, and exemplify to rural and urban residents alike the hope of social advancement; they also concentrate poverty and environmental degradation. Massive urban growth in developing areas during coming decades may bring hope and wellbeing to millions of people, or it may exacerbate suffering and misery for the majority of new urbanites. The welfare of billions of people depends directly on how the world prepares for this inevitable growth in developing areas.

The quality of governance and planning in these urban areas will thus have both local and global significance. The residents of cities that are economically unsuccessful are likely to be exposed to environmental health burdens; even cities that are successful in narrowly economic terms may, if they are not properly governed, do global environmental damage (as currently affluent urban centres already do).

While accommodating urbanization and urban growth will no doubt be difficult, efforts to prevent these developments are likely to make matters worse, and not just for the urban-dwellers. For reasons outlined in this book, the fundamental challenge is not to control the rate of urbanization, but rather to achieve a pace and pattern of urban development that is beneficial. The benefits must reach the urban poor as well as the elites, and must also be extended to both rural-dwellers and future generations. This challenge demands a proactive approach to urban planning which considers demographic and environmental futures while responding to current priorities. Such an approach demands, in turn, a sound understanding of urban development processes, locally, nationally and even internationally. This book is an attempt to contribute to this understanding.

Although it has not gone unnoticed, the urban transformation has yet to receive anything close to the attention it deserves. Of course, the *current* plight of cities and their slums, as well as the purported deterioration in their social and environmental conditions, are frequently highlighted. On occasion, at least, the productive potential of cities in the context of globalization has also been recognized. Yet the enormity of the impacts expected from urban growth in the developing world has not yet sunk in. Even less recognized is the fact that the future of developing-world cities – and, therefore, the very future of humanity – depends to a large extent on decisions that are taken *now* with respect to the organization of upcoming city growth.

This book proposes to reflect on several key strands in the larger story of 21st-century urbanization, with the aim of getting a better grasp on some of the actions that could be taken to make this process a more positive force for human development. The topics covered range over a wide spectrum of social, demographic, economic and environmental concerns. A recurring point is that, with a little support in the form of proper policies, urbanization can help to unshackle the bonds of perennial poverty, give people a better chance to live fuller lives and even help to deflect environmental damage. It is already a well-documented fact that, although the poor have been urbanizing even more rapidly than the population as a whole, the process of urbanization has helped to reduce overall poverty. But this record could improve significantly if better policies and proactive approaches were to replace the increasingly negative stances of policymakers to the urban transformation.

THE POTENTIALITIES OF THE NEW GLOBAL FRONTIER

Many policymakers and scholars still view urbanization as harmful and hope to somehow retard or even reverse it. To them, the concentration of poverty, slum growth, environmental problems and manifold social disturbances in cities paint a menacing picture. No one doubts that, in many countries, rural development priorities – which can play a vital role in reducing poverty and protecting the environment – do not receive the economic resources they deserve. The expert view, however, is all but unanimous: urbanization is not only inevitable but necessary if poverty is to be reduced in the developing world and global sustainability enhanced.

Cities will inevitably have an increasingly critical role in future development scenarios. Urbanization can be critical for economic growth, for reduction of poverty, for stabilization of population growth and for long-term sustainability. But realizing this potential will require a different mindset on the part of policymakers, a proactive approach and better governance than has been observed up to now.

Urban development is essential – if not in itself sufficient – for economic and social development. No country has ever achieved significant economic growth in the modern age by retaining its population in rural areas. Most increments in national economic activity already take place in urban areas. These cities and towns account for a growing share of national economic production because of their advantages in terms of proximity, concentration and scale. In the context of globalized economic competition, these advantages can be heightened.

Proximity and concentration make it easier and cheaper for cities to provide their citizens with basic social services, infrastructure and amenities. The higher intensity of economic activity in cities can foster employment and income growth, the starting points for improved social welfare. These potential benefits are often only partly realized, however, with urbanization being accompanied by unnecessary increases in inequality and fast-growing slums. Both urban and rural poor often lose out to urban elites. They also lose out when the residents of low-income urban neighbourhoods are prevented from securing the advantages of their urban location.

For better or worse, urbanization also constitutes a prime mover of cultural change, with an enormous impact on ideas, values, beliefs and social organization. For migrants, cities present new opportunities for access to diverse resources and knowledge in a wide range of areas. Cities allow greater flexibility in the application of social norms that traditionally impinge on freedom of choice, especially for women. They have the potential to provide more opportunities for social and political participation and new roads to empowerment, as evident in the rise of women's movements, youth groups, community associations and organizations of the urban poor in developing-world cities. Cities are also at the heart of local, national and global environmental change. While it is true that cities currently concentrate and exemplify the environmental problems produced by conventional development strategies, they are also critical elements in the solutions. Demographic concentration is likely to be essential to the preservation of the world's remaining rural ecosystems. The potential value of urbanization for long-term environmental sustainability is thus being increasingly recognized. Settlement patterns, geographic and ecological location, density, and urban management practices can all have an extraordinary impact on how urban growth affects the environment.

The demographic importance of cities is not limited only to their size and growth but also to their role in the future evolution of fertility rates and thus of global population growth trends. In almost all developing countries, the fertility transition occurs first and proceeds fastest in cities. Cities offer few incentives for large families. Moreover, access to health services, including reproductive health facilities, is typically better than in rural areas. Consequently, the pace of urbanization can be expected to have an important impact on the trajectory and timing of population stabilization in developing countries.

In short, social, economic, demographic and environmental outcomes for the future will hinge largely on what happens in the cities and towns of today's poor countries. Upcoming urban growth could, under the right policy framework, generate progress in all these domains. A new vision and improved governance, based on a better understanding of urban growth processes; better information; respect for the poor's right to the city; and enhanced participation by all sectors of urban society would help upcoming urban growth play multiple positive roles in improving people's lives.

FACTS, FALLACIES AND POLICIES ON URBAN GROWTH

To date, only a few countries and international agencies seem to have recognized the potential benefits of the new urban frontier. Progress has been hampered by the fact that urbanization and urban growth generally get bad press and are often viewed negatively by policymakers. Cities in developing countries tend to be viewed as unmanageable social cauldrons that concentrate not only people but also poverty and social disorganization. Much of this perception stems from misconceptions that need to be set right before more effective policies can be put into place. A brief review of key trends should help correct these misunderstandings and better set the stage for a fresh look at the new frontier.

First fallacy: All developing countries and regions are going through the same urban transition

Actually, there are large differences in the levels and patterns of urbanization between, and within, countries conventionally labelled as 'developing'. As seen in Figure I.1, the path of today's developing countries to urbanization and urban growth not only differs significantly from the past patterns of developed countries, but also varies considerably by region. For instance, most Latin American countries are well advanced in their urban transition; thus much could be learned from their experiences, both positive and negative. By contrast, several large, populous countries in Africa and Asia still have a predominantly rural base.

Among the three major developing regions, Latin America already has high levels of urbanization. Asia and Africa have initiated their urban transition at a much later date, with much larger population bases than was the case in Latin America. Consequently, as depicted in Figure I.2, Asia and Africa are projected to experience by far the largest expansion of absolute urban population. Between

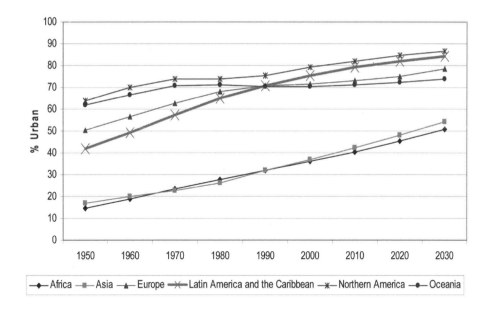

Figure I.1 *Percentage of the total population living in urban areas,
by region, 1950–2030*

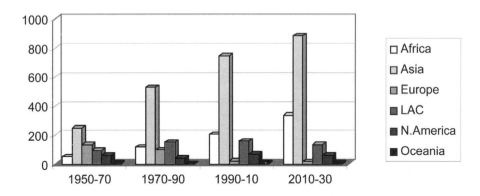

Figure I.2 *Absolute increases in urban population by world regions,
selected periods (000s)*

Source: United Nations, 2006 (see note 2).

2000 and 2030, Asia's urban population will nearly double – from 1.36 to 2.64
billion. Africa's is projected to more than double from 294 to 742 million, though
because of poor data, difficulties in taking account of the AIDS pandemic and
economic instability, this projection is particularly uncertain. Latin America's urban
population is expected to grow from 394 to 609 million. By 2030, Africa and Asia
will include almost seven out of every ten urban inhabitants in the world.

Second fallacy: Most urban growth is occurring in mega-cities

Much public attention in recent years has been centred on mega-cities, defined as urban centres with populations of 10 million or more. Actually, there are only 22 cities of that size today; the majority of them are dynamic and functional centres. Moreover, some of these larger cities have already shown a propensity for slower population growth. Still more important, cities of this size are *not* home to a large proportion of the world's urban population, nor are they expected to absorb a significant proportion of urban growth in the foreseeable future.

As shown in Figure I.3, smaller urban centres (those with less than 500,000 inhabitants) still contain more than half of the world's urban population. Moreover, they will continue to absorb about half of urban growth. Mega-cities, by contrast, account for only nine per cent of the current urban population, and this is not expected to change drastically in the future.

This distribution is of considerable importance for shaping policy, and a much closer look needs to be taken at the possibilities and difficulties of smaller urban centres. The good news is that smaller cities are likely to have more flexibility in terms of the direction of territorial expansion and, to some extent, the autonomy of decision-making. And in some cases they may be able to attract investments within the contexts of decentralization and globalized economic competition. The bad news is that smaller urban centres generally have more unaddressed problems in terms of adequate housing, piped water, sanitation, waste disposal and other services. Moreover, smaller urban centres tend to have fewer human, financial and

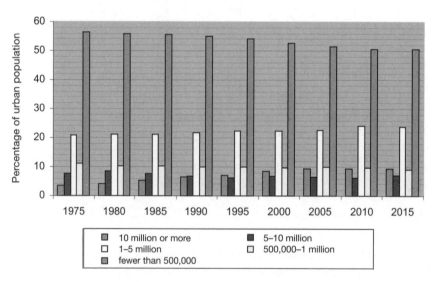

Figure I.3 *Percentage of world urban population by size class of settlement, 1975–2015*

Source: United Nations, 2006 (see note 2).

technical resources at their disposal. The combination of these characteristics makes them prime candidates for technical and financial support.

Third fallacy: The poor are a marginal minority in urban centres

The relationship between poverty and urbanization is complex and often misunderstood, which tends to perpetuate inadequate policies. On average, the residents of urban areas generally enjoy social and economic advantages relative to rural inhabitants. This disparity sometimes influences policymakers to favour solutions that try to resolve poverty in rural areas, while also attempting to prevent rural–urban migration, in the hope that this will prevent the transfer of poverty to cities. Yet the paradox is that, while urban poverty is growing and already much larger than generally depicted in global figures, the solutions to poverty, under good governance and proper policies, are more likely to be found in the economic dynamism of the cities.

It is important to look beneath the urban and rural averages in formulating pro-poor policies and programmes. Urban settlements in low- and middle-income countries almost invariably contain large pockets of poverty, and vulnerability can increase with rapid urban growth. The stark realities of slum life defy description and statistics. Large sections of the urban population in developing countries are malnourished, have below poverty-line incomes and face high infant and child mortality rates and large preventable disease and injury burdens. Global assessments tend to underestimate urban poverty by failing to account for the higher monetary cost of non-food needs. Moreover, poverty is growing rapidly in urban areas while decreasing in absolute terms in rural areas, partly because population growth in rural areas is slow or nil due to out-migration.

Urban policies therefore need to recognize the fact that the poor make up a large portion, and sometimes a majority, of the urban population in developing countries. According to UN-Habitat,[3] developing-world slums contain some 41 per cent of the urban population of these countries. About 72 per cent of urban populations in sub-Saharan Africa and 57 per cent of those in Southern Asia are slum-dwellers (UN-Habitat, 2006, p16). Furthermore, the percentage of slum-dwellers is largest in some of the subregions that are expected to experience the most substantial absolute urban growth over the coming decades.

It is of some relevance for policymakers that the poor make up an even larger component of *new* urban growth. Urban centres grow primarily through natural increase and through migration, and the poor tend to predominate in both these types of growth. Even though rural migrants generally benefit from the move, achieving higher standards of living than the rural average, many remain poor. Within urban areas, poor groups have higher rates of natural increase than the rest of the population.

Despite their numbers, poor people are often invisible to policymakers or are viewed by others as a marginal and temporary component of city life. Their needs are rarely prioritized in urban planning – which tends to be centred on making the city more functional for economic activity and for the needs of the middle and upper classes – and they fall through the cracks of formal real-estate markets. As a consequence, the poor often end up living on land that nobody else wants because it is too far from employment and services, too steep, too dangerous, too toxic, too ecologically vulnerable, or otherwise unacceptable for other uses.

This neglect of the needs of the poor is at the root of the appalling housing situations faced by slum-dwellers throughout the developing world. Shelter deprivation, lack of water and lack of sanitation all have important implications for people's lives. Lack of a decent shelter makes it much more difficult for poor people to take advantage of what the city has to offer. The neglect of the poor also makes it more difficult for the city to compete for productive investments, to generate a tax base, to create jobs and income, and, thus, to improve the overall quality of life.

Fourth fallacy: The poor are a drain on the urban economy

This commonly held view reflects a lack of understanding of the role that the urban 'informal' sector plays in urban and national economic growth. It is certainly the case that many of the urban poor work in informal activities. But in today's world, this sector is critical to the economy of developing countries – much of it is competitive and dynamic, well integrated into the urban and even the global economies. Informal activities can account for as much as two-thirds of urban employment in some countries and are a main source of employment and income for poor urban women.

However, a major consideration is that rural areas generally present even *fewer* options for gainful employment and for fulfilling minimal socioeconomic aspirations. Urban centres are more dynamic in generating economic activity and income. They inevitably have advantages of scale and proximity in terms of providing people with infrastructure and services.

Since the needs of the poor are not effectively addressed by urban administrations in poor countries, providing services for them has not generally strained budgets as much as attending to the needs of the better-off population. The fact that urban poverty is more visible and more politically volatile seems to be the primary implicit rationale for keeping people out of the cities. Unfortunately, such attitudes also lead to poor governance and to the failure to capitalize on the potential advantages that cities have to offer. Ultimately, treating 'rural' and 'urban' poverty as somehow separate is a short-sighted view of the problem. Successful urban development stimulates rural development and vice versa.

Fifth fallacy: Urbanization leads to environmental degradation

Economic and population growth create environmental pressures, not just in the locations where they occur but often in distant parts of the world. Since urbanization concentrates both people and economic activities, it is not surprising that it often gets blamed for creating these environmental pressures and the resulting degradation. Paradoxically, however, by concentrating these activities, urbanization often creates opportunities for reducing environmental pressures. Moreover, the local environmental health hazards associated with inadequate water and sanitation can be addressed more efficiently in urban areas due to returns to scale.

Transportation is one of the major sources of environmental burdens, and while urban settlements are transport hubs, urban clustering actually reflects the efforts of people and enterprises to reduce their need for transport. If people and enterprises were forced to stay in rural areas, then, for them to succeed economically, they would be likely to require more transportation than their urban counterparts. Well-planned urban settlement can have much lower built-over land requirements than rural alternatives, and compact urban development is less land-intensive than urban sprawl. Furthermore, concentrating environmentally harmful activities makes them not only more evident, but easier to control. Thus, while China's past policy of promoting 'town and village enterprises' had many successes, it was well known for creating severe environmental problems.

This is not to say that affluent urban centres are less of a threat to the global environment than are poor rural villages. On the contrary, while the living environment of affluent urbanites is typically far healthier than that of poor rural-dwellers, their 'ecological footprint' per capita is far greater. The fallacy is that it is urbanization itself that creates these environmental burdens. Indeed, where urban development is well managed, urbanization can help cushion the environmental impacts of economic growth.

In considering the alternatives to urbanization, it is also important to reflect on how these alternatives are to be achieved. It is all very well to posit an alternative where fewer people leave their rural homes and instead try to achieve their ambitions in rural areas. But how would this be accomplished? This leads to the last, and in some ways most fundamental fallacy.

Sixth fallacy: Governments should try to control rural–urban migration

The fact that urban poverty is readily visible to policymakers, some of whom view it as politically explosive, has in many countries led to anti-urban attitudes and policies.

It may seem sensible to suppress rural–urban migration to a level consistent with the availability of urban jobs and services. But on closer examination, the view that rural–urban migration is a principal cause of urban poverty proves to be misguided. Indeed, measures to curb urbanization can make both rural and urban poverty worse. Because rural areas generally present even *fewer* options for gainful employment and for fulfilling minimal socioeconomic aspirations, mobility is a strategy that households and individuals adopt to improve their lives and to reduce risk and vulnerability. Facilitating urbanization and increasing interaction between rural and urban areas, rather than trying to prevent or ignore it, can stimulate both rural and urban development. Ultimately, treating 'rural' and 'urban' poverty as somehow separate is a short-sighted view of the problem. Successful urban development and rural development are mutually beneficial.

Moreover, the implicit assumption that most governments have suitable policy tools for implementing planned changes in migratory flows is wrong. Policies that attempt to control migration flows directly are almost invariably punitive and economically costly. Policies that influence migration indirectly are almost invariably better if justified in terms other than the size of the impact on migration.

The best-known policies that have successfully controlled rural–urban migration have had to be very harsh. Many colonial policies limited the rights of rural-dwellers to come to urban areas, leading to a burst of migration in the wake of independence. In centrally planned regimes, rural–urban migration was often controlled tightly – as with the *Hukou* (household registration) system in China – but these controls have proved far harder to maintain with the loosening of markets. Apartheid South Africa instituted strict controls, but, again, these were dismantled with the decline of the authoritarian regime. In effect, measures to control internal migration have to be harsh when the migrants perceive clearly that they would benefit substantially from a move.

It is sometimes argued that a better way to control rural–urban migration is to invest in rural areas. However, even when it is sorely needed, rural investment does not necessarily reduce rural–urban migration – particularly if poverty is inhibiting people from migrating, as is often the case, or if the rural investment displaces rural-dwellers, as is also often the case. More important, the suitability of rural investment cannot be judged on the basis of its effects on migration, and to do so would be bad economics.

In any case, in demographic terms, the main cause of urban growth in most countries is not rural–urban migration but natural increase: the difference between births and deaths. Overall, some 60 per cent of urban growth is due to natural increase, with rural–urban migration and reclassification accounting for the remainder. As urbanization advances, the contribution of natural increase eventually becomes greater – even after factoring in the usual decline in fertility that accompanies urbanization. For instance, the current contribution of natural increase to city growth in the Latin American and Caribbean region is estimated to be 65 per cent, despite the significant reduction in urban fertility.

In situations where decision-makers are legitimately concerned with the rapid pace of urban growth, it may well make sense to assist women who want to lower their fertility – through social development, the empowerment of women and better access to health services, including reproductive health services. It is unlikely to make sense to try to prevent people from moving to urban areas.

ORGANIZATION OF THIS VOLUME

This book is divided into five parts, each examining a particular aspect of the urban challenge and containing between three and six chapters. The first part reviews the demographics of the urban transition and the importance of rural–urban relations. The next two parts focus on two of the major urban challenges of the 21st century: eliminating poverty and achieving environmental sustainability. These challenges must be met in changing demographic and social circumstances, and the fourth part considers several of the most significant of these changes. The challenges also vary across the world, and the final part explores the regional patterns of urbanization in parts of Africa, Asia and Latin America.

Each of these five topics is briefly summarized below. More detailed summaries, describing the content of individual chapters, are provided as introductions to each part.

Urban transitions

Although the demographics of the transition from rural to urban are comparatively well documented, there remain both real uncertainties and misconceptions. The three chapters of this part challenge the misconceptions and explore the uncertainties. The misconceptions range from the view that urban growth is predominantly the result of migration and is concentrated in mega-cities to the view that excessive rural–urban migration predominates in the emergence of slums and that the policy challenge is to reduce this migration. Uncertainties arise from the still crude nature of most spatial information and the enormous variety of local conditions and changes over time. The state of play is changing rapidly, however, and the coming decades are likely to see major advances in our understanding of urban transitions.

Shelter and urban poverty

Soon after the start of the 21st century, the world's urban population outnumbered its rural population. Over the course of the next few decades, the urban poor are likely to outnumber the rural poor. The pace of urbanization is likely to depend in large part on rates of economic growth and where this growth is concentrated.

However, the scale of urban and even world poverty will depend heavily on urban policies and development strategies. The four chapters in this part explore the experiences of the past and draw lessons for the future. While there have been many failed attempts to address urban shelter and poverty problems, there have also been notable successes. Special attention is paid to relations between organizations of the urban poor and their local governments, and to proactive planning for urban growth and expansion. If successful approaches to both of these can be combined effectively, the possibilities for addressing urban poverty in the 21st century will be greatly enhanced.

Urban growth and its challenge for sustainability

Urbanization is not in itself bad for the environment, and indeed provides many opportunities for improving people's living environments, reducing pressures on local ecosystems and even reducing global environmental burdens. Rapid and undirected urban growth does pose major environmental challenges, however, and these challenges are not being met. Instead, there has been an overly narrow focus on economic growth, and the positive environmental potential of urbanization is not being exploited. The chapters in this section both set out the challenges and examine different ways of addressing them. New ways of conceptualizing the relationship between urban development and the environment are described. Old debates, such as that surrounding urban sprawl, are re-examined. New threats, such as those from sea-level rise and more severe storms, are assessed. While there is still a long way to go in our understanding of urban growth and its challenge for environmental sustainability, these chapters make it clear that this is no excuse for inaction.

The changing face of urban demography and its potentialities

Ongoing rapid changes in fertility patterns, age composition and migratory behaviour in developing countries create a fast-changing panorama of opportunities and challenges in urban areas. A key consideration that is finally receiving its due in the literature, and that is explored herein, is that urbanization is, in itself, a prime factor in poverty reduction. Changing urban dynamics also present new options for enhancing women's and youths' empowerment, addressing the issues of ageing and confronting the AIDS epidemic. However, as the several chapters in this part make clear, policymaking will have to be refocused if developing countries are to take advantage of these potential benefits. Moreover, the importance of different community associations and social movements, including women's and youth groups, means that these will have to be given a larger role in decisions that affect them. It is also evident that making available reliable and updated information to local communities, to planners and to the media can help materialize the urban advantages by fostering the open discussion of strategies leading to more focused policies and more effective programmes.

Regional patterns of urbanization and linkages to development

There is enormous variation around the world in the patterns of urbanization and their linkages to development. Perhaps surprisingly, there is a large regional component to this variation. Within what is often termed the 'South', Latin American countries tend to be largely urban already; Asian countries are more likely to be rapidly both urbanizing and growing economically; sub-Saharan African countries are the least urban and many have been experiencing economic difficulties. But even regional generalization can be misleading. The urban areas of sub-Saharan Africa are perhaps not so lacking in opportunity as many would claim. China and India may both be large countries undergoing both rapid economic growth and urbanization – but the differences within as well as between them are enormous, and often their policy issues are very localized. On the other hand, the lessons from one region are often relevant to the others. Thus, for example, Latin American experiences illustrate the dangers in trying to inhibit urbanization, rather than turning it into a positive force, not only for economic development but also for reducing the poverty and environmental burdens that often accompany economic growth.

NOTES

1 For the sake of simplicity, we have tended to avoid referring to 'towns and cities' in this book; as is accepted practice, the term 'urban' applies to all manner of towns and cities defined as such by their respective countries, and the term 'cities' is used as shorthand for the more cumbersome 'towns and cities'.
2 Unless otherwise mentioned, all data in this chapter are based on United Nations (2006) *World Urbanization Prospects: The 2005 Revision*, Population Division, United Nations, New York, NY.
3 UN-Habitat (2006) *The State of the World's Cities 2006/7*, Earthscan, London.

Part I

Urban Transitions

INTRODUCTION

Among all the varied social and economic factors that propel urbanization in poor countries, the elemental demographic forces of fertility, mortality and migration are perhaps the most systematically documented. Since the late 1970s, the United Nations Population Division has issued a steady stream of reports (since 1990 titled *World Urbanization Prospects*) showing how the demographic rates are expressed in the sizes and rates of growth of town, city and urban populations. In spite of this quarter-century of focused effort on the part of the UN, however, even the academic literature on urbanization continues to be plagued by misunderstandings of the demographic components of growth, leaving policymakers without the guidance they need to correctly apprehend and respond to it. In addition, as urbanization proceeds it is thrusting into view unresolved conceptual and measurement concerns – What is meant by urban? By city? – that increasingly touch on fundamental concerns of governance and planning. The scientific and policy agendas intersect in the need to devise meaningful forecasts of city growth: much remains to be done on the scientific side to provide forecasts with errors small enough to be tolerable, and, for most poor countries, mechanisms are yet to be developed that will place spatially disaggregated demographic data and forecasts in the hands of local and regional planners.

The chapters in this part share a concern for these demographic complexities, but also ask how progress on the scientific front can be reflected in better planning, policies and governance. The main demographic features of the urban transition are reviewed in Chapter 1 by Montgomery, who draws upon the most recent data made available by the UN Population Division. This chapter examines two common misconceptions of urbanization that have injected biases into policymaking: the view that urban-dwellers in poor countries reside mainly in huge urban agglomerations (small cities and towns are far more important in numerical terms, yet receive far less attention) and the view that city growth is principally fuelled by rural-to-urban migration (natural increase is usually more important, suggesting that urban family planning programmes should have a fundamental role in urban-growth policies). The current state of city and urban forecasting is also discussed in this chapter, which closes with a discussion of new data and methods using remote sensing techniques, which have the potential to provide timely and useful guidance to policymakers if combined with disaggregated data from national censuses.

Tacoli, McGranahan and Satterthwaite emphasize the artificiality of separating urban from rural populations in development policy debates. This unfortunate but pervasive habit of thought has had the effect of obscuring the multiple linkages that connect rural to urban wellbeing. Among other things, productive agriculture stimulates the growth of producer services in nearby cities (especially in the provision of credit, tools and machinery) and can also stimulate demand for consumer goods (provided that access to land is sufficiently equitable to allow numerous rural households to partake of increases in incomes). Income growth in urban areas, in turn, stimulates demands for foods and high-value agricultural products; it also allows urban residents to transfer remittances to their rural families. As the authors point out, although the benefits of international remittances for the sending countries are now widely acknowledged, there is curiously little recognition of what are likely to be equally or more significant transfers stemming from internal migration. The general neglect of the benefits of internal migration is evident in what appears to be a hardening of anti-urban attitudes among policymakers, who often view migration as a factor that exacerbates urban poverty and needs to be directly controlled. Yet, as the authors argue, there is much empirical evidence indicating that rural-to-urban migrants themselves benefit from relocation, and very little evidence to suggest that migration drives up urban poverty.

In Chapter 3, Skeldon resituates the urban transition in the broader context of the demographic transition. As he notes, urbanization was a centrepiece in the early theoretical formulations of the demographic transition, establishing social and economic conditions that facilitate declines in both mortality and fertility rates. He observes that, while lower fertility and mortality are almost universally viewed in a positive light, urbanization is not similarly regarded, as clearly demonstrated in a review of anti-urban policies and measures taken to control internal migration in poor countries. These actions have rarely proven to be effective in either slowing or redirecting urban growth. Looking to the future, Skeldon foresees an era in which internal migration flows will slow and urban labour shortages begin to emerge in certain high-skill sectors, as may already be happening in the fastest-growing regions of coastal China. He speculates that international labour migration may come to play an increasingly important role in fostering growth and maintaining the vitality of city economies in poor countries.

1

The Demography
of the Urban Transition:
What We Know and Don't Know

Mark R. Montgomery

INTRODUCTION

As their urban populations continue to grow, poor countries will come under mounting pressure to rethink their development strategies and set priorities with both rural and urban interests in mind. Ideally, the demographic research community would assist in setting priorities by providing countries and international aid agencies with informative urban population estimates and scientifically credible forecasts of the pace and distribution of future growth. Although the urban transition has been in the making for decades, much remains to be done if demographers are to supply planners and policymakers with useful guidance, especially where the spatial dimensions of city growth are concerned.

In the first main section of this chapter, the long-standing problems of definition that influence urban population counts and growth rates are noted. As is discussed with reference to the estimates of absolute poverty in developing countries, these problems are not confined to demography: they spill over to contaminate measurement of other fundamental aspects of economic development. With this as background, the second section describes the main demographic features of urban and city growth, drawing upon the work of the United Nations Population Division. In reviewing this material, two points that have often escaped attention will be stressed: the continuing significance of small and medium-sized cities in the urban scene and the role of urban natural increase, which rivals and often outstrips migration as a source of city growth. As UNFPA (2007) makes clear, there are policy opportunities here that warrant careful consideration.

In the third section, the current state of urban demographic research is reviewed. As the developing world continues to urbanize, and both local and national planners struggle to anticipate and adapt to city growth, they will increasingly need to make use of disaggregated demographic data for small geographic units. From where will such disaggregated data come? In the past, the demographic research community has tended to neglect population censuses providing geographically detailed data in favour of national sample surveys, and the international agencies supporting census-taking have not given high priority to spatially disaggregated analyses of these censuses. In consequence, a large agenda lies ahead for those demographers who wish to ready their data sources and methods for the upcoming urban era.

URBAN DEFINITIONS MATTER

To understand the scientific foundations of the work of the United Nations, and see how urban definitions affect the framework in which policy is made, consider the case of Beijing. As have other countries, China has made frequent changes to its small-area administrative boundaries and the accompanying urban definitions (Chan and Hu, 2003; Chan, 2007). For 2000, the population of 'Beijing' was reported by China's National Bureau of Statistics to be 11.5 million. This count departed significantly from previous practice in that it included what is known as the 'floating population' of migrants who live in Beijing without having *de jure* urban registration status.[1] In geographic terms, Beijing is defined to take in the districts of the city proper, where some 8.5 million people live, as well as the full populations of the neighbouring 'city districts' (an additional 3 million), evidently because these districts are functionally linked to Beijing proper. But the populations of the city districts are more rural than urban, and if only their urban residents had been counted by the Chinese authorities, the Beijing total would have been 9.9 rather than 11.5 million. If the authorities had judged that the outlying counties of Beijing Province are also closely linked to the city of Beijing and added the urban residents of the small cities and towns in these counties to the 9.9 million, the population of Beijing would have been reported as 10.5 million persons.

Because China's total population is so large, revisions of this sort made across the country would affect urban population percentages and totals for the developing world as a whole and would, among other things, influence thinking about the relative magnitudes of urban and rural poverty. Based on recent research by Ravallion et al (2007), Figure 1.1 depicts the proportion of poor people among developing-country rural and urban populations, using the World Bank's US$1.08 per day absolute needs standard for rural areas, which is adjusted upward for urban areas by the country-specific ratio of urban to rural poverty lines. The percentage of the poor is shown over time both with and without China. Obviously, the

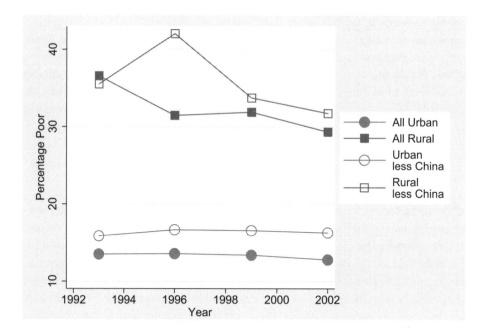

Figure 1.1 *Percentage of population living on less than US$1.08 a day in rural and urban areas, developing countries*

Source: Ravallion et al (2007).

definitions of urban and rural are of central importance here, in that alterations in China's definitions have the potential to shift large numbers of people between the urban and rural categories. Less obvious is the fact that the decision to count China's 'floating population' as urban on a *de facto* basis for 2000 differs from what was decided previously, with the surveys used by the World Bank to estimate poverty in China evidently taking these people to be rural residents (in accordance with their *de jure* status) rather than urban. Hence it is probable that the poverty rates for urban China are understated relative to what they would be if the floating population had been classified as urban.[2]

As this example suggests, multiple social, economic, administrative and political judgements come into play in the formulation of city definitions. It is not only national statistical authorities who have cause to make and remake their definitions. Urban researchers too are increasingly critical of the practice of declaring some places to be definitively urban and others rural, as evidence grows of the multiple linkages and flows across space of people, goods and information. Although the conventional, binary, urban–rural distinction still retains value, a consensus is emerging that future classification schemes will need to reserve a place for additional categories and degrees of urban-ness as well as the rural and urban ends of the spectrum (McGee, 1991; Champion and Hugo, 2004; Champion, 2006). Achieving homogeneity in urban definitions across countries has probably never been a feasible goal, and doubts are emerging as to whether it is, in fact, desirable. What continues to be desired, however, is a means of comparing the implications of alternative definitions, as will be discussed later in this chapter.

An Urban Landscape Emerges

This section offers a quantitative summary of the urban transition in developing countries, relying on data assembled by the United Nations Population Division.[3] It is no exaggeration to say that, over the past 40 years, the Population Division has been the sole source of internationally comparable city and urban estimates and projections. Much of the work has been carried out in-house, and the challenges that the UN faces in this endeavour are not well understood by the larger research and policy communities. The next section will take a closer look at the difficulties that plague this endeavour; here the main features of the urban transition as these are identified through the UN's data and methods will be surveyed.[4]

The scale of change anticipated for the upcoming decades can perhaps best be appreciated by examining Figure 1.2, which depicts the urban and rural population growth that has occurred since 1950 and the further growth expected to take place by 2024. In this figure, less developed regions (LDRs) are distinguished from more developed regions (MDRs). As can be seen, over the years from 2000 to 2024, the world's total population is projected to grow by 1.76 billion persons, with the greatest share of growth – some 86 per cent of the total – expected to take place in the cities and towns of developing countries. These near-term prospects stand in sharp contrast to what was experienced from 1950 to 1974, an era when rural growth still exceeded urban. These projections suggest that relatively little additional rural growth will occur in developing countries (an increase of some 190 million rural-dwellers in total from 2000 to 2024), and the UN anticipates that the rural populations of more developed countries will continue to decline.

Not surprisingly, given its dominance in terms of population overall, Asia now contains the largest total number of urban-dwellers among the major regions of developing countries and will continue to do so (Figure 1.3). By 2025, Africa is likely to have overtaken Latin America in terms of urban totals, moving into second place among the regions. The urban population of developing Oceania is also shown in the figure, but the totals for this region are very low in comparison with the other three regions, with only 1.92 million urban residents as of 2000 and 6.47 million urban-dwellers projected for 2050.

Figure 1.4 expresses regional trends in terms of annual growth rates. In the 1950s, 1960s and well into the 1970s, regional urban growth rates were in the

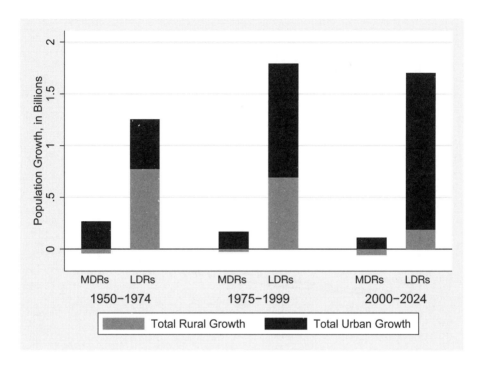

Figure 1.2 *Urban population growth in more developed regions (MDRs) and less developed regions (LDRs), 1950–2024*

Source: Provisional data provided by the United Nations Population Division (see note 4).

neighbourhood of four per cent per annum, although declines were already taking place in Latin America. (Growth rates for Oceania are shown for completeness.) Had the growth rates of this early era been sustained, the urban populations of the three major developing regions would have doubled roughly every 17 years. By 2000, however, urban growth rates had fallen considerably in each of these three regions. As the figure indicates, further growth rate declines are forecast for the first few decades of the 21st century, with urban Latin America projected to approach a state of zero growth.

Much as with population growth rates overall in developing countries, the urban growth rates in those countries before 2000 were substantially higher than the rates that were seen during comparable historical periods in the West, with the difference being due to lower urban mortality in present-day populations, stubbornly high urban fertility in some cases, and an inbuilt momentum in urban population growth that stems from the age and sex structures bequeathed by past growth (Montgomery et al, 2003). Even if the projected downward trends in growth rates come to pass, by 2050 urban growth rates in Africa will remain at

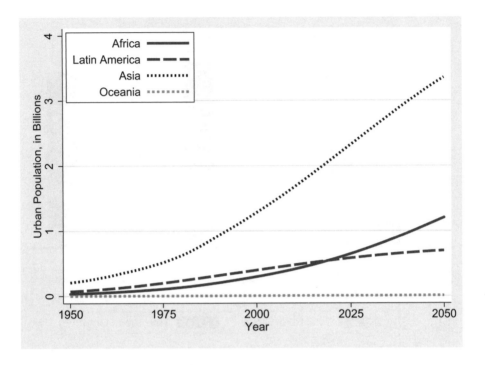

Figure 1.3 *Total urban population by region, developing countries*

Source: Provisional data provided by the United Nations Population Division (see note 4).

about two per cent per annum, a rate that would double the urban population of that region in 35 years.

In its programme, the United Nations also documents trends in the percentage of the urban population in national totals. In each of the developing regions, the urban percentage is advancing in a seemingly inexorable fashion, and by 2030 urban majorities are projected to emerge in both Asia and Africa. Despite what is often assumed, when compared with the historical experience in Western countries, these decade-to-decade changes in urban percentages – sometimes termed the *pace of urbanization* – are not especially large (Montgomery et al, 2003, Tables 3–5). The literature exhibits some confusion on this point, often failing to distinguish rates of urban growth, which are rapid by historical standards, from the pace of urbanization, which falls well within the historical bounds.

It is clear that one feature of today's urban transition has no historical parallel: the emergence of hundreds of large cities. In 1950, only two metropolitan areas in the world – the Tokyo and the New York–Newark agglomerations – had populations of 10 million or more. (Cities of this size are commonly called *mega-*

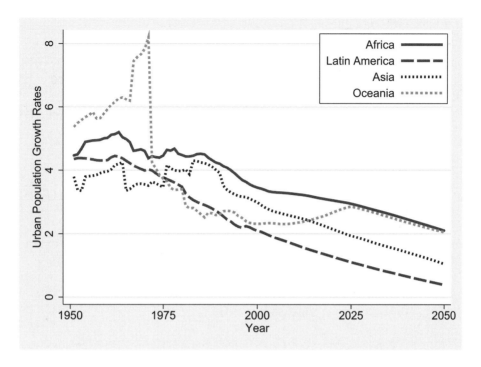

Figure 1.4 *Growth rates of total urban population by region, developing countries*

Source: Provisional data provided by the United Nations Population Division (see note 4).

cities.) By 2025, according to UN forecasts, the developing countries alone will contain 21 cities of this size and another 5 will be found in the more developed countries. Even more striking is the number of cities in the 1–5 million range. In 1950, only 33 such cities were found in the developing world; by 2025, it is projected, there will be a total of no fewer than 431 cities in this range. Most of the large cities in developing countries are in Asia, in keeping with its large urban totals, but both Africa and Latin America have a number of cities in the 1–5 million category.

This remarkable feature of the urban transition has attracted a great deal of attention in the popular press and appears to have fostered the impression that most urban residents of the developing world live in huge urban agglomerations. This is simply not the case. As Figure 1.5 shows, among all developing-country urban-dwellers living in cities of 100,000 and above, only 12 per cent live in mega-cities – about 1 in 8 urban residents. This is hardly a negligible figure, but it is only about half of the percentage of urbanites who live in smaller cities ranging from 100,000 to half a million.

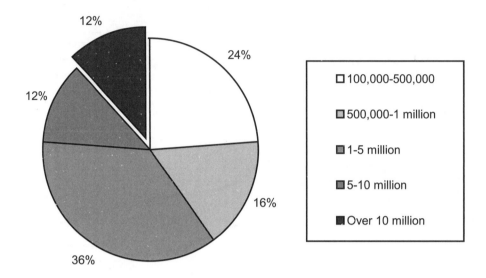

Figure 1.5 *Distribution of urban population by city size,
developing countries in 2000*

Source: Provisional data provided by the United Nations Population Division (see note 4).

As the Panel on Urban Population Dynamics has shown, smaller cities are generally less well provided with basic services, such as improved sanitation and adequate supplies of drinking water, than large cities (Montgomery et al, 2003). In smaller cities, rates of fertility and infant and child mortality can be little different from the rates prevailing in the countryside. Their municipal governments seldom possess the range of expertise and the managerial talent found in the governments of large cities. Yet, in an era of political decentralization, these smaller cities are increasingly being required to shoulder substantial burdens in service delivery and take on a larger share of revenue-raising responsibilities (Montgomery et al, 2003, Chapter 9). Given all this, it is surprising how often small cities have been neglected in policy discussions (but see UN-Habitat, 2006, for a treatment of the issues).

As Figure 1.6 shows for three large Asian cities, there is a tendency for city growth rates to decline with time. According to the estimates in the United Nations cities database, population growth rates in Jakarta were in excess of six percentage points annually in the early 1950s and rates in Seoul exceeded eight per cent. By the end of the century, however, Seoul's growth rate had fallen below zero and Jakarta's, although erratic, had dropped below four per cent. Meanwhile, growth

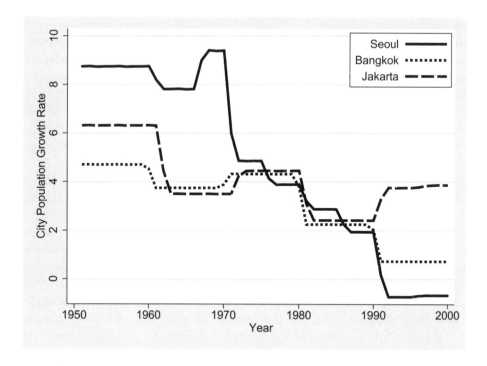

Figure 1.6 *City growth rates for Seoul, Bangkok and Jakarta, 1950–2000*

Source: Provisional data provided by the United Nations Population Division (see note 4).

rates for Bangkok wended their way downwards from over four per cent to about one per cent at the end of this period.

When confronted with time series of city growth such as these, urban economists are apt to offer explanations that emphasize how increasing city size drives up rents and the many costs of congestion, which thus discourage rural migrants and encourage businesses to consider relocation. Urban geographers are likely to stress the difficulties in locating and properly measuring the growth of large cities, noting that faster population growth in an urban periphery – which may or may not be recorded in the growth rate statistics – often accompanies slower growth in the city centre. But there is an additional and equally plausible explanation that receives far too little attention: the possibility that city growth is driven down over time by declines in urban fertility rates.

Research by the UN Population Division, based on a sample of countries providing two or more national censuses, allows urban population growth rates to be divided into a natural urban growth component – the difference between urban birth and death rates – and a residual one that combines net migration with spatial expansion (Chen et al, 1998). The results are strikingly at odds with the usual perception of the sources of urban growth. According to the UN findings, about 60 per cent of the urban growth rate in developing countries is due to natural growth; the remaining 40 per cent is due to migration and spatial expansion.[5] Recently, a very similar pattern was found for India over the four decades from 1961 to 2001, with urban natural growth again accounting for about 60 per cent of the total (Sivaramakrishnan et al, 2005, p32). Even in China, where the migration share is larger, natural growth is responsible for some 40 per cent of the urban growth rate.

As discussed in a recent UNFPA (2007) report, many developing-country policymakers have been apprehensive about rates of city growth in their countries, and they have not infrequently acted upon these concerns with aggressive interventions aimed at repelling rural-to-urban migrants and expelling slum residents. Such punitive policies have undoubtedly reduced the wellbeing of the urban poor and have probably caused more poverty than they have eliminated – and yet these policies have proven to be ineffective over the long term. More enlightened regional development policies, on the other hand, seldom generate the rapid changes in pace and spatial distribution that policymakers hope to achieve.

It is therefore surprising how little attention has been paid to a growth-rate policy of a very different character: urban voluntary family planning programmes. Over the past half-century, such programmes have compiled an impressive record of effectiveness across the developing world in facilitating fertility declines and reducing unwanted fertility. As will be shown in the next section, an empirical analysis of developing-country city growth and fertility suggests that, when national total fertility rates decline by one child, there is an associated decline of nearly one percentage point in the city population growth rates for that country. Hence, even if the health benefits of voluntary family planning programmes (in terms of reproductive health) are set aside by policymakers fixated on the need to slow city growth, these programmes deserve more attention than they have received. They offer an effective and humane alternative to the ineffective and brutalizing measures that have been applied all too often.

URBAN DEMOGRAPHIC RESEARCH: BASIC NEEDS

As urban scholars and demographers well know, the scientific basis for cross-country urban estimates and projections is adequate for identifying broad features and dominant trends, but, where the finer details are concerned, difficulties in conceptualization, definitional heterogeneities and measurement errors leave the science in a less than satisfactory state. Yet, as urbanization proceeds, it is precisely the finer details of the process – that is, the spatially disaggregated estimates and forecasts – that become urgently needed by policymakers. In view of the wealth of new data for developing countries that has entered the public domain in recent years, there now exists considerable potential for improvement in city population estimates and projections. Two developments are especially notable: urban data from a very large number of demographic surveys has greatly strengthened the basis for estimating the demographic components of urban growth and will continue to do so as these survey programmes proceed; and recent methodological advances have suggested new ways by which satellite imagery can be used to detect the spatial extent of urban areas, enabling the spatial dimensions of city growth to be quantified at relatively low cost (Angel et al, 2005; Balk et al, 2005; Small, 2005).

Although its cities database has not incorporated a spatial component to date, and its forecasting methods have essentially ignored urban fertility and mortality rates, the UN Population Division is now considering whether to re-establish its database on a firmly spatial footing. In the discussion that follows, the nature of the problems that vex the current version of the cities database are described, and then proposals for improving it and enhancing its spatial features are discussed.

Improving the cities database

The United Nations cities data take the form of a panel data set containing population counts for individual cities over time, generally recorded at irregular intervals. To organize its records, the United Nations has maintained three 'statistical concepts' that serve to define city boundaries. The term *city proper* refers to the formal administrative boundaries of a city as set out by local authorities. The *urban agglomeration* includes the city proper and also incorporates contiguous areas that are populated at urban levels of density. A number of countries (especially, but not exclusively, in Latin America) have adopted a more spatially elastic measure, categorizing their populations in terms of *metropolitan regions* that include rural-dwellers falling within the sphere of influence (or 'catchment area') of large urban places. Some countries have devised further variations on these boundary definitions, and the UN endeavours to fit them within its three-category framework.

Member countries of the United Nations are asked to provide city population data for urban agglomeration boundaries; however, they may respond with data coded in terms of city proper or metropolitan region or may provide the counts without any accompanying explanation of units. Where possible, these data are adjusted to conform to the agglomeration concept – but, of course, this is not always possible. Indeed, in only a small percentage of cases – 4.5 per cent in the provisional 2006 version of the UN's dat·hase – are all of the city's records expressed in terms of urban agglomerations. The city p·oper is a far more common concept in these data, with the populations of 39.8 per cent of cities being consistently recorded in this way. For another 23 per cent of cities, no information is available on the concept by which population is reported for any of the recorded dates, while in the remaining 32.5 per cent of cities the population time series mixes two or more boundary concepts.

The difficulties stemming from such mixed-unit time series are illustrated for Luanda, Angola, in Figure 1.7. The units in which this city's population was recorded are unknown for the 1950, 1960 and 1970 entries, whereas in 1982, population counts were provided for both the city proper and the urban agglomeration concepts. The next entry in the series is again of unknown type, and it is followed by one report on the agglomeration and a final record whose defining concept is not specified. In each new revision of *World Urbanization Prospects*, UN researchers succeed in eliminating some of these anomalous cases. Nevertheless, far more heterogeneity remains in the city time series than is commonly realized.

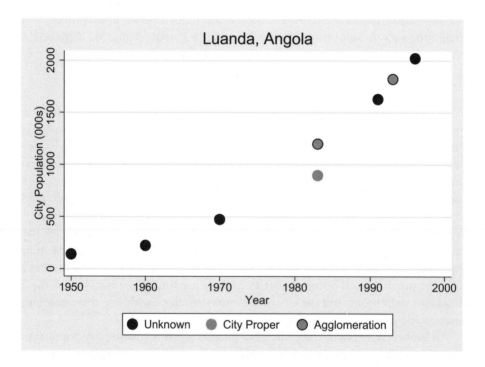

Figure 1.7 *City population time series for Luanda, Angola*

Source: Provisional data provided by the United Nations Population Division (see note 4).

Forecasting city growth

As part of the research summarized in *World Urbanization Prospects*, the UN Population Division prepares medium-term forecasts of both total urban and city-specific population growth. These forecasts are grounded in the city population series that have already been discussed, with all their attendant heterogeneity. For reasons that are not yet well understood, the UN forecasts, which are essentially extrapolations of each city's time series, have consistently projected city growth rates (and thus population sizes) that are too high. The tendency to over-project is not evident in the UN's forecasts of total population at the national level, but it persists in the city population forecasts despite the insertion of an algorithm in the forecasting model that is designed to slow projected growth rates as city size increases (recall Figure 1.6). The Panel on Urban Population Dynamics (Montgomery et al, 2003) explains the forecasting method and provides a critical review of the issues, as does Bocquier (2005).

The pattern of forecast error for total urban populations is illustrated in Table 1.1. The entries in this table refer to population-weighted averages of country-level percentage errors. As can be seen, the mean percentage forecast errors are large for the 20-year and 10-year forecasts. The 20-year forecast for Latin America that was made in 1980 proved to be 19.8 percentage points too high when the region's 2000 urban population was counted; the forecast for South Asia was 27.2 percentage points above the mark. Of course, as the forecast baseline moves closer to the 2000 end-line, some improvement in performance occurs, with the mean forecast error dropping to 5.4 per cent for Latin America for the decade-ahead forecast made in 1990. However, the error for South Asia remains 19.7 points too high even in the decade-ahead case. As Bocquier (2005) has noted, the tendency for over-projection that is exhibited by the UN forecasts raises doubt about the scale and pace of urban population change (if not the direction) that has been forecast for

Table 1.1 *Urban population forecast errors for 2000*

	Mean Percentage Forecast Errors (%)		
	1980–2000	1990–2000	1995–2000
Region			
East Asia and Pacific	3.9	26.7	−2.8
EAP excluding China	18.4	9.8	−0.4
Latin America and Caribbean	19.8	5.4	−0.9
Middle East and North Africa	13.3	6.8	8.5
South Asia	27.2	19.7	2.7
Sub-Saharan Africa	21.8	23.4	5.5
Level of Development			
Low	23.1	18.3	3.2
Lower Middle	6.9	26.1	−1.3
Lower Middle excluding China	25.6	9.9	3.7
Upper Middle	12.8	8.9	0.8

Source: Montgomery et al (2003).

the 21st century. Understanding the sources of forecast errors is a research priority of some urgency.

Given the uncertainties and measurement errors that plague the city population series in particular, it is clear that there are limits to how ambitious any forecast should strive to be. The UN Population Division has long couched its forecasting efforts in the most cautious of terms and has made plain its reservations about the proper scope of the effort. The United Nations (1980) warned that:

> *Projection of city populations is fraught with hazards. ... There are more than 1600 cities in the data set, and it is obviously impossible to predict precisely the demographic future of most of them. ... In most cases, national and local planners will have access to more detailed information about a particular place and could supply more reliable information about its prospects (p45).*

Even so, to an extent that probably could not have been foreseen in the early 1980s, several streams of new data – on demographic behaviour as well as on land cover, water supply and environment – have recently emerged. These new materials may well support more informed and credible city population estimates and projections than the experts of 1980 could have envisioned.

Exploiting new data

Although the United Nations operates a separate research programme in which it estimates and projects fertility and mortality rates at the national level, its city and urban projection methods have not incorporated fertility or mortality in any way, despite the UN's own finding that 60 per cent of urban growth is due to natural increase. The approach taken to city and urban projections thus ignores a large body of accumulated information on urban fertility and mortality rates, as well as some useful data on migration. Well over 200 nationally representative demographic surveys of developing countries have made their way into the public domain via the World Fertility Surveys (WFSs), first carried out in the late 1970s, and their two ongoing successor programmes, the Demographic and Health Surveys (DHSs), providing 154 surveys to date, and the Multiple Indicator Cluster Surveys (MICSs), with 43 surveys in their second round. Although the sample sizes of these surveys are too small to permit informative estimation of demographic rates at the city level, they are generally large enough to allow the rates to be estimated for the urban populations of the sub-national geographic region within which a city is located. With the aid of statistical tools, it is possible to further refine the estimates to take some city-specific characteristics (for example population size or coastal location) into account.

Table 1.2, based on data from the earlier 2003 revision of *World Urbanization Prospects*, may give an idea of the returns that can be secured from linking data

Table 1.2 *Panel data city growth regression models, developing countries*

	Ordinary Least Squares	Random Effects	Fixed Effects
Total Fertility Rate	0.602	0.685	0.887
(Z statistic)	(19.97)	(20.34)	(17.68)
Child Mortality Rate	−0.004	−0.005	−0.007
	(−5.53)	(−5.54)	(−4.49)
Constant	1.757	1.464	0.802
	(22.01)	(16.54)	(7.25)
Standard deviation of city effects α_u		1.184	1.907
		(27.71)	
α_{ffl}	2.662	2.394	2.381
		(107.08)	
log-likelihood	−18624	−18446	−16568

Source: Montgomery and Kim (2006).

on fertility and mortality rates to data on city growth. The time series of national total fertility and child mortality rates (provided by the United Nations) were used here rather than rates calculated from survey data for urban sub-national regions, which would have been preferred. The most interesting results are the fixed-effects estimates (the third column of the table), which introduce the equivalent of a control for all influences on a given city's growth rate that are constant over time. Even with such important sources of variation controlled, it can be seen that (with a coefficient of 0.887 on the total fertility rate) a decline in national fertility of one child is associated with a decline of nearly one percentage point in city growth rates. In addition to being demographically important, this association is highly significant in statistical terms. Although also statistically significant and in the expected direction, the effect of child mortality on city growth is substantially weaker. Taken together, these results provide further confirmation, if any is still needed, of the important role that natural increase plays in city growth.

To pursue this line of enquiry, links between the UN cities database and the demographic surveys would need to be established. Perhaps surprisingly, this is no easy task. The difficulty is that the WFSs, DHSs and MICSs contain very little by way of basic spatial identifiers to serve as the linking mechanism.[6] The WFSs of the 1970s and early 1980s somehow neglected to identify the city in which a sampling cluster was located (unless this happened to be the national capital or the only large city in an identified region), and the DHS and MICS programmes have unaccountably failed to rectify this error.[7] A further problem is that only the crudest summaries of migration histories are collected in these survey programmes, and the data available do not include the names (or even the regions) of former places of residence for migrants. This forecloses the possibility of calculating origin-to-destination estimates of migration rates. In short, the general neglect of space and geography in the major demographic survey programmes makes it far more difficult than it should be to link survey data on urban fertility, mortality, migration and the like to city-specific and other geographically coded information. This is a long-standing and serious flaw in the urban demographic record – although it would be fixable at trivial cost in future survey efforts.

Adding spatial content

In its current configuration, the UN's cities database gives the population of a given city at a point in time, but it does not show how that population is distributed over space. A first step in this direction is to organize population data according to the smallest geographic units ('building blocks') that are available. When population data are arrayed over space in reasonably fine detail, this enables a closer scrutiny of the areas lying on the peripheries of large cities, where much urban population growth is believed to take place, and gives planners and policymakers a view of the communities situated between large cities that are likely to fuse with neighbouring urban areas. Geo-coded data also provide a window on the smaller cities and towns, where, as already noted, a large percentage of urban residents live.

A systematic and thorough effort would be needed to create such geo-coded data sets for all developing countries. Although most developing countries continue to conduct national censuses, relatively few of them process their census data at the small-area level, and fewer still make any systematic effort to place the disaggregated population data in the hands of local planners and policymakers, many of whom have to operate with rudimentary data that lack spatial content. While geographic information systems are being developed at the national level, there will be an important interim role for international geographic data sets that are organized along similar lines. A model or template for such a database is provided by Center for International Earth Science Information Network (CIESIN) with their Global Rural–Urban Mapping Project (GRUMP), described in Balk et al (2005). The pay-off to the GRUMP approach is evident in the maps produced by McGranahan et al (2007), which depict the number of urban coastal inhabitants in developing countries who live within 10 metres of sea level, where they are likely to face rising risks from the storm surges and related phenomena that are expected to accompany global warming. As the developing world continues to urbanize, the efforts of planners and policymakers will become increasingly dependent on spatially disaggregated data such as these.

CONCLUSIONS

As has been argued in this chapter, a substantial workload lies in store for the demographic research community if it is to assemble the data and methods needed for the upcoming urban era. Considerable effort will be required to clean the city population time series of errors and resolve inconsistencies. The performance of the UN forecasts of city and urban growth has been heavily criticized in recent years, and there is now general agreement on the need for a thorough critical review of forecast errors and the development of new methods (Montgomery et al, 2003; Bocquier, 2005). Further effort will be needed to bring spatial specificity to the city population estimates in the form of geo-coded databases. Remote sensing methods will serve as a valuable supplementary tool, providing easily updated information on spatial extents, if not on population as such. In each of these domains, the city data will need to be scrutinized by a wider set of local, country-level and international experts than has been the case to date. For the past 40 years, far too much of the urban demographic research burden has rested with the United Nations Population Division. In view of the urban challenges ahead, it is time that these burdens are more widely shared.

NOTES

1   Chan (forthcoming) reviews estimates of the total number of such migrants in urban China, which have ranged as high as 144 million.
2   The implications for rural poverty are not clear: a migrant who falls below the urban poverty line may not be classified as poor according to the rural poverty line. See Chan (forthcoming) for discussion.
3   This section is adapted from a fuller discussion in the Montgomery and Balk (forthcoming) working paper.
4   The analysis that follows is based on provisional data made available to the author by the United Nations Population Division, representing an October 2006 snapshot of a database that is undergoing continual revision.
5   The 60/40 division reflects the situation of the median country in the UN's sample.
6   See the discussion in Montgomery et al (2003) on the amount of guesswork involved in linking DHS respondents to their cities when such identifiers are absent.
7   A promising recent development is that, in about half of the surveys in the DHS programme carried out since the late 1990s, geographic coordinates are collected for sampling clusters, thus providing a means of linking the clusters to other geographically coded data, including city boundaries. The MICS programme has not generally followed the lead of the DHSs in this respect.

REFERENCES

Angel, S., Sheppard, S. C. and Civco, D. L. (2005) *The Dynamics of Global Urban Expansion*, Transport and Urban Development Department, World Bank, Washington, DC

Balk, D., Pozzi, F., Yetman, G., Deichmann, U. and Nelson, A. (2005) 'The distribution of people and the dimension of place: Methodologies to improve the global estimation of urban extents', in *Proceedings of the Urban Remote Sensing Conference of the International*

Society for Photogrammetry and Remote Sensing, March 2005, International Society for Photogrammetry and Remote Sensing, Tempe, AZ

Bocquier, P. (2005) 'World urbanization prospects: An alternative to the UN model of projection compatible with mobility transition theory', *Demographic Research*, vol 12, article 9, pp197–236, www.demographic-research.org/volumes/vol12/9/12-9.pdf, last accessed 21 December 2007

Champion, T. (2006) 'Where do we stand? Lessons from the IUSSP Working Group on Urbanization', paper presented at the workshop 'Rethinking the Estimation and Projection of Urban and City Populations', 9–10 January 2006, Columbia University, New York

Champion, T. and Hugo, G. (eds) (2004) *New Forms of Urbanization: Beyond the Urban–Rural Dichotomy*, Ashgate, Aldershot, UK

Chan, K. W. (2007) 'Misconceptions and complexities in the study of China's cities: Definitions, statistics, and implications', *Eurasian Geography and Economics*, vol 48, no 4, pp383–412

Chan, K. W. (forthcoming) 'Internal migration and rural migrant labour: Trends, geography and policies', in M. Gallagher, C. K. Lee and A. Park (eds) *The Labour of Reform in China*, Routledge, London

Chan, K. W. and Hu, Y. (2003) 'Urbanization in China in the 1990s: New definition, different series, and revised trends', *The China Review*, vol 3, no 2, pp49–71

Chen, N., Valente, P. and Zlotnik, H. (1998) 'What do we know about recent trends in urbanization?', in R. E. Bilsborrow (ed) *Migration, Urbanization and Development: New Directions and Issues*, UNFPA and Kluwer Academic Publishers, New York, pp59–88

McGee, T. G. (1991) 'The emergence of *desakota* regions in Asia: Expanding a hypothesis', in N. Ginsburg, B. Koppel and T. G. McGee (eds) *The Extended Metropolis: Settlement Transition in Asia*, University of Hawaii Press, Honolulu, HI, pp3–26

McGranahan, G., Balk, D. and Anderson, B. (2007) 'The rising tide: Assessing the risks of climate change and human settlements in low elevation coastal zones', *Environment and Urbanization*, vol 19, no 1, pp17–37

Montgomery, M. R. and Balk, D. (forthcoming) 'The urban transition: Demography meets geography', Poverty, Gender and Youth Programme working paper, Population Council, New York

Montgomery, M. R. and Kim, D. (2006) 'Forecasting city growth rates in the developing world: Illustrative examples', paper presented at the workshop 'Rethinking the Estimation and Projection of Urban and City Populations', 9–10 January 2006, Columbia University, New York

Montgomery, M. R., Stren, R., Cohen, B. and Reed, H. E. (eds) (2003) *Cities Transformed: Demographic Change and its Implications in the Developing World*, The National Academy Press, Washington, DC

Ravallion, J., Chen, S. and Sangraula, P. (2007) 'New evidence on the urbanization of global poverty', Policy Research Working Paper No 4199, World Bank, Washington, DC

Sivaramakrishnan, K. C., Kundu, A. and Singh, B. N. (2005) *Handbook of Urbanization in India: An Analysis of Trends and Processes*, Oxford University Press, New Delhi

Small, C. (2005) 'The global analysis of urban reflectance', *International Journal of Remote Sensing*, vol 26, no 4, pp661–681

UNFPA (2007) *The State of World Population 2007: Unleashing the Potential of Urban Growth*, United Nations Population Fund, New York, NY

UN-Habitat (2006) *Meeting Development Goals in Small Urban Centres: Water and Sanitation in the World's Cities, 2006*, UN-Habitat and Earthscan, London

United Nations (1980) *Patterns of Urban and Rural Population Growth*, Population Studies No 68, Department of International Economic and Social Affairs, United Nations, New York

2

Urbanization, Poverty and Inequity: Is Rural–Urban Migration a Poverty Problem, or Part of the Solution?

Cecilia Tacoli, Gordon McGranahan and David Satterthwaite

INTRODUCTION

There is a general consensus among economists and urban scholars that urbanization plays a positive role in social and economic development. Historically, countries with the highest rates of economic growth have also been those with the most rapid increase in levels of urbanization, and cities are recognized as important drivers of overall economic development (Montgomery et al, 2003; Overman and Venables, 2005). Economies of scale and agglomeration economies in the production of goods and services reduce costs and support innovation. Proximity fosters synergies between different economic sectors, which can help optimize the use of resources and the disposal of wastes. Access to health services, education, basic infrastructure, information and knowledge are on average better in urban centres than in rural areas (UN-Habitat, 1996; Njoh, 2003; Champion and Hugo, 2004), although, as described later in this chapter, aggregate statistics can hide deep inequalities in access.

At the same time, however, there is a growing conviction among policymakers in rapidly urbanizing countries that migration should be controlled to prevent excessive urban growth.[1] This view is reinforced when the international development community treats poverty as a predominantly rural problem, which should be addressed by rural development.

It is perhaps not surprising that the better-off urban residents blame urban problems on low-income migrants. In many countries, urban growth has been accompanied by the rapid expansion of unplanned, underserved neighbourhoods with high concentrations of poor people. These neighbourhoods are considered by many to have very negative social and environmental consequences. Central and municipal governments cannot afford to provide the conventional urban infrastructure needed to accommodate these populations – the roads, drains, water pipes, schools, hospitals and other facilities considered necessary for sound urban development. Many of the residents of these neighbourhoods cannot find formal employment, and many of the residences themselves are on land not considered suitable for residential settlement or are not built to construction standards. Ideally, or so it would seem, rural–urban migration should be kept down to a level consistent with the availability of urban jobs and services.

This view may serve the interests of certain segments of the urban population, but it misrepresents the challenges and opportunities provided by urban growth and development. In many urbanizing countries, urban poverty is, indeed, an important and growing problem, even in countries, such as China, where rural poverty has been declining in recent years (Khan and Riskin, 2002). This chapter documents the challenges of urban poverty and argues that it still tends to be underestimated. Excessive migration is not the source of poverty, however, and measures to curb migration can easily make both urban and rural poverty worse. The arguments that portray excessive rural–urban migration as a cause of poverty are typically based on a number of misconceptions that need to be corrected.

First, the challenge of providing acceptable urban infrastructure and services to unacceptably poor urban-dwellers is as much a governance issue as a technical or financial one. A number of initiatives in low- and middle-income countries show that organizations of the urban poor can play a lead role in the provision of basic housing and infrastructure, provided their organizations are recognized and supported by local and central governments (see Chapters 4 and 7). Instead, groups of the urban poor are often thwarted in any attempts to improve infrastructure and service delivery. As described in the next section, regulations and standards only rarely serve to improve low-income neighbourhoods and more often render them informal or even illegal. The notion that it would have been better if the residents of these neighbourhoods had not moved to the urban areas in the first place reinforces the prejudice against them and decreases the likelihood that they will receive the support they need.

Second, while many residents of slums and other low-income neighbourhoods may work in the informal sector, this does not mean that they are not contributing to the urban economy. Up to the 1980s, much of the debate on how the urban poor make a living revolved around different conceptualizations of the informal sector. Initially described as a messy mix of marginalized activities, it was later understood that many parts of the informal sector are highly dynamic and not only respond to the needs of low-income and lower-middle-income communities and settlements, but are often well integrated into the urban economy and, in some cases, the global economy (Bromley, 1979; Bromley and Gerry, 1979; Moser, 1984). Further research has focused on urban household responses to crisis, especially to the structural adjustment programmes of the 1980s and 1990s (Kanji, 1995; González de la Rocha and Grinspun, 2001), underlining the crucial role played by the informal sector as a safety net for the often large numbers of retrenched workers following reform of the public sector. Moreover, there is evidence that, when migrants move to urban centres, they are making rational choices – even if the urban informal sector does have many disadvantages, it may be preferable to the rural alternatives.

Third, it can be very misleading to assume that it is rural–urban migrants who are populating the expanding low-income settlements. Patterns of urbanization closely reflect the geographical distribution of markets and their economic base. As described later in this chapter, the significance of rural–urban migration to urban growth varies among countries, depending largely on their economic performance and their level of urbanization. The main component of urban growth in many countries is now natural growth rather than rural–urban migration. Moreover, while there is an overall increase in people's mobility, the forms and directions of their movement are extremely diverse, with many people moving to and from urban areas or between different urban centres. Urban and rural poverty are often closely interlinked, but this should not be taken to imply that the urban poor are all, or even preponderantly, rural migrants.

Finally, one of the great conceptual mistakes in the development policy debates of the last 30 years has been to treat 'rural' and 'urban' poverty as somehow separate and to assume that they are in competition with each other for resources. In general, successful rural development will stimulate and support urban development and vice versa. There are some exceptions, but these do not invalidate this statement. And since mobility is primarily a strategy adopted by households and individuals to reduce risk and vulnerability, it is important that policies recognize its role in poverty reduction. The various implications of the many linkages between urban and rural poverty, and their impact on rural–urban migration and poverty in receiving areas, are examined later in this chapter.

URBAN POVERTY AS A GROWING AND UNDERESTIMATED CHALLENGE

The scale and depth of urban poverty are understated by most global assessments, either because they make no allowance for urban conditions (for instance poverty lines that make no allowance for the higher monetary cost of non-food needs) or through inappropriate measurements (for example data on sanitation services in urban areas that do not measure who has 'adequate' provision). Large sections of the urban population in developing countries are malnourished, have below poverty-

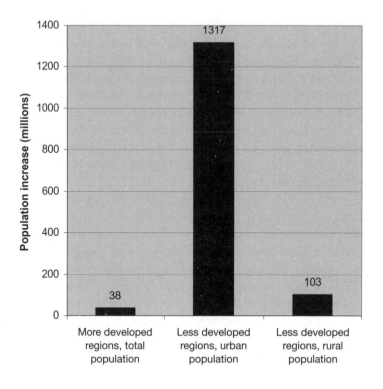

Figure 2.1 *Projected growth in the world's population, 2005–2025*

Source: United Nations (2006).

line incomes, and face high infant and child mortality rates and large preventable disease and injury burdens.

Globally, rural poverty still exceeds urban poverty, and this is especially so in most low-income countries. However, urban poverty now exceeds rural poverty in many middle-income countries and the scale of urban poverty is growing rapidly in many low-income ones. One simple reason for this is that a rapidly increasing proportion of the world's population live in urban centres. Between 1975 and 2005, the urban population of developing countries grew by 180 per cent while the rural population grew by 31 per cent. United Nations projections suggest that in the next two decades (2005–2025), the urban population in developing countries will increase by 1.3 billion while the rural population will increase by 103 million (see Figure 2.1).

According to most economic and social indicators, urban populations do better on average than rural populations. However, in all countries, most wealthy households live in urban areas; this improves urban averages and can hide the severe

Table 2.1 *Infant and under-five mortality rates in Kenya (per 1000 live births)*

Location	Infant mortality rate	Under-five mortality rate
Kenya (rural and urban)	74	112
Rural	76	113
Nairobi	39	62
Other urban	57	84
Informal settlements in Nairobi	91	151
Kibera	106	187
Embakasi	164	254

Source: APHRC (2002).

disadvantages faced by large sections of the urban population, as illustrated by data from Kenya on infant and under-five mortality rates (see Table 2.1) (APHRC, 2002). Problems are more serious in rural than in urban areas – and conditions in the capital, Nairobi, are better than in other urban areas. But infant and under-five mortality rates are much higher in the informal settlements, where around half of Nairobi's population lives. Kibera, in Nairobi, is one of Africa's largest informal settlements, with several hundred thousand inhabitants; at the time of the survey, nearly one child in five in Kibera died before its fifth birthday. In the wealthier parts of Nairobi, under-five mortality rates are likely to be one-tenth or even one-twentieth of this. The survey also found that the prevalence of diarrhoea with blood in children under three in the two weeks prior to the interview was far higher in Nairobi's informal settlements than among the rural population.

Even if indicators are better for urban populations than for rural populations, this does not imply that there is no need to address urban problems. In Chad, for instance, the infant mortality rate in 1997 was 99 per 1000 live births for urban areas and 113 for rural areas. In Mozambique, in 1997, it was 101 for urban populations and 160 for rural populations (Demographic and Health Surveys, undated). In these countries the rural infant mortality rates are higher than the urban, but the urban rates are also excessive. Moreover, if urban Chad and Mozambique face the same sort of intra-urban inequalities displayed in Kenya, there are likely to be urban neighbourhoods with rates well in excess of the rural averages. In many countries, the differences between the rural and urban infant and child mortality rates are not very great (Satterthwaite, 2007). This is surprising in that most urban areas have economies of scale and proximity in most of the measures that help reduce infant and child mortality rates (such as good provision of water, sanitation and healthcare).

A review of available data on malnutrition in developing countries by the International Food Policy Research Institute (IFPRI) shows that levels of childhood mortality, stunting and lack of weight are generally lower in urban than in rural areas, whereas acute malnutrition or wasting (as measured by low weight-to-height ratios) and morbidity from infectious diseases are often higher in urban areas.

However, there is considerable heterogeneity in poverty, morbidity, mortality and nutritional status in urban areas, and, generally, the intra-urban differentials in these are greater than the rural–urban differences (Ruel et al, 1998). Malnutrition among lower-income groups in urban areas may be very serious but hidden in any urban average because of the concentration of well-fed, middle- and upper-income groups.

Table 2.2 compares the proportion of the population with below poverty-line incomes in rural and urban areas. The proportion of the urban population that is below the poverty line is high – over half the urban population in Angola, Bangladesh, Chad, Guatemala, Haiti, Honduras and Niger. In many countries, there are no large differences in the proportions of the population with below poverty-line incomes or consumption in rural and urban areas; for some countries, the proportion in urban areas is actually higher than the proportion in rural areas (Honduras in 1993, Mongolia in 1995).

Poverty lines do not usually take into account the higher cost of most necessities in urban areas, especially in the larger cities (Satterthwaite, 2004). If they were adjusted to do so, in some countries there would possibly be an even higher proportion of below poverty-line households in urban areas.

Table 2.2 *Comparing the proportion of rural and urban populations that are below the poverty line*

Country	Year	Proportion of the population with below poverty-line incomes in:	
		Urban areas	Rural areas
Angola	2000	60.0	
Bangladesh	1995	61.0	
Chad	1995–1996	63.0	67.0
Egypt	1995–1996	22.5	23.3
El Salvador	1992	43.1	55.7
Guatemala	1989	61.4	85.4
Haiti	1980–1986	65.0	80.0
Honduras	1993	57.0	51.0
India	1994	30.5	36.7
Kenya	1997	49.2	52.9
Kenya (Nairobi)	1997	50.2	
Mongolia	1995	38.5	33.1
Niger	1989–1993	52.0	63.0
Nigeria	1992	30.4	36.4
Peru	1997	40.4	64.7
Sri Lanka	1990–1991	28.4	38.1
Yemen	1992	18.6	19.2
Zimbabwe	1996	46	72

Sources: Drawn mainly from World Bank (2003).

Socially and Legally Excluded Settlements and the Myth that These Are 'Migrant' Settlements

Despite the widespread recognition that urbanization is economically advantageous, there has long been concern that low-income countries are now urbanizing faster than appropriate to their economic status, especially in sub-Saharan Africa. This was expressed in the *World Development Report 1999/2000*: 'Cities in Africa are not serving as engines of growth and structural transformation. Instead, they are part of the cause and a major symptom of the economic and social crises that have enveloped the continent' (World Bank, 2000, p130). Such sentiments reinforce local prejudice, not so much against cities, as against the urban poor.

While researchers may express their concern with over-urbanization in terms of discrepancies between urbanization rates and economic performance, politicians and urban and international elites point to rapidly growing 'slums'. The residents clearly have not found adequate jobs, so the argument goes, or they would not be living in such conditions. They often lack basic services, creating unsanitary and unhealthy conditions. The ownership of land is often disputed, and informal 'owners' often control lands that are not formally theirs. The dwellings rarely conform to official zoning or building regulations. There are often social tensions surrounding these settlements and their inhabitants.

Many colonial governments explicitly prohibited rural-dwellers from moving to urban settlements without permission. With the exception of South Africa under apartheid, national governments, particularly in the post-colonial period, have generally avoided such overtly discriminatory policies. On the other hand, many inherited colonial legal and planning systems, and few planned for rapid urbanization or for the emergence of large-scale urban poverty. Most national governments have tried to utilize land-use planning and building regulations to restrict the development of urban slums, sometimes backing these up with evictions, which are still disturbingly common (du Plessis, 2005), and denying residents access to services such as water and sanitation.

In effect, these regulations have not provided a standard for low-income neighbourhoods to aspire to, but rather a stick to beat them with. An implicit justification for this discrimination has been that the slum-dwellers should not have moved to the city in the first place – that assisting slum-dwellers contributes to urban bias and over-urbanization, and that urban policies need to make rural–urban migration less, not more, attractive. However, as described in Box 2.1, many residents of these settlements are not rural–urban migrants, but are poor people who previously lived and worked in the city centre and who have been displaced by transformations in the urban space.

Box 2.1 From city centres to peripheral areas: Poor urban residents and marginalized settlements in Venezuela and Nigeria

In Caracas, population growth in the main urban core (Valley of Caracas) has been slowing down, while the peripheral municipalities within the Caracas Metropolitan Area are expanding at an accelerated pace. In part this is due to the overall growth of the metropolis and in part to the displacement of activities and residents from the city centre, which is increasingly dominated by modern business districts and high-income gated residential developments. In the peripheral metropolitan areas, vulnerable lower-middle-income groups can access loans at subsidized interest rates for the purchase of low-cost housing under the Housing Policy Act, while low-income groups are confined to illegal occupation of land, sometimes along railway lines, sometimes on abandoned and never-developed state industrial parks, and sometimes on unused municipal or privately owned land.

Ibadan Municipality consists of five local government areas and six peripheral local government areas where about one-third of the city's people live. Rapid population growth in the main city has resulted in increased demand for land and higher housing costs, which, in turn, have resulted in the outward movement of people from the main city to the city fringes. A small-scale study of low-income women in two peri-urban locations in the peripheral areas shows that about one-third of them had moved with their households from the city centre because of lower accommodation costs, lower costs of living in general, and better opportunities for petty trade and micro-enterprise.

Sources: Lacabana and Cariola (2003); Jaiyebo (2003).

Without any planned locations to populate, or economic resources to buy or rent their way into the formal housing markets, the urban poor are often marginalized, spatially, legally and, to some degree, economically. Spatially, their settlements are shifted to the urban periphery or along marginal lands within the urban centre – along railways or riversides, on steep slopes, or on other land environmentally unsuitable for development. Legally, the settlements are at the margins, in the sense that they break various codes and regulations, often to the point where residents are not allowed to receive public services, though not necessarily to the point where they can be legally evicted. Economically, low-income settlements are very much part of the urban economy, but with important 'imperfections' or discontinuities that, for example, prevent local residents from accessing loans at market rates. In effect, many of these settlements are influenced by plans but are not part of the plan. They are influenced by markets but do not formally constitute private property. Rather, they grew up where neither planners nor private property owners could easily stop them, in the interstices or margins of the urban fabric.

THE CONTRIBUTION OF RURAL–URBAN MIGRATION TO URBAN POPULATION GROWTH

Contrary to widespread perceptions, rural–urban migration is not usually the main component of urban population growth. On average, migration and reclassification of formerly rural areas as urban contribute around 40 per cent to urban growth, with the other 60 per cent due to natural growth (Chen et al, 1998). There are, however, significant differences in the rates of rural–urban migration both between countries and regions and over time within the same countries.

Table 2.3 presents estimates of the rates of urbanization (the annual increment in the percentage that is urban) and the rates of urban growth between 1975 and 2000 for Africa, Asia and Latin America. Ignoring differences in fertility and mortality, these figures imply that rural–urban migration (and reclassification) accounts for about half of urban growth in Asia, but only about 37 per cent in Africa (where natural population growth is particularly high) and about 30 per cent in Latin America (where the population is already preponderantly urban).

Overall, rural–urban migration rates tend to be higher in countries with growing per capita income levels. Estimates of rural–urban migration rates over three decades (the 1960s, 1970s and 1980s) suggest that migration rates in Asia as a whole are low but have continued to increase, while in Latin America they increased in the 1960s but declined in the 1970s and 1980s, and in Africa they have continuously declined since the 1960s (Chen et al, 1998). Although these estimates should be treated carefully because they are aggregates for large regions,[2] they highlight the link between rural–urban migration and economic growth – the declines in Latin America and Africa correspond to decades of economic stagnation. The recent high rates of urbanization in the eastern and south-eastern parts of Asia correspond to exceptionally high rates of economic growth. In China, the number of rural–urban migrants increased from just 2 million in the mid-1980s to 70 million in the mid-1990s and 94 million in 2002 (Ping and Pieke, 2003). In contrast, rural–urban migration is much less significant in sub-Saharan Africa, where, since the 1980s, economic crises and stagnation have somewhat reduced rural–urban inequalities in terms of incomes and opportunities,

Table 2.3 *Rates of urbanization and urban growth in Africa, Asia and Latin America*

Region	Rate of urbanization (%) (1975–2000)	Rate of urban growth (%) (1975–2000)
Africa	1.54	4.21
Asia	1.75	3.47
Latin America	0.84	2.76

Source: United Nations (2004).

resulting in increases in *urban–rural* migration (Jamal and Weeks, 2003; Potts and Mutambirwa, 1998).

It should be kept in mind, however, that international comparisons of urbanization – and of the importance of rural–urban migration and reclassification – are inherently inaccurate due to the wide differences in the national definitions of what constitutes an urban centre. This is especially the case for small towns: where population size is used, national cut-off points range between 200 and 50,000 (United Nations, 2002). Administrative status is also often utilized to define what constitutes an urban centre, again with wide variations among countries. Economic structure, often measured as the proportion of residents employed in non-agricultural sectors, sometimes in combination with other criteria such as population size and density, is the third and probably most accurate way to define urban centres. But since different countries use different criteria (either population size, administrative status or economic structure), generalizations should be treated with great caution, as indicated in Chapter 1.

Moreover, significant transformations in the shape of settlements have blurred the rural–urban distinction, with many settlements maintaining a rural administrative status despite becoming physically incorporated in extensive metropolitan regions, or clearly agriculture-based areas being incorporated within urban boundaries. Increased mobility and diversification of the income sources of rural households, with a growing proportion in non-farm work, mean that in many cases individuals live in one settlement but work in a different one, often an urban centre. In China, research in Jiangsu Province in the mid-1980s showed that daily commuters from surrounding rural villages accounted for up to 43 per cent of the daytime population of local small towns (Kirkby et al, 2000). In 1987–1988, four per cent of the urban workforce in India consisted of rural-based commuters, and this proportion has probably increased since then (Dyson and Visaria, 2005).

While there are essential differences between urban and rural contexts, among different rural contexts, and among urban contexts, as well as within urban centres themselves, especially large cities, it is important to recognize and understand the often-neglected crucial interdependencies between cities and countryside and the factors that determine the characteristics of poverty and vulnerability of their inhabitants. It is also important to recognize and understand the ways in which the many links between urban centres and rural settlements contribute to poverty reduction or increase poverty and vulnerability.

THE MULTIPLE LINKS BETWEEN URBAN POVERTY AND RURAL POVERTY

Rural and urban poverty are linked and do not merely compete with each other for resources. Successful rural development actually boosts urban development, and increasing levels of urbanization in agricultural regions are among the best indicators of successful rural development. At the same time, urban growth and urban prosperity increase demand for high-value agricultural produce, thereby raising farmers' incomes. Any strategy to reduce poverty needs to recognize that reducing urban poverty will generally help reduce rural poverty and vice versa.

Prosperous, high-value agriculture can greatly reduce both rural and urban poverty, although the extent of this depends heavily on the land-owning structure and on whether smallholders have access to local, national and regional markets. Many urban areas have had booming economies as a result of shifts in agriculture to higher-value crops, which supported much-increased demand for producer goods and services (for instance credit, farm machinery, storage and processing) and for consumer goods and services from more prosperous rural households. The more rural households earn a good return from this, the greater the stimulus to the economy of the local urban centre.

But agricultural development can also reduce access to land and water for significant sections of the rural population and thus increase rural poverty (and often increase migration to urban areas). Export-oriented commercial crops produced by large, mechanized farms may not reduce rural poverty if they generate relatively few adequately paying jobs. Increased competition for access to land and water may disadvantage smallholders, who may end up working as wage labourers, often on a seasonal basis and for low wages. Whole households or individual household members might have to move to urban centres, where limited skills confine them in the lowest-paid segments of the labour market. In such circumstances, unequal rural economic growth can increase urban poverty.

Seasonal wage labour in commercial agriculture is often a source of income for the urban poor. However, agricultural wage labour is possibly the lowest paid and most insecure occupation. Waged farm workers in Zimbabwe, for example, are among the poorest groups in the country's population, earning far less than the rural poverty line and the total consumption poverty line (Kamete, 1998). In high-income countries, seasonal agricultural labour is increasingly the preserve of migrant workers, often undocumented and exploited by gangmasters. For the urban poor, such work is likely to reduce their vulnerability in the short term, but not significantly reduce poverty levels.

Urban development has been shown in many contexts to contribute to the reduction of rural poverty and to stimulate rural development. Growing demand for high-value food products by urban consumers benefits farmers, especially smallholders, whose greater flexibility enables them to respond more effectively than large commercial farms. Moreover, rural households are able to invest in agricultural intensification and diversification by drawing on the money earned by individual members engaged in non-farm activities, often located in local small towns, and on remittances from those who migrate to more distant urban centres (Tiffen, 2003).

On the other hand, urban development can increase rural poverty by displacing large numbers of the urban poor to rural peripheries (for instance through forced relocations, as described earlier in this chapter) or by dispossessing rural-dwellers as their land is purchased for urban development at a fraction of its value and/or with very inadequate compensation. Whether or not a city's rapid economic growth increases, rural (and urban) poverty depends heavily on how governments manage this. If governments permit and support massive demolition and forced evictions of low-income populations and land-acquisition around cities with no protection for local (rural) populations, poverty is created or exacerbated.

RURAL–URBAN MIGRATION AND THE POVERTY IMPLICATIONS FOR RECEIVING AREAS

While rural–urban migration is the movement of most concern to policymakers and urban administrations, in many countries, the numbers of rural–rural migrants outstrip those of rural–urban migrants. In other cases, urban–urban migration is more important, and urban–rural movement may increase both for retirement purposes and because of increased difficulties in making a living in the city in times of economic crisis. To a large extent, the direction of migration flows reflects a country's level of urbanization and its economic base. Hence rural–rural migration is still the main type of movement in agriculture-based economies, especially in Africa and Asia, whereas urban–urban movement is more important in more urbanized regions such as Latin America (although with wide variations among countries). Patterns of migration are also increasingly influenced by the uneven spatial distribution of foreign investment, and this is especially the case in South-East Asia.

Rural–urban migrants are usually better educated and have more economic resources than those who stay behind in rural areas. Combined with severe urban inequalities, this often gives rural–urban migrants an economic advantage over the poorest urban groups. A review of the share of migrants among the urban poor in demographic and health surveys (DHSs) in 20 low- and middle-income countries found that the proportion ranged from 7 per cent in Nigeria to 43 per cent in Bolivia, with the share in 12 of the countries ranging between 25 and 35 per cent (Gardner and Blackburn, 1996). Of course, it is also likely that there is some element of self-selection of successful migrants, and that unsuccessful migrants do not stay in the urban centres, preferring to return to their home areas. This underscores the importance of rural-based safety nets for a segment of the urban poor.

It is often assumed that rural–urban migrants intend to settle permanently in urban centres. While this is certainly the case for many of them, a large number of rural residents only remain in urban centres for limited periods of time, either as a one-off stay or moving regularly every few months, often during periods when agricultural work is less intensive. Farmers in Viet Nam's Red River Delta go to Hanoi to work in the construction sector for a few months every year and then invest their earnings in agricultural production (Hoang et al, 2005). In Thailand, temporary migration, mainly to Bangkok and its surrounding areas, is estimated to account for one-third of all internal migration and is linked to the dry season, when labour demand for agricultural work decreases (Guest, 1998).

In many urban centres, the proportion of women-headed households is significantly higher than in the surrounding rural settlements, as economic survival in rural areas is problematic for women without a male partner, since they often lose their rights to land and have limited income-earning possibilities. Urban centres, with the opportunity for non-farm work, are a better option for these households. Although women's migration is also motivated by economic reasons, movement is to a large extent the result of gender inequalities that limit women's access to assets (especially land) and to activities in the rural non-farm sector other than the lowest-paid ones (Seppala, 1996).

Rural–urban migration is often viewed as a cause of environmental problems in urban centres. This relates to the assumption that rural–urban migrants are primarily responsible for urban growth (but see sections above for evidence that disproves this). Recent (and not-so-recent) migrants are also often thought to retain 'rural' behaviours, especially with regard to the disposal of household wastes and personal sanitation. The relationship between migrant status and attitude towards hygiene is unproven, however, whereas the relationship between illness and living in densely populated settlements, with limited or non-existing facilities such as water, sanitation and waste disposal, is widely recognized. So is the fact that the urban poor, regardless of their migrant status, suffer disproportionately from environmental problems because of the lack of services in the settlements where they live. They are also more likely to suffer disproportionately from natural disasters, as they often live on ecologically marginal areas such as steep slopes and areas prone to flooding.

For poor people, life in an urban centre can be full of uncertainty, either through loss of employment or insufficient earnings, loss of housing, especially in informal settlements, illness or death of working household members, which can dramatically affect the family's income, or, in many places, increases in violent crime and political instability. It is not unusual for poor urban households to maintain assets in their (rural) home areas as a safety net and possibly a place to go back to in their old age. Rural safety nets held by urban individuals or households in their 'home areas' are important in many instances, but this is often overlooked. For example, in Ethiopia, recent land legislation gives user rights to farmers, but these can be lost if the land is not cultivated for a certain period of time. In Viet Nam, migrants face a similar problem and usually resort to informal arrangements with relatives and neighbours, who cultivate the land on their behalf. Other entitlements can be lost by migrants: in Botswana, low-income urban migrants who invest in livestock in their home areas are not entitled to drought relief and other state subsidies, despite their contribution to local rural economies (Kruger, 1998). In China, debates on the reform of the household registration system are usually concerned with increasing freedom of movement; however, an important element in the debate is how to ensure that temporary migrants do not lose their entitlement to land, currently linked to their registration status (Ping and Pieke, 2003).

Data on population distribution does not provide information on the spatial distribution of people's assets and activities, and much of it comes from small-scale research on livelihoods and the role of mobility in reducing risk and accumulating assets. Understanding the spatial dimensions of livelihoods is, however, a key element of poverty reduction. A central issue for policymakers is whether multi-local livelihoods (that rely on assets and activities located in both rural and urban areas) are a transitional phase in a trend towards less spatially dispersed (and more urban) patterns, or whether this is likely to remain a relatively permanent feature. The latter view is supported by the significance of temporary movement and by the less important contribution of rural–urban migration to urban growth than is usually thought. In countries where economic stagnation has been a more or less constant feature of the past two decades, difficult living conditions in the cities may well be an important factor in making people spread their assets and activities to reduce risk. However, similar trends can also be seen in countries undergoing rapid economic growth (for example China and South-East Asia).

Conclusion: Rural–Urban Migration and Planning For – Rather than Against – The Urban Poor

Attempts to limit urban growth by controlling migration are misguided – in part because migration flows are logical responses to changing economic opportunities and in part because most urban population growth is actually from natural increase, not net rural-to-urban migration. The link between urban poverty and migration is also unproven. However, much more attention needs to be given to urban poverty and to ways of measuring it that reflect the true costs of living in a specific urban centre. At the same time, planners need to take into account the profound impact on the poor of transformations in the urban space, such as the reconstruction of city centres to host business and high-income residential developments. Without careful planning, the outcome of these projects is to displace the poor and increase their vulnerability by reducing their options for housing and employment. Careful planning also involves understanding that, for poor people (and in many cases for non-poor groups as well), spreading their assets and activities between urban centres and rural areas is a rational strategy to reduce their risks and accumulate assets. Rural–urban migration is thus part of the solution to reducing both rural and urban poverty, rather than a poverty problem. For national and local planners, recognizing the links between rural and urban people and economies is an important step to understanding how policies ranging from national economic strategies (and the spatial distribution of investments) to infrastructure development can contribute to rural and urban poverty reduction, or to its production.

NOTES

1   In 1996, 45 per cent of all governments were concerned with urban growth, a figure that rose to 52 per cent in 2003. African governments are clearly the most concerned: in 2003, 81 per cent declared that they were implementing policies to lower internal migration to urban centres, compared to 52 per cent in 1996 (United Nations, 2004).

2   As the authors note, caution is also dictated by the limited number of countries with data available and by the changing coverage of countries from one decade to the next, particularly in Africa and Asia.

REFERENCES

APHRC (2002) *Population and Health Dynamics in Nairobi's Informal Settlements*, African Population and Health Research Center, Nairobi

Bromley, R. (ed) (1979) *The Urban Informal Sector: Critical Perspectives on Employment and Housing Policies*, Pergamon Press, Oxford, UK, and New York

Bromley, R. and Gerry, C. (eds) (1979) *Casual Work and Poverty in Third World Cities*, John Wiley and Sons, Chichester, UK, and New York

Champion, T. and Hugo, G. (2004) 'Introduction: Moving beyond the urban–rural dichotomy', in T. Champion and G. Hugo (eds) *New Forms of Urbanization: Beyond the Urban–Rural Dichotomy*, Ashgate, Aldershot, UK

Chen, N., Valente, P. and Zlotnik, H. (1998) 'What do we know about recent trends in urbanization?', in R. E. Bilsborrow (ed) *Migration, Urbanization and Development: New Directions and Issues*, UNFPA and Kluwer Academic Publishers, New York, pp59–88

Demographic and Health Surveys (DHSs) (undated), STAT compiler, www.measuredhs. com, last accessed 1 November 2007

du Plessis, J. (2005) 'The growing problem of forced evictions and the crucial importance of community-based, locally appropriate alternatives', *Environment and Urbanization*, vol 17, no 1, pp123–134

Dyson, T. and Visaria, P. (2005) 'Migration and urbanization: Retrospect and prospects', in T, Dyson, R. Cassen and L. Visaria (eds) *Twenty-First Century India: Population, Economy, Human Development and the Environment*, Oxford University Press, Oxford, UK, pp108–129

Gardner, R. and Blackburn, R. (1996) *People Who Move: New Reproductive Health Focus*, Population Reports, Series J, No 45, Population Information Program, Johns Hopkins School of Public Health, Baltimore, MD

González de la Rocha, M. and Grinspun, A. (2001) 'Private adjustments: Households, crisis and work', in A. Grinspun (ed) *Choices for the Poor: Lessons from National Poverty Strategies*, UNDP, New York, pp55–87

Guest, P. (1998) 'Assessing the consequences of internal migration: Methodological issues and a case study on Thailand based on longitudinal household survey data', in R. E. Bilsborrow (ed) *Migration, Urbanization and Development: New Directions and Issues*, UNFPA and Kluwer Academic Publishers, New York, pp275–318

Hoang, X. T., Dang, A. N. and Tacoli, C. (2005) 'Livelihood diversification and rural–urban linkages in Vietnam's Red River Delta', Rural–Urban Working Paper No 11, International Institute for Environment and Development (IIED), London

Jamal, V. and Weeks, J. (1993) *Africa Misunderstood, or Whatever Happened to the Rural–Urban Gap?*, Palgrave Macmillan, London

Jaiyebo, O. (2003) 'Women and household sustenance: Changing livelihoods and survival strategies in the peri-urban areas of Ibadan', *Environment and Urbanization*, vol 15, no 1, pp111–120

Kamete, A. Y. (1998) 'Interlocking livelihoods: Farm and small town in Zimbabwe', *Environment and Urbanization*, vol 10, no 1, pp23–34

Kanji, N. (1995) 'Gender, poverty and economic adjustment in Harare, Zimbabwe', *Environment and Urbanization*, vol 7, no 1, pp37–56

Khan, A. R. and Riskin, C. (2002) *Inequality and Poverty in China in an Age of Globalization*, Oxford University Press, Oxford, UK

Kirkby, R., Bradbury, I. and Shen, G. (2000) *Small Town China: Governance, Economy, Environment and Lifestyle in Three Zhen*, Ashgate, Aldershot, UK

Kruger, F. (1998) 'Taking advantage of rural assets as a coping strategy for the urban poor: The case of rural–urban interrelations in Botswana', *Environment and Urbanization*, vol 10, no 1, pp119–134

Lacabana, M. and Cariola, C. (2003) 'Globalization and metropolitan expansion: Residential strategies and livelihoods in Caracas and its periphery', *Environment and Urbanization*, vol 15, no 1, pp65–74

Montgomery, M. R., Stren, R., Cohen, B. and Reed, H. E. (eds) (2003) *Cities Transformed: Demographic Change and its Implications in the Developing World*, The National Academy Press, Washington, DC

Moser, C. (1984) 'The informal sector reworked: Viability and vulnerability in urban development', *Regional Development Dialogue*, vol 5, no 2, pp135–178

Njoh, A. J. (2003) 'Urbanization and development in sub-Saharan Africa', *Cities*, vol 20, no 3, pp167–174

Overman, H. G. and Venables, A. J. (2005) 'Cities in the developing world', CEP Discussion Paper No 695, Centre for Economic Performance, London School of Economics, London

Ping, H. and Pieke, F. (2003) 'China migration country study', paper presented at the Regional Conference on Migration, Development and Pro-Poor Policy Choices in Asia, Dhaka, 22–24 June 2003, Department for International Development, London

Potts, D. and Mutambirwa, C. (1998) 'Basics are now a luxury: Perceptions of structural adjustment's impact on rural and urban areas in Zimbabwe', *Environment and Urbanization*, vol 10, no 1, pp55–76

Ruel, M. T., Garrett, J. L., Morris, S. S., Maxwell, D., Oshaug, A., Engle, P., Menon, P., Slack, A. and Haddad, L. (1998) 'Urban challenges to nutrition security: A review of food security, health and care in the cities', Food Consumption and Nutrition Division Discussion Paper No 51, International Food Policy Research Institute, Washington, DC

Satterthwaite, D. (2004) 'The under-estimation of urban poverty in low- and middle-income nations', IIED Working Paper on Poverty Reduction in Urban Areas No 14, International Institute for Environment and Development, London

Satterthwaite, D. (2007) 'In pursuit of a healthy urban environment in low- and middle-income nations', in P. J. Marcotullio and G. McGranahan (eds) (2007) *Scaling Urban Environmental Challenges: From Local to Global and Back*, Earthscan, London, pp69–105

Seppala, P. (1996) 'The politics of economic diversification: Reconceptualizing the rural informal sector in southeast Tanzania', *Development and Change*, vol 27, pp557–578

Tiffen, M. (2003) 'Transitions in sub-Saharan Africa: Agriculture, urbanization and income growth', *World Development*, vol 31, no 8, pp1343–1366

UN-Habitat (1996) *An Urbanizing World: Global Report on Human Settlements 1996* (HS/397/96A), Oxford University Press, Oxford, UK

United Nations (2002) *World Urbanization Prospects: The 2001 Revision*, Population Division, United Nations, New York

United Nations (2004) *World Urbanization Prospects: The 2003 Revision*, Population Division, United Nations, New York

United Nations (2006) *World Urbanization Prospects: The 2005 Revision*, CD-ROM Edition: Data in digital form (POP/DB/WUP/Rev.2005), Population Division, United Nations, New York

World Bank (2000) *Entering the 21st Century: World Development Report 1999/2000*, Oxford University Press, New York

World Bank (2003) *World Development Report 2003: Sustainable Development in a Dynamic World: Transforming Institutions, Growth and Quality of Life*, Oxford University Press, New York

3

Demographic and Urban Transitions in a Global System and Policy Responses

Ronald Skeldon

BACKGROUND

Two of the momentous changes that have occurred across much of the world over the last 200 years have been demographic: transitions to societies of low fertility and mortality (the demographic transition *sensu strictu*) and transitions to societies where a large majority of the population is concentrated in urban areas (the urban transition). These two transitions are not independent of each other, but neither are they associated in any neat or systematic way. Nevertheless, no highly urbanized society has high levels of fertility or mortality. One of the characteristics of these transitions is that, although the speeds, the dates of onset and the starting levels of the variables of the transitions have all been different, the overall trend, irrespective of political system or culture area, has been a shift towards lower fertility and mortality and an increasing concentration of population in urban areas.

In 1950, global fertility was around five children per woman, life expectancy was around 46 years and about 29 per cent of the world's population lived in cities (estimates in United Nations, 2007). By 2000, global fertility had declined to 2.7 children, expectation of life at birth was over 65 years of age and some 46.7 per cent of the world's population lived in urban areas. The United Nations estimates for the major world regions from 1950 to 2025 are given in Table 3.1. Although considerable variation exists within each of the major regions listed, the universality of a trend towards a low-fertility, low-mortality and urban society seems apparent.

Table 3.1 *Basic variables in the demographic and urban transitions, 1950–2025, world and major regions*

	1950–1955			1975–1980			2000–2005			2025–2030		
	TFR	e^0	Urban	TFR	e^0	Urban	TFR	e^0	Urban	TFR	e^0	Urban
World	5.02	46.4	29.0	3.92	60.2	37.2	2.65	66.0	46.7	2.21	71.9	57.5
Africa	6.75	38.5	14.7	6.61	48.7	25.4	4.98	51.6	36.2	3.30	59.8	47.9
Asia	5.87	41.0	16.8	4.19	59.1	23.3	2.47	67.5	40.4	2.01	74.1	59.3
Europe	2.66	65.6	50.5	1.97	71.3	65.6	1.41	73.8	71.7	1.61	78.2	76.6
LAC	5.88	51.4	42.0	4.48	63.0	61.2	2.52	72.0	75.4	1.97	77.1	83.1
N. America	3.46	68.8	63.9	1.78	73.4	73.8	1.99	78.5	79.1	1.83	80.9	85.7
Oceania	3.87	60.4	62.0	2.73	67.9	71.5	2.37	74.4	70.5	2.08	78.4	73.0

Note: Total fertility rates (TFR) and life expectancy at birth (e^0) are given as averages for the five-year period indicated; urbanization (urban) levels are given for the start year.
Sources: United Nations (2006b and 2007).

A critical question remains with reference to the urban, if not the demographic, transition: whether it is some inevitable part of a global process or whether it can be subject to policy intervention that can influence the rate or even the direction of change. It is assumed that lower mortality and fertility will be both a cause and a consequence of the present development aims of the global community, as expressed, for example, in the Millennium Development Goals. Hence the demographic transition is generally seen as a 'positive' and an integral part of development in its broadest sense.

Two examples illustrate this point. First, at the macro level, lower fertility will decrease the youth dependency ratio and generate age profiles more favourable to development in the medium term. Second, the empowerment of women is unlikely to occur without some reduction in childbearing, which will loosen them from patriarchal control and allow greater participation in activities beyond the home. The urban transition, on the other hand, has not necessarily been seen as a 'good', positive or integral part of development. On the contrary, it has often been considered undesirable, and measures have often been taken to slow or even reverse the trend. The concentration of population in cities, and particularly in large cities, has been seen to result in 'unbalanced' population distributions, an 'over-urbanization' that has seen the emergence of 'a planet of slums' in which one billion people struggle to find employment and which represents the real crisis of world capitalism (see Davis, 2006; also UNFPA, 2007, p16).

POLICIES AND REALITIES

The list of anti-urban policies that have been implemented is long but can generally be divided into two types: direct and indirect controls on the growth of large cities. Early assessments of such policies, as well as the thinking of the late 1970s, can be found in United Nations (1981) (see also Peek and Standing, 1982; Oberai, 1983). Direct controls focus on either (a) attempts to restrict population movements towards the cities from the countryside or small towns or (b) attempts to force migrants, or other city residents, back to small towns or rural areas. Bulldozing low-income settlements and forcing the residents out of the city, as was seen in Zimbabwe, is but a recent example of a strategy that was implemented in areas as different as apartheid-era South Africa, China and marginal urban areas around Latin American cities in the 1960s.

Among the most 'successful' of the direct control policies were those implemented in China in the 1960s and 1970s. Based on a household registration system (*Hukou*), rural residents were not allowed to change their place of registration without state sanction (Mallee, 1995). This system could only be effective in the context of a socialist economy, in which no free market for food existed: people could only obtain the basic staple grain at their place of registration. State control was reinforced through a series of mass campaigns that literally saw millions of people forced to move from the city to the countryside, particularly in the infamous 'sending down' flows of 1960–1961 and 1966–1967. Although many of those displaced trickled back, the policies were effective over the short term in limiting the growth of cities in China. One observer concluded that the level of urbanization in the absence of the direct policies that were implemented would have been at least twice that which was observed in the early 1980s (Banister, 1987, pp326–327).

However, with the emergence of market reforms from 1979, which allowed people to purchase grain in 'free' markets, the registration system as an effective control of migration to the cities began to break down. The result was that, after years of control, a huge migration was unleashed, perhaps 'the largest peacetime movement of people in history' (Murphy, 2002, p1). The proportion of the population of China classified as living in urban areas soared from 19.4 per cent in 1980 to 44.5 per cent in 2005, when some 532 million people were estimated to be living in towns and cities (United Nations, 2006b).

Non-socialist economies, too, have attempted to restrict access to cities, for example the Indonesian policy to 'close' Jakarta in 1970, when it had a population of about 3.9 million and was the 23rd largest urban agglomeration in the world. However, by 2005, Jakarta was estimated to have reached 13.2 million and was the 9th largest city in the world (United Nations, 2006b). And it was not just in large countries that anti-urban attitudes were found. Policies to restrict migration to Port Moresby in Papua New Guinea date from the 1960s. The movement was seen to be 'detrimental to village life', with migrants in the city viewed as unemployed vagrants, whether this was true or not, who were to be repatriated home (Oram, 1976, pp168–169). Most of them simply returned to the city as soon as they could.

Perhaps the most dramatic attempt to reverse the tide of urbanization, however, was seen in Cambodia after the Khmer Rouge overthrew the US-backed military junta in 1975 and ordered the populations out of the cities. Phnom Penh, which had been a thriving city of some 600,000 before the war in Indochina, but was swollen by many hundreds of thousands of people fleeing the bombing in the countryside, was virtually turned into a ghost city within a matter of days. Over three million people who had been living in cities were suddenly forced into the countryside. Over one million were killed. While this was one of the greatest human tragedies of the era, the impact on urbanization over all but the shortest period of time was negligible. The proportion of the population living in urban areas declined over the period 1970–1975 from 11.7 to 10.2 per cent, although these figures should be treated with some degree of caution. By 1980, following the Vietnamese invasion, the proportion had increased to 12.4 per cent; conflict and economic stagnation continued over the following decade, with the proportion urban still only 12.6 per cent in 1990. That proportion rose to 19.7 per cent by 2005, when Cambodia was showing one of the fastest rates of urbanization in South-East Asia (all urban estimates from United Nations, 2006b).

Other countries that pursued 'closed city' policies were South Africa and Namibia under apartheid, where access to cities was strictly policed (Simon, 1992, p107). The proportion of the population that was classified as urban in South Africa remained remarkably stable from 1960 to 1985, rising from 46.6 to 49.4 per cent, but it had increased to 59.3 per cent by 2005 (United Nations, 2006b) after the racist system was swept away by 1990. The majority of African governments, however, attempted to reduce migration to the cities through less extreme measures (Becker et al, 1994, p120), although these anti-urban attitudes had their roots in earlier colonial practices to limit the number of Africans living permanently in towns (see Nugent, 2004, p59; Davis, 2006, pp51–55).

In Africa, and elsewhere, more common direct policies were those that tried to improve conditions in the areas of origin so that rural-dwellers did not have to move to the cities. However, attempts at rural development through the construction of roads and the raising of education levels had the opposite effect. These improvements, along with projects to raise rural incomes, provided more people with the means to migrate: access to cities, information and cash. Rural development, initially at least, tended to accelerate rather than reduce mobility from the villages. Furthermore, the limited development funds available were often concentrated in a relatively small number of locations, and these tended to be in urban areas: the urban bias that has been attributed to so much of development efforts (Lipton, 1977).

Governments of newly independent states saw their priority as centralizing power and were reluctant to disperse scarce funds to remoter areas where their control might be more tenuous. Hence, despite aspirations to limit migration to the cities, the result of the development policies implemented by governments was to increase such movement. Again, the consequences of the migration were often misconceived: migrants in urban areas and the circulation of migrants between urban and rural areas could have positive effects on the development of both urban and rural sectors, as well as for the migrants themselves (Skeldon, 1990; Becker et al, 1994).

An important variant of rural development policies to channel potential migrants away from the largest cities was that which was designed to divert migrants to alternative rural destinations by opening up new areas of agricultural land in settlement frontiers. One of the most ambitious attempts was in Indonesia – the *transmigrasi* programme which aimed to move millions of farmers from the densely populated central island of Java to the outer islands of the archipelagic state, particularly to Sumatra and Sulawesi. Although begun under the Dutch, *transmigrasi* reached its height in the 1980s, when almost 600,000 families were moved to outer islands, more than twice the number moved since the inception of the programme some 70 years before (Hugo, 1997, p238). However, this flow was occurring at precisely the same time that the growth of the urban population of Indonesia was also peaking: it rose by over 22 million over the decade (United Nations 2006b, p78). Thus, relative to the flow to the urban areas, the numbers of those being moved into new rural settlements were quite small.

Many other countries have implemented policies of agricultural settlement, the objective of which was to divert rural migrants from going to the largest cities. The movement of people into the dry zone of Sri Lanka from the densely settled highlands of the south-western part of the island in the 1960s and 1970s; the movement of people eastwards in the Malayan peninsula from the concentrations along the western side; the movement of poor migrants from the northern border areas of Viet Nam into the central highlands far to the south; and the movements into the upper Amazon from the highland communities in Ecuador, Peru and Bolivia are but four examples. These schemes often had more to do with the extension of state control over areas where its influence was weak than with a real commitment to limiting the size of the largest cities. The financial costs of establishing these new settlements were usually substantial, and environmental destruction in these often marginal areas could be great. (These issues are reviewed in Skeldon, 1990, pp200–201.) Clashes between new settlers and indigenous inhabitants also raised significant political and human rights issues. More central to the concerns of this chapter, however, is the fact that these attempts to create alternative destinations for potential rural–urban migrants had little impact on either slowing the pace or decreasing the level of urbanization.

Indirect policies to influence the distribution of the population usually revolve around measures that lower the cost of land or utilities outside the capital city or provide tax benefits for establishing enterprises in small towns as opposed to the largest cities. Administrative measures and planning procedures attempt to divert businesses or government departments away from the national or state capitals in order to decentralize economic and bureaucratic activity. For these to be effective, however, an efficient and transparent bureaucratic organization must exist that few developing countries possess. Also, the decentralization of business or administrative activity might not make economic or political sense. In developed societies that follow a neo-liberal agenda focused on the market, concentration will continue until the costs rise to a level that might encourage the emergence of a new pattern. Initially, agglomeration and economies of scale may ultimately make more economic and political sense than idealized schemes to generate a more even spread of urban places. The apparent benefits as well as the disadvantages of concentration are well reviewed in Montgomery et al (2003, p312), which sums up the debate by arguing that urban spatial concentration must be one cause of national economic growth, even if its exact contribution is not yet known.

The debate about the advantages or disadvantages of agglomeration usually focuses primarily on economic benefits and costs. Nevertheless, political issues also loom large. Decentralizing investment towards distant smaller towns or rural areas, no matter how beneficial in economic terms this might be, can provide support to potentially rival or competing interest groups. Hence a basic tension can exist between concentrating investment and keeping power in the centre or diffusing investment that might lead to more decentralized power that could threaten the integrity of fragile states. Few governments, whether more autocratic or more open, are willing to take this risk. Yet continued migration to mega-cities concentrates populations that can be increasingly difficult to control and are in a position to threaten governments. Hence the basic dilemma: to decentralize to produce a more equitable distribution of investment – a strategy that may not stop the migration towards the largest cities and may support rival factions – or to maintain a strategy of agglomeration that will also concentrate disaffected groups but in areas where they can be more easily confronted.

Governments since the early 1980s, an era of increasing globalization, have leaned more towards accepting the continuing migration to cities rather than implementing policies that are designed to divert or slow the flows. The reasons for this are clear. When cities were relatively small, net migration was an important component of total growth. As cities expanded in population, the natural increase of the primarily youthful populations grew in importance as a component of growth, even though urban fertility was generally lower than rural fertility (United Nations, 2001a). Although adequate recent time-series data to demonstrate the case are scarce, those that are available suggest that, in areas of high fertility, the importance of natural increase grows over time. Conversely, as urban fertility declines to below replacement levels over a long period of time, the importance of net migration rises once again.

The emphasis in policy thus switches away from largely futile attempts to divert migration flows towards dealing with the consequences of that migration and integrating migrants and low-income urban natives into the economic and social fabric of the urban areas. How this is best done, however, remains the subject of considerable debate. One line of thinking that dates from the work of Turner (1968) and Mangin (1967) in the 1960s is best expressed in the work of De Soto (1989). This approach emphasizes the role of self-help: the poor and recent arrivals in cities, if granted tenure to land, are best placed to create their own settlements, employment and security, with minimum government assistance. Others are critical of this approach because of the abrogation of the state from its responsibilities and because it has led to substandard construction, higher prices and potential for local abuse, as outlined in the polemic of Davis (2006). Irrespective of the merits of the various arguments, the policy emphasis over recent decades has primarily focused on the best ways to improve welfare in low-income urban settlements for all residents, irrespective of their origins, rather than on attempting to influence the direction of migration. After all, the right to freedom of movement has been accepted by all states as a universal human right.

Thus attempts to limit either the growth of cities in general or the concentration of population or activity in the largest of these cities may be counterproductive. The transition to an urban society based on large cities appears unstoppable, even if history has shown that it is possible to slow or even to reverse that process for short periods of time. Policy interventions to try to divert the process of urbanization are unlikely to be effective or even desirable. Yet even in 2005, almost three-quarters of governments in the developing world still thought that they should implement policies to reduce internal migration into urban agglomerations (United Nations, 2006b, p24). Over half the governments in the developing world thought that a major change in the distribution of their population was desirable. The proportions of governments in the developed world who felt that migration into urban agglomerations should be reduced was slightly lower, at 61 per cent, but just over one-third of developed-country governments considered that a major change in their population distribution was desirable.

Thus, in the developing world in particular, a fear of large cities still exists, together with concern about perceived disruption brought about by rural-to-large-city migration. The current debate on international migration and development, in which the benefits are emphasized as much as the costs of migration, does not yet appear to have permeated into the discourse on internal migration and development (see, for example, GCIM, 2005; United Nations; 2006a). Internal and international migrations remain essentially separate areas of research and policy. Yet clear linkages exist between the two types of migration, both in terms of the real impact of the one on the other and in terms of policy formulation.

A SECOND URBAN TRANSITION?

Just how urban can societies become? United Nations (2006b) estimates place proportions of between 75 and 85 per cent as about the limits of urbanization in the most-developed societies and in their urban projections through to 2030. However, at these levels, any distinction between rural and urban becomes largely meaningless, as the population still remaining in 'rural' areas will be mostly part of the urban world by virtue of modern technologies of transportation and communication. Yet that urban world, given the direction of the demographic transition, cannot go on expanding indefinitely. The transition to very low levels of fertility, with the resulting ageing societies, and mortality rising as the population ages, has been termed the 'second demographic transition' (van de Kaa, 1987). Ultimately, if these trends persist, the mainly urban populations must start to shrink, a trend that will first be seen at the national level. However, the nature of the migration process leading to urbanization is also changing, and it is perhaps appropriate to think of a 'second urban transition' as well. This transition, as with the demographic transition, begins in the developed world and may eventually diffuse into the periphery, as the fertility levels of developing countries also dip below replacement levels.

The transitions in developed societies of destination

The second demographic transition will bring very low levels of fertility, to the extent that the urban populations will not be replacing themselves. As important, however, is the draining of the pool of potential rural–urban migrants in the rural sector, which has supplied the cities with labour.

To take Japan as an example, between 1947 and 1990, some 28 million new jobs in industrial areas were created, but 13 million in agriculture and forestry were lost (Totman, 2000, p472). Over this period, the rural population of Japan was drained to the extent that, by the 1990s, virtually half of the total land area was classified as 'severely depopulating'. Some 40 per cent of Japan's rural population and over 60 per cent of its farmers are currently over 65 years of age. Japan's fertility had fallen below replacement level by 1960, and the number of young adults, who are those most likely to migrate, has been declining since 1970. Nationally, in 2003, the number of young adults (20–34 years old) was over 5 per cent less than in 1970. The number of internal migrants in Japan has also steadily decreased over recent decades, from 4.2 million interprefectural migrants in 1970 to 3.4 million in 1980, 3.2 million in 1990 and 2.7 million in 2003, and many of these, perhaps the majority, were within the urban sector itself.

The conclusion seems inescapable: the supply of that 'ultimate resource', population, from internal sources is decreasing, and, if the cities are to maintain their growth and demographic dynamism, other strategies will be required. Of course, a reduction in population may not necessarily be negative for the urban future, but, in a competitive globalizing world, labour shortages, and specifically skilled labour shortages, appear to characterize the global city. A central part of any second urban transition is the extension of the migration fields overseas and the substitution of internal migration and natural increase with international migration.

This transition is the urban counterpart of the 'migration turnaround', in which countries shift from being economies of net emigration to economies of net immigration (Abella, 1994). In southern Europe, Spain, Portugal, Italy and Greece have all gone through this shift from emigration to immigration in recent decades, and in Asia, Japan, South Korea, Taiwan, Province of China, and increasingly Malaysia and Thailand appear to be following suit, though often not in a neat and tidy way (see, for example, the results of some of the work summarized in Skeldon, 2006b; see also King et al, 1997; Fielding, 2004).

A shift from net emigration to net immigration does not imply that out-migration from a country ceases. In fact, out-migration could theoretically increase in tandem with even greater increases in in-migration. Out-migration continues as skilled nationals move overseas as part of global corporate expansion, governmental and non-governmental development aid programmes, or simply to compete in global markets. For example, the UK has a similar proportion of its population overseas as those countries more commonly associated with emigration, such as Mexico or the Philippines, even if the types of emigrants are quite different (see Sriskandarajah and Drew, 2006). Much of this global movement is circular, whether of longer or shorter duration, and is centred around the largest or global city (Sassen, 1991). The city is central in this process: it is the conduit, and very often the origin, of much of the emigration; it, or its immediate surrounding areas, is also the primary destination of the immigration that can be expected in the second urban transition.

However, international migration is not simply a substitute for all internal migration. In the context of skilled migration, for example, many of the skills could not in the past and cannot at present be sourced locally. A significant circulation of brains is moving from one city to another, often within the networks of trans-national corporations, but also independently, as those with specific skills sell themselves on the global market. Doctors move from the UK to the US and Australia, but doctors in Australia move to the UK. Doctors are moving from developing countries such as Ghana and South Africa to Europe and North America, but doctors from Cuba are moving to Ghana and South Africa to practise in places where local doctors are unprepared to work (OECD, 2003, p128). Expatriate Indian doctors go back to their country of origin on both short and longer terms. All these examples illustrate a growing trend towards the circulation of skills at a global level, centred on a hierarchy of cities. Those circulating belong increasingly to a trans-national class (Sklair, 2001), with perhaps more in common with each other than with their less skilled and less mobile compatriots.

Two provisos are immediately warranted. First, international migrants are unlikely to compensate demographically for the reductions in the labour force: the numbers required would just be too large either to be successfully integrated socially or to be accepted politically by the host population (United Nations, 2001b).

Hence, city populations are still likely to decline in the context of low fertility and the exhaustion of local sources of migrants. However, the skills that relatively small numbers of migrants supply are essential if the city is to remain competitive in the global economy. It should also be stressed that no clear separation between skilled and unskilled migratory systems can be sustained, as the skilled require services that the less skilled supply: office cleaners, laundry services, restaurant workers and so on. Demand for many of the latter, too, will be met through international migration.

Second, it can be argued that some cities have always been significant destinations for international migration. The great cities of North America and the settler societies of Australia and New Zealand are cases in point. However, a clear difference exists between the relatively recent cities created through international migration in settler areas and those in long-established settlements in Europe and Asia. Although the latter cities may also have experienced previous waves of migration from other countries, their recent dependence upon foreign sources of supply in the context of sustained low fertility and limited availability of local labour has created a new situation. In some ways, they are taking on the profile of the cities in settler societies but without the long tradition of immigration or institutions to deal with immigrants. This difference between the settler and non-settler cities clearly demonstrates the different pathways through the urban transition. However, both have moved to a position where they are in competition for skilled and unskilled labour from external sources in a global economy.

Coleman (2006) has proposed the idea of a 'third demographic transition', in which low fertility, combined with high immigration, have come to transform the composition of national populations in developed economies. While the arguments have clear parallels with those made in this chapter, Coleman does not accord centrality to the role of the city in the process or consider the changing balance between internal and international migrations. Thus, the idea of a second urban transition may convey a more vivid idea of the spatial processes involved.

The transitions in developing countries of origin

The second urban transition has different implications for cities in the developing world. Several countries currently classified as 'developing' are well on their way through both the first demographic and the urban transitions. The boundary between 'developed' and 'developing' is constantly changing, with an increase in the number of countries in the former category and a reduction in the number in the latter. These countries are to be found particularly in Asia, such as China, India, Malaysia and Thailand, but can also be expected in other parts of the world, perhaps South Africa, Brazil or Mexico. Hence cities at specific locations in the developing world are, like those in the developed world, likely to emerge with a labour deficit.

It might seem strange to argue that the demographic giant, China, will experience labour shortages. Nevertheless, two million job vacancies were already reported in the south-east coastal region of China in 2004 (*Economist*, 9–15 October 2004), and labour shortages spread north into the Yangtze River and the north coastal region in 2005 (Wang et al, 2005). To an extent, these shortages reflect bottlenecks in the internal labour market within China for certain types of labour, but more recent evidence suggests that the shortages may have structural components as well.

China's accession to the World Trade Organization and programmes to diffuse development more widely into the interior have created opportunities closer to the areas of origin of internal migrants. The result has been severe labour shortages in coastal regions and increases of around 25 per cent in the basic wage in Shenzhen, for example (*International Herald Tribune*, 3 March 2006). China will not yet be seeking to import workers from overseas, but already the era of cheap labour in China appears to be ending. China, like the other developed economies in Asia, has seen a precipitous decline in fertility, from 4.9 children per woman in the early 1970s to 1.7 in the period 2000 to 2005, and United Nations projections envisage China's population starting to decline after 2030. That decline will lead to a slowdown in the rate of growth of the labour force and, if China follows the Japanese pattern, to a slowing in internal migration. The idea that the rural areas will be drained of their population might seem far-fetched given current levels of unemployment and underemployment in rural China. Nevertheless, the speed of economic growth and social transformation in that vast country has been astonishing, and assuming that the current growth continues – and that in itself is a big if – it is surely not inconceivable that pressures to import labour may emerge in certain cities within a generation.

However, it is clear that not all cities or countries in the developing world will necessarily follow the above pattern. In towns that began as administrative centres of external powers, with linkages back to metropolitan areas that were stronger than those to their immediate hinterlands, different patterns are likely to emerge. The fragility of post-independence economies in Africa, for example, has not allowed many of the urban areas to develop a strong production base, and they remain mainly centres of extractive industries or administration.

The economic and political crises of the 1970s and early 1980s saw rural–urban income differences contract; migration to the cities slowed and, in countries such as Ghana, a significant return of migrants back to rural areas took place (Songsore, 2003, p112; Potts, 1995). Nevertheless, in Ghana, levels of urbanization increased slowly, from 29 per cent in 1970 to 32.9 per cent in 1985, despite high rates of natural increase in the towns, because of reduced rural–urban migration.

In recent years, improving economic performance in Ghana saw annual GDP growth per capita increase. The average for the period 1975 to 2003 was only 0.4 per cent per annum, but that increased to an average of 1.8 per cent per annum for the last part of that period, 1990–2003 (UNDP, 2005, p268). Ghana's level of urbanization was estimated to have reached 47.8 per cent by 2005 (United Nations, 2006b), and its fertility had declined to 4.39 births per woman by that year. This figure was high by Asian standards, but down by some 34 per cent since the mid-1970s and less than the average for Africa of 4.97.

With fertility still high throughout Africa, and urbanization levels also increasing, the question must be the extent to which the continued concentration of population in towns is sustainable in the context of levels of economic growth that are low at best. The annual average growth in per capita GDP between 1990 and 2003 for sub-Saharan African countries as a whole was 0.1 per cent, and for the period 1975–2003 it was negative, at –0.7 per cent (UNDP, 2005). In this context, Ghana is one of the better performers, but for many countries the urbanization is based on very weak foundations. A reversal of migration in a period of economic downturn, as seen in the 1980s, is certainly a possibility, with any continued growth of towns largely based on natural increase. However, given the demand for labour in other parts of the world, as discussed above, and the fragility of the migration fields in many of these countries, it is possible that the internal movements will develop into international movements. While this conclusion is purely speculative at this stage, such an outcome would represent the origin side of the migration equation in the second urban transition as hypothesized above.

These migrations need not be primarily directed towards the cities in the present most-developed parts of the world, although some will be – they will also be targeted at the new centres emerging in Asia, the Middle East and in parts of Africa itself. Again, international migration substitutes for internal migration. Any such transition in migration need not simply be from the towns to destinations in other countries, in other words internal migrants moving into unemployment in local towns and then moving on to seek jobs in another country in a stepwise progression. Some movements will evolve directly from rural origins to international destinations, as observed in some countries in Asia (Skeldon, 2006a). In this way, many towns in the periphery of the developing world may become short-circuited from their hinterland in the second urban transition and enter a period of stagnant growth.

CONCLUSION: THE TRANSITION AND URBAN DEVELOPMENT

The evolution of this second urban transition will be predicated upon the continuation of globalization and current patterns of uneven development. Global foreign development investment (FDI) is still very much concentrated in the developed world. Africa still accounts for only about three per cent of global FDI, with over one-quarter of that tiny proportion concentrated in North Africa. Sub-Saharan Africa is still only tenuously linked to the global system, even if these links appear to be growing. Investments are still focused primarily on oil and other minerals, with increasing amounts coming from China. The latter's trade with

Africa quadrupled between 2001 and 2005 to US$40 billion, and China is now Africa's third largest trading partner after the US and France (Furniss, 2006, p55). However, investments in extractive activities make a weak foundation on which to build a solid urban economy.

Moreover, the importation of cheap manufactured goods from China appears likely to undermine local urban production systems. Reports are emerging that the termination of the Multi-Fibre Agreement at the end of 2004 has led to Chinese imports replacing locally produced clothing. The value of clothing and textiles in five African countries fell by 17 per cent in 2005, with significant job losses in Kenya, South Africa and Lesotho, as well as a reported 350,000 in Nigeria (Furniss, 2006, p58). Increased trade brings increased migration, and large numbers of Chinese traders and entrepreneurs are to be found throughout sub-Saharan Africa. But if history teaches anything, it is that reverse migration will also occur. As China and other Asian economies move through the second demographic and urban transitions, is it too far-fetched to envisage significant flows of African labour eastward? If programmes of temporary migration of labour give rise to later more settled migration of people, such a scenario will have significant consequences for the patterns of both Asian and African urban development.

The role of the city is central in the demographic transition. Prior to the industrial revolution, towns were demographic 'sinks' where the populations experienced high mortality and were in constant need of replenishment by migration from surrounding areas. With the decline in mortality rates and a rise in fertility, natural increase became a more significant relative component of urban growth, while migration remained important. The decline in fertility to very low levels in the post-industrial era has seen the shift back to the importance of migration as the dominant component of urban growth, but with the significant difference that national reservoirs of labour have become exhausted and the migration field extended to other countries. In London at the beginning of the 21st century, some 2.2 million people, or 30 per cent of the population, had been born outside of England. Of the social and linguistic groups that could be identified as non-indigenous, some 50 communities had populations of 10,000 or more, and over 300 languages were identified as spoken by the residents of the city. Some 36 per cent of the population of New York was foreign-born in 2000, representing 2.9 million people, again with a high degree of diversity in origin (City of New York, 2004). None of the new cities of immigration in Asia can yet match this degree of diversity or level of immigration. For example, according to Benton-Short and Price (2005), only about 2.4 per cent of the population of Tokyo may be foreign-born.

An integral part of this transition from internal to international sources of migrants is the emergence of new dynamic centres of urban development away from the traditional developed world. Beginning, and as yet still concentrated, in East Asia, such centres are emerging in parts of South Asia, Gulf States such as Dubai, parts of Latin America and even in sub-Saharan Africa, for example in South Africa, Ghana and Nigeria. The process of globalization underlies this shift. Declining fertility, slowing labour-force growth and the rising cost of labour have forced labour-intensive industries out of core industrial countries to locations overseas and laid the basis for the emergence of new urban complexes that themselves would embark upon the demographic and urban transitions.

While it is accepted that '[in] general terms, urban evolution seems to follow the same pattern all over the world' (Geyer, 2002, p11), it has been argued in this chapter that there are several pathways through the transition. Significant shifts in the pattern of the leading components of urban growth, fertility and migration, occur through the transition, to the extent that a distinction between a first and a second urban transition seems warranted. As fertility declines, a gradual shift from national to international sources of labour occurs in the most-developed parts of the world. As the process continues to evolve, more centres emerge to compete with the early ones, and they, too, go through this transition. Given a sustained demand for labour in these cities, their migration fields extend ever further into the periphery and, where development remains weak, migration to local urban centres shifts to regional or even global movements, leaving the local towns short-circuited. Some whole regions in the periphery may begin to depopulate in the same way as the rural areas throughout the developed world have done, and their urban centres may stagnate.

Forecasting accurately what may or may not happen in an urban future is always fraught with difficulty. Urbanization will continue throughout most of the world, although patterns in developed and less developed regions may differ. But any continuation into a second urban transition will depend upon the persistence of present processes of globalization, and this is by no means guaranteed. Globalism itself may collapse (Saul, 2005). The present direction of development may be unsustainable, and global warming will cause rises in sea levels that will threaten most of the global cities in the world. The evidence for such heroic speculation, however, remains weak. During the first urban transition, which involved essentially internal migration to cities, policy seems to have been largely ineffectual in affecting the course of migration to cities over all but the short term. During the second transition, which involves international migration, policy will play a much more significant role, as, indeed, it has done for global migration in general since the end of the Second World War (Hatton and Williamson, 2005).

Policy on international migration is the responsibility of national governments, yet it is city governments that have to administer and provide for the majority of international arrivals. One of the intriguing and as yet unknown dimensions of future policy is the relative role of metropolitan and national governments. Whether there is collaboration or contradiction between them will determine the effectiveness of future migration management in the cities. Irregular migration to developed economies draws parallels with internal movements to cities in earlier contexts. Ultimately, the underlying economy is the driver of migration, and no guarantee exists that future attempts to regulate population movement to the largest cities will be any more successful than in the past.

REFERENCES

Abella, M. (ed) (1994) 'Turning points in labour migration', *Asian and Pacific Migration Journal*, vol 3, no1, special issue

Banister, J. (1987) *China's Changing Population*, Stanford University Press, Stanford, CA

Becker, C. M., Hamer, A. M. and Morrison, A. R. (1994) *Beyond Urban Bias in Africa: Urbanization in an Era of Structural Adjustment*, Heinemann, Portsmouth, NH

Benton-Short, L. and Price, M. (2005) 'Global immigrant pathways', presentation at brownbag lunch on Global Immigrant Gateways, 11 November 2005, George Washington Centre for the Study of Globalization, Washington, DC

City of New York (2004) *The Newest New Yorkers, 2000: Immigrant New York in the New Millennium*, Department of City Planning, City of New York, New York

Coleman, D. (2006) 'Immigration and ethnic change in low-fertility countries: A third demographic transition', *Population and Development Review*, vol 32, no 3, pp401–446

Davis, M. (2006) *Planet of Slums*, Verso, London

De Soto, H. (1989) *The Other Path: The Invisible Revolution in the Third World*, Harper and Row, New York

Fielding, A. J. (2004) 'The "new immigration model" applied to Japan', paper presented at the Joint East Asian Studies Conference, British Association for Japanese Studies, 6–8 September 2004, Leeds, UK

Furniss, C. (2006) 'Dossier: China in Africa: The hungry dragon and the dark continent', *Geographical*, vol 78, no 12, pp53–61

GCIM (2005) *Migration in an Interconnected World: New Directions for Action: Report of the Global Commission on International Migration*, Global Commission on International Migration, Geneva

Geyer, H. S. (2002) 'Fundamentals of urban economic space', in H. S. Geyer (ed) *International Handbook of Urban Systems: Studies of Urbanization and Migration in Advanced and Developing Countries*, Edward Elgar, Cheltenham, UK, pp3–18

Hatton, T. J. and Williamson, J. G. (2005) *Global Migration and the World Economy: Two Centuries of Policy and Performance*, MIT Press, Cambridge, MA

Hugo, G. (1997) 'Population change and development in Indonesia', in R. F. Watters and T. G. McGee (eds) *Asia Pacific: New Geographies of the Pacific Rim*, Hurst and Company, London, pp223–249

King, R., Fielding, A. J. and Black, R. (1997) 'The international migration turnaround in southern Europe', in R. King and R. Black (eds) *Southern Europe and the New Immigrations*, Sussex Academic Press, Brighton, UK, pp1–25

Lipton, M. (1977) *Why Poor People Stay Poor: Urban Bias in World Development*, Temple Smith, London

Mallee, H. (1995) 'China's household registration system under reform', *Development and Change*, vol 26, no 1, pp1–29

Mangin, W. P. (1967) 'Latin America's squatter settlements: A problem and a solution', *Latin American Research Review*, vol 2, no 3, pp65–98

Montgomery, M. R., Stren, R., Cohen, B. and Reed, H. E. (eds) (2003) *Cities Transformed: Demographic Change and its Implications in the Developing World*, Panel on Urban Dynamics, National Research Council, National Academy Press, Washington, DC

Murphy, R. (2002) *How Migrant Labour is Changing Rural China*, Cambridge University Press, Cambridge, UK

Nugent, P. (2004) *Africa since Independence: A Comparative History*, Palgrave Macmillan, Basingstoke, UK

Oberai, A. S. (1983) *State Policies and Internal Migration: Studies in Market and Planned Economies*, Croom Helm, London

OECD (2003) 'The international mobility of health professionals: An evaluation and analysis based on the case of South Africa', in *Trends in International Migration 2003*, Organisation for Economic Co-operation and Development, Paris, pp115–151

Oram, N. D. (1976) *Colonial Town to Melanesian City: Port Moresby, 1884–1974*, Australian National University Press, Canberra

Peek, P. and Standing, G. (eds) (1982) *State Policies and Migration: Studies in Latin America and the Caribbean*, Croom Helm, London

Potts, D. (1995) 'Shall we go home? Increasing urban poverty in African cities and migration processes', *The Geographical Journal*, vol 161, no 3, pp245–264

Sassen, S. (1991) *The Global City: New York, London, Tokyo*, Princeton University Press, Princeton, NJ

Saul, J. R. (2005) *The Collapse of Globalism and the Reinvention of the World*, Atlantic Books, London

Simon, D. (1992) *Cities, Capital and Development: African Cities in the World Economy*, Belhaven Press, London

Skeldon, R. (1990) *Population Mobility in Developing Countries: A Reinterpretation*, Belhaven Press, London

Skeldon, R. (2006a) 'Interlinkages between internal and international migration and development in the Asian region', *Population, Space and Place*, vol 12, no 1, pp15–30

Skeldon, R. (2006b) 'Recent trends in migration in East and Southeast Asia', *Asian and Pacific Migration Journal*, vol 15, no 2, pp277–293

Sklair, L. (2001) *The Transnational Capitalist Class*, Blackwell Publishing, Oxford, UK

Songsore, J. (2003) *Regional Development in Ghana: The Theory and the Reality*, Woeli Publishing Services, Accra

Sriskandarajah, D. and Drew, C. (2006) *Brits Abroad: Mapping the Scale and Nature of British Emigration*, Institute for Public Policy Research, London

Totman, C. (2000) *A History of Japan* (second edition), Blackwell Publishing, Oxford, UK

Turner, J. F. C. (1968) 'Uncontrolled urban settlement: Problems and policies', in United Nations, *International Social Development Review*, vol 1, United Nations, New York, pp107–130

UNDP (2005) *Human Development Report 2005: International Cooperation at a Crossroads: Aid, Trade and Security in an Unequal World*, UNDP, New York

UNFPA (2007) *The State of World Population 2007: Unleashing the Potential of Urban Growth*, UNFPA, New York

United Nations (1981) *Population Distribution Policies in Development Planning* (ST/ SOA/Ser.A/75), Population Studies No 75, Department of International Economic and Social Affairs, United Nations, New York, NY

United Nations (2001a) *The Components of Urban Growth in Developing Countries* (ESA/ P/WP.169), Population Division, United Nations, New York

United Nations (2001b) *Replacement Migration: Is it a Solution to Declining Populations?* (ESA/P/WP.160), Population Division, United Nations, New York

United Nations (2006a) *International Migration and Development: Report of the Secretary General* (A/60/871), United Nations, New York

United Nations (2006b) *World Urbanization Prospects: The 2005 Revision*, Population Division, United Nations, New York

United Nations (2007) *World Population Prospects: The 2006 Revision*, Population Division, United Nations, New York

Van de Kaa, D. (1987) 'Europe's second demographic transition', *Population Bulletin*, vol 42, no 1, pp1–59

Wang, D., Cai, F. and Gao, W. (2005) *Globalization and Internal Labour Mobility in China: New Trend and Policy Implications*, Institute of Population and Labor Economics, Chinese Academy of Social Sciences, Beijing

Part II

Shelter and Urban Poverty

INTRODUCTION

The great majority of the world's wealthy people live in and around urban centres, but so do a growing share of those living in poverty. While cities are often described as economic powerhouses, access to their power is very unequal, and rapid urban growth is often accompanied by growing economic inequalities. Deprived urban-dwellers not only receive lower incomes, they often pay higher prices and face more social and political obstacles than their wealthier neighbours. It has been estimated that the number of urban-dwellers who lived on less than a dollar a day rose from 240 to 290 million between 1993 and 2002, while those living on less than two dollars a day went from 690 to 750 million (Ravallion et al, 2007). On the other hand, UN-Habitat has estimated that in 2001 almost a billion urban-dwellers lived in slums, and faced serious deficiencies in one or more of the following: tenure, water, sanitation, housing quality and crowding (UN-Habitat, 2003). While such statistics should be viewed with considerable scepticism, and are not strictly comparable, more detailed research also suggests that in urban areas shelter poverty – the inadequacy and insecurity of homes and basic services – is more severe than income poverty, and that both are growing in absolute terms.

A central theme of this book is that the benefits of urbanization and urban development need to be both recognized and seized, and this certainly applies to poverty issues. On the one hand, urbanization and urban development do typically benefit poor groups, in both rural and urban areas. On the other hand, they could be far more beneficial. Treating slums as a symptom of over-urbanization can reinforce policies that make poverty worse. A more positive stance towards urbanization and urban development is only a start, however. It is important to understand why so many efforts to address urban poverty have failed in the past, and also to find better ways for the future. This is what the chapters in this section set out to do.

The 20th century saw a heated debate over the relative merits of markets and governments, which extended to the question of providing basic urban shelter and services. For a large share of the world's urban poor, however, neither markets nor governments delivered – and nor, for that matter, did public–private partnerships. In Chapter 4, McGranahan, Mitlin and Satterthwaite start off by reviewing past public and private failures. Many public failures can be explained by a combination of unrealistic standards, inadequate funding and politics that provide little leverage to poor groups. While private failures have a somewhat different logic, often the same factors that undermine public provisioning also undermine private provisioning. Thus, for example, the same informal settlements that are ill-served by the public sector are ill-served by the private sector too.

To overcome these public and private failures, McGranahan, Mitlin and Satterthwaite argue in Chapter 4 in favour of a progressive pragmatism that, rather than trying to identify some idealized approach or set of 'best practices' that can be rolled out internationally, builds on approaches that have been shown to work locally. With this in mind, they review the experience with upgrading the property rights of the urban poor, improving access to finance and organizing civil society. Many of the more successful initiatives are those that have managed to promote local control, to encourage incremental improvements and to support alternative forms of community organization. More generally, they suggest that there are critical roles for government in working constructively and routinely with slum-dwellers, creating the basis for more efficient and equitable land and housing markets, and developing physically and financially realistic strategies for accommodating future urban growth.

While Latin America is no longer urbanizing at anything like the rate of Asia and Africa, its recent history provides insights into the challenges that rapid urbanization and urban growth can bring. Unfortunately, as Smolka and Larangeira describe in Chapter 5, much of Latin America's experience with informal settlements has been a series of lessons in what not to do. The attitude of different governments towards informal settlement has varied from accommodating to punitive, but few have managed to address the causes of informality. In particular, neither forced evictions, nor upgrading, nor land titling have provided the means for bringing the inhabitants of informal settlements into an acceptable relationship with government, or created efficient and fair land and housing markets.

Two interrelated barriers that prevent the regularization of informal settlements are the impossibility of securing sufficient funds to finance equitable programmes of the required scale and the conflict and speculative expectations that often arise when changes are being considered. Smolka and Larangeira argue that the best means of overcoming the financial barrier is to find a way to tap the increase in land values provided by regularization, and to use some of this increase to finance the programme itself. Preventing conflict and speculative expectation, on the other hand, requires involving all parties in the process, including landowners, developers and final occupants. They describe two innovations that have promised to address these challenges.

Regularizing informal settlements is one thing; preventing the emergence of new informal settlements is another. Both of the first two chapters in this section make the case for forward-looking policies designed to bring the supply of serviced land into line with the growing shelter requirements. This challenge is even more central to Chapter 6, in which Angel provides a concrete example of how to provide land for the urban poor in a context of rapid urban expansion, using the experiences of five mid-sized cities in Ecuador. He argues that to ensure that residential land for the urban poor remains affordable, municipalities should provide the public goods necessary for a well-functioning urban land market. They must ensure that accessible urban land remains in ample supply in the coming years, thus avoiding speculative increases in land prices. Municipalities must also expand their city limits; plan for an arterial infrastructure grid and obtain the land rights for the right of way of the entire arterial grid using available laws while minimizing unilateral expropriation; and extend better infrastructure services to the urban population – especially to poor families living in marginal settlements.

In short, Angel argues that keeping housing affordable requires keeping land prices affordable. This is an attractive strategy for visionary mayors that can be carried out with a relatively low amount of investment *if it is carried out early enough*. Looking to the future, this should also be an important demonstration project for the large number of cities in developing countries that now face strong population pressures.

In particularly difficult economic or political circumstances, identifying the means to achieve affordable housing does not provide the basis for eliminating urban shelter poverty. Governments often face little pressure to plan for the poor of today, let alone those of the decades to come. Whether they face constructive pressure depends on both how the low-income residents themselves organize to meet their collective needs and how they engage with the governmental, non-governmental and private agencies that can help them meet these needs. Organizations of the urban poor are central to Chapter 7, in which Carolini describes the growing roles these organizations have played in recent decades. She argues that it is misleading to think of these organizations in terms of conventional dichotomies, such as 'bottom–up' versus 'top–down' or 'process' versus 'product'. Rather, success is often based on strategies that combine the two in innovative ways: where self-help from 'below' helps to bring forth more effective assistance from 'above'; where achieving a well-defined 'product' for the community contributes to a longer-term 'process' of organizational strengthening.

While the chapters in this section focus on different aspects of the urban shelter challenge and suggest different strategies, all are relatively optimistic about the potential for reducing urban poverty, even in rapidly growing settlements. As a first step, it is important not to misinterpret slums and other low-income settlement as evidence of over-urbanization. In order to address the challenge, however, it is important to make better use of the poverty-reducing potential of urban development. The principles, lessons and examples provided in these chapters at least begin to indicate how this can be done.

REFERENCES

Ravallion, M., Chen, S. and Sangraula, P. (2007) *New Evidence on the Urbanization of Global Poverty*, Development Research Group Working Paper No 4199, World Bank, Washington, DC

UN-Habitat (2003) *The Challenge of Slums: Global Report on Human Settlements 2003*, United Nations Human Settlements Programme, Nairobi

4

Land and Services for the Urban Poor in Rapidly Urbanizing Countries

Gordon McGranahan, Diana Mitlin and David Satterthwaite

INTRODUCTION

Despite the many advantages urban settlements provide, their poorest residents often live in exceptionally unpleasant and unhealthy conditions. This was so when industrial urbanization started in earnest in the 19th century and continues to this day. In low- and middle-income countries, it is the case for the 900 million or so urban inhabitants of what UN-Habitat (2003a) refers to as 'slums'.[1] These deprived urban-dwellers typically live in worse environments than their income alone would dictate. Their demands for shelter and environmental services are not well met by markets, which favour areas where property rights are well defined and people are willing and able to pay for the full range of household services. These same shelter demands also tend to be poorly met by governments, whose public services rarely reach more than a small fraction of those living in slums and whose regulations often work against solutions that the urban poor can afford themselves. Perhaps it should be no surprise that in an era where market- and state-led models compete for pre-eminence, the shelter problems of the urban poor have rarely been addressed effectively.

Low-income settlements often contravene existing building codes, zoning regulations and even property laws – at least in part because the codes, regulations and laws were not developed with the needs of the urban poor in mind, let alone with their involvement. Public services are often lacking, and utilities are often actively discouraged from providing them. Unfounded fears of over-urbanization can make matters worse, as they provide an excuse for fatalism for policymakers. Governments often deflect criticisms of their failings by claiming, without evidence, that improving conditions in informal settlements will attract more migrants. Governments may even claim that it is migrants who are creating the problems in the first place. However, taking a more positive attitude to urbanization is clearly not enough. Conventional approaches to improving informal settlements do not need to be expanded, they need to be transformed. The limitations of both public and private solutions need to be reassessed, along with the notion that these limitations can be overcome by public–private 'partnerships'.

There are inspiring examples of approaches, many grounded in organizations of the urban poor (OUPs), that have managed to overcome the obstacles to addressing basic shelter and service deprivation. While these approaches have worked in a wide range of circumstances, however, they remain the exception. Although they have reached considerable scale in some cities and nations, they have only reached a small proportion of those in need. Looking to the future, it is clear that not only do successful approaches need to be scaled up, but steps also need to be taken now to avoid a new generation of slums from forming – not by stopping urbanization, but by accommodating urban growth more efficiently and equitably.

The first two sections below reassess the failure of both public and private solutions to urban shelter and service deprivation. These are followed by a section that assesses the scope of what could be termed progressive pragmatism, transcending the public–private and formal–informal divides and finding ways to help OUPs improve their own conditions. The final section looks briefly to the future.

THE FAILURE OF PUBLIC-SECTOR SOLUTIONS

In the industrializing countries of the 19th century, urban poverty grew to unprecedented levels. Recent evidence suggests that, with early industrialization, urban mortality and morbidity rates actually increased in England, only declining in the late 19th century when local governments became more responsive to the needs of the urban poor (Szreter, 2005). The 'sanitary revolution' was an important factor in this decline and helped to enlist broader support for government-led urban-improvement efforts designed to improve public health and prevent the outbreak of major epidemics.

It was in the 20th century, however, that government spending came to account for an appreciable share of economic activity, even in market economies. This occurred primarily in the wealthier countries, with little apparent effect on their economic growth (Lindert, 2004). The 20th century also saw the distinction between central planning and market mechanisms become a central issue in global geopolitics. This ensured that the debate over the roles of the public and private sectors was highly ideological and as influenced by international politics as by local experiences.

Towards the end of the 20th century, along with the decline of centrally planned economies, there was a reaction against the growing role of government within the more affluent market economies. The rise of neo-liberalism was a defining feature of Western politics in the 1980s and 1990s, particularly in the US and its closest allies. Through structural adjustment programmes and other conditionalities of development assistance, however, the policy impact of this political shift was more evident in low- and middle-income countries than in the countries of its origin (Stiglitz, 2002). The pressure to reduce the role of government extended to the urban services that had helped to justify the expansion of the state in the 19th century. The World Bank, for example, began to promote increased private-sector participation in water and sanitation provision, and by the 1990s, large concession contracts were being developed for water and sanitation utilities in selected major cities in Asia and Latin America, including Buenos Aires, Jakarta and Manila (Finger and Allouche, 2002; Budds and McGranahan, 2003).

The failure of governments to provide for the urban poor does not explain why private-sector participation came to be so vigorously promoted, but it does help to explain the initial lack of resistance. From the perspective of the urban poor, two common and mutually reinforcing public failures have been that:

1   The urban poor are often marginalized (spatially, legally and politically) by land-use planning designed and undertaken in the name of the public interest.
2   Better-off groups often capture the benefits of public programmes developed in the name of the urban poor.

It would be misleading to present the policy issues surrounding deficient urban shelter and services as if governments and development agencies were always concerned with how best to assist deprived residents. In many cities, the more lively debate in the corridors of power, if not in the pages of reports, has been over how to prevent the poor from settling in the expanding 'slums'. As described in Chapter 2, this issue is often bound up with fears about excessive rural–urban migration and over-urbanization and the (often incorrect) belief that informal settlements and slums are migrant settlements.

Concern with over-urbanization can easily become a liability for poor groups. If underserved and degraded neighbourhoods are taken to reflect over-urbanization, then this can be used to justify more restrictive plans, limiting the amount of land zoned for residential development, raising the standards required for authorization for new residential developments and not providing the infrastructure that might encourage residential development. Under such conditions, urban land-use planning does not serve the poor but marginalizes them.

On the other hand, many government programmes have been designed with the express purpose of providing land, housing or services for the urban poor. During the 1960s and 1970s, government housing and public service programmes were instituted in urban Africa, Asia and Latin America, often influenced by similar programmes in Europe (Hardoy and Satterthwaite, 1989). Typically, the goal was to provide housing and services of an acceptable standard, and at affordable prices, for those who would otherwise be forced to do without. However, with a few exceptions, the levels of public funding needed to mount programmes of sufficient scale to meet the demand were not forthcoming. Moreover, problems resulted from overly centralized approaches, with little involvement on the part of the intended beneficiaries. These limitations were recognized at the time and in some programmes a greater focus was placed on supporting the involvement of poorer groups in designing and implementing measures (Mangin, 1967; Turner, 1968 and 1976).

Where desirable public housing was supplied, it was typically secured by better-off groups – if not immediately, then after changing hands. The tendency for non-poor households to 'capture' public housing intended for the poor followed a time-honoured tradition: high standards and low prices were justified on the grounds that everyone deserves adequate provision at an affordable price; limited public resources ensured that supplies at the prescribed standard could not meet demand at the prescribed price; and politics ensured that the better-off, or groups with influence on government, were first in line. In many cases, the political compromise between those who claimed to represent the interests of the urban poor and those who did not resulted in policies that claimed to represent the urban poor but actually did not.

The sites and services and upgrading programmes that became popular in the 1970s reduced the contradiction between big ambitions and little funding. They were based on the recognition that settlements built by the residents, with the help of local artisans, often suited the needs of the urban poor better than expensive units designed by experts and built by contractors. Providing secure tenure was also stressed. Unfortunately, this period also saw a growing concern with 'urban bias' in the donor establishment, resulting in decreased funding for urban programmes. Urban bias refers to a tendency for governments, dominated by urban elites, to favour urban areas in both public spending and pricing policies (Lipton, 1977). But while urban elites do undoubtedly skew policies, their interests only sometimes overlap with those of the urban poor. On the other hand, attempts to correct urban bias often harm the urban poor. With declining public funding, even upgrading programmes were often unsuccessful (see, for example, Cabanas Díaz et al, 2000).

In principle, extending services alone should further reduce contradictions between big ambitions and small funding. The 1980s were proclaimed the international drinking water and sanitation decade, and governments set themselves the goal of achieving universal provision of safe water and sanitation. For some time, the standard model for providing water and sanitation services in affluent cities had been the public utility. With its water and sewer pipes, the public utility had also become the model for extending services to the urban poor. Unfortunately, just as public housing programmes were often 'captured' by more affluent residents, so were improvements in urban services. Water and other services are often subject to heavy price controls and limited subsidies, with the result that even well-run utilities could not afford to make their services widely available.

Generally, the politics of public housing and service provision do not favour loosely organized groups of low-income residents, whose principal political tools are electoral politics or protests. Housing developments and water networks are extended incrementally, making them susceptible to clientelistic politics, with politicians using improved housing or services as political favours or to gain strategically important support. The price of water is more amenable to both electoral and protest-based influence, but keeping the price of water affordable is of no avail to those who cannot gain access to the network. Indeed, if a low official price reduces water supplies, it is likely to increase water prices in secondary markets. In many low- and middle-income countries, the urban public utilities not only failed to serve the poor, but also failed to manage their networks efficiently and were unable to account for a large share of the water that went into the piped water network (UN-Habitat, 2003b).

There are various lessons that can be drawn from the failure of so many public authorities to extend land and services to the urban poor. The lesson drawn by the World Bank and a number of other development-assistance organizations was that, wherever possible, government bureaucracy and regulation should be replaced with private enterprises and flexible markets. But this same conclusion was being drawn in relation to virtually every area of government provisioning (Batley and Larbi, 2004). It was a conclusion informed as much by the decline of the Soviet Union as by experience with urban land and services. Unfortunately, public failure is not a good basis for private success.

THE FAILURE OF PRIVATE-SECTOR SOLUTIONS

Proponents of private-sector solutions have long argued for more private provision of housing and public service delivery. Starting in the 1990s, such policies have been adopted and promoted by the World Bank and other international development agencies, to considerable effect. More recently, building on the case made by Hernando De Soto (2000), there has been talk of turning the 'informal' capital of the poor into legally supported assets with which they can take advantage of national and international markets (Ishengoma and Kappel, 2006). In practice this has often been taken to mean land titling, despite its limitations (Payne and Majale, 2004). There is, however, a broader question of whether the informal sector can provide the basis for private solutions to shelter and service deficiencies and whether this can be furthered by efforts to support or transform the informal sector.

From a market perspective, urban land, housing and services represent a large number of distinct demands, which can be met through different markets. This section, however, will focus on water provision, examining the role of private-sector participation, in both its formal and informal guises. The relevant markets are somewhat different from those for land, housing and other services, but many of the issues are analogous. Private solutions have not proved to be the panacea their proponents claimed, particularly where the public sector has not been able to provide public solutions. Moreover, informal systems play a critical role but have their own, often severe, limitations.

In recent centuries, there have been numerous controversies over the choice between public and private water provisioning. During the last decades of the 20th century, this debate became global. At one extreme, proponents argued that increasing private-sector involvement would solve the failures plaguing public water utilities, including their inability to reach large sections of the urban poor. At the other, critics portrayed privatization as a dismantling of the policies and institutions needed to achieve universal coverage. Both proponents and critics often ignored the many barriers to provision that have nothing to do with who operates the utility (McGranahan and Satterthwaite, 2006).

The received wisdom in public policy circles in the mid-20th century was that water networks were natural monopolies and provided public health benefits. Left to themselves, private monopolists would overcharge, under-provide and ignore the public health priorities. The public sector had to take control to prevent the abuse of monopoly powers and therefore serve the public interest.

In the 1980s and 1990s, however, proponents of private-sector involvement launched a sustained critique of public utilities and their failures and promoted several private alternatives. They argued that public utilities were inefficient and open to manipulation by politicians pursuing short-term political ends. Low water tariffs, far from helping the urban poor, were turning water distribution into patronage and undermining the financial basis for extending water to low-income settlements. Privately run utilities, on the other hand, would be cost-conscious, apolitical and demand-responsive. Competition for concessions would introduce market discipline, and regulation would help to prevent the abuse of monopoly powers. Private capital would be invested in utility upgrading and expansion.

However, once private-sector participation reached significant levels, some of the more ambitious claims became unconvincing (Budds and McGranahan, 2003). Far from depoliticizing water and sanitation provision, private-sector participation sparked political controversy. It changed but did not remove patronage and corruption. The competition for water concessions often involved little more than a handful of multinationals. The level of private investment was disappointing (Hall and Lobina, 2006). And many contracts encountered problems.

Empirical evidence on the impact of private-sector participation is mixed (Clarke et al, 2004; Kirkpatrick et al, 2004). This should not be surprising: many of the obstacles to improving water and sanitation provision have nothing to do with whether utility operators are private or public. A public sector having difficulties creating the right regulatory environment for public utilities is also likely to have trouble regulating private utilities. Residents with insecure tenure, for example, living in difficult-to-reach locations and lacking sufficient funds to invest in connections, can have just as much trouble convincing private utilities to connect them as convincing public ones. Public utilities can be forced to face commercial pressures whereas, under certain contractual arrangements, privately operated utilities can be protected from these same pressures. Thus the distinction between private and public utilities is not nearly so straightforward as is often implied.

While advocates of private-sector participation and public–private partnerships were rightly critical of public provisioning, they were wrongly optimistic about private provisioning. To make matters worse, the public–private controversies diverted attention from the problems that both privately and publicly operated utilities face – and from the places that neither reach.

Somewhat revealingly, the proponents of private-sector participation neglected the small and often informal water enterprises that have for centuries operated in low-income settlements. Such vendors often provide low-quality service at a high price, but their contributions could be improved, and they operate in markets far closer to the competitive ideal than do the water multinationals (McGranahan et al, 2006). Historically, the goal of public utilities has been one of replacing rather than assisting small water enterprises. Governments have been concerned with prohibiting them from selling 'overpriced' or 'substandard' water, rather than encouraging them to invest or compete more vigorously. Moreover, by suppressing water vending, authorities make it still more difficult for deprived residents to obtain water, drive up the market price and increase the risk that the water will be contaminated. As a means of providing water, small vendors may be a failure, but in many circumstances they need to be part of the solution – as does the public sector. The challenge is not to determine whether private or public provisioning is inherently better, but to find the means of improving provisioning, recognizing the economic limitations and political predilections of the various different institutions involved.

PROGRESSIVE PRAGMATISM AND TRANSCENDING THE PUBLIC–PRIVATE DIVIDE

In the face of the debate over the relative merits of private, market-driven solutions and public, state-led solutions, it is tempting to argue for a third way – and, indeed, an approach labelled the 'Third Way' did gain popularity around the turn of the millennium (Giddens, 1998). The challenge, however, is not to identify yet another idealized model of how land and services should be delivered to deprived urban residents, but to support approaches that can be shown to work locally.

The market model may be right in emphasizing how important it is for the residents' own desires for a secure and healthy home to drive improvement efforts. Deprived urban residents are in a constant process of seeking housing security. Their shelters provide them, simultaneously, with a home, security for their belongings, safety for their families, a place to strengthen their social relations and networks, a place for household enterprises or local trading and service provision, and a means to access state-provided basic services. For those who own their homes, investing in them is also a means of building up the value of their most important asset – and one that can be drawn on in emergencies. To provide effective support that has both scale and longevity, public–private and non-profit agencies need to work with the investments that families are already seeking to make and to respond to their demands. It is a mistake, however, to assume that markets are always the best means of achieving this. Markets are just one possible avenue through which urban residents can pursue their needs, and where markets are not operating to the advantage of the urban poor, it is important to consider alternatives, including local organizations.

The public sector model, on the other hand, may be right in emphasizing the importance of collective action and the public interest. Improving conditions in deprived urban neighbourhoods requires collaboration. Many service deficiencies create severe public health problems – as when, for example, one household's bad sanitation creates health risks for neighbouring homes. Many infrastructure improvements need to be coordinated among neighbours and thus contribute to the public good, at least locally. To provide effective support, it is important to recognize these public dimensions. Again, however, it is a mistake to assume that the state is always the best means of achieving this. Somewhat similarly, the public-sector advocates may be correct in claiming that deprived urban-dwellers deserve far better shelter and services, but adopting high standards, and embedding them in a punitive regulatory system, may actually make their provision less likely.

The distinction between public and private institutions captures a very small fraction of institutional diversity (Ostrom, 2005). Government agencies and regulations, along with private enterprises and markets, come in an enormous variety of sizes and forms and often display divergent logics. The same governments that have policies and regulations that exclude poor urban groups from access to land and services will also typically have programmes and projects designed to give them better access. Electoral democracy can help make government more accountable to the urban poor, but it is neither a necessary nor a sufficient condition for resolving urban land and service failures. Similarly, competitive markets can help make private enterprises more responsive to the urban poor, but only in certain limited circumstances. Civil society groups and institutions are equally complex and diverse. They can be critical in improving conditions in deprived urban neighbourhoods, since markets are often too individualized to drive collective action and government agencies are often too distant or unrepresentative.

While it is impossible to generalize about what practices work locally to benefit deprived urban residents, there are three principles that a great many successful projects have followed within local communities: promote local ownership, encourage incremental improvements and support alternative forms of community organization within low-income settlements.

The importance of local ownership has long been recognized. This may be achieved by providing local residents with greater security in the use of their own resources (for example by taking measures to increase tenure security), with better access to finance, or with some decision-making authority over public or collective shelter and service projects.

The importance of allowing or even encouraging incremental improvements is less obvious, but this is often a necessary condition for local ownership. Outsiders almost inevitably control large, one-off projects, which typically require large subsidies. Incremental improvement can be more responsive to local priorities and more amenable to the very uneven cash flows and time budgets that come with informal livelihoods. Problems can also be created by this approach, as when piped water is introduced without drains, but, generally, improvements are more feasible when they are undertaken incrementally.

Support for alternative forms of community organization is probably the most difficult principle to apply effectively, but it can be critically important, particularly when participatory processes are being relied upon to achieve local ownership. As observed in a book on deepening democracy, the participatory processes often associated with dialogic democracy are of limited value if the deprived groups do not secure some countervailing power with which to pursue their agendas (Fung and Wright, 2003). Disorganized and impoverished groups are rarely in a position to take advantage of participatory exercises. Moreover, disorganized communities are not in a position to launch projects, or even to handle financing if it is made available.

Before turning explicitly to issues of organizing civil society, the following section reviews strategies for upgrading the property rights of the urban poor and expanding their access to finance. It should be recognized, however, that such strategies are unlikely to be effective unless deprived groups have sufficient political leverage to influence the details of the land and finance programmes developed in their name.

Upgrading the property rights of the urban poor

Since the lack of security in land and housing is a major source of shelter and service problems, an obvious strategy for improving conditions in informal settlements is to upgrade residents' property rights to land. Many land regularization programmes have been designed for this purpose. Such approaches have been reinvigorated by the work of Hernando De Soto (2000), who argues that if low-income residents can gain formal ownership of their informal property, they will be in a much better position to reap the benefits of the market – by, for instance, securing access to loans by using their property as collateral. In accordance with this thinking, for example, a new policy to legalize property was established in Peru in 1996, and, by 2000, more than one million title deeds had been issued (Calderón, 2004).

In the right circumstances, land regularization can improve access to land, housing and services. Where land tenure problems are preventing informal settlements from receiving public services, land regularization will stimulate public investment. Somewhat ironically, however, given that market-based arguments are often the ones that have been used to promote land titling and regularization, land regularization will not always stimulate private investments by the owners. Households without formal tenure may invest because *de facto* tenure is already secure, or in the belief that investments will actually enhance their security by creating a legitimate neighbourhood that is politically as well as physically harder to destroy. On the other hand, even formal land ownership may not be sufficient collateral for lenders who really have little interest in repossessing houses. Up to 2002, only 17,324 families in Peru who had obtained title deeds under the new policy had gained access to mortgage loans, representing a mere 1.3 per cent of the total title deeds allocated during the process (Calderón, 2004). In short, the relationship between land regularization and investment needs to be understood locally, not assumed internationally.

In some cases, land regularization has been a component of a more integrated programme to address the shelter needs of the urban poor. In Central America, the Swedish International Development Cooperation Agency (Sida) has been funding state programmes to support local governments in improving the provision of infrastructure and services in low-income settlements. Programmes to provide essential services also encourage the active participation of residents. Additional components assist in providing microfinance for income generation and housing improvements. As of 2005, one of these programmes, in Nicaragua, had financed 558 projects, mobilizing US$14 million and generating 8000 jobs per year (Stein and Castillo, 2005).

Improving access to financing for shelter

Especially where rental markets are not operating effectively for the poor, obtaining financing can be an important but difficult step on the way to acquiring affordable and secure housing. Purchasing a house, land or even just building materials typically represents a large share of a poor household's income. Saving is difficult. Low- and middle-income households generally find it difficult to obtain bank loans and mortgages. Informal sector loans may be easy to get, at least for small sums, but are almost inevitably costly. Not surprisingly, then, many attempts to improve shelter and services in low-income urban areas have focused on finance.

Microfinance

Microfinance, conventionally targeting small enterprises, has also been applied to shelter (Ferguson, 1999; Malhotra, 2003; Daphnis and Ferguson, 2004). Microfinance agencies charge rates that are higher than bank rates but less than informal lenders. At the risk of over-generalizing, typical loans are up to US$500, loan periods are generally between three and five years, and a wide range of non-formal collateral is used. Shelter microfinance loans are more often given for incremental improvements to existing housing than for the core dwelling (Malhotra, 2003).

The loans tend to be oriented towards borrowers living in well-established settlements where residents have already secured tenure or where there is little risk of eviction. The Grameen Bank, originally founded in Bangladesh in the mid-1970s, and now active in over 40 countries, has an extensive housing loan programme of over half a million loans providing for core units. However, it requires that borrowers first purchase land and, for this reason, does not operate its programme in urban areas. Unfortunately, this means that many shelter-deprived urban-dwellers are not in a position to make use of microfinance, as the lenders consider their locations to be too high a risk. Nor is shelter microfinance able to assist households that are relatively secure to improve their access to services, as this requires significant collective investment. Shelter microfinance agencies, for the most part, do not have resources to assist communities to work together and manage the kind of group loans that such activities require. Loans are sometimes granted for service improvements, but these are household-level investments in, for example, toilets, bathrooms and water/sewerage connections to nearby mains.

Extending the mortgage market

There has been some success in 'down-marketing' mortgage finance by encouraging formal mortgage companies to make their products more accessible to low-income families – but here the limits are even more apparent than with microfinance. In Mexico, an expertise in supporting repayments through flexible loan collection practices has helped companies to reach lower-income households who depend on informal incomes (Pickering, 2000). The rapid expansion of housing lending in some of the more rapidly growing Asian economies is also indicative of both increasing household incomes and the down-marketing of mortgage finance (Watanabe, 1998). However, a number of studies suggest that mortgage finance (which is provided for a completed, formally produced house) is not relevant for the lowest 30 to 60 per cent of income earners in countries in Asia, Latin America and North Africa (UN-Habitat, 2005). The relevance of such forms of mortgage finance is even less in sub-Saharan Africa (except South Africa), due to low incomes and little formal housing provision.

Loans from developers

Where rules and regulations encourage it, private developers can provide legal but comparatively low-cost land subdivisions. In El Salvador, for example, low-cost subdivision regulations established in the early 1990s helped stimulate a low-income land development industry of 200 firms (Ferguson and Navarrete, 2003). The developers sold 12–15 year loans, with repayments of about US$15–25 a month, and these came to account for more than half of the growth of low-income housing. Many developers also offered additional loans for constructing housing. The key reforms here were not so much in the financial regulations as in the regulation of developments. In many countries much poorer than El Salvador, however, this sort of low-cost, incremental development is not allowed, let alone promoted. Furthermore, there are, of course, many urban households that cannot afford anything like US$20 a month, so this model, too, is of limited relevance in very low-income areas.

Government loans and subsidies

In the Philippines, the Community Mortgage Programme offers the residents of low-income neighbourhoods facing eviction access to low-interest loans for the purchase of land, with upgrading taking place over a longer period. This client group has ensured that the programmes financed are oriented to those in need. The programme has reached over 100,000 families over the last 20 years (Porio and Cristol, 2004). However, the dependence on loans, albeit subsidized, means that poorer families have struggled to maintain their participation in these upgrading activities (Porio et al, 2004). Other loan programmes, for a range of income groups, are provided by governments in countries across Asia and Latin America, though few have reached this scale or income group. Much rarer are the larger unit subsidies offered by countries such as Chile and South Africa. Both programmes have now reached over one million families and provide for a completed housing unit with only a small additional contribution required from the poorest families. While achieving significant scale, however, there have been very similar reservations about both programmes. Both use commercial contractors and have tended to minimize land costs and maximize building activities; hence the new housing is often built on the periphery of cities, improving the material condition of housing but increasing spatial exclusion (Jiron and Fadda, 2003; Baumann, 2004). Moreover, while some of the households reached may be very poor, the governments involved are in successful middle-income nations with comparatively well-financed governments.

Organizing civil society

While most of the initiatives described above can be viewed as lying somewhere along a continuum between public- and private-sector provisioning, it would be very misleading – though not uncommon – to treat private profit-seeking enterprise and government as the only two organizational forms that can work to provide urban-dwellers with land and services. A wide range of civil society organizations are also involved, some rooted within the low-income areas themselves (grassroots organizations), others from outside. Recent decades have seen the explosive growth of professional and semi-professional civil society organizations and non-governmental organizations (NGOs).

Civil society organizations, land and housing

In many cases, the more professional civil society organizations work within existing government programmes to enhance their effectiveness. Hence, in the Philippines, a group of NGOs is working with communities that are accessing the loans of the Community Mortgage Programme. These NGOs act as professional support agencies, working together with local government to aid community organizations and assist in the quality of physical improvements. The Thai parastatal agency, the Community Organizations Development Institute, which supports a nationwide upgrading programme, also works with and assists many NGOs, as well as grassroots organizations.

Most other initiatives can be grouped into three types: those that are primarily defensive and which work mainly against evictions; those that seek to organize people to work within the market through housing cooperatives and other market mechanisms; and those that seek state support for agendas defined by the land- or service-deprived communities.

Some NGOs provide advice on legal and campaigning strategies to reduce the likelihood of eviction and to help groups defend themselves in such cases. These NGOs may also work to change national and international law in order to reduce the likelihood of eviction and increase the possibility of compensation (or the amount paid). The Centre for Housing Rights and Evictions (COHRE) provides an international network for local groups and the NGOs that support them.

Housing cooperatives have not been widely used by the poor, because they tend to follow formal requirements and hence be relatively expensive. But they can be a solution for those with slightly higher incomes who cannot afford private housing. Cooperative strategies were used in Zimbabwe and have been expanding (albeit at a slow rate) in countries such as Kenya. However, the numbers remain very small, and it is likely that cooperatives will be overtaken by individualized market-based routes as the latter develop and provide basic units more cheaply.

A particularly significant initiative to assist the urban poor in finding government support for people's own development programmes is provided by the 14 grassroots organizations and networks of low-income, homeless and shack-dwellers that are affiliates of Shack/Slum Dwellers International (SDI). These are located primarily in southern and east Africa, and Asia, with one further member in west Africa and another in Brazil. All these support women in low-income settlements to organize themselves through savings schemes. These schemes draw members together through daily savings activities and regular lending. Savings groups discuss local priorities, which include tenure security and access to basic services, and how they might be achieved. Different settlement-level savings schemes affiliate across cities to be able to identify existing resources (available land and subsidy programmes) and negotiate with politicians, political parties and civil servants. As a result of this work, long-term tenure has been secured for about 150,000 families over the last 15 years, and housing improvements have taken place for at least half these families (D'Cruz and Satterthwaite, 2005) (see Box 4.1 for more details).

Civil society actions are not restricted to NGOs, and an alternative strategy, less used by formal NGOs and more favoured by social movements and grassroots organizations, is that of land invasions. FEGIP (Federação de Inquilinos e Posseiros do Estado de Goiás), a federation of tenants and land occupiers in the state of Goiania, Brazil, is a particularly notable example, with about 200,000 people having been assisted to invade public land and secure tenure (having previously been tenants) (Barbosa et al, 1997). In many settings, complex relationships have developed between popular land invasion, private land development and political power. Hence, while invasions might appear to be organized by civil society, in practice this may not be the case. Land invasions are less widely used now than in the past, in part because only less-well-located land is open to being invaded.

Civil society organizations and acquiring basic urban services

The residents of under-serviced neighbourhoods recognize their need for basic services such as water, sanitation, drainage (in some areas), waste collection and schools. They can try to secure access to such services through markets, from public agencies or utilities, or through their own work. Small-scale entrepreneurs often emerge to provide services in the absence of the state. There is no profit in providing public goods that are non-excludable (for example drainage channels), however, so these goods and services are not supplied by private entrepreneurs unless residents organize themselves and create a collective demand, or a public agency contracts them to provide the service. Even where small-scale private solutions do emerge, they may need to connect to the piped networks and hence suffer further problems due to inadequate public investments. Small-scale water vendors often simply collect water from the nearest public point and transport it to low-income areas. Waste collectors, it is hoped, dump the waste at public sites.

Many civil society initiatives involve neighbourhood associations seeking to improve public services in their areas. These associations lobby, pressure and coerce local councillors and politicians to provide them with the services they require. However, they often end up accepting the generally inadequate provision and simply lobby for further improvements at the next election.

Faced with this wasteful and health-damaging situation, a range of professional civil society organizations have sought to intervene to improve access to services. Their contributions include:

- assistance to the informal private sector (loans and technical advice);
- campaigns to improve public services (often associated with anti-privatization); and
- support to neighbourhood groups wanting to install their own community-managed services.

The most significant programme (in terms of scale and, arguably, the radical nature of their approach) is that of the Orangi Pilot Project in Pakistan, which developed a model of lane sanitation in which local residents met all the costs of the infrastructure within the neighbourhood, with technical assistance being provided by the project staff. After 20 years of experimentation and replication, the model is now being rolled out in 27 towns and cities across the country and is being adopted within the national sanitation policy (Hasan, 2006a and 2006b). In terms of social organization, lanes establish committees, which are then networked into area associations, which in turn work with state agencies to ensure adequate provision of sewer mains into which they can connect.

The 14 federations of the urban poor (see Box 4.1) working within SDI are frequently drawn into addressing neighbourhood-level services such as water and sanitation. Specific plans differ, depending on the availability of state subsidies and the strictness with which building and land subdivision regulations are maintained. In some countries, there are state subsidies available for infrastructure improvements, and the strong local organizations, combined with national-level federation activities, have enabled SDI affiliates to secure access to such subsidies. In other contexts, particularly in sub-Saharan Africa, the local savings groups have to finance neighbourhood infrastructure themselves, using soft loans and their own labour to reduce costs to a minimum (Mitlin, 2003).

Communal or public provision of water – through public taps or water kiosks – has long been seen as a 'solution' for poorer groups. This method of supply works better than communal provision for sanitation, as households can store water in their homes and avoid queues or the need to fetch water at night. Communal or public provision for sanitation is never ideal, but, in many places, it is the best compromise between better provision, what can be afforded and what can be managed locally. It is cheaper than household provision and often much easier to provide in existing high-density settlements (Burra et al, 2003).

In Thailand, the Danish International Development Agency (Danida)-financed Environmental Community Activities Fund worked within the office of the Thai Government's Community Organizations Development Institute (CODI) to finance local community improvements in infrastructure and services (along with other neighbourhood improvements such as building renovation). In this case, improvements were primarily grant-financed and were designed to strengthen local and city networks, which were able to use the grants as catalysts for a broader programme of upgrading (Boonyabancha, 1999).

Box 4.1 Federations of the urban poor

There is a long history of federations formed by groups from within the urban poor that seek political change and, where political circumstances permit, negotiate resources and government programmes that benefit their members. But over the last two decades, a new kind of federation has emerged, formed by savings groups set up by the inhabitants of 'slums'. These federations are not lobbying government for 'solutions' but are actively engaged in developing solutions themselves and are offering governments partnerships to implement these at scale. They are unusual in the central role that women play in all of them, including offering women leadership positions. They are also unique in the way that the different national federations learn from and support each other. These federations have developed a model for addressing urban poverty that they share with each other and assist each other in implementing – supported by the small umbrella organization Shack/Slum Dwellers International (SDI), of which they are all members.

The catalyst for this new kind of federation was the National Slum Dwellers' Federation in India. The head of this federation, Jockin Arputham, was a community leader who, from the early 1960s, had fought to protect the 'slum' where he lived, and other 'slums', from being bulldozed (Arputham, 2006). In the early 1980s, Arputham and other slum leaders in India recognized the need to go beyond this fight to protect their settlements. They also understood the state's incapacity to actually deliver alternatives that met their needs. So they began to develop their own solutions, to demonstrate to government the kinds of housing and basic service programmes that worked for slum-dwellers and to show their own capacity to work with governments in implementing these at scale. This change coincided with the emergence of a federation of savings groups formed by women pavement-dwellers in Mumbai, Mahila Milan, who were supported by a recently formed, local NGO, SPARC (Society for the Promotion of Area Resource Centres). These three organizations formed an alliance that, since 1985, has been demonstrating to governments through concrete projects – for instance for new housing, for community mapping and for public toilets – how to address the needs of their members.

The intervention model that this alliance developed spread to many other urban centres in India through a growing programme of community-to-community exchanges; exchanges also developed between nations as new slum/shack-dwellers' federations formed and sought to learn from each other. This programme was formalized and expanded by the creation of SDI in 1996.

Addressing urban poverty requires strong local grassroots organizations able to negotiate for resources, design appropriate development solutions, implement those solutions in conjunction with the local authorities and strengthen accountable representative organizations through this process. Strengthening local organizations is critical as it enables the local groups to maintain and develop their capacities, allowing them to deepen the participatory democratic process. Successive rounds of negotiations and implementation enable the people-centred development process to grow.

To simplify, the intervention model includes the following steps:

- Build local grassroots organizations around daily savings. These organizations are based on savers, who collect funds from their members and provide loans, develop the capacity to handle finance, and create the foundation for collective action.

- Prioritize women and develop an understanding of the need for women's involvement. Daily savings help establish processes that are pro-women and pro-poor (because men and the not-so-poor, in general, are not keen on the regularity or even tedium of daily saving). The central role of women can help to ensure that the process is need-oriented and that the organization can establish a pragmatic, collective focus that is powerful but non-violent.
- Understand needs through detailed household surveys (enumerations) and local mapping. This settlement-wide process provides the information base for groups to consolidate their work and plan for improvements (Patel et al, 2002; Weru, 2004).
- Develop a mass base across each settlement (enumeration and lending activities help to draw groups together).
- Foster an understanding of local capacities. Savings, financial contributions, activities such as land searches (to identify sites that can be used for new housing) and incremental improvements help give residents a sense of their own ability and reduce dependency.
- Develop a consciousness of solidarity between groups of the urban poor and a commonality of interests. Community exchanges within each city and among cities help to establish the sense of solidarity. All urban poor groups suffer from isolation, but women savers are keen to collaborate and to learn from each other, so this is a relatively easy process.
- Encourage city and national federation leaders to become political negotiators. Though not party-political, federation leaders learn to use electoral pressure and how to work with official negotiations and through a mass presence on the ground.

Looking to the Future

Historically, urban planning and land-use regulations have often contributed to the creation of large, informal settlements or slums, whose residents are typically deprived of environmental services. There is now international agreement that it is important both to avoid the creation of new slums and to upgrade or transform existing ones. To meet these challenges, however, it is important that governments and international agencies stop regarding slums as a symptom of over-urbanization and stop using land-use policies as a means of curbing urban growth. Instead, governments will need to:

1 work constructively and routinely with existing slum-dwellers to solve problems locally;
2 create the basis for land and housing markets that reallocate resources efficiently and equitably; and
3 develop physically and financially realistic strategies for accommodating future urban growth.

While, as described in previous sections, there is no one recipe for success, many of the most successful efforts to improve conditions in deprived urban areas build on the efforts of the residents themselves. Key principles include local ownership, incremental improvement and more effective community-level organization. Unfortunately, although successes have been sufficiently widespread to justify optimism about what can be done, they are not sufficiently common to justify much optimism about what will be done. Looking to the future, it is critical to improve the political basis for negotiation between organizations of the urban poor and local governments. This will need the support of both national governments and international agencies. It will also need the support of NGOs that are willing to help organizations of the urban poor to represent their own interests to local and national governments, rather than claiming to represent those interests themselves. But, perhaps most important, it will require organizations of the urban poor to develop and spread more effective strategies, as has been done by the federations of the urban poor described in Box 4.1.

Looking to the future, it will be a challenge for many urban and national authorities to ensure that sufficient land is made available for new housing (and in doing so provide legal alternatives to 'informal settlements' that lower-income households can afford), that land markets are functioning efficiently and fairly, and that the growing demand for services can be met. This will require careful planning, locally, citywide and nationally. At first glance, this would seem to be a very different challenge from that of upgrading or transforming existing slums. After all, future urban residents cannot negotiate directly for their stake in urban development in the way that existing groups can – at least if they are allowed to do so.

But even looking to the future, it is important to develop better relations between deprived residents and their governments in the present. Good relationships need to be developed and institutionalized over time and are far too rare in the present. Moreover, while adequate supplies and markets for land, housing and services are critical, they are not in themselves sufficient. Housing and land-use regulations that the urban poor cannot afford to meet; infrastructure and utility charges which they cannot or will not pay; developments that require large-scale relocations – these can quickly drive low-income settlements into illegality or informality. They can also lead to stand-offs, where residents refuse to move and governments refuse to support their stay. Eventually, they can be used to justify evictions. Planning for the future does not just mean working out how future needs will be met, but also providing a sound foundation for resolving future disputes, at least in part by improving current practices.

NOTE

1 UN-Habitat (2003a) uses the term 'slum' to refer to neighbourhoods, or, in some cases, even individual homes, that lack access to safe water, access to sanitation, secure tenure, durability of housing and/or sufficient living space.

REFERENCES

Arputham, J. (2006) Personal communication

Barbosa, R., Cabannes, Y. and Morães, L. (1997) 'Tenant today, *posseiro* tomorrow', *Environment and Urbanization*, vol 9, no 2, pp17–42

Batley, R. and Larbi, G. A. (2004) *The Changing Role of Government: The Reform of Public Services in Developing Countries*, Palgrave Macmillan, Basingstoke, UK

Baumann, T. (2004) 'Housing finance in South Africa', report for UN-Habitat Housing Finance Programme, UN-Habitat, Nairobi

Boonyabancha, S. (1999) 'The urban community environmental activities project and its environment fund in Thailand', *Environment and Urbanization*, vol 11, no 1, pp101–116

Budds, J. and McGranahan, G. (2003) 'Are the debates on water privatization missing the point? Experiences from Africa, Asia and Latin America', *Environment and Urbanization*, vol 15, no 2, pp87–114

Burra, S., Patel, S. and Kerr, T. (2003) 'Community-designed, -built and -managed toilet blocks in Indian cities', *Environment and Urbanization*, vol 15, no 2, pp11–32

Cabanas Díaz, A., Grant, E., Vargas, P. I. D. and Velásquez, V. S. (2000) 'El Mezquital: A community's struggle for development', *Environment and Urbanization*, vol 12, no 1, pp87–106

Calderón, J. (2004) 'The formalization of property in Peru, 2001–2002: The case of Lima', *Habitat International*, vol 28, no 2, pp289–300

Clarke, G. R. G., Kosec, K. and Wallsten, S. (2004) 'Has private participation in water and sanitation improved coverage? Empirical evidence from Latin America', Policy Research Working Paper No WPS3445, World Bank, Washington, DC

Daphnis, F. and Ferguson, B. (2004) *Housing Microfinance: A Guide to Practice*, Kumarian Press, Bloomfield, CT

D'Cruz, C. and Satterthwaite, D. (2005) 'Building homes, changing official approaches: The work of the urban poor organizations and their federations and their contributions to meeting the Millennium Development Goals in urban areas', Poverty Reduction in Urban Areas Series Working Paper No 16, International Institute for Environment and Development, London

De Soto, H. (2000) *The Mystery of Capital: Why Capitalism Triumphs in the West and Fails Everywhere Else*, Bantam Press, London

Ferguson, B. (1999) 'Microfinance of housing: A key to housing the low- or moderate-income majority?', *Environment and Urbanization*, vol 11, no 1, pp185–200

Ferguson, B. and Navarrete, J. (2003) 'A financial framework for reducing slums: Lessons from experience in Latin America', *Environment and Urbanization*, vol 15, no 2, pp201–216

Finger, M. and Allouche, J. (2002) *Water Privatization: Trans-National Corporations and the Re-Regulation of the Water Industry*, Spon Press, London

Fung, A. and Wright, E. O. (2003) *Deepening Democracy: Institutional Innovations in Empowered Participatory Governance*, Verso, London and New York

Giddens, A. (1998) *The Third Way: The Renewal of Social Democracy*, Polity Press, Cambridge, UK

Hall, D. and Lobina, E. (2006) *Pipe Dreams: The Failure of the Private Sector to Invest in Water Services in Developing Countries*, Public Services International Research Unit, London

Hardoy, J. E. and Satterthwaite, D. (1989) *Squatter Citizen: Life in the Urban Third World*, Earthscan, London

Hasan, A. (2006a) 'Orangi Pilot Project: The expansion of work beyond Orangi and the mapping of informal settlements and infrastructure', *Environment and Urbanization*, vol 18, no 2, pp451–480

Hasan, A. (2006b) 'The sanitation programme of the Orangi Pilot Project: Research and Training Institute (OPP-RTI), Karachi, Pakistan', paper presented at the World Urban Forum, UN-Habitat, Vancouver, 19–23 June 2006

Ishengoma, E. K. and Kappel, R. (2006) 'Economic growth and poverty: Does formalization of informal enterprises matter?', GIGA Working Paper No 20, German Institute of Global and Area Studies, Hamburg, Germany

Jiron, P. and Fadda, G. (2003) 'A quality of life assessment to improve urban and housing policies in Chile', paper presented at The World Bank Urban Research Symposium 2003, Washington, DC, 15–17 December

Kirkpatrick, C., Parker, D. and Zhang, Y-F. (2004) 'State- versus private-sector provision of water services in Africa: An empirical analysis', paper presented at the Center on Regulation and Competition 3rd International Conference, 'Pro-Poor Regulation and Competition: Issues, Policies and Practices', Cape Town, South Africa, 7–9 September

Lindert, P. H. (2004) *Growing Public: Social Spending and Economic Growth since the Eighteenth Century*, Cambridge University Press, Cambridge, UK

Lipton, M. (1977) *Why Poor People Stay Poor: Urban Bias in World Development*, Temple Smith, London

Malhotra, M. (2003) 'Financing her home, one wall at a time', *Environment and Urbanization*, vol 15, no 2, pp217–228

Mangin, W. (1967) 'Latin American squatter settlements: A problem and a solution', *Latin American Research Review*, vol 2, no 3, pp65–98

McGranahan, G., Njiru, C., Albu, M., Smith, M. D. S. and Mitlin, D. (2006) *How Small Water Enterprises (SWEs) can Contribute to the Millennium Development Goals: Evidence from Accra, Dar Es Salaam, Khartoum and Nairobi*, Water, Engineering and Development Centre, Loughborough University, Loughborough, UK

McGranahan, G. and Satterthwaite, D. (2006) 'Governance and getting the private sector to provide better water and sanitation services to the urban poor', Human Settlements Discussion Paper, Theme: Water, No 2, International Institute for Environment and Development, London

Mitlin, D. (2003) 'A fund to secure land for shelter: Supporting strategies of the organized poor', *Environment and Urbanization*, vol 15, no 1, pp181–192

Ostrom, E. (2005) *Understanding Institutional Diversity*, Princeton University Press, Princeton, NJ

Patel, S., d'Cruz, C. and Burra, S. (2002) 'Beyond evictions in a global city: People-managed resettlement in Mumbai', *Environment and Urbanization*, vol 14, no 1, pp159–172

Payne, G. and Majale, M. (2004) *The Urban Housing Manual: Making Regulatory Frameworks Work for the Poor*, Earthscan, London

Pickering, N. (2000) *The SOFOLES: Niche Lending or New Leaders in the Mexican Mortgage Market?*, Joint Center for Housing Studies, Harvard University, Cambridge, MA

Porio, E. and Cristol, C. (2004) 'Property rights, security of tenure and the urban poor in Metro Manila', *Habitat International*, vol 28, no 2, pp203–219

Porio, E., Crisol, C. S., Magno N. F., Cid, D. and Paul, E. N. (2004) 'The Community Mortgage Programme: An innovative social housing programme in the Philippines and its outcomes', in D. Mitlin and D. Satterthwaite (eds) *Empowering Squatter Citizen: Local Government, Civil Society, and Urban Poverty Reduction*, Earthscan, London, pp54–81

Stein, A. and Castillo, L. (2005) 'Innovative financing for low-income housing improvement: Lessons from programmes in Central America', *Environment and Urbanization*, vol 17, no 1, pp47–66

Stiglitz, J. E. (2002) *Globalization and its Discontents*, W. W. Norton and Company, New York

Szreter, S. (2005) *Health and Wealth: Studies in History and Policy*, University of Rochester Press, Rochester, NY

Turner, J. F. C. (1968) 'Housing priorities, settlement patterns and urban development in modernizing countries', *Journal of the American Institute of Planners*, vol 34, pp354–363

Turner, J. F. C. (1976) *Housing by People: Towards Autonomy in Building Environments*, Marion Boyars, London

UN-Habitat (2003a) *The Challenge of Slums: Global Report on Human Settlements 2003*, Earthscan, London and Sterling, VA

UN-Habitat (2003b) *Water and Sanitation in the World's Cities: Local Action for Global Goals*, Earthscan, London

UN-Habitat (2005) *Financing Urban Shelter: Global Report on Human Settlements 2005*, Eathscan, London

Watanabe, M. (ed) (1998) *New Directions in Asian Housing Finance*, International Finance Corporation, World Bank, Washington, DC

Weru, J. (2004) 'Community federations and city upgrading: The work of Pamoja Trust and Muungano in Kenya', *Environment and Urbanization*, vol 16, no 1, pp47–62

5

Informality and Poverty in Latin American Urban Policies

Martim O. Smolka and Adriana de A. Larangeira[1]

INTRODUCTION

Adequate housing for the urban poor is looming as a major challenge for the 21st century. According to UN-Habitat (2006), there were almost a billion slum-dwellers in the world in 2005. If current trends continue, the slum population will reach 1.4 billion by 2020. Recent analyses of satellite images corroborate the leading role of informal occupations in the rapid geographical extension of cities in the developing world (Angel et al, 2005).

In comparison with the developing regions of Africa and Asia, the Latin American continent underwent an early urban transition, and it has already accumulated considerable experience in dealing with rapid slum growth. Although the results of policy efforts have rarely been ideal, much can be learned from Latin America's trials and errors. This chapter reviews some of the major approaches adopted and attempts to derive key recommendations from them.

In spite of public efforts to deal with the growth of informal settlements since the early 1960s, and of more intensive efforts during the last decade, the number of slum-dwellers in Latin America increased from 111 to 127 million between 1990 and 2001 (ECLAC, 2004, p276). Approximately 44 per cent of the region's urban population lives in precarious settlements, experiencing inadequate living conditions in regard to building quality, access to basic services, such as sewage and public lighting, and proper titling (MacDonald, 2004).

Some Latin American countries have had more than a century of short-sighted urban policies, ranging from outright repression, removals and relocation to full recognition, large-scale housing projects, serviced sites and basic services, on-site selective support for self-improvements, and direct public investments in settlement upgrading.[2] These policies did not significantly alleviate the problem and, in many circumstances, further fuelled the growth of informal settlements.[3]

Recognition of policy failure, and of the structural inability to address the issue at its current scale, has generated tolerance towards informal settlements. The consequent rampant growth of informality has impacts beyond their direct occupants. Indeed, informality disrupts the functioning of land markets (unfair competition given the higher profitability of informal land schemes), pushes up land prices (more restrictive land-use regulations to 'protect' areas from informal occupations) and generates increased difficulties in providing services, especially for the poor, because of the restricted tax base and the higher cost of servicing informally occupied areas. In short, informality begets more informality.[4]

This chapter argues that the magnitude and persistence of informality in Latin American cities is, to a large extent, the product of ineffective policies over the last 40 years. It begins with a brief review of how public attitudes evolved regarding informality, discusses some of the misunderstandings that have largely been responsible for short-sighted and self-defeating policies, and concludes by highlighting the need for a shift in emphasis from mitigation towards addressing the causes of informality.

INFORMALITY: A TRANSITORY PHENOMENON?

In the late 19th and early 20th centuries, informal settlements were seen as a transitory phenomenon, expected to fade away with economic growth and modernization. This assumption proved to be deeply mistaken: informal settlements not only failed to disappear, but grew in number, size and density of land occupation, becoming the rule, rather than the exception, for city growth in Latin America.

Far from being isolated and infrequent events, the informal occupation of public and private vacant lands, hillsides, swamps, risky and/or environmentally protected areas, and the like has provided the only alternative 'housing solution' for lower-income groups since the mid-1800s. This practice greatly intensified with the quickening of urbanization in the region after the 1950s.

Contrary to conventional wisdom, informal land occupations are, by and large, the object of 'regular' market operations, widely promoted by so-called 'pirate' or informal developers. This is now a highly profitable business (outcompeting formal developers) and the prevailing form of land acquisition in urban peripheries, as well as in most inner-city consolidated informal settlements (Abramo, 2006).

Squatting and 'Land Takeovers'

The persistence of squatting has been fuelled by a number of factors. The most obvious is an inadequate supply of affordable housing to meet the needs of rapidly growing, low-income urban populations. This increase results from a combination of natural growth in urban areas and the influx of rural–urban migrants in search of economic opportunities. In some countries, other factors, such as natural disasters or wars, also affect the mismatch between population growth and the provision of urban infrastructure and services.

Though inevitable and generally predictable, the rapid urban growth that has marked Latin America for the last half-century was rarely, if ever, planned for. Sooner or later, public administrators were forced to accommodate the massive increase in poor inhabitants, at much higher social and financial costs than would have been the case if proactive measures had been in place. This 'accommodation' frequently took the form of tolerance or even facilitation of apparently spontaneous land takeovers that contributed to forming and increasing an informal 'housing stock'.

Nevertheless, occupiers of informal settlements were often held responsible for their precarious living conditions. This classic example of 'blaming the victim' diverted attention from public responsibility for the problem. Some of the public measures ultimately taken in response took an extreme form: slum eviction.

Forced Eviction and Resettlement

The long-lasting 'transitory' condition of informal settlements was widely interpreted as both a social and a political threat. Due to their poor sanitary conditions, slums and tenement houses were declared hazardous for public health,[5] thus justifying forced evictions, often in association with modernizing and/or cosmetic urban reform plans. These knock-down, eviction-cum-displacement policies have been the most radical response to the underlying presumption of informal settlements as a problem.

With the accelerated growth of informal settlements, more structured and systematic actions were set in motion, particularly those aimed at eviction. In Pinochet's Chile, for example, low-income groups were massively eradicated from areas at odds with their paying capacity. In general, eviction takes the form of displacement and is accompanied by relocation if minimal rights for informal occupants are recognized. Such relocations, involving financial subsidy systems, left easily recognizable footprints on the peripheries of practically all Latin American metropolitan areas. The case of attempts to eliminate slums and move people into high-rise apartment buildings by Venezuelan President Pérez Jiménez is emblematic (Bolivar, 2003).

Although forced evictions are no longer a leading practice in Latin America, isolated episodes are still being reported in Argentina, Brazil, Colombia and Peru (COHRE, 2006). More subtle contemporary market-driven evictions and displacements ('here's an offer you can't refuse'), closely related to economic pressures, are now replacing conventional forced evictions and affecting overall accessibility to serviced land (Durand-Lasserve, 2005).

The negative effects of all such forced evictions and displacements extend far beyond the move itself, given longer commuting times, higher costs, loss of neighbourhood support networks and inability to meet monthly payments. The latter result in the '*passa-se uma casa*' syndrome.[6] Those who remain after the evictions face the 'City of God' fate: in other words, fast degradation of the built environment and lack of integration into the surrounding urban tissue.

In short, intervention was again faulty in the case of subsidized displacements: even when generous open or hidden subsidies were provided in 'resettlement programmes', they were either insufficient to cover more than a small fraction of the needs, or they were rapidly appropriated by other social groups, rather than by the originally targeted group.

UPGRADING PROGRAMMES

The counterpoint for earlier eviction policies has taken the form of regularization and slum upgrading programmes. This strategy frames informal settlements as a solution, rather than a problem. It recognizes the spontaneity and creativity of people and takes into account their efforts and investments as the 'capital' that could be leveraged in existing settlements. Regularization programmes are thus claimed to be cost-effective, not only in financial terms, but also in avoiding the political costs associated with eviction.

Re-democratization processes in most Latin American countries encouraged reassessment of the traditional model of large-scale housing projects in favour of 'progressive and participatory' methods to gain access to housing, as in Argentina, and for upgrading, as in several other countries.

Despite some official resistance, a plethora of such initiatives were started in the early 1990s,[7] albeit under dramatically variable conditions, in that many included support and follow-up to the families involved. To be feasible, these programmes were typically limited to clusters of 50 to 200 dwellings (Pelli, 1997).

Though well intentioned, however, these initiatives were as short-sighted as their predecessors, underestimating the difficulties of simultaneously managing multiple interventions to attend to the massive demands.[8] UN-Habitat accurately diagnosed the difficulties in scaling up these experiences:

> *Many existing good practices for shelter and services delivery can rarely get past the demonstration or pilot phase and tend not to be replicable.*

> *The main reasons for this are the lack of clear institutional linkages,*
> *the lack of economic sustainability and a failure to reinvest. New*
> *initiatives are often perceived as threats to existing structures in local*
> *administrations. Internal resistance to change is exacerbated by turf-*
> *wars and failure to share information among all stakeholders within*
> *the administration.* (UN-Habitat, 2002, p5)

Many of the regularized settlements (and their surrounding areas) ceded to pressure for more housing by increasing their size and density, largely through informal means. The infrastructure and urban services thus implemented were, in turn, found to foster new invasions, leading to overburdening and to the premature degradation of settlements. As a result, inner-city informal areas were consolidated through a strong process of densification (Abramo, 2007). Moreover, these areas were rarely integrated into the local fiscal system or fully granted secure land tenure. Even upgraded settlements had an incomplete formal status, and their social stigma remained unchanged.

Tangible improvements in living conditions were undoubtedly achieved in some of these settlements, but they had limited, if any, impact on the city as a whole: They did not noticeably affect land-market dynamics or overall access to urban services. To be sure, these programmes were clearly an improvement over the older paradigm in which informal settlements were simply eradicated. The objective of urban and social integration has, however, not been met, and the limited scale of programme implementation was insufficient to produce significant impacts. Living conditions may have improved in limited areas, but overall access to serviced land and housing conditions for the city as a whole worsened.

THE MASSIVE TITLING APPROACH

Over the last decade, almost all countries and cities in the Latin American region have introduced titling programmes separate from programmes aimed at upgrading existing settlements or new housing initiatives. Freehold titles were expected to wake 'sleeping capital', the term proposed by De Soto (2000).

In Peru, the titling programme sponsored under this approach issued 1,393,096 titles between 1996 and 2004 and was heralded as a great success.[9] More careful assessments, however, indicate that the programme's central tenets were not verified in practice and that it had less-publicized negative implications (Calderón Cockburn, 2003 and 2005a).

Formalization of property rights did not necessarily lead to access to the credit that was supposed to automatically integrate slum-dwellers into the urban economy and support economic growth. For most credit agencies, a steady job is more important than freehold titles as collateral. After four years of operation (with 76 per cent of titles already issued), only 1.6 per cent of titleholders had obtained loans through the banking system using their property titles as collateral.[10] Newly regularized residential and commercial properties remained in the same precarious conditions as before. This was shown by both their physical condition and the continued social exclusion of the inhabitants. The objectives of the programme had clearly not been met.

It is revealing that the inhabitants of informal settlements themselves seem to have little, and decreasing, faith in such titles. Two surveys conducted 18 years apart in Rio's *favelas* clearly reaffirm their low opinion (Cavallieri, 2003). Over and above their failure to meet intended objectives, titling programmes seem to induce at least two unanticipated negative impacts. First, freehold titles facilitate the disposal of individual properties, thus weakening community cohesiveness and collective actions. Second and concomitant, the relatively low cost of the title, ease of acquisition and supposed advantage of the 'unrestricted' exercise of property rights generate, in practice, the underutilization of newly regularized plots. In Peru, for instance:

> *Authorities have been very lax about allowing people to take possession of two plots. Today, a person can own a plot of land and not live on it. Consequently, in some settlements, 20 per cent of the plots are empty and 10 per cent have a floating population.* (Calderón Cockburn, 2007, p4)

Freehold titling programmes isolated from urban upgrading processes end up increasing the cost of land transactions, generating a formal market for substandard land and reducing the already scarce access to adequate land for the urban poor. In short, rather than being a first step in the process of urban inclusion, massive land titling consolidates and formalizes urban exclusion (Ramirez Corzo and Riofrío, 2005).

It is thus of some concern that major financing agencies are now focusing on freehold land titling programmes when accumulated experience in the field seems to highlight the limitations of this approach as well as its unintended consequences for informality itself.

LACK OF POLICIES OR SHORT-SIGHTED POLICIES?

This brief review of the evolution and scope of public policies towards informality reveals that, by and large, they have generally failed to address the fundamental determinants of informality itself: dysfunctions of urban land markets and the corresponding misguided public policies. The latter cover a wide range, including elitist land-use regulations with which lower-income populations are unable to comply; lack of sanctions for pirate land developers, especially on urban peripheries; the absence of fiscal instruments to discipline the functioning of urban land markets; the arbitrary distribution of benefits and charges from increases in land value resulting from public intervention; high transaction costs imposed by inefficient bureaucratic procedures; and the 'clientelistic' use of the operational capacity of public administration, including tolerance towards the occupation of publicly owned land. All of these ultimately not only affect the causes but also deepen the negative effects of informality.

Thus the magnitude and persistence of informality in Latin American cities stems from the paucity of *good* land policies, rather than the absence of policies. Critical issues are often overlooked in the public policy agenda, and actions are often based on incorrect information. This is particularly important since the object of intervention seems to be ever changing – a moving target.

MISCONCEPTIONS

Informality is a multidimensional phenomenon that results from a variety of causes and contributing factors. Better analyses and more accurate diagnoses would lead to the design of more consistent and effective policies. Many misunderstandings, in the form of myths, prejudices and ill-informed 'truths', seriously distort the views of otherwise well-intentioned policymakers.

The lack of a legal property title, for example, does not necessarily mean that land was acquired outside the market, as is often assumed. Access to land in urban peripheries, and even in the more consolidated informal settlements, is nowadays obtained predominantly through market transactions. Land invasions, which historically typified most slums, are no longer the most prevalent form of obtaining land. Regardless of the type of land use or the quality of houses produced, irregular housing is advertised, sold and rented in an operating market (Bogus and Pasternak, 2003). Even invaded land is commercialized, as in the so-called organized invasions, where the rights to occupy an area are granted for a fee. This has obvious policy implications: focusing on places (rather than on processes) may simply reinstate informality through 'drawer contracts'.[11]

Another misconception is to perceive informal settlements as occupied exclusively by homogeneous groups: the poor. As seen in Rio de Janeiro, consolidated inner-city slums have a more heterogeneous socioeconomic composition than formal neighbourhoods (Abramo, 2007, p20). Moreover, there is ample evidence that poor people live in formal areas and non-poor people in informal areas (Smolka, 1992). A recent study of the 401 largest Brazilian municipalities found no correlation between an increase in urban poverty and the increase in informality between 1991 and 2001 (Biderman and Smolka, 2007). The population living in informal areas is larger than the total number of poor people: This has obvious implications for occupants' willingness and capacity to pay for services and property taxes as a way of legitimizing their land tenure (Smolka and De Cesare, 2006).[12]

It is also an error to assume that all slum-dwellers are stable, long-term residents. Significant movement in and out of *favelas* is associated with both vibrant land markets and socioeconomic mobility (Abramo, 2007). This overlooked fact, together with the observed high prices of property in consolidated informal areas, suggests that the occupation of these areas results less from residents' incapacity to pay than from the inability of the 'formal market' to provide products with the set of attributes that are demanded. These attributes range from flexible credit conditions adaptable to an irregular stream of income to progressive building permits accommodating higher densities or allowing shops in residences.

Moreover, it is wrong to assume that living in informal settlements is free, or even cheap. From both individual and collective viewpoints, informality has many associated costs, often higher than those in formal areas of the city. Many informal occupants realize that private provision of basic services through informal means is likely to be more costly and unreliable than that provided as a counterpart to the payment of a property tax: water from truck distributors, for example, often costs from three to five times as much as piped water services in equivalent formal areas. Thus:

> *Ironically, it is the affluent groups who benefit most from under-pricing of basic services such as water supply, as the poor are rarely connected to municipal services and have to rely on the informal market. Generally the poorest residents pay the highest unit price for services such as water and energy.* (UN-Habitat, 2002, p8)

The price per square metre in informal land subdivisions is also typically higher than in formal ones, given what is provided. The price is set within the margins in which the informal developer operates. Its lower limit is determined by the price of land acquired at its agricultural value, plus the costs of subdivision, provision of minimum services (for example electricity) and infrastructure (for example dirt streets), other indirect costs (for example security), and commercialization costs. The upper limit is established by the competitive price of the closest formal developer. Informal 'developers' thus operate under quasi-monopolistic conditions. Final prices are set higher (relative to formal land) not only due to higher profit margins, but also because the operation is less efficient.

All of these conditions have profound implications for addressing what is considered the most critical barrier to mitigating informality: the lack of a sustainable flow of financial resources.

SUSTAINABILITY OF PROGRAMMES

The insufficiency of financial resources is frequently given as justification for pitifully inadequate public actions. Programme developers and managers typically assume that the only way to finance regularization programmes is to adapt their initiatives to limited borrowed funds. This attitude leads to a failure to take advantage of the opportunities presented by informality itself in developing effective and sustainable programmes.

In effect, significant additional costs are accrued when the lack of proactive actions generates the need for substantial curative or remedial public investments. This is the case when public intervention tries desperately to follow the kaleidoscopic trail of urban shortages left by the process of informal land occupations instead of acting in anticipation of urban expansion.[13] As a result, public investment is prioritized for regularization. This sends positive signals to informal market operations and further intensifies the pace of informal expansion. Plots can be produced more expeditiously in informal than formal developments.[14]

Moreover, there is a clear mismatch between social and private costs and benefits. Surprisingly, cost-recovery mechanisms are rarely considered as market-correcting mechanisms in the design of programmes, or at least as alternatives or complements to loans. While some Latin American programmes apply property taxes[15] and levies on value increments resulting from public investment – albeit in a rather symbolic form[16] – such initiatives rarely take place in association with upgrading or regularization. This underlines their isolation and disconnection from the broader urban policy framework and thus undermines their potential effectiveness.

INVOLVEMENT OF PRIVATE AGENTS

Demystifying informality and confronting the primary causes of its persistence requires a closer look at the role played by public and private initiatives. Despite increasing coverage of basic urban infrastructure (sewerage, piped water and so on), and despite the significant decrease in regional rates of urban growth, the supply of serviced land at affordable prices is still insufficient, thus perpetuating informality. Some of the factors contributing to the illegal, irregular, informal and clandestine activities that provide access to urban land remain untouched. These include failure to foresee inevitable urban growth; inadequate urbanistic norms and regulations; ill-balanced spatial distribution of urban infrastructure and services; an unfettered culture of urban delinquency and indiscipline; the prejudices of credit agencies towards low-income land development projects; and cutbacks in the provision of public housing.

All this reduces the motivation for private formal developers to participate in the low-income market. They cannot compete with informal developers. They also find it more profitable to concentrate on the high-income segment of the market, where effective demand is renewed through product innovations that draw on the higher propensity of these groups to pay. Public agents, in turn, tend to concentrate more on curative rather than on proactive policies, even though the former are more costly per benefited family than fully serving even larger plots of land in new developments (Smolka, 2003).

A complex interdependence of the formal and informal markets has thus been established, leading to an equilibrium of sorts. High-income families pay a premium to avoid the negative conditions of slums. Low-income families pay a premium to access well-located land that is not suited for occupation by the formal market (either because of environmental regulations and/or low market value due to noise pollution, proximity to landfills and garbage dumps, etc.) without complying with the conditions imposed on formal markets or incurring the full costs of urbanistic norms and regulations.

REVISITING CONVENTIONAL MODELS

Public responses to informality have generally left the nexus of the problem untouched, thereby favouring its perpetuation. By tolerating informality, local administrations recognize their inability to offer an alternative and rely on future regularization of land occupations to solve the problem. The higher this expectation, the higher the premium land subdividers are able to charge. Or, assuming that low-income families cannot afford the costs of housing that complies with urbanistic norms and regulations, policymakers offer upfront (open or hidden) subsidies to the developer or the final consumer.

Given the intensification of regularization programmes on the one hand and the scale of public funds needed to subsidize all housing deficits on the other, both approaches seem to lead to higher land prices, thus feeding back on informality. To break this vicious circle, alternative approaches are needed, based on the principle that increases in land prices generated by government interventions should be used to finance the housing programme itself, and that speculative expectations can be neutralized by the involvement of all parties participating in the resulting projects (landowners, developers and final occupants).

TWO PROMISING INNOVATIONS

Ongoing experiments that effectively address the above challenges include Operación Nuevo Usme in Bogota and the Gonzalo Vallejo Restrepo Macro-Project in Pereira, both in Colombia, and the Social Urbanizer project in municipalities of the Porto Alegre Metropolitan Region in Brazil. These initiatives demonstrate the feasibility of publicly conceived alternatives for the provision of affordable and competitively priced serviced and titled land that comply with established urbanistic norms and regulations in a sustainable, self-funded mode.

These projects are complex operations that combine a set of new legal instruments. In the Colombian projects, the municipality not only acquires land on which to develop community facilities and serviced plots for low-income housing projects, it also establishes vectors of urban growth and some control over the form and intensity of land use and occupation. Landowners (whether or not they are land developers) share in the land-value increments generated by large-scale development projects. Those who contribute land to the project (voluntarily or otherwise[17]) are preferably compensated in the form of serviced land in proportion to their contributions. Through this mechanism – a type of land readjustment scheme oriented to low-income people – the original landowners receive a lower share of the resulting increase in land value, albeit at a lower risk than in conventional models, since market demand is guaranteed by the public agency.

In both Colombian projects, a pivotal role is played by the application of land management instruments and plans with equitable distribution of costs and benefits (a kind of land readjustment); public participation in land-value increases resulting from administrative acts; and public land acquisition provisos and other fiscal obligations associated with the fulfilment of the social functions of private property. Value-capture instruments, such as the sale of building rights and the internalization of these funds in the targeted areas, are additional instruments foreseen in the Brazilian experiment.

In the Social Urbanizer case, emphasis is placed on negotiated partnerships among potential developers (overcoming, on the one hand, resistance of formal developers to operating in lower-priced markets and, on the other, constraints that push developers to informality), public agencies (managing, financing, providing urban infrastructure and so on) and low-income families seeking housing solutions.

The Social Urbanizer is an instrument to discipline land markets and finance urban development. Instead of simply eliminating informal land developers, it recognizes their knowledge and abilities, engaging them in the provision of formal housing alternatives under the guidance of the public sector. A 'win–win situation' is negotiated in which developers offer legal products and avoid the risks of clandestine operations; end-users receive legal lots for the same or lower prices than they would pay for informal ones; and the public sector is able to orient urban development towards the most appropriate areas for occupation, reducing the costs of investment in infrastructure and services.[18]

Land-value increments generated in the process of informal-land subdivision – a common procedure on the periphery of Latin American cities – would be sufficient to cover most costs of *ex ante* land development.

These initiatives propose changes in the established perverse practices that negatively impact low-income families and sustainable urban development. These are promising avenues to dealing with informality. Such policies rely on instruments that, to a great extent, change the rules of the urban land-markets game. But they are far from constituting a 'silver bullet'. Many other ingredients are needed.

FINAL CONSIDERATIONS

Seen in retrospect, the approaches described in this chapter have had minimal success in dealing with housing needs under conditions of rapid urban growth. On the one hand, it is clear that not regularizing informal settlements is unacceptable: doing nothing about the housing problem is sheer social irresponsibility. On the other, the model based on the complete tolerance of informality and glorifying it as an efficient way of providing access to housing is also problematic.

Existing regularization programmes have focused primarily on correcting the visible *effects* of informality without touching on the *causes* of its persistent growth. Programmes dedicated exclusively to titling can claim only meagre results compared to their proposed objectives. Upgrading programmes have also proven to be much too expensive (when fully implemented) and thus insufficient to confront the increasing level of informal occupancy. In practice, policy focus has been swinging capriciously between improving living conditions and regularizing property tenure, as though they were mutually exclusive. Even within the limits of curative approaches, they have rarely been reconciled as two inherent aspects of a single phenomenon.

Even at their best, currently applied strategies for regularization are insufficient and unsustainable. The simple fact that, despite decreased rates of urban growth, there are over 130 million people in Latin America now living in substandard conditions, and that current initiatives for regularizing settlements show no sign of significantly reducing that number, underscores this inadequacy.

Proactive policies require *prima facie* actions towards improving the supply of serviced land at pace with social need. This supply, in turn, depends on 'producing' new land through investment in infrastructure and services, and on 'utilizing' the existing stock of serviced land by making actual use of vacant lands in terms of intensity/density and zoning types. In this sense, proactive action requires decision-makers to better understand the slack created by urban land-market distortions and other 'institutional discontinuities' that are filled in by informal activities. This may involve, *inter alia*:

- reviewing citywide land-use regulations, making them less elitist and more 'poor-friendly';
- prioritizing universal access to basic urban infrastructure and services before promoting upgrading in isolated urban fragments;
- relying on more democratic procedures for the definition and scheduling of public interventions aiming at a more equitable urban development;
- promoting initiatives that, wherever possible, formalize 'the informal' (for example recognition of the expertise of informal developers) and informalize the formal (as in more flexible credit schemes), thereby avoiding situations in which only pirate developers benefit from collectively generated land-value increments;

- narrowing the gap between private and social costs and benefits of informal activities through more responsible use of subsidies and fiscal charges;
- introducing more effective price-correction mechanisms (for example through so-called value-capture instruments, whereby benefits and charges of servicing land are socially redistributed); and
- reducing the information asymmetry among actors to facilitate negotiated outcomes.

In sum, mitigating the effects and eliminating the causes of informality policies require a broader view. Informality is not just a problem of a segment of society or of the city, but the very essence of the conditions of urbanization in developing countries. A less paternalistic perspective should be taken, admitting that, if properly identified and managed, land-value increments associated with the informal occupation of land could be mobilized for the provision of housing solutions. To that effect, authorities must also develop the technical skills to identify and measure land-value increments derived from urban development and formulate efficient mechanisms to capture these increases and invest them in benefits for the community.

To actually devise meaningful strategies, implement feasible policies and achieve consistent outcomes, local authorities must set aside certain prejudices against private formal and informal developers and the inevitable mediation of existing 'markets'. They must also consider that low-income families often have the willingness and capacity to pay for land. Indeed, they already pay dearly for non-serviced land and for the costs incurred in the long years before regularization is achieved. Finally, local authorities must set the groundwork for and even facilitate negotiations among affected landowners, inhabitants of informal settlements and developers to devise more creative, innovative, socially acceptable and responsible solutions. This is the agenda required not only for future work in Latin America but, even more critically, to address the conditions of massive urban growth in Africa and Asia.

NOTES

1   The authors gratefully acknowledge suggestions by Julio Calderón and George Martine but take full responsibility for any remaining errors and omissions in this chapter.
2   In Peru, titling programmes began as early as 1961, when the share of informal occupations was 17 per cent. After almost 40 years of policies, this share had reached 38 per cent (Calderón Cockburn, 2005).
3   Informality refers to illegal (lack of proper tenure rights), irregular (non-compliance with urbanistic norms and regulations) and clandestine (not licensed) activities to access and occupy urban land, which typically lacks minimal services and infrastructure. Slums tend to accumulate all these attributes.

4   These arguments are developed more fully in Smolka (2005).

5   Health conditions were often used simply as a pretext to demobilize (or remove) spatially delimited movements organized around broader social, political or cultural issues.

6   This 'for sale' sign refers to dwellers trying to sell housing units they never really wanted to purchase in the first place and who are looking for more suitable housing 'solutions' (Valladares, 1978). They will possibly form new slums elsewhere, in even worse environmental conditions.

7   Although participatory upgrading programmes have existed since the late 1960s, it was only in the 1990s that they were adopted as a relevant policy option to address the housing needs of the poor.

8   See, for example, the case of Promeba (Argentina). The reduced scale of operations is noteworthy: the 55,380 families included in the programme represent only 2.1 per cent of the 2,640,871 precarious dwellings in the country (Romagnoli and Barreto, 2006).

9   These results are especially significant given the small number of titles issued by most titling programmes in Latin America.

10   In fact, credit was more often obtained from public than private banks. In addition, no preferences were granted to holders of title deeds awarded by Cofopri. Moreover, those in possession of registered title deeds were not more inclined to apply for formal loans, and their disapproval rate was higher than that of other groups of proprietors whose title deeds were supposedly less secure (Calderón Cockburn, 2007).

11   A non-official contract whereby occupancy rights are transferred at a price to a third party.

12   As suggested by Smolka (2005), new occupants of informal subdivisions in urban peripheries pay very high prices for land when there is an expectation of regularization. In other words, they are already paying 'taxes' insofar as the informal subdivider capitalizes that expectation in the price charged for the land.

13   Even in Curitiba, internationally acknowledged as an example of good urban management, a recent study detected 13,136 households on irregular sites, corresponding to 2.8 per cent of the city's total population. To resettle all these families in new subdivisions with basic urban infrastructure and $27m^2$ houses would require an investment of approximately US$183 million, equivalent to almost twice Curitiba's entire revenue from 2005 property taxes. This same amount spent on new serviced land would accommodate from 30,000 to 50,000 families on plots of $250m^2$!

14   This is true even in Porto Alegre, widely known for a succession of socially responsible administrations. The approval of a new subdivision takes an average of three years. Ten projects were approved between 1998 and 2002, during which time 100 new irregular subdivisions were registered (Alfonsin, 2004). Thus informal production was at least ten times faster than formal.

15   It is easy to demonstrate mathematically that the introduction of property taxes at rates currently applied in formal areas would be sufficient to cover at least 60 per cent of the costs of upgrading.

16   Of the ten cities included in a study of Brazilian *favelas*, only one (Goiânia) had any cost-recovery mechanism (Larangeira, 2002).

17 If landowners refuse this offer, they are compelled to sell their property to the municipality at prices equivalent to those that prevailed before development began; that is, they are deprived of any benefit that the operation itself may have produced in the area.
18 Unfortunately, the Social Urbanizer pilot project in Porto Alegre was aborted when a different political party was elected to the local government in recent elections. Nevertheless, the initiative made sufficient progress to convincingly demonstrate the viability of public–private partnerships to provide serviced land to low-income groups (see Smolka and Damasio, 2005). It is currently being implemented in other municipalities in the Porto Alegre Metropolitan Area.

REFERENCES

Abramo, P. (2006) 'Teoria econômica da favela: Quatro notas preliminares sobre a localização residencial dos pobres e o mercado imobiliário informal', unpublished paper, Instituto de Pesquisa e Planajemento Urbano e Regional, Universidade Federal do Rio Janero, Rio de Janeiro, Brazil

Abramo, P. (2007) 'Faculty profile', *Land Lines*, vol 19, no 1, Lincoln Institute of Land Policy, Cambridge, MA

Alfonsin, B. (2004) 'Para além da regularização fundiária: Porto Alegre e o Urbanizador Social', in B. Alfonsin and E. Fernandes (eds) *Direito à Moradia e Segurança da Posse no Estatuto da Cidade: Diretrizes, Instrumentos e Processos de Gestão*, Fórum, Belo Horizonte, Brazil, pp281–291

Angel, S., Sheppard, S. C. and Civco, D. L. (2005) *The Dynamics of Global Urban Expansion*, Transport and Urban Development Department, World Bank, Washington, DC, available at http://siteresources.worldbank.org/INTURBANDEVELOPMENT/ Resources/dynamics_urban_expansion.pdf, last accessed 27 September 2007

Biderman, C. and Smolka, M. O. (2007) 'Informality: Urban poverty neither necessary nor sufficient', work in progress, Lincoln Institute of Land Policy, Cambridge, MA

Bogus, L. M. M. and Pasternak Taschner, S. (2003) 'A cidade dos extremos: Desigualdade socioespacial em São Paulo', *Cidades, Comunidade e Território*, no 6, pp51–71

Bolivar, T. (2003) 'Entrevista concedida a Irenees', www.irenees.net, accessed 1 October 2006

Calderón Cockburn, J. (2003) *Propiedad y Crédito: La Formalización de la Propiedad en el Perú*, PGU-Habitat, Quito

Calderón Cockburn, J. (2005) *La Ciudad Ilega: Lima en el Siglo XX*, Fondo Editorial de la Facultad de Ciencias Sociales, Serie Tesis, 1ª ed, Universidad Nacional Mayor de San Marcos, Lima

Calderón Cockburn, J. (2007) 'After formalization, what's next? Notes about the consolidation of human settlements in low-income areas', paper presented at the Fourth Urban Research Symposium 2007, World Bank, Washington, DC, 14–16 May

Cavallieri, F. (2003) 'Favela-Bairro: Integração de áreas informais no Rio de Janeiro', in P. Abramo (ed) *A Cidade da Informalidade: O Desafio das Cidades Latino-Americanas*, Livraria Sette Letras/FAPERJ, Rio de Janeiro, pp265–296

COHRE (2006) *Desalojos en América Latina: Los Casos de Argentina, Brasil, Colombia y Perú*, Centro por el Derecho a la Vivienda y contra los Desalojos, Porto Alegra, Brazil

De Soto, H. (2000) *El Misterio del Capital*, El Comercio, Lima

Durand-Lasserve, A. (2005) 'Market-driven displacements and the perpetuation of informal settlements in developing cities', paper presented to the sixth N-AERUS Research Conference on Cities in the South, 'Promoting social inclusion in urban areas', Lund, Sweden, 16–17 September

ECLAC (2004) *The Millennium Development Goals: A Latin America and Caribbean Perspective*, Economic Commission for Latin America and the Caribbean, Santiago

Larangeira, A. (2002) *Estudo de Avaliação da Experiência Brasileira de Urbanização de Favelas e Regularização Fundiária: Relatório Final*, IBAM/Cites Alliance, Rio de Janeiro, Brazil

MacDonald, J. (2004) 'Pobreza y precariedad del hábitat en ciudades de América Latina y el Caribe', (LC/L.2214-P), Serie Manuales No 38, División de Desarrollo Sostenible y Asentamientos Humanos, CEPAL, Santiago

Pelli, V. S. (1997) 'La necesidad de clarificación y replicabilidad', *Revista Vivienda Popular*, Facultad de Arquitectura de la Universidad de la República, Montevideo

Ramirez Corzo, D. and Riofrío, G. (2005) 'Land titling: A path to urban inclusion? Policy and practice of the Peruvian model', paper presented to the sixth N-AERUS Research Conference on Cities in the South, 'Promoting social inclusion in urban areas', Lund, Sweden, 16–17 September

Romagnoli, V. and Barreto, M. A. (2006) 'Programas de mejoramiento barrial: Reflexiones sobre fundamentos y pertinencia de sus objetivos a partir de un análisis del PROMEBA (Argentina) y su implementación en la ciudad de Resistencia (Provincia del Chaco)', *Cuaderno Urbano*, no 5, pp151–176, Resistencia, Argentina

Smolka, M. O. (1992) 'Mobilidade intra-urbana no Rio de Janeiro: Da estratificação social à segregação residencial no espaço', *Revista Brasileira de Estudos Populacionais*, vol 9, no 2, pp97–114

Smolka, M. O. (2003) 'Regularização da ocupação do solo urbano: A solução que é parte do problema, o problema que é parte da solução', in P. Abramo (ed) *A Cidade da Informalidade: O Desafio das Cidades Latino-Americanas*, Livraria Sette Letras/FAPERJ, Rio de Janeiro, Brazil, pp119–138

Smolka, M. O. (2005) 'El funcionamiento de los mercados de suelo en América Latina: Conceptos, antecedentes históricos y nexos críticos', in J. L. Basualdo, *Manejo de Suelo Urbano. Posibilidades y Desafíos en el Desarrollo de la Ciudad de Corrientes*, Lincoln Institute of Land Policy, Instituto de Vivienda de Corrientes, Corrientes, Argentina

Smolka, M. O. and Damasio, C. P. (2005) 'The social urbanizer: Porto Alegre's land policy experiment', *Land Lines*, vol 17, no 2, Lincoln Institute of Land Policy, Cambridge, MA

Smolka, M. O. and De Cesare, C. M. (2006) 'Property taxation and informality: Challenges for Latin America', *Land Lines*, vol 18, no 3, Lincoln Institute of Land Policy, Cambridge, MA

UN-Habitat (2002) 'Cities without slums', HSP/WUF/DLG.I/ Paper 4, paper presented to the World Urban Forum, Nairobi, 29 April–3 May

UN-Habitat (2006) *The State of the World's Cities 2006/7: The Millennium Development Goals and Urban Sustainability*, Earthscan, London

Valladares, L. (1978) *Passa-se Uma Casa: Análise do Programa de Remoção de Favelas do Rio de Janeiro*, Zahar, Rio de Janeiro, Brazil

6

Preparing for Urban Expansion: A Proposed Strategy for Intermediate Cities in Ecuador[1]

Shlomo Angel[2]

THE DYNAMICS OF GLOBAL URBAN EXPANSION AND ITS IMPLICATIONS

This chapter focuses on the provision of land for the urban poor in a context of rapid urban expansion. It describes a methodology and provides a concrete demonstration of how the land needs of the poor can be effectively met, using examples from five mid-sized cities in Ecuador.

A recent World Bank study (Angel et al, 2005) focused on the declining density of the built-up area in cities and the far-reaching implications of this in the face of continued urban growth. It provided, for the first time, tables and global estimates on the key parameters of urban expansion in developing countries. Preliminary estimates indicate that, if average densities continue to decline as they did during the 1990s, the built-up areas of cities of more than 100,000 people will increase from 200,000km² in 2000 to more than 600,000km² in 2030:

> *In other words, by 2030 these cities can be expected to triple their land area, with every new resident converting, on average, some 160 square metres of non-urban to urban land during the coming years.* (Angel et al, 2005, p1)

Table 6.1 provides preliminary estimates of population and built-up area totals for regions and city size groups for two time periods, 1990 and 2000. The annual

Table 6.1 *Preliminary estimates of population and built-up area totals for regions, income groups and city size groups, 1990–2000*

Category	Urban population (>100,000)			Built-up area (km²)		
	1990	2000	Annual % Change	1990	2000	Annual % Change
Developing Countries	1,394,533,000	1,665,035,000	1.8	145,800	206,900	3.6
Industrialized Countries	540,701,000	572,893,000	0.6	152,500	202,100	2.9
Region						
East Asia & the Pacific	336,214,000	410,903,000	2.0	21,900	43,900	7.2
Europe	350,776,000	353,722,000	0.1	66,600	81,400	2.0
Latin America & the Caribbean	234,459,000	288,937,000	2.1	33,700	42,600	2.4
Northern Africa	44,997,000	54,765,000	2.0	4500	5900	2.8
Other Developed Countries	337,202,000	367,041,000	0.9	120,800	159,600	2.8
South & Central Asia	278,205,000	332,207,000	1.8	15,500	24,200	4.6
South-East Asia	91,019,000	110,279,000	1.9	3600	6700	6.4
Sub-Saharan Africa	180,735,000	227,930,000	2.3	19,100	28,800	6.1
Western Asia	81,627,000	92,142,000	1.2	12,700	15,800	2.2
City Population Size						
100,000–528,000	585,330,000	655,294,000	1.1	98,300	136,300	3.3
528,000–1,490,000	482,319,000	539,682,000	1.1	63,300	90,400	3.6
1,490,000–4,180,000	449,160,000	547,268,000	2.0	65,400	90,600	3.3
More than 4,180,000	418,423,000	495,685,000	1.7	71,400	91,700	2.5
Total	1,935,233,000	2,237,928,000	1.5	298,300	409,000	3.2

Source: Angel et al (2005) Table IV-1, p55, based on weighted averages of the 90-city sample.

growth in population and built-up area in Latin America and the Caribbean were 2.1 per cent and 2.4 per cent respectively. The annual growth in population and built-up area in lower-middle-income countries such as Ecuador were 2.0 per cent and 5.4 per cent respectively; the annual growth in population and built-up area in cities with populations between 100,000 and 528,000 were 1.1 per cent and 3.3 per cent respectively.

Table 6.2 provides preliminary estimates of average density and built-up area per person for regions and city size groups for the same two time periods. Average densities in Latin America and the Caribbean changed from 6955 persons per km^2 in 1990 to 6785 per km^2 in 2000, an annual decrease of 0.3 per cent. Average densities in cities with populations between 100,000 and 528,000 changed from 5955 persons per km^2 in 1990 to 4810 per km^2 in 2000, an annual decrease of 2.1 per cent. The implications of these findings are challenging:

> *It is of the utmost importance to all stakeholders – be they ordinary citizens or planners and decision-makers in the public, private or civic sectors – to ensure that adequate quantities of public goods are put in place in a timely fashion, before it is too late; that there are adequate lands for absorbing the expected population growth; that there is an adequate capacity of urban trunk roads than can carry public transport; that there are adequate supplies of drinking water and effective means of sewage disposal; that sensitive lands are protected from development; and that there is effective protection of open space. None of these are likely to be provided at adequate levels without concerted public action.* (Angel et al, 2005, p73)

The conclusion arrived at by Angel et al is unambiguous: cities that experience population and economic growth will also need to prepare for expansion of their urban perimeters:

> *This in itself is an important finding, because it is quite common to hear of urban planners and decision makers speaking of their cities as exceptions to the rule, asserting that other cities will grow and expand and their city will not, simply because it is already bursting at the seams, and because they think that further growth is objectionable. ... The key issue facing public-sector decision-makers – at the local, national and international levels – is not whether or not urban expansion will take place, but rather what is likely to be the scale of urban expansion and what needs to be done now to adequately prepare for it.* (Angel et al, 2005, p90)

Table 6.2 *Preliminary estimates of average density and built-up area per person for regions, income groups and city size groups, 1990–2000*

Category	Average built-up area density (persons/km²)			Average built-up area per person (m² per person)		
	1990	2000	Annual % change	1990	2000	Annual % change
Developing Countries	9560	8050	-1.7	105	125	1.7
Industrialized Countries	3545	2835	-2.2	280	355	2.3
Region						
East Asia & the Pacific	15,380	9350	-4.9	65	105	5.1
Europe	5270	4345	-1.9	190	230	1.9
Latin America & the Caribbean	6955	6785	-0.3	145	145	0.3
Northern Africa	10,010	9250	-0.8	100	110	0.8
Other Developed Countries	2790	2300	-1.9	360	435	2.0
South & Central Asia	17,980	13,720	-2.7	55	75	2.7
South-East Asia	25,360	16,495	-4.2	40	60	4.4
Sub-Saharan Africa	9470	6630	-3.5	105	150	3.6
Western Asia	6410	5820	-1.0	155	170	1.0
City Population Size						
100,000–528,000	5955	4810	-2.1	170	210	2.2
528,000–1,490,000	7620	5970	-2.4	130	165	2.5
1,490,000–4,180,000	6870	6040	-1.3	145	165	1.3
More than 4,180,000	5860	5405	-0.8	170	185	0.8
Global Average	6485	5470	-1.7	155	185	1.7

Source: Angel et al (2005) Table IV-2, p57, based on weighted averages of the 90-city sample.

URBAN GROWTH AND EXPANSION IN ECUADOR

Most of the larger intermediate cities in Ecuador are growing rapidly and are expected to double (or more than double) their populations and triple (or more than triple) their built-up areas in the next 25 years. Five intermediate cities in the country are the focus of this chapter. They have not been selected for study because of any particular attribute, other than the fact that they are cities in developing countries that are presently experiencing rapid growth. The author visited these cities in an exploratory mission for the World Bank in late 2005 to examine possible strategies for ensuring that affordable land for housing the poor remains in ample supply in the coming years. The cities visited were Eloy Alfaro Durán, a rapidly growing outer suburb of Guayaquil; Milagro, an agricultural-export centre about an hour east of Guayaquil; Santo Domingo, a transport hub in the centre of the country; Sangolqui, an outer suburb of Quito; and Riobamba, a provincial centre on the Andean plateau, half way between Quito and Guayaquil. In all five cities, the author interviewed municipal officials, mostly from the cadastre, planning, public works and finance departments, obtained documents and maps, and visited settlements on the urban periphery.

At present, there is no shortage of affordable plots for the urban poor in these intermediate cities. Most residential plots are currently supplied by private landowners or developers who subdivide and sell minimally serviced land and, to a lesser extent, by land invasions. However, to ensure that residential land for the urban poor will remain affordable, municipalities must make certain that accessible urban land remains in ample supply in the coming years, so that land prices will not be subject to speculative increases. To meet this challenge, municipalities must actively prepare for urban expansion by:

- expanding their city limits;
- planning for an arterial infrastructure grid – in the order of 800–1000 metres in width – in the areas of expansion;
- employing the services of highway engineers to locate the required 25–30-metre-wide right of way for the infrastructure grid on the ground; and
- obtaining the land rights for the right-of-way of the entire arterial grid, using available laws while minimizing unilateral expropriation.

This chapter provides the background and the rationale for pursuing this strategy at the present time.

There are four aspects of the pattern of urban growth in Ecuador that merit attention: the urban–rural balance, the distribution of the urban population, urban growth rates and the distribution of urban growth.

In 2003, for example, only 61.8 per cent of the Ecuadorian population lived in cities, compared with 76.8 per cent in Latin America and the Caribbean and

81.1 per cent in South America as a whole. In South America, only Guyana and Paraguay were less urbanized than Ecuador. Indeed, Ecuador is still a rural country compared to most other South American countries, relying as it does on agriculture as its main export: 57 per cent of all exports in 2003 were of agricultural products (ITC, undated).

The distribution of the urban population in Ecuador is highly skewed towards the larger cities. In 2001, of a total urban population of 7.0 million in cities with 10,000 or more people, 48.5 per cent resided in the two primate cities – Guayaquil (2.0 million) and Quito (1.4 million). Thirteen secondary cities with populations between 100,000 and 300,000 housed an additional 30.2 per cent of this population (2.1 million), while 31 tertiary cities with populations between 20,000 and 100,000 housed an additional 15.6 per cent (1.0 million). Cities with populations between 10,000 and 20,000 people housed only 390,000 people, or 5.5 per cent of the total (INEC, 2001, Tables 2 and 4).

While declining, the urban growth rate in Ecuador is still the fourth highest in South America, at 2.3 per cent between 2000 and 2005. Urban growth continued to account for almost all population growth in the country. Primary cities in Ecuador grew at a slower rate than smaller cities – 2.4 per cent per annum between 1990 and 2001, when the average annual growth rate in each of the other city size groups was in the order of 3.1 per cent per annum. One city, Eloy Alfaro Durán, grew very rapidly, at a rate of more than 7 per cent per annum; if continued, this rate would *double* its population in a single decade.

Table 6.3 provides population, built-up area and density figures for the five intermediate cities studied. Sangolqui, the smallest of the five, is a relatively rich and low-density suburb of Quito, with no informal settlements or invasions. Milagro is the only city with a reported population growth rate lower than two per cent,

Table 6.3 *Populations, built-up areas and densities in five intermediate cities in Ecuador*

City	Population 1990	Population 2001	Annual growth (%)	Population 2006	Urban area (km²)	Built-up area (km²)	Density[3] (persons per km²)
Sangolqui	35,386	56,794	4.30	70,104	32	19	3664
Milagro	93,637	113,440	1.74	123,684	30	21	5816
Riobamba	94,505	124,807	2.53	141,403	29	17	8177
Eloy Alfaro Durán	82,359	174,531	6.83	242,821	59	29	8273
Santo Domingo	114,422	199,827	5.07	255,871	73	44	5863

Sources: Population data for 1990 and 2001 are from the census; the 2006 population estimates were obtained by linear extrapolation of census data; urban area and built-up area estimates are from interviews in municipalities.

although municipality officials and a recent cadastre, which found 50,000 occupied residential properties, dispute this census figure.

Since none of the five intermediate cities studied here was in the global sample of cities analysed by Angel et al (2005), gross estimates were made of the current built-up areas of these cities, while the parameters of the global study were used only to estimate their future growth. Table 6.4 provides population, density, built-up area and urban area projections for 2030. These projections were based on the assumptions that: urban population growth in Ecuador will decline between 2000 and 2030 at the rates estimated by the United Nations (2004); the share of the urban population in these five cities will grow at the same rate as it did between the two latest census periods (0.15 per cent per annum); built-up area densities will decline at a rate of 2 per cent per annum; the population of Milagro was underestimated and was in the order of 150,000, and not 113,000, in 2001; and the urban limits will encompass one-third more area than the built-up area, to account for open space and vacant lands.

Preliminary estimates suggest that, by 2030, Eloy Alfaro Durán, Santo Domingo, Milagro and Sangolqui will require a *threefold* increase in their present urban areas to accommodate their projected population and built-up area increases. Riobamba will require a *doubling* of its urban area. This expansion will require the conversion of adequate lands from rural to urban use on the periphery of these cities. In all five cities examined, the officially designated limits of the urban area will have to be expanded to accommodate the projected increase in the built-up areas.

Table 6.4 *Population, density, built-up area and urban area projections for 2030 for the five intermediate cities in Ecuador*

| City | Population 2030 | Density 2030 | Built-up area 2030 | Urban area 2030 | Growth ratios 2005–2030 | | | |
					Population	Density	Built-up area	Urban area
Sangolqui	140,850	2211	64	85	2.0	0.6	3.3	2.7
Milagro	251,773	3510	72	96	2.0	0.6	3.4	3.1
Riobamba	195,611	4935	40	53	1.4	0.6	2.3	1.8
Eloy Alfaro Durán	635,466	4993	127	170	2.6	0.6	4.3	2.9
Santo Domingo	569,138	3538	161	214	2.2	0.6	3.7	2.9

Source: Based on data in Table 6.3.
Note: Areas measured in km^2 and density in people per km^2.

ACCESS TO RESIDENTIAL LAND FOR THE
URBAN POOR IN ECUADOR

In general, it appears that there are no shortages of *raw* land for residential development in Ecuadorian cities at the present time (Jarrin, 1997). It is abundantly clear, however, that there are serious shortages of *serviced* urban land for low-income housing in the formal sector, with the result that a great share of land subdivision and sale takes place in the informal sector – either through land invasions or through informal land subdivisions which do not conform to zoning and subdivision regulations. The prevalence of invasions varies considerably from city to city. There were no invasions in Santo Domingo, for example, in 2005 and 2006, while there were five invasions (and no formal land subdivisions) in Milagro in 2006 alone.

The availability of land for informal-sector housing varies from city to city, as do land prices. In some secondary cities on the coast, for example, more than 70 per cent of residential land is under informal sector occupation, compared to only 25 per cent for secondary cities in the sierra (MIDUVI, 1994, Table 6, p15). In Quito, raw land in illegal subdivisions sold for US$4/m^2 in 2000, partially serviced land in established informal settlements sold for US$15–25/m^2, land for middle-income housing sold for US$50–60/m^2, and land in upper-income, fully serviced subdivisions sold for US$100/m^2 or more. There are still numerous illegal subdivisions where cheap land can be found within the city limits.

To reach *below-median* households in Ecuador at the present time, serviced or partially serviced plots should cost US$1660–3300[4] – in other words US$14–28/m^2 for a 120m^2 plot or US$8–17/m^2 for a 200m^2 plot. To reach the lowest 20 per cent of the income-earning households, serviced or partially serviced plots should cost US$660–1330 – in other words US$6–11/m^2 for a 120m^2 plot or US$3–7/m^2 for a 200m^2 plot. These numbers help explain why the informal sector continues to be the main supplier of residential land for the poor. They also explain, in stark terms, the challenge facing the formal sector in going downmarket to develop progressive urbanizations that can effectively compete with what the informal sector now offers.

In the five intermediate cities studied, unserviced land prices in informal settlements were somewhat higher than those observed on the outskirts of Quito in 2000, but were still affordable by the lowest income decile. In Milagro, for example, the average price in an illegal subdivision was US$8/m^2, or US$960 for an 8 metre by 15 metre plot. In Santo Domingo, the average price in an illegal subdivision was US$10/m^2, and plots of 120m^2 were sold for US$1200, payable at US$20 per month for five years at the local savings bank (Caja de Ahorros). In Riobamba, plots without services in illegal subdivisions sold for US$4/m^2.

Compared to other countries, a very high percentage of the urban households in Ecuador live in unauthorized housing communities without legal title documents.

In 1994, 48.1 per cent of the urban population in Ecuador lived in marginal settlements and 34.7 per cent of the urban population did not have legal tenure (MIDUVI, 1994, Tables 6 and 7). This compares with a value of 25 per cent for cities in Latin America and the Caribbean, 16 per cent for lower-middle-income countries and 4 per cent for the world as a whole (Angel, 2000, p328).

In Quito, the population in marginal settlements – mostly informal land subdivisions and not invasions – amounted to 30 per cent and the population without legal land titles to 18 per cent. In other cities of the sierra, the population in marginal settlements amounted to 25 per cent and the population without legal tenure to 13 per cent. In Guayaquil, the population in marginal settlements amounted to 60 per cent and the population without legal tenure to 45 per cent. Illegal invasions of private lands, with political support, have been going on in the city for 60 years. In other cities on the coast, 70 per cent of households lived in marginal settlements, and 56 per cent did not have legal title documents (MIDUVI, 1994, Tables 6 and 7, pp15–16).

The absence of legal title documents continues to impede housing market transactions at full value, to prevent the use of the house as collateral for loans, to limit investment in house improvements, to diminish residential mobility, to give rise to property-related disputes, to prevent effective property taxation, and to create an overall environment of illegitimacy and disrespect for the law (World Bank, 1998). Titles, on the other hand, increase the value of houses, although it is not exactly clear by how much. A recent study of the effect of titling on the house values of 400 families in Guayaquil concluded that informal property rights in older communities can effectively substitute for formal titles: thus it makes more sense to focus on titling in young, disorganized communities (Lanjouw and Levy, 1998).

Data on the quality of residential infrastructure is also available from the 1990 and 2001 censuses (INEC, 2001). In 2001, 96.6 per cent of all urban homes in Ecuador had electricity, compared with 95.4 per cent in 1990; 84.6 per cent had a water connection on their plot, compared with 75.8 per cent in 1990; 66.6 per cent had piped sewage disposal, compared with 61.6 per cent in 1990; 64.5 per cent had garbage collection services, compared to 69.0 per cent in 1990; and 43.7 per cent had telephones, compared with 24.7 per cent in 1990 (INEC, 1990 and 2001, Table 2). Water rates for those dwellings with a water connection varied between US$0.06 and US$0.30/m^3, as against US$1.80/m^3 for water delivered by truck, but many of those with a permanent water connection experienced an irregular water supply. In most intermediate cities, a large percentage of the roads in residential communities were unpaved. In Milagro, for example, 61 per cent of roads were paved with laterite and 21 per cent not paved at all.

There is a clear need to extend better infrastructure services to the urban population and especially to poor families living in marginal settlements. People are willing to pay for better basic services – water, sewerage, drainage and paved roads – in these settlements. In Riobamba, for example, the municipality, in partnership with several communities, is negotiating a loan with a commercial bank for upgrading infrastructure.

Municipalities are presently burdened with the obligation of providing residential infrastructure for their residents but are seriously lacking in adequate resources to meet this obligation. Water shortages are especially acute, and two municipalities – Santo Domingo and Eloy Alfaro Durán – have initiated large water purification projects with international loans. Large numbers of roads remain unpaved, and there is virtually no sewerage and minimal sewage treatment in low-income residential communities. Improving the quality of infrastructure in the years to come will hinge on enlisting the collaboration of communities as well as their monetary contributions. This will take time, and, for now, while the poor can afford to settle on minimally serviced lands, they cannot expect a full complement of urban services to be present when they first occupy the land. Municipal services are likely to be provided gradually, as funds and loans become available, and will hinge on the ability of municipalities (or private-sector intermediaries) to recover a substantial portion of the full cost of providing these services.

MAKING MINIMUM PREPARATIONS FOR URBAN EXPANSION

The problem of access to land for the urban poor in the intermediate cities of Ecuador is largely a longer-term problem affecting the city as a whole. As accessible urban land around these cities becomes scarcer, land prices are likely to rise, making building sites unaffordable for the poor. Keeping housing affordable requires keeping land prices affordable. This implies that there needs to be an adequate supply of urban land so that land speculation is kept to a minimum and land prices remain affordable. If municipal governments can ensure that there is a viable land market on the urban fringe of cities, then they can stay out of the direct acquisition of land for affordable housing, or sites and services of any kind, and let the market offer land at affordable prices for all segments of society, including the poor.

This, in turn, requires that municipal governments provide the *public goods* necessary for a well-functioning urban land market on the fringe of cities. They must ensure that there is an adequate amount of land for urban use, a basic arterial infrastructure network and a regulatory framework to ensure ordered development of this land in line with municipal objectives. The latter requires the development of new regulations and procedures that are negotiated and agreed upon between municipalities and private-sector informal developers, so as to ensure that informal subdivisions are better planned and that a minimum amount of urban services are provided. There will be an effort to transform these informal developers into 'social urbanizers', utilizing recent experiences from Brazil, Colombia and El Salvador. Possible collaboration between municipalities and informal developers may involve the provision of training in project layout, the certification of urbanizers, and the provision of lines of credit or subsidies for infrastructure.

Developers or communities typically plan (and later develop) *tertiary* infrastructure networks at the city-block level within land subdivisions. At the national level, central governments act to plan and provide *primary* inter-city roads and rail transport. The arterial or *secondary* road system within cities, however, is a public good that is typically under-supplied. It is this road system that is also the location of trunk infrastructure services – water mains, sewers and storm drains, and cable and telephone networks. It is also the road network that serves public bus transport and provides the right of way for light rail transport. It is usually the responsibility of municipalities to ensure that a connected network of such arterial roads is properly planned and developed as the city expands outwards.

The main reason that the secondary road system is under-supplied is what is known in economics as the 'free rider' problem. The cost of tertiary roads within land subdivisions is typically included in the price of the land and is recovered when the land is sold to its future occupants. Primary roads are typically financed by central government budgets and as of late, part of their cost is recovered from tolls. Municipalities typically provide secondary roads free of charge, and their cost cannot be recovered from tolls. Secondary roads are classic public goods and their cost needs to be recovered, to the extent possible, from property taxes or from general taxation. Given the very limited budgets of municipalities and their limited ability to borrow funds, it is of utmost importance, therefore, to minimize the cost of bringing the secondary road network into being.

If municipalities wait too long before acquiring land for secondary roads, it becomes too expensive to acquire. Clearly, once land subdivisions spring up haphazardly and land is occupied, it is virtually impossible to introduce new secondary roads, and they remain in permanently short supply. It is of prime importance, therefore, to secure the right of way for such an arterial infrastructure network far in advance of development, when land prices are still low and when there is little or no need for the demolition of structures of any kind.

What is needed is the early acquisition of the right of way for an entire network of roads that will serve the projected urban area. Two parameters are particularly important here: (a) the width of these rights of way will need to be in the order of 25–30 metres and (b) the roads will need to be spaced in the form of an *urban grid*[5] some 800–1000 metres apart, so that people can walk to a bus stop from any location within the urban area in less than 10 minutes. This means that the road network will enclose 'super blocks' of an average size of 60–100 hectares. These super blocks will, in turn, contain road networks that serve individual subdivisions, neighbourhoods, and commercial, industrial and civic areas, as well as parks and open spaces.

Urban grids of arterial roads can be found in a number of cities around the world. However, in order to support public transport that is within walking distance of any interior location in a super block, the grid spacing cannot exceed one kilometre. The projected densities in the five cities studied – 3500 to 5000 people per square kilometre (except for the city of Sangolqui) – are all above the thresholds required for a bus system or, more generally, for a public-transit-oriented urban lifestyle (Holtzclaw, 1994).

The organization of urban expansion within new city limits – with super blocks that form a rectangular grid, a connected set of radial and peripheral roads, or something in between – will advance the ordered development of the urban territory. This does not mean that there will not be a need for more detailed zoning, land-use planning, or regulations concerning density and building codes, however. All it will do is provide an underlying organization for the orderly expansion of the city. It will provide municipal planners with a key tool for organizing future development and a starting point for more comprehensive city planning. For once, they will be ahead of those subdividing land rather than trailing them.

The acquisition of the right of way for the entire network of arterial roads carrying trunk infrastructure will distribute access to land throughout the urban fringe, preventing the speculation that typically occurs when the number of roads is in short supply. It will also act to unify the city and to prevent the formation of large and isolated low-income neighbourhoods. The placement of the right of way of roads is expected to modestly increase land values beyond the present rural land values of US$1–6/m^2, and this will increase property taxes. But the increase in price is likely to be relatively limited, given the large amount of land that will be brought into the urban land market. It is expected that the municipalities will be able to repay the cost of acquisition through the increase in property taxes in the rural periphery as a result of the project.

Preparing cities for expansion with an urban grid also empowers municipalities to direct development away from lands that should remain undeveloped because of their sensitive habitat, because of their value as open space, or because of the dangers of landslides or floods. It will still not prevent development in areas designated as open space, however, if municipalities do not delimit these areas, reduce the amount of land to be protected to a minimum and then apply aggressive measures to protect it from development. Such measures may include fencing and guarding the lands or bequeathing the land to civic organizations that could protect them with campaigns and volunteers. Simply declaring lands as open space not to be developed is unlikely to be an effective enough measure where most development takes place illegally or informally.

All of the cities studied, with the possible exception of Riobamba, have large haciendas on the urban periphery. However, available cadastral data for the rural areas surrounding the city of Milagro, summarized in Table 6.5, shows that the average size of rural properties is only 5.6 hectares and the average size of small rural properties is 2.7 hectares. In Canton Durán, to take another example, the average size of rural properties is 12.7 hectares. There is, therefore, no need to apply complicated procedures such as *land readjustment* to obtain land for roads and primary infrastructure networks. The Ecuadorian law pertaining to the acquisition of land for public use allows for acquiring up to 10 per cent of each property for public use as a servitude without pay. It also allows for using up to 35 per cent of

Table 6.5 *The size distribution of rural properties in Canton Milagro*

Size Range (hectares)	Number of properties	Average size (hectares)	Total area (hectares)	Percentage of total
0–10	6566	2.47	16,243.38	39.2
10–50	801	18.59	14,892.50	35.9
>50	65	158.34	10,292.34	24.8
Total Canton	7432	5.57	41,428.22	100.0

Source: Municipality of Milagro, Cadastral Department (2006).

each parcel for public purposes once the land is developed, and this land can be reserved in advance by marking a lien on its title. The proportion of land that needs to be expropriated for a 30-metre right-of-way grid at a one-kilometre spacing is 6 per cent; for an 800-metre grid spacing it is 7.5 per cent. It has been estimated by several cadastral directors that the majority of the right of way in each city could be acquired without pay and without forced expropriation.

What are the possible risks of pursuing this strategy of preparing these cities for urban expansion at the present time? One possible risk is that municipalities, swamped with short-term commitments and obligations, will not be willing to devote sufficient manpower, resources or political capital for pursuing this project. This is a serious risk, of course, but the indications from the author's visit to these municipalities are that there is a great deal of willingness to carry it out. All of the cities have new administrations that are keen to make their mark and new mayors who are interested in a broad vision of their cities. They would lend substantial support to the project, particularly if it can be implemented during their terms of office.

A second possible risk is that the enlargement of the urban boundaries and the marking of the rights of way of roads will provide a signal to the real estate market that the city will grow and expand, and that consequently this will lead to speculation and to a substantial rise in land prices. Indeed there is surely going to be some rise in land prices, as well there should be. But increases are likely to be moderate, because a very large area will be added to the city, and because speculative pressures on land prices at the present time are very low. Executing the project in five cities is likely to see different results in different cities, and it will be important to study these results with the aim of explaining the variations in land price increases between them. All cities have now completed (or almost completed) maps of current land values that will act as baseline data for a future study of the effects of the project on land values.

A third possible risk is that the increases in the availability of land on the urban periphery will have the opposite effect – that of lowering land prices, thereby leading to development at lower densities. This is unlikely to happen. Land prices are quite low at the present time, and densities of development are not far from global norms.

Finally, a fourth possible risk is that the cost estimates for the expropriation of lands for the rights of way are inaccurate, and that the actual costs will be much higher. To address this, it may be necessary to obtain a better estimate, with a local study of these projections. All these risks must be properly assessed before moving ahead with the proposed strategy, but they do appear to be manageable.

CONCLUDING REMARKS

Although this chapter should be understood as an interim report on work in progress, it has shown that a practical strategy aimed at ensuring that access to land for the urban poor in the intermediate cities in Ecuador remains ample and affordable is possible. There is a serious commitment on the part of officials in all the municipalities visited to pursue this strategy vigorously in the months and years to come. Municipal officials from two more intermediate cities – Machala and Manta – have now joined the initiative. Officials from these seven municipalities met with international and local experts, including the author, for a workshop on this subject. They have started to delimit new expansion areas based on preliminary population and built-up area projections, planning the arterial road networks in the new expansion areas, refining legal tools for acquiring the rights of way for the arterial road networks, and estimating the budgets needed for implementation. There is no doubt among the great majority of participating municipal officials (with the possible exception of those in Sangolqui) that this is a strategy with a potentially high rate of return on investment.

The strategy should be an attractive one for visionary mayors and can be carried out with a relatively low amount of investment *if it is carried out early enough*. It is also an important demonstration project for a large number of cities in developing countries that now face strong population pressures. Given the scale of upcoming urban growth in other developing countries, particularly in Asia and Africa, and given the large share of poor people in that growth, the need for such strategies appears critical.

NOTES

1   This chapter is based on a recent World Bank study on the global dynamics of urban expansion and a follow-up mission to Ecuador to help design a strategy for responding to that expansion. All opinions, findings or inaccuracies herein are the sole responsibility of the author and do not reflect the views, policies or practices of the World Bank.
2   The author wishes to thank Fernando Argüello, Monica Quintana and Rodrigo Torres for their support and suggestions.
3   Density is measured as a ratio of the population to the built-up area, not the 'urban area' (the administrative area within the city limits).

4   Assuming that the income distribution now is the same as it was in 2000 and that the cost of land forms up to a third of total house and land price.
5   For a description of the main characteristics and advantages of this kind of grid, see Farvaque-Vitkovic and Godin (1998).

REFERENCES

Angel, S. (2000) *Housing Policy Matters: A Global Analysis*, Oxford University Press, New York

Angel, S., Sheppard, S. C. and Civco, D. L. (2005) *The Dynamics of Global Urban Expansion*, Transport and Urban Development Department, World Bank Washington, DC, available at http://siteresources.worldbank.org/INTURBANDEVELOPMENT/Resources/dynamics_urban_expansion.pdf, last accessed 27 September 2007

Farvaque-Vitkovic, C. and Godin, L. (1998) *The Future of African Cities: Challenges and Priorities for Urban Development*, World Bank Report No 18408, World Bank, Washington, DC, pp103–104

Holtzclaw, J. (1994) 'Using residential patterns and transit to decrease auto dependence and costs', Natural Resources Defense Council, New York, quoted in A. Bertaud (2002) 'Clearing the air in Atlanta: Transit and smart growth or conventional economics', Table 1, p9, http://alain-bertaud.com/images/AB_Clearing_The_Air_in%20Atlanta_1.pdf, last accessed 27 September 2007

INEC (1990) *V Censo de Población y de Vivienda*, Instituto Nacional de Estadística y Censos, Quito

INEC (2001) *VI Censo de Población y de Vivienda*, Instituto Nacional de Estadística y Censos, Quito

ITC (undated) 'Comparison of Ecuador's export statistics with those of partner countries, by product group, for 2003', International Trade Centre, based on COMTRADE data of the United Nations Statistical Division, www.intracen.org/countries/structural05/ecu_8.pdf, last accessed 27 September 2007

Jarrín, A. M. (1997) 'Ecuador: Removiendo obstáculos críticos para la provisión de vivienda', *Urbana Consultores*, 3 April, Quito

Lanjouw, J. O. and Levy, P. I. (1998) 'Untitled: A study of formal and informal property rights in urban Ecuador', Center Discussion Paper No 788, Economic Growth Center, Yale University, New Haven, CT

MIDUVI (1994) 'Política nacional de desarrollo urbano, vivienda y saneamiento ambiental', Ministerio de Desarrollo Urbano y Vivienda, Quito

United Nations (2004) *World Urbanization Prospects: The 2003 Revision*, Population Division, United Nations, New York

World Bank (1998) 'Project appraisal document on a proposed loan in the amount of US$60.7 million to Venezuela for a Caracas slum-upgrading project', Report No 17924, World Bank, Washington, DC

7

Organizations of the Urban Poor and Equitable Urban Development: Process and Product[1]

Gabriella Y. Carolini

INTRODUCTION: REVALUATING DEVELOPMENT WORK

When there is pressure for immediate action on an issue or for implementation of a policy, discussions in international development circles tend to be polarized on orientation and approach (for example top–down versus bottom–up). All interested practitioners and advocates have been perceived at one time or another as forwarding their own leadership above that of others in addressing the various challenges posed in advancing economic development and social justice. This has certainly been the case in the planning and upgrading of settlements in the rapidly growing cities of the Global South. International organizations and financial institutions, along with national and local governments, are often perceived as too top–down in their approach or overly technocratic. Concurrently, community-based organizations and their supporting non-governmental organizations (NGOs) have been seen as too idealistic about their capacity and too narrowly focused to address the scale of planning and upgrading needed in their cities. And though recent years have seen the acknowledgement of the virtues of partnership and of different actors' capacities to serve the cause of 'development', there remains a fundamental ideological siding in opinions of who should – or can – best lead.

This positioning is emblematic of a power struggle – whether or not it is recognized as such by any party in the debate. The true intentions and capacities of different actors in development may lie somewhere in between their claims and the criticisms of others. Regardless of their position in the current power paradigm, most actors would agree that time is better spent recognizing and using the different strengths of interested parties. However, recognizing and using other actors' strengths is anything but a simple or non-political task. It would imply, for one thing, that there is common understanding or definition of strengths: in short, a shared system of valuation. In reality, acknowledging another group's capacities might appear to lessen one's own, and certainly not all actors see the same capacities as strengths. This complicates any notion of shared recognition and coordinated action. Thus, collaborative work, while nominally diplomatic, is often the most contentious of propositions. Successful collaboration requires a revisiting of what are understood to be the priorities and accompanying valuation of development. Nowhere is this clearer than in the valuation or prioritization of development strategies. Strategies can comprise 'product' and 'process' goals, or what are often termed the hardware (product) and software (process) of development.[2] However, depending on an actor's value system and perception of development priorities, only one of these goals (product or process) is placed in the foreground.

Clarity on what is meant by product and process can be evasive. Traditionally, product and process are separated by two differences in character: time and tangibility. Product is present or not, in other words it can be captured in a photo; process is ongoing in nature, in other words it requires filming. Product is also usually understood to mean tangible results or targets, such as trunk infrastructure, paved sidewalks, higher literacy rates or lower morbidity. In short, product tends to refer to that which can be quantitatively measured. Process, on the other hand, is typically used as a catch-all term describing contextual factors which enable 'product', for example transparency, good governance, participation, voice and civic-mindedness. While there have been efforts to quantifiably measure such intangible factors, they are fundamentally difficult to capture in numerical form. This difficulty often results in the relegation of 'process' goals to the background of development strategies.

Such definitions of product and process are, however, overly static. One could argue that process is a product of development while also understanding that product is part of the development process. The reflexive nature of this interplay turns the distinctions between product and process on their head. Like other traditional dualist notions in development dialogues (rural–urban, private–public and so on), the product–process axiom presents a false dichotomy. Yet what remains clear is that current processes of development are undervalued and products of development incompletely understood. This is very much the case where the work of organizations of the urban poor (OUPs) is concerned. The next section of this chapter outlines a fuller vision of the development product–process continuum that OUPs generate. The remainder of the chapter builds a case for how critical a nuanced understanding and more comprehensive valuation of the work of such community organizations in addressing today's urban challenges are to ensuring equitable urban development in the face of estimated urban population (and spatial) growth.

CAPTURING COMMUNITY CAPITAL

Much has been written and discussed about bottom–up development and participatory planning. In the process, OUPs continue to gain recognition in international development dialogues. The first operational recommendation from the UN Millennium Project's task force on slums was for governments 'to acknowledge the organizations of the urban poor wherever they exist and to work with their strategies' (UN Millennium Project, 2005, p3). This recommendation reflects an increasing acknowledgement and documentation of the successful improvements made through participatory and locally led projects in slums. By comparison, the call to improve the lives of one million slum-dwellers by Target 11 of the Millennium Development Goals (MDGs) was generally considered minimalist.

Unlike many of the other MDG targets, the general reaction to Target 11 was that it would be easily achieved. One million slum-dwellers' lives would be improved whether or not there were any newly coordinated actions introduced. Around the world, community-based OUPs were already achieving that goal – striving, innovating and pushing ahead to improve the quality of living conditions in their neighbourhoods. Such improvements have been achieved through their own community projects and through partnerships with governmental and non-governmental actors. It was in part because of this reality that the UN Millennium Project Task Force on Target 11 proposed a more ambitious and meaningful formulation: 'By 2020, improving substantially the lives of at least 100 million slum dwellers, while providing adequate alternatives to new slum formation' (UN Millennium Project, 2005, p3).

However, despite the recognition of OUPs in such development discourses, too often in practice their work is understood and valued only through a one-dimensional lens – that of short-term results or, in the traditional (incomplete) sense, product. OUPs certainly 'produce' results in a relatively short time – from as little as one day or week to two or three years. But to recognize their work in only this shorter-term timeframe is to miss a significantly important aspect of the strategies of OUPs and their critical role in equitable urban development. In longer-term frameworks, the value of OUPs in the development 'process' gains currency. Yet what OUPs generate over both the shorter and longer terms transcends the static product–process axiom. A better description of their contribution is that they generate *community capital*, where community capital is defined as both a product and a process. It is the mobilization of community cohesion towards a productive goal or improvement in the physical or non-physical lives of community members. Its importance to equitable development lies in its transformative power.

What exactly does the community capital of OUPs transform? The answer is decision-making processes and planning and implementation of development projects. Through their productive cohesion, OUPs have been able – over time – to start balancing other voices at decision-making tables that impact the lives of the urban poor. OUPs have also used their community capital for more immediate goals, such as organizing volunteer construction teams to dig trenches for sewerage pipes. Within the scope of the work required in planning for future urban population growth and the inevitable struggle for power in expanding spaces, the facilitation and the empowerment of such community capital as manifested in OUPs will become more acutely important to developing socially just cities. The next section highlights an important portfolio of examples of the work that 'capitalized' OUPs have achieved.

WHAT ARE OUPs DOING FOR TODAY AND FOR TOMORROW?

It can be helpful to think of OUPs as engaging in two broad areas of work, namely service provision[3] and neighbourhood improvement. The provision of basic services is perhaps where OUPs gain the most notice, as well as criticism. The services in which such groups have engaged include the provision of water, sewerage and drainage and the creation of community toilets, healthcare services and waste collection, using various innovative methods and mobilization techniques. The experiences of OUPs in these areas are as diverse as are the informal settlements around the world; a few of them are highlighted in Box 7.1.

BOX 7.1 BASIC SERVICE PROVISION BY OUPs

Water services: Guatemala City, Guatemala

Guatemala City is the largest city in Central America, with a population of over 2.5 million. El Mezquital is an informal settlement in the capital city; it was created in 1984 with a planned land invasion by roughly 1500 families. The settlers managed to resist eviction and began to establish a system of governance within the community, with a number of community management boards overseeing subdivisions of the settlement and sending representatives to a settlement-wide association. Lacking national assistance for water provision, the settlement-wide association of El Mezquital established a cooperative organization to tend to the community's basic service needs. The organization – COIVEES – dug the settlement's first well and organized the provision of two large water tanks with the help of international donors. After ten years, in 1994, COIVEES secured support from the national Government of Guatemala, as well as continued support from UNICEF and new funding from the World Bank. The organization was able to extend its water delivery service to so-far-unreached parts of the settlement and constructed another two water wells.

After many years of striving to gain official recognition, COIVEES now operates and maintains good quality water provision – in addition to many other services – for almost all of the families living in El Mezquital. In addition, it has trained other community-based organizations of neighbouring informal settlements on how to provide basic services like water, thus extending the scope of its own impact.

Sources: Cabanas Díaz et al (2000); UN-Habitat (2003).

Community toilets: Kanpur, India

In 1993, the Kanpur Slum Dwellers Federation – a community-based federation – conducted a community survey and found that in 228 slums, home to over 450,000 people, 66 per cent had no toilets and another 21 per cent had inadequate toilet facilities. With the help of the Slum Dwellers Federation of Mumbai, the Kanpur Federation embarked on a toilet-building programme in one settlement along the railway. Their initial success encouraged the group to join with a 600-woman-strong slum and pavement dwellers collective called Mahila Milan to build another toilet facility in Burma Shell (along Kanpur's railway line). While their first facility was torn down by the railway authorities, another one, built on municipal land at the settlement's edge, was more successful. It holds ten toilet seats, is connected to the municipal sewer line, and contains a water storage tank, sink and bathing enclosures. Mahila Milan in Kanpur also built another ten-seat toilet facility in the Shiv Katra settlement on the edge of Kanpur City. These facilities all utilize a pay-and-use system to generate funds for maintenance and upkeep; they provide a critical service as a result of the work of partnerships between community-based organizations.

Source: Burra et al (2003).

Sewerage system: Maputo, Mozambique

Roughly two-thirds of the population in Maputo's unplanned settlements live without access to a formal sewage system. In 2000, a community-based organization – ADASBU – was established in the neighbourhood of Urbanizacão with the help of Médecins sans Frontières (MSF) to address this lack of provision locally. With MSF's technical support and equipment, ADASBU was able to provide drainage services to the neighbourhood using a special vacuum, a storage tanker and a mini-tractor to pull it. The initial project envisioned disposing of the drained waste from settlement latrines into a neighbouring sewerage line; however, this plan was rejected by the national ministry in charge of sewerage. The compromise plan was for the waste to be held in ADASBU's yard until a municipal suction truck collected it. Although ADASBU's work is currently being challenged by the volatility of fuel costs, the organization is one of the few groups in Maputo that now have an official contract with the municipality for sewage collection. The community being serviced also contributes funds to ADASBU's continued work.

Sources: Schaub-Jones (2005); Langa (2006).

Refuse collection: São Paulo, Brazil

In 1989, with the help of the Catholic foundation, the Fraternal Assistance Organization (OAF), a cooperative of street people who scavenged refuse was formed in the city of São Paulo. Though not based in a particular neighbourhood or settlement, this cooperative, COOPAMARE, is still very much a 'community' organization, with a central facility located in the neighbourhood of Pinheiros. In a city that produces over 20,000 tons of refuse per day, COOPAMARE started by scavenging the plentiful recyclables from São Paulo's settlements and private-sector establishments. Some estimates have put COOPAMARE's recyclable collections at 100 tons a month – or roughly half of what the official recycling programme in the city of São Paulo collects. The cooperative weighs, packs and sells these materials, enabling its members to earn a modest living. COOPAMARE's model has been duplicated throughout the city and Brazil, a compliment but also a constraint in that the competition that emerged has led to a revision of the work strategy of the cooperative, which now focuses on collecting recyclables from partners, with whom there are special agreements.

Sources: Brazilian Recycling Commitment (1996); Rolnik and Cymbalista (2004).

Caring for the ill: Nairobi, Kenya

The grassroots women's group federation GROOTS Kenya is engaged in a wide range of activities in members' communities. One of the main services the federation provides within the informal settlement of Mathare in Nairobi is providing assistance for women suffering from HIV/AIDS. The organization trained 120 local caregiving members, and roughly 20 still work in Mathare, regularly visiting HIV/AIDS-infected women in their households, often bringing them food, and helping them to better care for themselves and their families.

Sources: Sustainable Development Issues Network (2005); FAO (2006).

In addition to basic service provision, as highlighted in Box 7.1, OUPs also work towards the improvement of their neighbourhoods, both physically and socially, via collective action in such realms as land development, shelter improvements, security and savings. Box 7.2 highlights two such activities: land invasions and community surveying (or mapping). The first is perhaps one of the most important (and controversial) exercises in which community organizations of the urban poor have engaged. Land invasions are typically staged in a context of informality or illegality. However, such organized development or invasion of land highlights the need for proactive measures and demonstrates the capacity of OUPs to help improve their living conditions in the absence of socially inclusive, affordable and accessible formal housing or land development programmes. While community surveying or mapping is not as controversial or illegal an activity, it too seeks to fill a void that formal efforts have fallen short of addressing – that is, formally recording the full scale of livelihoods, activities, services and needs in informal or substandard settlements.

Box 7.2 Communities engaging in neighbourhood planning and improvement

Land development and invasions

There are several examples of communities from one part of a city or peri-urban area planning the invasion of vacant or unoccupied land that has potential for residential development (though such land is often potentially hazardous as a residential site). In some cases, especially in parts of South America, for example in Brazil, community organizations have even consulted municipal guidelines on how far apart housing units should be, how wide to set streets and so on in order to facilitate formal upgrading later.

Witwatersrand Metropolitan Region, South Africa

Located outside Johannesburg, in the eastern portion of the Witwatersrand Region, Wattville is an old, extremely overcrowded African township. A community organization was formed in 1985, in part to address the crowding issue and the need for more land. This organization, the Wattville Concerned Residents Committee (WCRC), made several attempts to engage with local government authorities regarding their land needs and housing shortage. In 1990, after many years of a lack of response from government and repression of the community organization, the WCRC agreed to invade a vacant site south of Wattville, to be named Tamboville. The invasion, though somewhat stymied by police, forced more fruitful negotiations with local authorities, which then agreed to apportion the Tamboville land for low-income housing. As a result of post-land-invasion negotiations, the WCRC was invited to form part of a joint technical committee with local authorities to administer the Tamboville development project – which became a strategic model of planned land invasion in the area.

Source: Royston (1998).

Community surveys and mapping for improvements

Across the globe, communities of the urban poor, along with supportive NGOs, are documenting their own living conditions – their needs and their community assets – in an effort to improve their lives. These exercises serve two basic purposes: they build knowledge systems that reflect real local expertise (community knowledge) and they help strengthen community groups by building relationships among community residents and by establishing the community as a formal stakeholder in political and planning processes in the city (Kretzmann and McKnight, 1997). A few examples of such activities are highlighted here:

Phnom Penh, Cambodia

Starting out as a savings group in 1994, the Solidarity and Urban Poor Federation in Phnom Penh has carried out a number of surveys of members' communities. The community enumerations gather and analyse data, including population size and density, shelter location and risk, tenancy, availability and method of securing water, sanitation, electricity, and occupations and incomes.

Source: Asian Coalition for Housing Rights (2001).

Dar es Salaam, Tanzania

With the assistance of the UK-based charity WaterAid, an umbrella community-based organization called the People's Voice for Development (PEVODE), comprising seven communities in the Temeke municipality of Dar es Salaam, was established in 1998. Since its inception, PEVODE has mobilized water-user associations and engaged in community mapping of five of the seven member communities of Temeke to study how residents were dealing with a water and sanitation crisis. PEVODE itself was trained in this exercise with the help of WaterAid and representatives from other OUPs from South Africa (the Homeless People's Federation) and Zimbabwe (Dialogue on Shelter) which had community mapping experience. PEVODE led the survey and mapping of the communities and gathered information on population figures, the physical layout and boundaries of different communities, illnesses, and water and sanitation access. These data have fed both the community's own knowledge base and that of local government planning and service agencies, as well as the programmatic knowledge of international organizations such as WaterAid.

Source: Glöckner et al (2004).

Nairobi, Kenya

A federation of the urban poor in Kenya, Muungano wa Wanvijiji, works closely with a supporting NGO, the Pamoja Trust, to develop plans to secure basic services and security of tenure. In the settlement of Huruma, Pamoja and federation members from the Huruma villages of Kambi Moto, Mahiira, Redeemed, Ghetto and Gitathuru carried out a community survey and mapping exercise with the Nairobi City Council. All of the data were collected by residents of Huruma itself and included information on population and household size, tenancy, income strategies, household expenditures, and water and sanitation access and use. The survey and mapping exercise was the first step in the regularization process of these settlements.

Source: Weru (2004).

OUPs as a Silver Bullet?

Both the provision of basic services and the engagement in general neighbourhood improvements require large investments of time, energy and savvy from members of OUPs. While some of this work shows immediate benefits to the community, much of it tends to require dedication over more than just a few months – though even this scale of measurement is a short-term one. It is thus not unreasonable to ask whether the community capital underwriting an OUP can sustain the development journey and whether it can infinitely grow or be replicated. This section pursues a discussion of some of the key challenges facing OUPs, both in their formation and their work.

One of the first questions often posed with regard to the potential of OUPs to manage development goals centres on their size and potential for achieving large-scale improvements. Some studies point to the population size of a settlement as a measurable indicator of successful community-managed development projects and services, noting that smaller populations demonstrate better management outcomes (Doe and Sohail Khan, 2004). However, as shown in the documented cases discussed in the previous section alone, successful OUPs range from those starting out as very small savings group collectives of proximate neighbours to significantly large national federations of slum-dwellers and their international networks (Patel and Mitlin, 2002). Perhaps a more serious working constraint within OUPs is that time and energy are taken for granted. Though some OUPs break even or make some profit from the services they provide, many – and almost all at early stages – function because of the voluntary efforts of the urban poor themselves. Ironically, those that can least afford non-income-generating labour are most involved. Yet the energy capacity of the urban poor continues to be perceived as either boundless or idle and thus always available to engage in community organizing and management of projects and services (Berner and Phillips, 2005).

Another dynamic in which time plays a factor in the success of OUPs is that of generations and tenure. While some informal settlements are long established and culturally homogeneous, many others represent great crossroads of cultural, generational and ethnic diversity and are reminders of the fact that residents are also dynamic – moving in, out and around settlements in cities when necessary or desired (Botes and van Rensburg, 2000; Williams, 2004; Berner and Philips, 2005). Though this diversity does not equal adversity, it does indicate that attention must be paid to issues of representation and voice even within community OUPs. A number of studies have pointed to the challenges of working beyond the interests of self-selected local leaders or the domination of OUPs by the relatively powered members of a community (Lind, 1997; Tendler, 1997; Stall and Stoecker, 1998; Botes and van Rensburg, 2000; Jellinek, 2003; Gugerty and Kremer, 2004; Rakodi, 2004; Berner and Phillips, 2005). This call for representational analysis does not so much challenge the purpose, form or work of OUPs as point to the need for self-evaluation in those organizations, as well as a role for external partners who can help facilitate the representation of the most marginalized groups in communities, such as women and children.

Indeed, gender roles play an important part in a culturally nuanced understanding of how OUPs form and on what issues they work. From the early 20th-century community settlement houses in the US and the UK to the building of community toilets in India in the late 1990s, women have been central to both the organizational and substantive character of community-based organizations. However, as Lind (1997) relates, their participation in OUPs requires adding more work to their already heavy domestic chores – and for neither work are they remunerated. Some studies, in fact, contend that work within a community is, in certain respects, considered an extension of work in the household, and thus in some cultures it is easily relegated to the arena of women's labour (Stall and Stoeker, 1998). Other studies argue that cultural marks on behaviour and practices are variable in both space and time and that some aspects of cultural practice are more influenced by space than others. For example, shared perspectives on labour division according to sex have a high correlation with physical or geographic clusters. In other words, what your neighbours do or think matters for what kind of work you perceive is acceptable for women or men (Guglielmino et al, 1995). As such, it is, in part, an understanding of gender roles in family and community structures and in socioeconomic and political ideologies that determines what facilitates (and constrains) women's or men's participation and success in community-level collective action (Lind, 1997).

Two short examples are illustrative of this point. Though NGOs have often targeted women in facilitating the creation of empowered community-based organizations, when one such NGO-supported women's OUP in Mumbai tried to negotiate for materials at a hardware store for their community toilet block construction, shopkeepers did not seriously attend to them (Burra et al, 2003). In Indonesia, a group of female social workers were central in the design phase of a locally initiated NGO's research and action programme in five informal communities in Jakarta. However, once the community-based NGO attracted the attention of powered elites outside the community, men in the organization took greater control of the direction of the work and of external communications (and fired the initial group of female social workers) (Jellinek, 2003).

In these examples, as in many others, women's role as grassroots organizers *within* the community appeared acceptable and helped in the establishment of a community-based organization or OUP. However, once women had to negotiate with actors *outside* their community, they – and to some extent the groups they led or helped form – faced greater cultural obstacles to and biases against their work due to power struggles and adherence to the culturally acceptable gendered division of labour. Using this example of a gender lens, it is evident that, while an initial challenge can create community capital sufficient to form an OUP and propel its work, there are also more contextual cultural challenges to OUPs that may both facilitate and constrain the work in which they engage.

Ensuring self-regulation and reflection, enabling external partners and supportive cultural environments are essential for the success of OUPs. Nonetheless, governmental and international finance agencies can play a pivotal role in alleviating some of the burdens (time, energy and so on) faced by community OUPs by entering into dialogues with such groups in a cooperative manner (in other words not predetermining work programmes and roles) and helping to secure technologies and larger infrastructure networks that could facilitate OUPs' diverse work strategies and programmes. In this way, governments help and learn and benefit from OUPs, but OUPs also help and learn and benefit from governments and other interested actors. Such interaction can help create an environment in which building a shared system of valuation in development has a chance.

Conclusion: Building a Constituency for Change

Though the numerous success stories of the work of OUPs in improving their own lives are encouraging, in consideration of their impact on planning for tomorrow's urban population, it is important to understand that this work exists in a larger context of political transformation. The general purpose of OUPs is not to replace the work of government, though such organizations and their supporting NGOs often engage in services that governments normally provide in regularized or upper-income settlements. Even in instances of OUP programmatic success, a good climate of governmental support is typically necessary to enable their work strategies – whether by allowing groups to build and improve on municipal lands or by providing such groups with institutionalized space and a voice in planning processes. As one account of community empowerment in Sri Lanka illustrates, it is not enough that communities simply organize themselves; they need to be linked with higher levels of government administration in their neighbourhoods, cities and provinces to ensure that these groups have recognized power to act (Dayaratne and Samarawickrama, 2003). Getting 'linked in' or formal recognition, however, tends to take time.

As eccentric designer and innovator Buckminster Fuller once said, 'You never change things by fighting the existing reality. To change something, build a new model that makes the existing model obsolete' (Fuller, undated). Fuller's words have resonance for the process of empowerment and change in decision-making that OUPs and their supporting NGOs have stirred. OUPs are creating 'new models' of development by helping bring to light alternative strategies of development that work – showing that top–down and bottom–up models are both obsolete. These groups are showing that development initiatives have to flow in both directions simultaneously. They recognize that many governments, after many internal and external struggles, have provided key institutional space and support for collaborative efforts. This hard-fought-for movement to the circular – where product is process and process is product – is arguably where community OUPs have had the greatest sustainable impact on planning and governance for the future just city.

Yet this fuller understanding of the work of OUPs remains somewhat elusive in development debates. Instead, they are portrayed as bottom–up development proponents alone. In reality, OUPs and their development strategies represent a veritable social movement and must be understood as such. Much like the movements for independence, racial and gender equality, and religious freedom, the social movements of the urban poor have discovered a transformative medium in the form of community organizations. Furthermore, today's community OUPs have found an innovative means of extending their reach in lessons learned and shared – through supportive networks. Networks of OUPs can find an institutional home and support through dedicated government programmes and agencies, as has happened in Thailand and Brazil (Boonyabancha, 2004; Rolnik and Cymbalista, 2004). They are also formed through the help of NGOs that concentrate on bridging like-minded or similarly situated community groups, as in India (Patel and Mitlin, 2004).[4] In a growing number of instances, networks of OUPs are forming across local and international borders through exchanges among supporting NGOs and community representatives, as in Pakistan, South Africa, the United Republic of Tanzania and Zimbabwe (Alimuddin et al, 2004; Glöckner et al, 2004).

Such networks and the information exchanges they spur provide OUPs with precedent-setting examples for reference in negotiations with other development actors. They also encourage regularized knowledge documentation and fund-raising or financial pooling, in addition to providing a supportive forum for discussion of internal and external challenges to organization. Networks are increasingly used as a support in the transitions many OUPs experience as they grow more successful and are forced to address the question of their work objectives, the scales on which they wish to engage and the partners they must choose. Through such network development, OUPs are moving the discourse away from a debate about the strengths and weaknesses of particular organizations or particular development orientations and towards an era of coordinated development practice that finally capitalizes on and better supports the (rapidly) growing constituency and drive of the urban poor.

NOTES

1   This chapter was originally conceived as a background paper for the UNFPA's *The State of World Population 2007* report. In its revised form, the arguments presented here benefited greatly from the comments and suggestions of Gordon McGranahan, head of the Human Settlements Group at the International Institute for Environment and Development, and from discussions with numerous participants at the Rockefeller Foundation's Global Urban Summit in Bellagio, Italy, in July 2007.
2   See Moser (1989) and Botes and van Rensburg (2000) for more on this point.
3   For a more detailed framing of the different ways in which organizations engage in the acquisition of basic urban services in poor neighbourhoods, see Chapter 4.
4   See Chapter 4 for more information on the alliance formed in India and its role in the emergence of Slum/Shack Dwellers International.

REFERENCES

Alimuddin, S., Hasan, A. and Sadiq, A. (2004) 'The work of the Anjuman Samaji Behbood in Faisalabad, Pakistan', in D. Mitlin and D. Satterthwaite (eds) *Empowering Squatter*

Citizen: Local Government, Civil Society and Urban Poverty Reduction, Earthscan, London

Asian Coalition for Housing Rights (2001) 'Building an urban poor people's movement in Phnom Penh, Cambodia', *Environment and Urbanization*, vol 13, no 2, pp61–72

Berner, E. and Phillips, B. (2005) 'Left to their own devices? Community self-help between alternative development and neo-liberalism', *Community Development Journal*, vol 40, no 1, pp17–29

Boonyabancha, S. (2004) 'A decade of change: From the Urban Community Development Office to the Community Organization Development Institute in Thailand', in D. Mitlin and D. Satterthwaite (eds) *Empowering Squatter Citizen: Local Government, Civil Society and Urban Poverty Reduction*, Earthscan, London

Botes, L. and van Rensburg, D. (2000) 'Community participation in development: Nine plagues and twelve commandments', *Community Development Journal*, vol 35, no 1, pp41–58

Brazilian Recycling Commitment (1996) 'Case study: Educational kit for the promotion of recycling cooperatives in Brazil', paper for the Urban Management Programme (UMP)/Swiss Agency for Development and Cooperation (SDC) Collaborative Programme on Municipal Solid Waste Management (MSWM) in Low-Income Countries, presented at the Workshop on Micro-Enterprises Involvement in Municipal Solid Waste Management in Developing Counties, Cairo, 14–18 October

Burra, S., Patel, S. and Kerr, T. (2003) 'Community-designed, -built and -managed toilet blocks in Indian cities', *Environment and Urbanization*, vol 15, no 2, pp11–32

Cabanas Díaz, A., Grant, E., del Cid Vargas, P. I. and Sajbin Velásquez, V. (2000) 'El Mezquital: A community's struggle for development', Working Paper on Poverty Reduction in Urban Areas No 1, International Institute for Environment and Development, London

Dayaratne, R. and Samarawickrama, R. (2003) 'Empowering communities in the peri-urban areas of Colombo', *Environment and Urbanization*, vol 15, no 1, pp101–110

Doe, S. and Sohail Khan, M. (2004) 'The boundaries and limits of community management: Lessons from the water sector in Ghana', *Community Development Journal*, vol 39, no 4, pp360–371

FAO Sub-Regional Office for Southern and East Africa (2006) *Reclaiming Our Lives*, Human Sciences Research Council Press, Cape Town

Fuller, B. (undated) quotation cited on the home page of the Buckminster Fuller Institute website, www.bfi.org, accessed 30 June 2008

Glöckner, H., Mkanga, M. and Ndezi, T. (2004) 'Local empowerment through community mapping for water and sanitation in Dar es Salaam', *Environment and Urbanization*, vol 16, no 1, pp185–198

Gugerty, M. and Kremer, M. (2004) 'The Rockefeller effect', Poverty Action Lab Paper No 3, Massachusetts Institute of Technology, Cambridge, MA

Guglielmino, C. R., Viganotti, C., Hewlett, B. and Cavalli-Sforza, L. L. (1995) 'Cultural variation in Africa: Role of mechanisms of transmission and adaptation', *Proceedings of the National Academy of Sciences*, vol 92, pp7585–7589

Jellinek, L. (2003) 'Collapsing under the weight of success: An NGO in Jakarta', *Environment and Urbanization*, vol 15, no 1, pp171–280

Kretzmann, J. and McKnight, J. L. (1997) *Building Communities from the Inside Out*, ACTA Publications, Skokie, IL

Langa, E. (2006) 'Participation in urban environmental management: A participatory approach from sustainable urban development in Maputo', Master's thesis in Environmental Management, Aalborg University, Aalborg, Denmark

Lind, A. (1997) 'Gender, development and urban social change: Women's community action in global cities', *World Development*, vol 25, no 8, pp1205–1223

Moser, C. (1989) 'Community participation in urban projects in the third world', *Progress in Planning*, vol 32, no 2

Patel, S. and Mitlin, D. (2002) 'Sharing experiences and changing lives', *Community Development Journal*, vol 37, no 2, pp125–136

Patel, S. and Mitlin, D. (2004) 'Grassroots-driven development: The alliance of SPARC, the National Slum Dwellers Federation and Mahila Milan', in D. Mitlin and D. Satterthwaite (eds) *Empowering Squatter Citizen: Local Government, Civil Society and Urban Poverty Reduction*, Earthscan, London

Rakodi, C. (2004) 'Representation and responsiveness: Urban politics and the poor in ten cities in the South', *Community Development Journal*, vol 39, no 3, pp252–265

Rolnik, R. and Cymbalista, R. (2004) 'Communities and local government: Three case studies in São Paulo, Brazil', Paper No 14, UNRISD Democracy, Governance and Human Rights Programme, United Nations Research Institute for Social Development, Geneva

Royston, L. (1998) 'South Africa: The struggle for access to the city in the Witwatersrand region', in A. Azuela, E. Duhau and E. Ortiz (eds) *Evictions and the Right to Housing: Experience from Canada, Chile, the Dominican Republic, South Africa and South Korea*, International Development Research Centre, Ottawa

Schaub-Jones, D. (2005) 'Sanitation partnerships: Beyond storage: On-site sanitation as an urban system', BPD Sanitation Series, Building Partnerships for Development in Water and Sanitation, London

Stall, S. and Stoecker, R. (1998) 'Community organizing or organizing community? Gender and the crafts of empowerment', *Gender and Society*, vol 12, no 6, pp 729–756

Sustainable Development Issues Network (2005) 'Slum-dwellers doing it in the slum', *Taking Issue*, vol 5, issue 4, p3

Tendler, J. (1997) *Good Government in the Tropics*, John Hopkins University Press, Baltimore, MD

UN-Habitat (2003) *Water and Sanitation in the World's Cities*, Earthscan, London

UN Millennium Project (2005) *A Home in the City*, Task Force on Improving the Lives of Slum Dwellers, Earthscan, London and Sterling, VA

Weru, J. (2004) 'Community federations and city upgrading: The work of Pamoja Trust and Muungano in Kenya', *Environment and Urbanization*, vol 16, no 1, pp47–62

Williams, L. (2004) 'Culture and community development: Towards new conceptualizations and practice', *Community Development Journal*, vol 39, no 4, pp345–359

Part III

The Social and Sustainable Use of Space

Introduction

Although urban localities occupy only a minute part of the Earth's surface, there are huge social and environmental implications to where, why and how cities are built and land is incorporated into the urban make-up. This part begins with a broad overview of the relationships between urban growth and global environmental change. In Chapter 8, Sánchez argues that a better understanding of these interactions requires, above all, a more comprehensive vision of urban sustainability. He notes that fragmented approaches to urban planning have hampered effective solutions. Similarly, he points out that the perception that the negative consequences of global environmental change will occur in the long term, and thus do not require immediate attention, is also misleading. Local processes that affect or are being affected by regional and global biophysical processes also require actions (mitigation and adaptation) in the short term.

To help stimulate a broader approach, Sánchez offers a multidimensional conceptual scheme for the study of the interactions between urban areas and global environmental change (GEC). He shows how the biophysical system results from interactions between regional and global biophysical and chemical processes and local, regional and global socioeconomic and geopolitical development. He then examines in greater detail how urban areas interact with GEC through land cover and climate changes. This discussion depicts an alarming scenario of vulnerabilities, especially for developing countries and the poorer segments of the urban population, urging not only more effective integrated action but also a greater focus on equity issues.

Climate change is particularly critical for coastal areas, which tend to have more fragile ecosystems and yet be more urban than inland areas. Overall, low elevation coastal zones contain some 2 per cent of the world's land and 10 per cent of its population. In Chapter 9, McGranahan, Balk and Anderson focus on urban settlements in such areas and the risks from flooding and storm damage that climate change poses for their growing populations. Though mitigation of climate change may be the best means of reducing such threats, urban settlement is highly path-dependent; thus urban coastal settlements established in the past and present are likely to attract more urban coastal settlement in the future. Out-migration from some of the most threatened coastal regions may eventually be called for. Timely measures to prevent urban development in risky locations are also critical.

Dense littoral populations can also be a burden on coastal ecosystems, many of which are already under stress, and the loss of ecosystem services can make urban settlements more prone to disaster. Many of the risks from climate change could be reduced by more appropriate land-use patterns and regulation of residential and commercial activities. In many cases, there may be measures that can address present problems while also providing a means of adapting to climate change. These are an obvious place to start, even if such coincidences of interest are unlikely to be sufficient to form the basis for all of the adaptive measures needed.

The geographical setting and ecological resources of urban locations affect the success of individual urban centres, and, in an increasingly urban world, the location of urban populations also has environmental significance at larger scales, including globally. In Chapter 10, Balk, McGranahan and Anderson estimate the rates of urbanization and urban growth by ecological zone. They find that, while continental, regional and country-level views are significant to the understanding of environmental processes, ecological zones are more environmentally relevant. The latter take on special significance in light of changing environmental conditions and the possibility that urbanization trajectories will come into conflict with these environmental shifts.

While coastal zones are more urbanized than other zones, and home to the largest urban areas of most nations, other zones, such as inland water and dryland areas, are also important and vulnerable and are home to large numbers and growing shares of urban population. Future urbanization, in Africa and Asia in particular, is expected to be high in many of these other zones, as well, raising the bar for environmentally sustainable development under varying conditions of resource scarcity.

Chapter 11 looks at urban sustainability from the standpoint of one of the most talked-about features of modern city growth: urban sprawl. Hogan and Ojima review the debate from the perspective of the challenges that sprawl raises for the sustainability of expected urban growth in coming decades. Originating as an aspect of suburbanization in North America during the post-World War II years, sprawl became a volatile political issue by the end of the 20th century. Its appearance in Europe – where compact cities have a long tradition – and, especially in developing countries, is related to contemporary lifestyles and does not bode well for harmonizing environmental quality with population concentration.

Criticism of sprawl has been strong in terms of both social and environmental consequences. Sprawl is associated with longer daily travel times and less family time, a health burden that includes greater stress, pollution from increased traffic, loss of green space, increased water use, and ecosystems compromised by fragmentation. The authors discuss the methodological difficulties of measuring sprawl; review related polemics on compact versus dispersed cities; and emphasize the importance of the morphology of urban growth. Form, as well as size, is held to be a crucial component of urban sustainability. The authors conclude that not all forms of dispersed urbanization can be considered sprawl and that other forms of dispersion are still insufficiently understood.

Overall, it seems clear from these different contributions that, although most interest has so far been focused on the ecological footprint of cities in terms of their production and consumption patterns, preparing for a sustainable urban transition will require much greater attention to where and how cities grow and how they are administered. A new vision, inspired by both global concerns and local perspectives such as those outlined in this part, will have to emerge and, in turn, spawn better informed and more participative regional responses to the challenges of rapid urban expansion.

8

Urban Sustainability and Global Environmental Change: Reflections for an Urban Agenda

Roberto Sánchez-Rodríguez

INTRODUCTION

The destiny of today's societies is increasingly tied to the evolution of their urban areas. Fostering balanced growth in dynamic urban areas is undoubtedly challenging. Various contradictory needs and actions affect the daily functioning of cities and determine the types of urban space created, as well as their environmental impacts. Rapidly growing cities in poor countries are the most affected by the difficulties of achieving sustainable urban growth. Unemployment and underemployment, environmental degradation, deficiencies in urban services and housing, deterioration of existing infrastructure, lack of guaranteed access to the natural resources vital to urban life, and an alarming increase in violence are but a few of the problems they face.

All of these issues are aggravated by the rapid growth of populations and urban spaces, as well as by imbalances in urban structure and accumulated deficits in the construction, expansion and operation of public services. Economic and financial crises further exacerbate these problems. The overall result has been the formation of fragmented and segregated urban spaces that increase social exclusion and deficiencies in the functioning of urban areas while also aggravating environmental problems (Lopes de Souza, 2001; Pirez, 2002; Moser and McIlwaine, 2005).

During the last 15 years, urban sustainability efforts have sought to balance three critical functions of urban areas: as engines of economic growth, as loci of improved social wellbeing and as agents of environmental change. For the most part, however, urban sustainability continues to be more a normative ideal than an operational reality. Most approaches emphasize the economic aspects (urban areas as centres of wealth production), giving limited attention to environmental protection and social wellbeing.

A more effective approach to urban sustainability should recognize, and somehow deal with, the complexity of the dynamic interactions among socioeconomic, geopolitical and environmental processes at local, regional and global levels. Current approaches to sustainable development that tend to consider urban issues in a fragmented manner should be replaced with multidimensional perspectives capable of generating an integrated perspective of complex and dynamic urban realities (Pelling, 2003).

Fragmented approaches are frequently the result of the technical exercise of planning, of simplifying complex urban realities in order to facilitate the design and implementation of actions aimed at the resolution of immediate problems, such as in public services, housing, transportation, urban economy and environmental pollution. This fragmented vision overlooks the wide range of multidimensional social, economic, political, cultural and biophysical interactions behind each urban problem. Issues of natural resource supply, ecological services and environmental pollution cannot be considered in isolation from their broader social, economic and cultural contexts (Bryant and Wilson, 1998; Gibbs and Jonas, 2000).

This chapter seeks to contribute to an integrated multidimensional vision of urban sustainability and to a better understanding of the interactions between urbanization and global environmental change (GEC). A central argument made here is that urban sustainability in the 21st century requires looking beyond the local scale in order to foster a dynamic perspective of the interactions between the local, regional and global biophysical and social processes that are generated by, and that affect, urban areas.

One specific goal of this chapter is to help change the perception that, since the negative consequences of GEC will occur in the long term (25, 50 or 100 years from now), they do not require immediate attention. Such a view fails to recognize that the local processes that are affecting and being affected by regional and global biophysical processes also require actions (mitigation and adaptation) in the short term to reduce their negative consequences. Since such actions are linked both directly and indirectly to current urban and environmental problems, investments in solving them could help to mitigate or adapt to the negative consequences of GEC – if their design took into consideration their interactions with regional and global processes. The good news is that many of those actions do not require additional costs to the programmes currently focusing on planning for the urban future.

THE INTERACTIONS BETWEEN URBAN AREAS AND GLOBAL BIOPHYSICAL PROCESSES

The negative effects that urban areas have on the global environment have drawn considerable attention, especially in regard to the effects of greenhouse gas emissions and the so-called 'heat island effect' on climate change (IPCC, 2001). A series of international, regional and local initiatives have prioritized the reduction of greenhouse gas emissions in urban areas. However, the biophysical and chemical processes associated with GEC also have negative but less-recognized impacts on urban areas.

Figure 8.1 presents a graphic representation of a conceptual scheme for the study of the interactions between urban areas and global environmental changes. The scheme is based on two premises. The first is that urban systems result from alterations made to the landscape as a result of social processes expressed in physical space by the built environment. The impacts of the urban system on the biophysical system, or those of the biophysical system on urban space, will be different, depending on the type of space created (for example a well-serviced area as opposed to a slum area). The type of built landscape and the social groups occupying it have different capacities to cope with, adapt to and resist the impacts of GEC or to generate those impacts. This distinction is important when addressing equity issues in urban sustainable development. Moreover, the biophysical system is, in reality, the result of interactions between regional and global biophysical and chemical processes and local, regional and global socioeconomic and geopolitical ones. For instance, alterations to the water or carbon cycle – responsible for climate change and other aspects of GEC – are the result of such interactions.

The second premise is the recognition of a bidirectional relationship between urban areas and biophysical systems, as shown by the short light-grey arrows in Figure 8.1. One side depicts the manner in which the urban system impacts on the biophysical system. Greenhouse gas emissions of urban origin – from transportation, industry and services – and heat emissions, including heat islands, are clearly responsible for this impact. Other factors, such as changes in land use and land cover directly or indirectly caused by the urban system, also impact on the biophysical system but receive less attention. The demand for construction materials, food, energy, water and other natural resources cause changes in land use and land cover. For example, the high urban demand for wood and food has caused deforestation and the associated increases in CO_2 emissions, while the demand for water produces alterations in the water cycle of large areas. The other short light-grey arrow illustrates how the biophysical system impacts on the urban area. Natural disasters are one of the most visible results, but there are other impacts on urban form and function (the urban economy and social activities) and on health that are relevant to daily urban life and future urban sustainability.

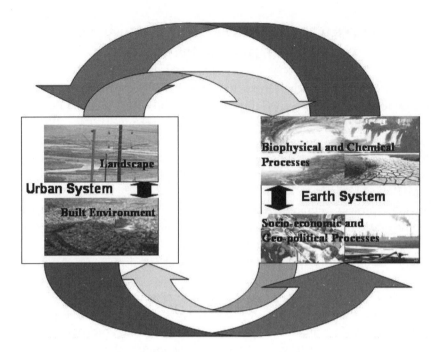

Figure 8.1 *The interactions between urban areas and global environmental change:*
A conceptual framework

Source: Sánchez-Rodríguez et al (2005).

Figure 8.1 also presents a second bidirectional flow (the dark-grey arrows) between the urban system and the biophysical system. It illustrates the dynamic nature of these non-linear processes. Society, like nature, often has unexpected responses to sudden shocks. Cities are complex systems where unexpected reactions to extreme events are part of a wide array of feedback loops that result from such interactions with GEC. This second group of impacts occurs as a consequence of the first. For example, increases in temperature (heat waves) can cause a large increase in energy use in many urban areas, thus elevating the emission of greenhouse gases and the impact on the biophysical system. Extreme climatic events, such as floods or droughts, can intensify migration to urban areas, resulting in changes to land use and land cover. These changes, in turn, cause a new series of impacts on the biophysical system and subsequently on urban areas.

The interactions between GEC and urban areas can be classified into two main broad areas: land-use and land-cover change, and climate change. These are examined briefly in the following sections.

LAND-USE AND LAND-COVER CHANGE

Cities are increasingly the sites of most economic growth, a fact that has been accentuated by globalization. This concentration of economic activity is associated with rising incomes and consumption patterns. Both of these consequences tend to increase pressure on natural resources at the regional and global levels. Although urban production and consumption processes may originate in an urban area, their impacts are usually not confined within the city's boundaries. Urban dynamics have the potential to affect social, cultural, economic and ecological processes in lands that are both near and distant from the urban core (Eaton et al, 2007).

To fulfil their needs, urban systems have 'zones of influence' well beyond the immediate urban area. Cities depend on vast resources for the supply of critical ecological services, from the supply of inputs (for example food, energy, water and building materials) to the provision of ecological services (for example wildlife corridors, microclimate and buffer areas to protect against flooding). Outlying areas also suffer the same negative consequences as urban areas (for example pollution, urbanization pressures and land-use changes, and degradation of natural resources).

'Peri-urban areas' satisfy many of these needs and also provide essential services to both the urban and outlying areas.[1] In the most general sense, the development of peri-urban areas involves a complex adjustment of social and ecological systems as they become absorbed into the sphere of the urban economy. Land-use and land-cover changes are associated with the provision of these ecological services and natural resources (Tratalos et al, 2007). Thus GEC and globalization affect the pool of natural resources and ecosystem services upon which urban systems rely (the bidirectional arrows in Figure 8.1).

The rapid rate of change in rural and peri-urban areas demands greater attention in order to understand how urban–rural land-use dynamics will be affected by different levels of GEC and the social responses to them. Globalization is not only a driving force in the growth of cities; at the same time, it facilitates the extension of a city's area of influence over larger geographical areas and even across national boundaries. Studies on urban metabolism have documented fluxes of energy, water, food and construction materials. However, little attention has been paid to the locus of those resources or to the environmental and socioeconomic consequences of urban growth at the local, regional and global levels, including the changes in the landscape.[2]

An additional concern for the future is that the rapid transformation of the rural and peri-urban areas providing such services could change them to urban or other land uses without due consideration of their critical role for the long-term sustainability of the city or for the Earth's ecosystem. The extensive transformation of wetlands or forests near urban areas, for instance, has significant consequences at the local level (on microclimate, the hydrological cycle, habitats and biodiversity, and so on) and affects basic biophysical processes at the regional and global levels (carbon and hydrological cycles and biodiversity). Ultimately, such alterations impact on GEC.

CLIMATE CHANGE

The transformation of human societies has always been intimately related to climate. The development and collapse of civilizations have strong links with environmental management and, in particular, with climate management (Diamond, 2005). For centuries, technological advances have gradually transformed the capacity for adaptation to adverse climate conditions, particularly evidenced in the form and location of human settlements (housing and urban space). Changes have been particularly dramatic in the last century: the adoption of technology such as air-conditioning and central heating has facilitated the prioritization of aesthetics over more functional aspects in architecture and urban design and adaptation to climate.

Changing cultural patterns, influenced by the growth of capitalist consumer societies, and by their rapid spread throughout the 'global society', have further induced the abandonment of traditional knowledge on how to adapt to local climate conditions. These new patterns are based on significant energy costs (for example air-conditioning or new materials) and new architectural and urban forms. Climate change and climate variability often aggravate the deficiencies of poor adaptation to climatic conditions and increase dependence on artificial coping mechanisms.

Direct climate impacts, however, are not the only component of GEC that shape the form and growth of the built environment. Indirect changes can also have an effect. Sea-level rise in coastal areas has an impact on the shape and form of urban areas, as well as on their vulnerability to inundation. Better knowledge and understanding of these interactions would provide useful information to national and local decision-makers about the way that biophysical processes shape the construction, form and function of the built environment. Such knowledge would be useful in influencing growth and sustainable development policies for urban areas in both rich and poor countries, and also assist them in adapting to the potential negative consequences of climate change.

The effect of an increase in the temperature of an urban area in comparison to its surroundings is a particularly important component in the relationship between urban areas and climate (Rosenzweig et al, 2005). The size of the urban centre and its type of urbanization and land use are some of the factors that determine the urban heat island (UHI) effect. As population centres grow in size, from village to town to city, they tend to have a corresponding increase in average temperature – between 2 and 6°C hotter than the surrounding countryside – thereby increasing the demand for air-conditioning. Moreover, as a result of UHIs, monthly rainfall is greater in upwind parts of the urban area compared to areas downwind.

The UHI effect is often aggravated by urban designs and forms that neglect the climatic conditions of the locales and that provoke the loss of green areas which previously had a cooling effect (Bochaca and Puliafito, 2007). These problems are particularly prominent in the urban areas of poor countries located in the tropics. Current urbanization trends in those countries, together with the impacts of climate variability and climate change, can exacerbate the already stressed conditions caused by UHIs. Unfortunately, most of the existing studies on UHIs have been conducted in temperate zones, while most future urban growth will occur in the global South (Corbella and Magalhaes, 2007).

One of the most evident negative consequences of extreme climatic events is the growing number and magnitude of climate-related disasters in urban areas during the last few decades. The damage caused by hurricanes and other extreme climatic events has had a high social, economic and environmental cost and is often associated with unplanned and incomplete urban growth, often in risk-prone areas, and with severe modifications of the natural landscape (Mirza, 2003; Pelling, 2003). Such changes have increased the number of people who are vulnerable to hurricanes and tropical storms, droughts, landslides, floods, and so on.

The rates and patterns of ongoing urban growth, as well as increases in urban poverty, are key elements in the rising vulnerability of cities to the negative consequences of climate change (Cross, 2001; Pelling, 2003). The transformation of the global economy has also triggered important changes in the urban dynamics of the largest cities in poor countries since the 1970s. These transformations are driven by foreign direct investment, large-scale movement of capital, and structural adjustment programmes that tend to redefine the economic base of these urban areas and recast their territorial patterns (the bidirectional flows between cities and social and biophysical processes shown in Figure 8.1). The results are highly segregated urban spaces and expanded urban growth in risk-prone areas, along with severe deficiencies in the provision of public services.

Poverty, income inequality and segregation are key elements in the vulnerability of urban populations to the negative consequences of GEC (Satterthwaite, 2007). Urban areas are indeed highly vulnerable in crises and disasters: sudden supply shortages, heavy environmental burdens or major catastrophes can quickly lead to serious bottlenecks or emergencies for a vast number of people or exacerbate conditions for the socially weakest groups (Wisner, 2004). Constraints and conflicts may acquire multiple dimensions, as they arise amid poorly coordinated planning and response, increased subordination to the influence of the globalized economy, growing socioeconomic disparities, and intensifying environmental burdens. As stated earlier, realistic actions in confronting these problems would require a multidimensional and multi-scale approach.

The scientific debate around the frequency and intensity of extreme climatic events has not been thoroughly settled, but it is clear that natural disasters have become more frequent during the last two decades. This is due in part to the rapid increase in vulnerability and exposure of larger numbers of urban inhabitants, as well as to landscape modifications that aggravate the impact of extreme climatic events in urban areas. Lessons learned from the impact of natural disasters caused by frequent extreme climatic events have not yet been translated into a systematic body of knowledge on the vulnerability of urban areas to those events, nor into effective adaptation to their negative consequences in poor countries (Burton et al, 2002). Decisions affecting urban growth largely neglect the interaction of local issues with broader processes. Current trends of urban growth in conditions of growing socioeconomic disparities favour the increased impact of natural disasters in urban areas.

The interactions between climate change and urban areas include myriad other processes that are not given sufficient consideration. Some of these interactions do not have as dramatic consequences as those associated with climate-related natural disasters, but they still have significant consequences for urban life and functioning. For example, changes in average and extreme temperatures, or in the intensity and length of seasons, can have significant consequences for important economic activities in some urban areas (for example tourism); the productivity of workers; the use of urban space for social activities (due to the comfort index); water supply, distribution and quality; energy demand; and human health.

Climate change can also modify migration patterns between rural and urban areas or within urban areas. Drought, flooding and other consequences of climate change can be strong drivers of these demographic changes. Migration is often a desperate means of alleviating extreme pressure on livelihoods, particularly among low-income groups. It is also a coping and adapting mechanism in response to GEC. The rapid rate of urbanization in the developing world, together with the size of the population and the associated social conditions (a large increase in poverty and inequity during recent decades), makes the interactions between climate change, migration and settlement patterns a key issue.

As noted above, one of the alarming prospects of climate change is its impact on sea-level rise and the potential consequences for coastal urban areas (McGranahan et al, 2007). As shown in Chapter 9, despite their low levels of urbanization, Africa and Asia have many coastal cities that contain much of their urban population. This reflects historical patterns of urban growth: major cities in Africa and Asia, as well as in Latin America, grew as ports and export nodes of raw materials during their colonial periods. In other regions of the world, many cities of different sizes are also located in coastal zones.

The most evident impact of sea-level rise in those areas is flooding, particularly when combined with extreme climatic events. Other impacts include salt intrusion into bodies of fresh water – threatening critical resources used to supply water to urban areas – and modifications to landscape and ecosystems critical in the supply of ecological services and natural resources to urban areas (food, energy, building materials, microclimate and biodiversity). Sea-level rise could also trigger new waves of migration to inland urban areas (environmental refugees).

Impacts on human health are among the most important consequences of climate change in urban areas. Urban living conditions make residents, particularly in poor countries, vulnerable to severe deficiencies in the supply and operation of public services, infrastructure, sanitation and health services. Even in normal times, many urban inhabitants already face environmental problems, while suffering from malnutrition, poor housing, and other conditions associated with poverty and inequity. All of these aggravate the negative consequences of changes in urban biophysical processes. For example, changes in temperature and precipitation can expand tropical vector-borne diseases (for example malaria, dengue and yellow fever) into areas currently unaffected by them (Haines et al, 2006; Few, 2007). They can also speed up the spread of disease in already affected areas.

The dearth of urban services (for example of drainage and solid waste collection), coupled with dense living conditions and changes in temperature and precipitation, also fosters the reproduction of mosquitoes, increasing the hazards for human health. Deficiencies in housing and other conditions (for example lack of infrastructure, public services and urban design) in poor countries can also aggravate the negative consequences of high temperatures, increasing the morbidity and mortality associated with heat stress. Inadequate infrastructure and transportation in urban areas can exacerbate the consequences of climate change on local air pollution (tropospheric ozone). Changes in climate and the water cycle could affect water supply, water distribution and water quality in urban areas, with important consequences for the expansion of water-borne diseases in poor countries.

THE QUEST FOR URBAN SUSTAINABILITY

The above discussion illustrates some of the challenges of urban growth, particularly in poor countries. The interactions between local urban, social and environmental problems and the impacts of global changes (social and biophysical) on cities create an alarming scenario. 'Sustainable development' offers a widely accepted framework for urban planning that should result in positive social change and more balanced paths of growth for cities. But this framework has to move from rhetoric to action if it is to become a useful tool in orienting urban growth.

New approaches to urban sustainability should be based on integrated perspectives and an awareness of their multi-scale connections. These approaches should create change through continuous learning and adaptation (Mog, 2004) and should focus more attention on three issues: the advancement of knowledge based on integrated perspectives; greater attention to equity as a key component of sustainability; and identification of the institutional changes needed to promote urban sustainability. This section addresses these issues.

The development of new approaches to urban sustainability is supported by the rich legacy of urban studies, which have a long tradition in various disciplines.

Still missing, however, are sustained efforts to create and apply integrated and multidimensional perspectives on urban issues, taking advantage of the accumulated knowledge of these various studies. The multidimensional approach coincides with increasing efforts to conduct interdisciplinary (Petts et al, 2008) and transdisciplinary (Luks and Siebenhüner, 2007) studies on topics related to sustainable development, and it also coincides with the study of various aspects of global environmental problems. Breaking with the culture of excessive specialization in favour of interdisciplinary and transdisciplinary thinking is admittedly not easy. Yet there is at least a growing recognition of the need to complement disciplinary visions with integrated multidimensional perspectives in the study and management of the current and future urban reality. Adequate consideration of the various time/space aspects of those perspectives can contribute to the construction of better theories and methods (Bai, 2007).

This knowledge can be useful in helping local officials and stakeholders in cities to recognize how local processes are affecting or are being affected by broader processes. Investments in solving current problems could help to mitigate and adapt to the negative consequences of GEC through integrated knowledge of urban problems. But it is important that urban investments neither increase the vulnerability of individuals and social groups to the negative consequences of climate change nor diminish the opportunities for urban sustainable development (Pritchett and Woolcock, 2004). An integrated perspective would also help identify the unintended consequences of actions in terms of equity, a key component in urban sustainable development.

Intragenerational and intergenerational equity is recognized as a central component of sustainability and one of its most critical features for the future, given growing levels of inequality within and among societies. Scholars emphasize the importance of addressing equity concerns in the study of the risks posed by climate change and their connection to development challenges, particularly in poor countries (Tol et al, 2004; Thomas and Twyman, 2005; Paavola and Adger, 2006). The close association of vulnerability and equity is highlighted by studies that draw attention to factors influencing the capacity of individuals or groups to anticipate, cope with, resist and recover from the impact of a natural hazard (Wisner, 2004). These factors (assets, sources of livelihood, class, race, ethnicity, gender and poverty) are also part of the discussion of social justice presented in approaches seeking higher states of social wellbeing, such as in sustainable development.

A number of scholars have also begun to stress the importance of incorporating equity as a key element in the discussion of climate change. Adger et al (2005) reassert the fact that the risks from climate change for present-day societies result from previous actions in disturbing the climate system, as discussed in the first part of this chapter. They also highlight the key role played by unequal distributions of power within the institutions that manage resources in creating and exacerbating vulnerabilities. For Adger et al, present-day adaptations often reinforce existing inequalities and do little to alleviate underlying vulnerabilities; thus measures to reduce poverty and increase access to resources could reduce vulnerability to climate variability and climate change. Thomas and Twyman (2005) also highlight the fact that climate change does not occur independently of other processes impacting upon poor societies, and draw attention to how the interface of climate change and development can enhance existing inequalities.

Attention has also been drawn to distributional issues of adaptation, recognizing possible externalities at other geographical and temporal scales (the second set of bidirectional flows presented in Figure 8.1). Adger et al (2005) highlight the risk that actions that are effective for one agent may produce negative externalities and spatial spillovers, potentially increasing impacts on others or reducing their capacity to adapt. (Similar concerns have been expressed before about development and sustainable development.) This underlines the importance of incorporating the consideration of contradictions, conflicts and imbalances within and among societies in the discussion of vulnerability, adaptation to climate change and urban sustainability.

Recent studies have emphasized this need. Tompkins and Adger (2005), for example, propose that any response to climate change must be cognizant of wider development pressures and goals, instead of focusing solely on single-system management. They highlight the relationships among assets, institutions and society, the role of cultural and regional differences among societies, and the importance of public policy in responses to different hazards and different types of climate change.

The above discussion underlines the need for institutional changes to respond to the challenges created by GEC and to enhance opportunities for urban sustainability (Evans, 2001, p275). Scientific contributions that provide a better understanding of the wider range of sustainable development challenges (including the socioeconomic, cultural and political aspects traditionally considered under the umbrella of development, as well as environmental issues embedded in biophysical processes at both the local and global scales) make an important contribution in this direction. However, the difference between understanding and acting is great (van den Hove, 2007), and institutional change should target both.

Institutional change can be a lengthy process (Spangenberg et al, 2002). A better understanding of responses to GEC (mitigation, vulnerability and adaptation) is required and the way these issues are introduced to stakeholders and decision-makers could be improved. Making explicit the connections between vulnerability and adaptation to current urban problems and urban sustainability can be an effective method of achieving this goal. The advantage of this approach is that it presents an integrated vision of urban sustainability that stakeholders and decision-makers can relate to their daily lives and areas of concern.

By the same token, institutions could play a significant role in helping urban systems to cope with, and adapt to, the negative consequences of GEC. Recent attention to the role of institutions in building sustainable development initiatives in urban areas provides a useful framework for this discussion (Button, 2002; Spangenberg et al, 2002). There are several research areas worth considering in this regard: bridging the gap between the domain of science and those of policy and practice in order to use available scientific knowledge in the design of adaptations to GEC and development policies (Hordijk and Baud, 2006); taking advantage of the attention to climate change to foster changes in institutions and better respond to the needs of society in the 21st century; generating governance processes that include a broader participation of civil society in opening opportunities for urban sustainability; and overcoming the reluctance and obstacles of institutions to change and updating their structure, focus and actions to meet the challenges of the 21st century.

CONCLUSION

This chapter began by stating that the destiny of societies is intrinsically linked to the growth of their urban areas. Ultimately, urban concentrations are not, per se, the prime source of environmental threats; they are simply the geographical space in which the contradictions in our pursuit of 'development', the social conflicts and relationships, and the clash between society and nature are expressed most intensely. The problems in cities are a reflection of the inequity within and among societies. Proposing alternatives for a better future (sustainable development) implies a process of social change.

This chapter seeks to contribute to a broader discussion of social change, recognizing the interactions of social and biophysical processes and their connections at different scales, from local to regional to global. Addressing the complex reality of cities in the 21st century – in conditions of growing socioeconomic disparities and the increasing negative impacts of GEC – creates challenges that should not continue to be neglected or addressed through fragmented actions. Sustainable development can be a useful tool in this direction. This chapter suggests a realistic approach to sustainable development by creating change through continuous learning and adaptation and institutional change. There is urgency in these changes: The size, scale and form of cities and their likely future growth trajectories will be critical to GEC and to the sustainability of societies.

NOTES

1   Peri-urbanization refers to a highly dynamic process whereby rural areas, both close to and increasingly distant from city centres, become enveloped by, or transformed into, extended metropolitan regions (Mbiba and Huchzermeyer, 2002; Aguilar et al, 2003). Land speculation often plays a large role in these gradual changes.
2   For a discussion of differentiated environmental impacts by city size and income level, see McGranahan et al (2005).

REFERENCES

Adger, W. N., Arnell, N. W. and Tompkins, E. V. (2005) 'Successful adaptation to climate change across scales', *Global Environmental Change*, vol 15, no 2, pp77–86

Aguilar, A. G., Ward, P. M. and Smith Sr., C. B. (2003) 'Globalization, regional development and mega-city expansion in Latin America: Analysing Mexico City's peri-urban hinterland', *Cities*, vol 20, no 1, pp3–21

Bai, X. (2007) 'Integrating global environmental concerns into urban management: The scale and readiness arguments', *Journal of Industrial Ecology*, vol 11, no 2, pp15–29

Bochaca, F. and Puliafito, E. (2007) 'Dry island effect on intermediate cities: The case of the city of Mendoza', in R. Sánchez-Rodríguez and A. Bonilla (eds) *Urbanization, Global Environmental Change and Sustainable Development in Latin America*, International Aluminum Institute, Instituto Nacional de Ecología and UNEP, Sao Jose de los Campos, Brazil, pp81–111

Bryant, R. V. and Wilson, G. A. (1998) 'Rethinking environmental management', *Progress in Human Geography*, vol 22, no 3, pp321–343

Burton, I., Huq, S., Lim, B., Pilifosova, O. and Schipper, E. (2002) 'From impacts assessment to adaptation priorities: The shaping of adaptation policy', *Climate Policy*, vol 2, no 2, pp145–159

Button, K. (2002) 'City management and environmental indicators', *Ecological Economics*, vol 40, no 2, pp217–233

Corbella, O. and Magalhaes, M. (2007) 'Conceptual differences between the bioclimatic urbanism for Europe and the tropical humid climate', *Renewable Energy*, vol 1, pp6–9

Cross, J. (2001). 'Mega-cities and small towns: Different perspectives on hazard vulnerability', *Global Environmental Change Part B: Environmental Hazards*, vol 3, no 2, pp63–80

Diamond, J. (2005) *Collapse: How Societies Choose to Fail or Succeed*, Viking Penguin, New York

Eaton, R. L., Hammond, G. P. and Laurie, J. (2007) 'Footprints on the landscape: An environmental appraisal of urban and rural living in the developed world', *Landscape and Urban Planning*, vol 83, no 1, pp13–28

Evans, P. (ed) (2001) *Liveable Cities? Urban Struggles for Livelihoods and Sustainability*, University of California Press, Los Angeles, CA

Few, R. (2007) 'Health and climate hazards: Framing social research on vulnerability, response and adaptation', *Global Environmental Change*, vol 17, no 2, pp281–295

Gibbs, D. and Jonas, A. (2000) 'Governance and regulation in local environmental policy: The utility of a regime approach', *Geoforum*, vol 31, no 3, pp299–313

Haines, A., Kovats, R. S., Campbell-Lendrum, D. and Corvalan, C. (2006) 'Climate change and human health: Impacts, vulnerability and public health', *Public Health*, vol 120, no 7, pp585–596

Hordijk, M. and Baud, I. (2006) 'The role of research and knowledge generation in collective action and urban governance: How can researchers act as catalysts?', *Habitat International*, vol 30, no 3, pp668–689

IPCC (2001) *Climate Change 2001: Impacts, Adaptation and Vulnerability: Summary for Policymakers and Technical Summary of the Working Group II Report*, Intergovernmental Panel on Climate Change, Geneva

Lopes de Souza, M. (2001) 'Metropolitan deconcentration, socio-political fragmentation and extended suburbanization: Brazilian urbanization in the 1980s and 1990s', *Geoforum*, vol 32, no 4, pp437–447

Luks, F. and Siebenhüner, B. (2007) 'Transdisciplinarity for social learning? The contributions of the German socio-ecological research initiative to sustainability governance', *Ecological Economics*, vol 63, nos 2–3, pp418–426

McGranahan, G., Marcotullio, P. J., Bai, X., Balk, D., Braga, T., Douglas, I., Elmquist, T., Rees, W., Satterthwaite, D., Songsore, J. and Zlotnik, H. (2005) 'Urban systems', in R. Hassan, R. Scholes and N. Ash (eds) *Ecosystems and Human Wellbeing: Current Status and Trends*, Millennium Ecosystem Assessment, Island Press, Washington, DC, pp795–825

McGranahan, G., Balk, D. and Anderson, B. (2007) 'The rising tide: Assessing the risks of climate change and human settlements in low elevation coastal zones', *Environment and Urbanization*, vol 19, no 1, pp17–37

Mbiba, B. and Huchzermeyer, M. (2002) 'Contentious development: Peri-urban studies in sub-Saharan Africa', *Progress in Development Studies*, vol 2, no 2, pp113–131

Mirza, M. (2003) 'Climate change and extreme weather events: Can developing countries adapt?', *Climate Policy*, vol 3, no 3, pp233–248

Mog, J. (2004) 'Struggling with sustainability: A comparative framework for evaluating sustainable development programmes', *World Development*, vol 32, no 12, pp2139–2160

Moser, C. and McIlwaine, C. (2005) 'Latin American urban violence as a development concern: Towards a framework for violence reduction', *World Development*, vol 34, no 1, pp89–112

Paavola, J. and Adger, W. N. (2006) 'Fair adaptation to climate change', *Ecological Economics*, vol 56, pp594–609

Pelling, M. (2003) *The Vulnerability of Cities: Natural Disasters and Social Resilience*, Earthscan, London

Petts, J., Owens, S. and Bulkeley, H. (2008) 'Crossing boundaries: Interdisciplinarity in the context of urban environments', *Geoforum*, vol 39, no 2, pp593–601

Pirez, P. (2002) 'Buenos Aires: Fragmentation and privatization of the metropolitan city', *Environment and Urbanization*, vol 14, no 1, pp145–158

Pritchett, L. and Woolcock, M. (2004) 'Solutions when the solution is the problem: Arraying the disarray in development', *World Development*, vol 32, no 2, pp191–212

Rosenzweig, C., Solecki, W., Parshall, L., Chopping, M., Pope, G. and Goldberg, R. (2005) 'Characterizing the urban heat island in current and future climates in New Jersey', *Global Environmental Change Part B: Environmental Hazards*, vol 6, pp51–62

Sánchez-Rodríguez, R., Seto, K. C., Simon, D., Soleki, W. D., Kraas, F. and Laumnan, G. (2005) *Science Plan: Urbanization and Global Environmental Change*, IHDP Report No 15, International Human Dimensions Programme on Global Environmental Change, Bonn, Germany

Satterthwaite, D. (2007) 'In pursuit of a healthy urban environment in low- and middle-income nations', in P. Marcotullio and G. McGranahan (eds) *Scaling Urban Environmental Challenges: From Local to Global and Back*, Earthscan, London

Spangenberg, J. H., Pfahl, S. and Deller, K. (2002) 'Towards indicators for institutional sustainability: Lessons from an analysis of Agenda 21', *Ecological Indicators*, vol 2, nos 1–2, pp61–77

Thomas, D. S. G. and Twyman, C. (2005) 'Equity and justice in climate change adaptation amongst natural-resources-dependent societies', *Global Environmental Change*, vol 15, no 2, pp115–124

Tol, R. S. J., Downing, T. E., Kuik, O. J. and Smith, J. B. (2004) 'Distributional aspects of climate change impacts', *Global Environmental Change*, vol 14, no 3, pp259–272

Tompkins, E. L. and Adger, W. N. (2005) 'Defining response capacity to enhance climate change policy', *Environmental Science and Policy*, vol 8, no 6, pp562–571

Tratalos, J., Fuller, R. A., Warren, P. H., Davies, R. G. and Gaston, K. (2007) 'Urban form, biodiversity potential and ecosystem services', *Landscape and Urban Planning*, vol 83, no 4, pp308–317

Van den Hove, S. (2007) 'A rationale for science–policy interfaces', *Futures*, vol 39, no 7, pp807–826

Wisner, B. (2004) 'Assessment of capability and vulnerability', in G. Bankoff, G. Frerks and D. Hilhorst (eds) *Mapping Vulnerability: Disasters, Development and People*, Earthscan, London, pp183–194

9

Risks of Climate Change for Urban Settlements in Low Elevation Coastal Zones

Gordon McGranahan, Deborah Balk and Bridget Anderson

INTRODUCTION

This chapter focuses on urban settlements in low elevation coastal zones (LECZs) and the risks that climate change poses for their growing populations.[1] In order to help assess these risks, the settlement patterns of populations living in areas that are less than 10 metres above sea level and contiguous to the coast are examined. Urban settlement is central to this analysis since coastal areas tend to be more urban than inland areas, and urbanization can contribute to the movement of populations towards the coast.

Climate change is expected to increase the risks of flooding and storm damage that are associated with living in LECZs. Mitigating climate change may be the best means of preventing these risks, but it is too late to rely solely on mitigation. Preventing excessive migration into LECZs that are prone to climate-related hazards will therefore be important. Out-migration, or at least movement within LECZs, will be necessary in some areas, although this can be costly and difficult to implement without causing severe disruptions. Modification of the prevailing forms of coastal settlement in order to protect local residents will also be needed.

In addition to being at risk from coastward hazards, littoral populations can be a burden on coastal ecosystems, many of which are already under stress. As has been shown elsewhere, coastal systems are more densely populated, in both urban and rural areas, than any of the other zones defined for the Millennium

Ecosystems Assessment – except for the urban systems themselves (McGranahan et al, 2005). This is a further reason for monitoring and adapting coastal settlements, particularly since, in some circumstances, the loss of ecosystem services can make urban settlements more prone to disaster, amplifying the risks of climate change.

Despite the spatial nature of urban development – and its relation to environmental conditions such as coastal hazards – urbanization is often analysed without a spatially explicit framework (Montgomery et al, 2003). Previous studies using moderate-resolution spatial data have shown that, historically, populations have preferred to live within 100 kilometres of coasts and near major rivers (Small and Nicholls, 2003; Small and Cohen, 2004). But a systematic global assessment of urban areas in a narrower coastal band – in other words those at risk from events related to climate change – has not been undertaken. The study reported on in this chapter, however, has started to fill that gap and begins to examine the implications of urban coastal settlement for vulnerability to climate change. It integrates recently constructed, spatially explicit global databases (CIESIN et al, 2006; ISciences, 2003) and analyses them to assess the distribution of population and settlement size in LECZs.

This chapter first examines the critical issues involving urban settlement in LECZs and the risks of climate change. It then reviews the methodology used for data integration and analysis. The findings are presented for different groups of countries (for example by region and by economic status) and for some of the countries with particularly large populations or population shares in LECZs. For China and Bangladesh, some of the changes between 1990 and 2000 are presented. The chapter ends with a summary discussion, emphasizing some of the implications of these findings.

COASTAL RISKS, URBANIZATION AND CLIMATE CHANGE

Though cities are distributed widely, coastal ecosystems are disproportionately urban (McGranahan et al, 2005). Urban disasters and environmental hotspots are already located disproportionately in coastal areas (Pelling, 2003; Dilley et al, 2005). Climate change will exacerbate both, even as urbanization and declining agricultural employment continue to draw people towards the coasts. Rising sea levels will increase the risk of floods, and stronger tropical storms may further increase the hazard. Low-income urban groups living on flood plains are already at risk and are especially vulnerable both to climate-related hazards and to disruptive evictions. Fragile ecosystems are also vulnerable both to climate change and to human responses to climate change. Prevailing economic incentives fail to reflect the environmental risks of coastal settlement. This, combined with the long lead times required to alter both climatic and demographic processes, makes it important to act now, even in areas where the risks have not yet started to rise. Adapting the forms of local settlements is also likely to be less costly if undertaken early, although, given existing uncertainties, some measures may be rendered inappropriate or soon become obsolete.

Coastal locations and human settlement

Human populations have long been drawn to coastal locations, which provide many resources and trading opportunities, even though they expose residents to various hazards. Historically, the attraction of coasts has been particularly strong among trading nations, and the recent expansion of international trade – and the continuing decline in agricultural employment – has also contributed to population movements towards the coast. China's ongoing economic boom, for example, is one of the clearest examples of trade-related coastward movement, although one could argue that government economic policies have been as important as market pressures in causing this (Han and Yan, 1999; McGranahan and Tacoli, 2006).

Environmental damage and climate-related risks

The concentration of populations and economic activities on and near the coast has had serious environmental consequences. Urban systems have radically altered the flows of water, energy and materials, transforming the pre-existing ecosystems (Rakodi and Treloar, 1997; Timmermann and White, 1997). The review of coastal systems undertaken for the Millennium Ecosystem Assessment concluded that these ecosystems, both onshore and offshore, are both among the most productive in the world and among those most threatened by human settlement (Agardy et al, 2005). Moreover, many coastal populations are at risk from flooding – particularly when high tides combine with storm surges and/or high river flows. Between 1994 and 2004, about one-third of the 1562 flood disasters and half of the 120,000 people killed and 98 per cent of the 2 million people affected by them were in Asia, where there are large population agglomerations in the flood plains of major rivers (for example the Ganges–Brahmaputra, Mekong and Yangtze) and in cyclone-prone coastal regions (for example the Bay of Bengal, the South China Sea, Japan and the Philippines) (Few and Matthies, 2006).

Poorly managed urban development

Some features of urban development increase the risk of flooding. Water drains more rapidly from built-over land, increasing peak flows. In many parts of the world, developers have drained wetlands, which sometimes reduces malaria prevalence or opens up valuable land for urban development, but which also removes a buffer against tidal floods. Particularly in delta regions, land compaction, subsidence due to groundwater withdrawal and reductions in the rate of sediment deposition (due to water regulation) can lead, in effect, to sea-level rise (Ericson et al, 2006). When urban planning ignores or works against the worst-off residents, they are likely to be made especially vulnerable. In cities of low-income countries, poor people are often forced (implicitly or explicitly) to settle in flood plains or other hazard-prone locations, as they cannot afford more suitable alternatives (Hardoy et al, 2001). However, even in New Orleans sharp inequalities were evident (Dreier, 2006).

Climate change exacerbates coastal risks

As noted in the literature, climate change will increase the risk of flooding, as well as causing other environmental damage in coastal areas (Nicholls, 2002; Klein et al, 2003; Nicholls et al, 2007). The estimates of sea-level rise in the Special Report on Emissions Scenarios of the Intergovernmental Panel on Climate Change (IPCC) range from 22 centimetres to 34 centimetres between 1990 and the 2080s (Nicholls, 2004). Far faster sea-level rise (more than a metre per century) could result from accelerated melting of the Greenland ice sheet or the collapse of the West Antarctic ice sheet, although this is not considered likely during the 21st century (Nicholls et al, 2007). It has been estimated that, in the absence of any other changes, a sea-level rise of 38 centimetres would increase fivefold the number of people affected by storm surges (Nicholls et al, 1999).

Economic incentives and the environmental risks of coastal settlement

Few of the environmental disadvantages of coastal urbanization are reflected in the economic incentives that drive urban development. Moreover, the economic advantages typically ascribed to urban agglomeration are based primarily on the benefits that come from the clustering of people and enterprises and only secondarily on the natural features that make some locations more attractive than others (Fujita et al, 1999; Fujita and Thisse, 2002; Henderson and Thisse, 2004). Most urban infrastructure is immobile and long-lasting, making rapid shifts in location very costly. Moreover, successful urban settlements tend to become nodes of growth, attracting more enterprises and people. As a result, urban settlement is highly path-dependent; thus urban coastal settlement past and present is likely to attract more urban coastal settlement in the future.

Early action is critical

Both climatic change and population movements are long-term, cumulative processes that are far more easily shifted slowly than rapidly. The IPCC predicts that anthropogenic warming and sea-level rise will continue for centuries even if greenhouse gas concentrations are stabilized (IPCC, 2007). The sooner emissions can be reduced, however, the better. Somewhat similarly, past urban development and demographic trends influence the direction of population movements well into the future. Timely measures to prevent urban development in risky locations are therefore critical, especially since adapting infrastructure in existing settlements is extremely expensive if it has to be undertaken rapidly.

Migration can be an effective response to climate change

The risks to human settlements could be reduced if people and enterprises could be encouraged to move away from the coast, or at least from the most risk-prone coastal locations (this would also reduce the pressures human settlements place on coastal ecosystems). Unfortunately, current population movements are in the opposite direction. Given the character of urban development, and that the factors driving coastward movement are still poorly understood, turning these flows around is likely to be slow, costly or both. In particular, there is the danger that ill-considered or politically short-sighted measures to shift population from coastal areas will impose unnecessary economic costs on key enterprises in those areas and fail to provide the basis for viable alternatives inland or in more appropriate coastal locations. A better understanding of the causes of urban change and more appropriate interventions and policies are sorely needed, and the earlier the better.

Effective adaptation of existing coastal settlements is inherently local

While mitigation can be undertaken anywhere in the world, and migrants can move away from high-risk locations, most adaptation is inherently localized to the threatened settlements. As noted in a recent report:

> *Adaptation to climate change requires local knowledge, local competence and local capacity within local governments. It needs households and community organizations with the knowledge and capacity to act. It also requires a willingness among local governments to work with lower-income groups.* (Satterthwaite et al, 2007, pviii)

Climate change risks vary widely among different coastal settlements or even among residents of a single settlement. Many of these can be reduced by more appropriate land-use patterns and a greater capacity to relocate residential and commercial activities economically and equitably. Urban planning needs to facilitate and, in some cases, regulate this process. The current failure of urban planning agencies or urban land markets to address land distribution economically or equitably, and the resulting tendency for a large share of the population in many urban centres to live in housing of questionable legality, is a major obstacle to adaptation to climate change.

National and international support and information for local adaptation

Adaptation involves very different measures from those required for mitigation, and there is no reason to link the two or to make support for adaptation conditional on mitigation. Given the extremely unequal international contributions to greenhouse gas emissions historically, however, international funding for local adaptation is imperative (Roberts and Parks, 2007). Thus, assessing the risks of climate change not only to target national, regional and local policy efforts but also to mount international responses is crucial.

THE INTERNATIONAL DISTRIBUTION OF URBAN SETTLEMENT IN LECZS

This section examines the distribution of human settlement in LECZs. The populations and land areas assessed are estimated using the methods summarized in Box 9.1 and described in more detail in the article on which this chapter is based (McGranahan et al, 2007).

BOX 9.1 METHODOLOGY FOR ESTIMATING URBAN AND RURAL POPULATIONS IN THE LOW ELEVATION COASTAL ZONE[2]

Defining LECZs

LECZs are defined as land area under 10 metres in altitude (above the middle of the tide) and contiguous with the coastline. The 10-metre cut-off was chosen over smaller elevations to avoid implying greater precision in our estimates than current data can provide. It does not and should not be taken to suggest that everyone living in such zones is at risk. The sea level is not expected to increase by anything like 10 metres in the foreseeable future. Tides, storm surges, subsidence, saline intrusion and various other processes will combine to ensure that the maximum altitude of impact is several metres higher than the metres (or fractions of a metre) of sea-level rise resulting from climate change. There will also be economic and social consequences for people living in the vicinity of physically affected areas. However, neither the physical impacts on coastal settlement nor their social and economic consequences will be confined to a clearly identifiable altitude or to the same altitude in different coastal locations. Combined with the inaccuracies in even the best international estimates of elevation and the spatial distribution of population, this makes it difficult to justify using a cut-off of less than 10 metres. In short, while the LECZ represents an area where the coastal risks of climate change should be taken seriously, the LECZ boundary does not represent a well-defined risk threshold. As with most global studies, in any given locality, local data and information could be used to provide refined estimates.

Estimating the urban and rural land areas and populations in LECZs

This study integrates recently developed spatial databases of (1) finely resolved global population distribution, (2) urban extents and (3) elevation data to produce country-level estimates of urban land area and population in LECZs. By overlaying geographic data layers, the urban and rural populations and land areas inside and outside of LECZs are calculated for every country and then used to calculate summary statistics. Shuttle Radar Topography Mission (SRTM) data were used to delineate the LECZs, including the land area contiguous with the coast up to 10 metres in elevation. Urban extents were taken from the Global Rural–Urban Mapping Project (GRUMP) of Columbia University's Center for International Earth Science Information Network. These urban extents were primarily delineated using the US National Oceanic and Atmospheric Administration's night-time lights satellite data (city lights 1994–1995), verified with additional settlement information, and represent urban agglomerations including surrounding suburban areas. Population and land area were also taken from GRUMP, which provides these data as gridded surfaces based on geo-referenced census data. Population is allocated to rural areas or, in the case of urban populations, to its identified urban extent. All data are expressed at 1km resolution. Figure 9.1 illustrates the spatial overlap of urban extents and the LECZ in southern Viet Nam.

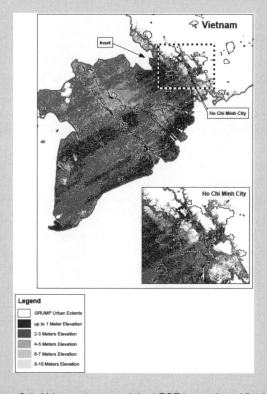

Figure 9.1 *Urban extents and the LECZ in southern Viet Nam*

Source: Figure from McGranahan et al (2007), updated using finer resolution (90-metre) elevation data.

Table 9.1 *Population densities inside and outside LECZs,
by region, 2000*

	Population density in LECZ (Persons/km²)	Population density outside of LECZ (Persons/km²)	Average population density (Persons/km²)
Africa	293	25	27
Asia	529	106	118
Europe	103	31	33
Latin America	73	23	24
Australia and New Zealand	22	3	3
North America	44	16	17
Small Island States (SIS)	98	132	126
World	235	43	47

Source: Based on LECZ data generated from GRUMP for McGranahan et al (2007).

Regional differences

Overall, LECZs contain some 2 per cent of the world's land and 10 per cent of its population, based on estimates for 2000. As illustrated in Table 9.1, the population densities within LECZs are higher than those outside them in all regions except for the small island states.

Of about 630 million people living in LECZs, 360 million are urban. This implies an urbanization level of 60 per cent, compared to a world urbanization level of slightly less than 50 per cent. In somewhat different terms, LECZs include 10 per cent of the world's population and 13 per cent of its urban population. Table 9.2 presents the urban and rural populations and land areas in the LECZs, along with the shares that these figures represent.

Asia accounts for about one-third of the world's land in LECZs, but, because of far higher population densities, it accounts for two-thirds of the urban population and almost three-quarters of the total population in the LECZs. The region with the highest share of its total land area in the LECZ is, not unexpectedly, the Small Island States, with about 16 per cent – about eight times the world average.[3] What is more surprising is that the share of the total population of the Small Island States that are in the LECZ is, at 13 per cent, only 3 per cent above the world average, while the urban population share, also at 13 per cent, is the same as the world average. By way of contrast, Africa, the only region with as little as 1 per cent of its land in the LECZ and with one of the lowest population shares in the LECZ, has 12 per cent of its urban population there.

While more affluent countries tend to be more urban, and urban settlements are more likely to be on the coast, there is no indication that these regions have

Table 9.2 *Population and land area in the LECZ, by region, 2000*

Region	Population and land area in LECZ				Share of population and land area in LECZ			
	Population (millions)		Land (000 km²)		Population (%)		Land (%)	
	Total	Urban	Total	Urban	Total	Urban	Total	Urban
Africa	56	31	191	15	7	12	1	7
Asia	466	238	881	113	13	18	3	12
Europe	50	40	490	56	7	8	2	7
Latin America	29	23	397	33	6	7	2	7
Australia and New Zealand	3	3	131	6	13	13	2	13
North America	24	21	553	52	8	8	3	6
Small Island States	6	4	58	5	13	13	16	13
World	634	360	2,700	279	10	13	2	8

Source: McGranahan et al (2007), p23.

a higher share of their populations in the LECZ (this is covered in more detail in McGranahan et al, 2007). There are marked differences in the population shares of the LECZ of two politically important income-related groups engaged in climate change negotiations: the least developed countries (LDCs) – 50 very low-income countries whose economic status is explicitly recognized as making them particularly vulnerable – and the 30 mostly high-income countries of the Organisation for Economic Co-operation and Development (OECD). The differences, however, are the opposite from what one might expect. The LDC group has a particularly high share of both its total population and urban population in the LECZ (14 and 21 per cent respectively), despite a comparatively modest land share (1.2 per cent). OECD countries, in contrast, only have 10 per cent of their overall population and 11 per cent of their urban population, with about 2.8 per cent of the land, in the LECZ. This result is largely due to Bangladesh, an LDC with an extremely large population in the LECZ, and may well reflect the importance of accidents of geography.

Countries with the largest urban populations or urban population shares in the LECZ

The countries that rank highest in the size of their urban population in the LECZ (see Table 9.3) are mostly countries that also rank high in their overall urban population. Indeed, four of the top five countries – China, India, Japan and the US – rank in the top five in terms of overall urban population. Indonesia is also highly ranked: with the fourth largest urban population in the LECZ, it has the eighth largest urban population overall. By way of contrast, most of the countries with

Table 9.3 *Ranking of countries with the largest urban population counts and shares in the LECZ, 2000*

Top ten	Ranked by urban population in the LECZ			Ranked by share of urban population in the LECZ		
	Country	Urban population in the LECZ		Country[4]	Urban population in the LECZ	
		counts (000)	% of urban in LECZ		counts (000)	% of urban in LECZ
1	China	78,278	18	Suriname	291	98
2	India	31,515	10	Guyana	249	93
3	Japan	29,022	26	Bahamas	214	87
4	Indonesia	22,721	28	Netherlands	10,126	76
5	US	20,282	9	Bahrain	450	76
6	Bangladesh	15,429	50	Viet Nam	12,862	74
7	Viet Nam	12,862	74	Thailand	12,471	60
8	Thailand	12,472	60	Liberia	291	60
9	Egypt	11,262	24	Senegal	2353	53
10	Netherlands	10,126	76	Djibouti	274	52

Source: Based on LECZ data generated from GRUMP for McGranahan et al (2007).

large urban shares in the LECZ have very small urban populations. The exceptions are The Netherlands, Viet Nam, Thailand and Senegal, for all of which the urban population in the LECZ not only accounts for more than half their total urban population but also for millions of people. Combined with Bangladesh, where about half of the country's urban population is in the LECZ, these countries would appear to pose special challenges, and it is notable that all but The Netherlands are low- or lower-middle-income countries.

Distribution of settlements of different sizes

Just as the LECZ has a greater share of the world's urban population than of its rural population, it also contains a greater share of large urban settlements (and their inhabitants) than of small urban settlements. As illustrated in Figure 9.2 and Table 9.4, however, while the share of settlements intersecting the LECZ increases sharply with settlement size, the share of the population in the zone increases more gradually. Thus, for the world as a whole, the share of settlements intersecting the LECZ increases steadily from 13 per cent among urban settlements with populations under 100,000 to 65 per cent among cities of over 5 million. By contrast, over the same range, the share of population living in the LECZ only increases from 7 to 21 per cent. These tendencies are evident in most regions and illustrate the dangers of focusing on large cities simply because they are more likely

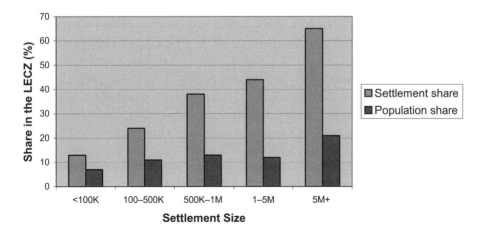

Figure 9.2 *The shares of urban centres intersecting the LECZ and of urban populations residing in the LECZ, by urban settlement size*

Source: Based on Tables 5 and 6 in McGranahan et al (2007), pp30–31.

Table 9.4 *Shares of urban centres intersecting the LECZ and shares of urban populations residing in the LECZ, by urban settlement size and region*

Region	<100K		100–500K		500K–1M		1–5M		>5M	
	A	B	A	B	A	B	A	B	A	B
Africa	9	5	23	15	39	20	50	18	40	10
Asia	12	8	24	13	37	14	45	16	70	32
Europe	17	6	22	7	37	11	41	6	58	12
Latin America	11	6	25	8	43	12	38	7	50	6
Australia and New Zealand	44	16	77	20	100	26	100	10	NA	NA
North America	9	4	19	7	29	6	25	5	80	13
Small Island States	51	18	61	11	67	13	100	12	NA	NA
World	13	7	24	11	38	13	44	12	65	21

Note: A: share of urban centres in the size category intersecting the LECZ;
B: share of total urban population in the size category living in the LECZ.
Source: Based on Tables 5 and 6 in McGranahan et al (2007), pp30–31.

to intersect the coastal lowlands: as one would expect, large cities that intersect the coastal lowlands tend to have a smaller share of their population in the LECZ than do smaller urban centres.

CHANGES IN LOW ELEVATION COASTAL SETTLEMENT BETWEEN 1990 AND 2000: THE EXAMPLES OF CHINA AND BANGLADESH

China is the country with the largest population in the LECZ, and Bangladesh has the third largest. Moreover, China is one of the more rapidly urbanizing countries, with particularly fast urban growth along the coast, while Bangladesh contains one of the most populous delta regions in the world and already has almost half (46 per cent) of its population in the LECZ. The settlement patterns in both of these countries raise serious concerns about the need for adaptation to climate change to start as soon as possible.

As illustrated in Table 9.5, in both Bangladesh and China, the population in the LECZ grew at almost twice the national rate between 1990 and 2000. Moreover, in both countries, the urban populations in the LECZ grew particularly rapidly. Indeed, the urban population growth in China's LECZ was more than three times the national rate, although the GRUMP estimates of China's urbanization rate for the period are lower than the estimates from the United Nations and the Chinese census (see note 44 in McGranahan et al, 2007).

Thus, even as the seaward hazards associated with climate change are increasing, the areas most at risk are experiencing particularly high population growth. Some of this may be due to urbanization, but the predominantly rural population of Bangladesh's LECZ is growing at an even faster rate than the country's urban average. The movement towards the coast in China is linked to urbanization, but it is also being driven by a trade-oriented economic strategy and policies that favour urban development along the coast.

China's rapid urbanization and coastward population movement, and the economic liberalization and growth that are driving these demographic trends,

Table 9.5 *Urban population counts and growth between 1990 and 2000 for China and Bangladesh, by total and in the LECZ*

Country	Population (000)		Annual growth rate
	1990	2000	1990–2000
China	1,138,676	1,262,334	1.04
Urban	336,577	423,730	2.33
LECZ	119,103	143,880	1.91
Urban LECZ	56,059	78,278	3.39
Bangladesh	110,024	123,612	1.17
Urban	23,097	26,865	1.52
LECZ	50,568	62,524	2.14
Urban LECZ	11,686	15,429	2.82

Source: McGranahan et al (2007), p32.

date back to the early 1980s (McGranahan and Tacoli, 2006). The geographical advantages of coastal development have been enhanced by the creation of special economic zones in coastal locations. It has been estimated that the advantages conferred by geography were about equal to those conferred by preferential policies (Demurger et al, 2002 and 2004). By amplifying the advantages of coastal settlement through their special economic zones, China has not only attracted more people to the coast but is establishing an urban structure that will continue to attract people there far into the future.

Overall, the risks of climate change are clearly far more threatening and intractable for Bangladesh than for China. Only about one-fiftieth of China's land area is in the LECZ, compared to more than two-fifths of Bangladesh's. Nevertheless, China, too, faces potentially serious threats, the evolution of which depends on policy agendas that do not as yet treat climate change as a serious issue.

Summary Discussion

From an environmental perspective, there is a double disadvantage to excessive coastal settlement. First, uncontrolled coastal development is likely to damage sensitive and important ecosystems and other resources. Second, coastal settlement, particularly in the lowlands, is likely to expose residents to hazards such as sea-level rise and tropical storms, both of which will probably become more serious with climate change. Yet the LECZ is more densely settled and urban than inland areas. Moreover, there is a legitimate concern that continued urbanization will draw still greater populations and population shares into the LECZ.

Looking to the future, the responses to the growing risks to coastal settlements should include mitigation, migration and modification. To avoid severe disruptions, measures for each of these need a long lead time. As the effects of climate change become increasingly clear, the location of coastal settlements most at risk should also become evident. Unfortunately, by that time, most of the easier options for shifting settlement patterns, and modifying them so that they are better adapted to the hazards of climate change, will have been foreclosed. Large companies may be able to shift the location of their activities relatively quickly, using the same procedures that have allowed them to adapt to economic globalization. Others will not find it so easy. Moreover, it is already evident that settlements in the coastal lowlands, and particularly those in low-income countries and those also at risk from tropical storms, are especially vulnerable.

Particularly as the need for action becomes more urgent, care will be needed to prevent government responses themselves from being inequitable or unnecessarily disruptive economically. Economically successful urbanization is typically based on the decentralized decisions of economic enterprises and families, supported by their governments. When governments try to decide centrally where urban development should occur or where people should migrate, a range of political interests can intrude, favouring economically unviable locations and/or land-use regulations that are particularly burdensome to the urban poor. Adaptation cannot be left to the market, but nor should it be left to arbitrary central planning.

In many cases, there may be measures that can address present problems while also providing a means of adapting to climate change. These are an obvious place to start, even if such coincidences of interest are unlikely to be sufficient to form the basis for all of the adaptive measures needed.

At the national level, measures to support previously disfavoured inland urban settlements, away from the large cities on the coast, might not only reduce risks from climate change but also support a more balanced and equitable pattern of urban development. In China, for example, giving inland urban settlements the support needed to redress the imbalance caused by the creation of special economic zones along the coast would not only help reduce coastward migration but would also reduce the increasingly severe regional inequalities that threaten China's national integrity.

Alternatively, among coastal settlements in low-income countries, those that find more equitable means to resolve the land problems that so often push their poorest urban residents to settle informally on unserviced and environmentally hazardous land (such as flood plains) will also be in a far better position to adapt to the risks of climate change. More generally, measures that support more efficient and equitable resolution of existing land issues are likely to provide a better basis for addressing the land issues brought on by climate change.

Vulnerable settlements in low-income countries clearly deserve international support in these and other measures to adapt to climate change. If climate change were simply an unfortunate accident of nature, such support could be justified on ethical grounds. In fact, climate change is closely associated with the past and present lifestyles of high-income groups in high-income countries. This makes it doubly important that the governments of these countries contribute to adaptation as well as to mitigation. It also implies that this assistance for adaptation should be viewed as additional to, rather than as part of, conventional development aid. Furthermore, assistance which responds to existing local needs, contributes to other development goals and can be locally driven is the most likely to succeed.

NOTES

1   This is an abridged version of our *Environment and Urbanization* article (McGranahan et al, 2007), edited and in some places added to so as to focus the presentation more directly on the principal themes of this book. A significant part of the text is taken from the article verbatim, or with only minor modifications, but the article is only cited when it includes materials that have not been reproduced in this chapter. Where tables are reproduced from the article, the article is given as the source, while unsourced tables are from the same data set but were not included in the original.

2   More details on the methodology can be found in McGranahan et al (2007). For access to the data and related publications, see CIESIN (undated).
3   For the purposes of Tables 9.1, 9.2 and 9.4, this group has 65 members, 32 of which are not listed as Small Island States in the IPCC regional listing.
4   Countries with an urban population of less than 100,000 were excluded from this list.

References

Agardy, T., Alder, J., and Dayton, P. (2005) 'Coastal systems', in R. Hassan, R. Scholes and N. Ash, (eds) *Ecosystems and Human Wellbeing: Current Status and Trends: Findings of the Condition and Trends Working Group*, Millennium Ecosystem Assessment, Island Press, Washington, DC, pp513–549

CIESIN (undated) 'Low elevation coastal zone (LECZ): Urban–rural estimates', Socioeconomic Data and Applications Center, Center for International Earth Science Information Network, Columbia University, New York, http://sedac.ciesin.columbia.edu/gpw/lecz.jsp, last accessed 17 December 2007

CIESIN, IFPRI, World Bank and CIAT (2006) 'Global Rural–Urban Mapping Project (GRUMP), alpha version: Urban extents grids', Global Rural–Urban Mapping Project, Socioeconomic Data and Applications Center (SEDAC), Columbia University, Palisades, NY, http://sedac.ciesin.columbia.edu/gpw, last accessed February 2006

Demurger, S., Sachs, J. D., Woo, W. T., Bao, S. M. and Chang, G. (2002) 'The relative contributions of location and preferential policies in China's regional development: Being in the right place and having the right incentives', *China Economic Review*, vol 13, no 4, pp444–465

Demurger, S., Sachs, J. D., Woo, W. T., Bao, S. and Chang, G. H. (2004) 'Explaining unequal distribution of economic growth among China provinces: Geography or policy?', in A. Chen, G. G. Liu and K. H. Zhang (eds) *Urbanization and Social Welfare in China*, Ashgate, Aldershot, UK, pp269–306

Dilley, M., Chen, R. S., Deichmann, U., Lerner-Lam, A. L. and Arnold, M. (2005) *Natural Disaster Hotspots: A Global Risk Analysis*, World Bank, Washington, DC

Dreier, P. (2006) 'Katrina and power in America', *Urban Affairs Review*, vol 41, no 4, pp528–549

Ericson, J. P., Vorosmarty, C. J., Dingman, S. L., Ward, L. G. and Meybeck, M. (2006) 'Effective sea-level rise and deltas: Causes of change and human dimension implications', *Global and Planetary Change*, vol 50, nos 1–2, pp63–82

Few, R. and Matthies, F. (eds) (2006) *Flood Hazards and Health: Responding to Present and Future Risks*, Earthscan, London

Fujita, M. and Thisse, J-F. (2002) *Economics of Agglomeration: Cities, Industrial Location, and Regional Growth*, Cambridge University Press, Cambridge, UK

Fujita, M., Krugman, P. R. and Venables, A. (1999) *The Spatial Economy: Cities, Regions, and International Trade*, MIT Press, Cambridge, MA

Han, S. S. and Yan, Z. X. (1999) 'China's coastal cities: Development, planning and challenges', *Habitat International*, vol 23, no 2, pp217–229

Hardoy, J. E., Mitlin, D. and Satterthwaite, D. (2001) *Environmental Problems in an Urbanizing World*, Earthscan, London

Henderson, J. V. and Thisse, J-F. (eds) (2004) *Handbook of Regional and Urban Economics: Volume 4: Cities and Geography*, Elsevier North-Holland, Amsterdam

IPCC (2007) 'Summary for policymakers', in S. Solomon, D. Qin, M. Manning, Z. Chen, M. Marquis, K. B. Averyt, M. Tignor and H. L. Miller (eds) *Climate Change 2007: The Physical Science Basis. Contribution of Working Group I to the Fourth Assessment Report of the Intergovernmental Panel on Climate Change*, Cambridge University Press, Cambridge, United Kingdom and New York, NY

ISciences (2003) 'SRTM30 Enhanced Global Map: Elevation/Slope/Aspect' (release 1.0), ISciences, Ann Arbor, MI

Klein, R. J. T., Nicholls, R. J. and Thomalla, F. (2003) 'Resilience to natural hazards: How useful is this concept?', *Global Environmental Change Part B: Environmental Hazards*, vol 5, nos 1–2, pp35–45

McGranahan, G., and Tacoli, C. (2006) 'Rural–urban migration, urban poverty and urban environmental pressures in China', contribution to the China Council Task Force on Sustainable Urbanisation Strategies, International Institute for Environment and Development, London

McGranahan, G., Marcotullio, P. J., Bai, X., Balk, D., Braga, T., Douglas, I., Elmquist, T., Rees, W., Satterthwaite, D., Songsore, J. and Zlotnik, H. (2005) 'Urban systems', in R. Hassan, R. Scholes and N. Ash (eds) *Ecosystems and Human Wellbeing: Current Status and Trends*, Millennium Ecosystem Assessment, Island Press, Washington, DC, pp795–825

McGranahan, G., Balk, D. and Anderson, B. (2007) 'The rising tide: Assessing the risks of climate change and human settlements in low elevation coastal zones', *Environment and Urbanization*, vol 19, no 1, pp17–37

Montgomery, M. R., Stren, R., Cohen, B. and Reed, H. E. (eds) (2003) *Cities Transformed: Demographic Change and its Implications in the Developing World*, Panel on Urban Dynamics, National Research Council, National Academy Press, Washington, DC

Nicholls, R. J. (2002) 'Rising sea levels: Potential impacts and responses', in R. E. Hester and R. M. Harrison (eds) *Global Environmental Change*, Issues in Environmental Science and Technology, vol 17, Royal Society of Chemistry, Cambridge, pp83–107

Nicholls, R. J. (2004) 'Coastal flooding and wetland loss in the 21st century: Changes under the SRES climate and socioeconomic scenarios', *Global Environmental Change*, vol 14, no 1, pp69–86

Nicholls, R. J., Hoozemans, F. M. J. and Marchand, M. (1999) 'Increasing flood risk and wetland losses due to global sea-level rise: Regional and global analyses', *Global Environmental Change*, vol 9, supplement 1, ppS69–S87

Nicholls, R. J., Wong, P. P., Burkett V., Codignotto, J. O., Hay, J. E., McLean, R. F., Ragoonaden, S. and Woodroffe, C. D. (2007) 'Coastal systems and low-lying areas', in M. L. Parry, O. F. Canziani, J. P. Palutikof, P. J. van der Linden and C. E. Hanson (eds) *Climate Change 2007: Impacts, Adaptation and Vulnerability. Contribution of Working Group II to the Fourth Assessment Report of the Intergovernmental Panel on Climate Change*, Cambridge University Press, Cambridge, UK, pp315–356

Pelling, M. (2003) *The Vulnerability of Cities: Natural Disasters and Social Resilience*, Earthscan, London

Rakodi, C. and Treloar, D. (1997) 'Urban development and coastal zone management: An international review', *Third World Planning Review*, vol 19, no 4, pp401–424

Roberts, J. T. and Parks, B. C. (2007) *Climate of Injustice: Global Inequality, North–South Politics, and Climate Policy*, MIT Press, Cambridge, MA

Satterthwaite, D., Huq, S., Reid, H., Pelling, P. and Romero-Lankao, P. (2007) 'Adapting to climate change in urban areas: The possibilities and constraints in low- and middle-income nations', Human Settlements Discussion Paper, International Institute for Environment and Development, London

Small, C. and Cohen, J. (2004) 'Continental physiography, climate and the global distribution of human population', *Current Anthropology*, vol 45, no 2, pp269–277

Small, C. and Nicholls, R. J. (2003) 'A global analysis of human settlement in coastal zones', *Journal of Coastal Research*, vol 19, no 3, pp584–599

Timmermann, P. and White, R. (1997) 'Megahydropolis: Coastal cities in the context of global environmental change', *Global Environmental Change*, vol 7, no 3, pp205–234

10

Urbanization and Ecosystems: Current Patterns and Future Implications

Deborah Balk, Gordon McGranahan and Bridget Anderson[1]

INTRODUCTION

Much international assessment and reporting on urbanization and urban population trends falls into one of two camps. The first distinguishes urban and rural areas and populations and then reports and evaluates information about urban populations for larger political units, such as countries and continents, and globally (Satterthwaite, 2005; United Nations, 2006). The second focuses on particular urban areas or city-regions, and often includes spatial analysis of urban expansion. Special attention is often given to mega-cities (see, for example, Cohen 1993; Fujita and Thisse, 2002), but there are also case studies of urban settlements of all sizes. Something important is lost between these two approaches, especially when it comes to monitoring the environmental implications of urbanization. There is a need for a perspective of urbanization that is both spatial and global and allows the environmental settings of urbanization and urban growth to be considered at country, continental and global scales.

Human population is not uniformly distributed across physically (Small and Cohen, 2004), politically or economically defined regions. Urban areas are particularly unevenly distributed (Montgomery et al, 2003; McGranahan et al, 2005; United Nations, 2006). Of cities of 500,000 persons or more, most are located in low- and middle-income countries. Yet, within these countries, only 12 per cent of the urban population lives in 'mega-cities'. Further, the vast majority of urban centres are relatively small, with a quarter of the urban population living in cities of between 100,000 and 500,000 persons. Of large cities – those greater than 1 million persons – Asia has far more (over 180 as measured in 2000) than any other continent.

Urban settlements develop primarily because of the advantages associated with the clustering of people and markets and only secondarily because of the geographical attraction of particular locations (Fujita and Thisse, 2002; Henderson and Thisse, 2004). The geographical setting and ecological resources of urban locations can be critical, however. Not only can they affect the success of individual urban centres, but, in an increasingly urban world, the location of urban populations also has environmental significance at larger scales, including globally. This suggests the need to examine where urban settlements are growing, not only in economic and political terms, but also in geographical and ecological terms.

A major research programme – the Millennium Ecosystem Assessment – took a first pass at evaluating urban areas with respect to other ecologically defined areas (McGranahan et al, 2005). Ecosystems are the suppliers of 'ecosystem services', in other words benefits that individuals derive from ecosystems (Hassan et al, 2005). The locations of population clusters and markets are, undoubtedly, influenced by the paths through which these services and related products can be transported and distributed, though there has been little research on this relationship.

In this chapter, we extend the analysis of urban trends in the Millennium Ecosystem Assessment, placing particular emphasis on identifying the ecologically defined areas where urban growth and urbanization will take place if current trends continue. Environmental conditions and ecological services can also be expected to change over time, and climate change can be expected to have a major but differentiated influence on local conditions and services, which may in turn influence urban trends. Modelling such feedback is well beyond the scope of this chapter, however.

Ecosystems and Ecological Zones

Ecosystems can be identified at various scales and often resist mapping. An ecosystem can be defined as 'a dynamic complex of plant, animal and microorganism communities and the nonliving environment interacting as a functional unit' (Hassan et al, 2005, pvii). In reporting on ecosystem conditions and trends, the Millennium Ecosystem Assessment selected 10 reporting categories amenable to mapping: marine, coastal, inland water, forest, dryland, island, mountain, polar, cultivated and urban. For ease of presentation, we have chosen to call these reporting categories ecological zones.

Ecological zones differ in their dominant form, internal diversity and level of resources, as well as their extent and distribution across the Earth's land surface. The largest ecological zone in terms of land area is dryland (46 per cent), whereas the urban and coastal zones occupy a small fraction of the Earth's land area (3 per cent and 5 per cent respectively) (McGranahan et al, 2005, Table 27.4). These ecological zones are not mutually exclusive: coastal areas may also be cultivated or forested, for example. More directly relevant to this chapter, urban areas are embedded within or overlap all of the other land-based ecological zones, including the coastal zone.

An area's combined ecosystem characteristics, and how they are treated, influence the vulnerability of both the ecosystems (Kasperson et al, 2005) and the inhabitants that depend on them (Levy et al, 2005). Furthermore, ecological zones influence and are influenced by human settlement patterns. Different combinations of ecosystems provide living environments, ecosystem services and other natural resources that are more or less supportive of human habitation and economic activity. Coasts, for example, may provide easy access to other locations, and the points of overlap between inland and coastal zones can attract urban settlements that serve as nodes in long-distance trading systems. Agriculture, on the other hand, is typically associated with dispersed rural populations, although successful agricultural systems often support large urban populations, and when agriculture becomes more capital-intensive, rural population densities may fall. Industrial developments also both draw on and threaten ecosystem services, and, while most large industrial establishments are in or near urban centres, where there are large labour supplies, their location is also influenced by the resources and services available in the surrounding zone.

Data

In this chapter, urban ecological zones are considered in relation to seven other ecological zones: dryland, forest, mountain, inland water, cultivated, coastal and a more vulnerable coastal subset called a low elevation coastal zone (LECZ).[2] This analysis requires that all data are spatial. Several spatial databases form the basis for the descriptive analysis which follows, as shown in Table 10.1.

Method

The data in Table 10.1 combined to calculate the estimates of urban land area and population by ecosystem. The methodology is fairly simple: after aligning coastal boundaries, population and urban extents grids (raster data, expressed at 30 arc second resolution) overlay ecosystem grids to construct estimates of population and land area by the various ecosystems and are summarized by country and continents. This chapter adopts the same methods used in McGranahan et al (2005 and 2007) but also includes population estimates for 2025. To estimate future population, or even change in population from 1990–2000, in each ecosystem, we

Table 10.1 *Underlying data sources and concepts*

Category	Central concept	Boundary limits for mapping
		Ecosystem
Coastal *Hassan et al (2005)*	Interface between ocean and land, extending seawards to about the middle of the continental shelf and inland to include all areas strongly influenced by the proximity to the ocean.	Area between 50 metres below mean sea level and 50 metres above the high tide level or extending landward to a distance 100 kilometres from shore. Includes coral reefs, inter-tidal zones, estuaries, coastal aquaculture and seagrass communities.
Coastal, low elevation *McGranahan et al (2007)*	Same as 'coastal' but with emphasis on lower-lying coastal areas at risk of seaward hazards associated with climate change.	The contiguous area along the coast that is less than 10 metres above sea level.
Cultivated *Hassan et al (2005)*	Lands dominated by domesticated plant species, used for and substantially changed by crop, agroforestry or aquaculture production.	Areas in which at least 30 per cent of the landscape comes under cultivation in any particular year. Includes orchards, agroforestry and integrated agriculture–aquaculture systems.
Dryland *Hassan et al (2005)*	Lands where plant production is limited by water availability; the dominant uses are large mammal herbivory, including livestock grazing, and cultivation.	Drylands as defined by the Convention to Combat Desertification, i.e. lands where annual precipitation is less than two-thirds of potential evaporation, from dry sub-humid areas (ratio ranges 0.50–0.65) through semi-arid, arid and hyper-arid (ratio <0.05), but excluding polar areas; drylands include cultivated lands, scrublands, shrublands, grasslands, semi-deserts and true deserts.
Forest *Hassan et al (2005)*	Lands dominated by trees; often used for timber, fuelwood and non-timber forest products.	A canopy cover of at least 40 per cent by woody plants taller than 5 metres. The existence of many other definitions is acknowledged, and other limits (such as crown cover greater than 10 per cent, as used by the Food and Agriculture Organization of the United Nations) will also be reported. Includes temporarily cut-over forests and plantations; excludes orchards and agroforests where the main products are food crops.

Inland water *Hassan et al (2005)*	Permanent water bodies inland from the coastal zone, and areas whose ecology and use are dominated by the permanent, seasonal or intermittent occurrence of flooded conditions.	Rivers, lakes, flood plains, reservoirs and wetlands; includes inland saline systems. Note that the Ramsar Convention considers 'wetlands' to include both inland water and coastal categories.
Mountain *Hassan et al (2005)*	Steep and high lands.	As defined by Mountain Watch using criteria based on elevation alone, and, at lower elevations, on a combination of elevation, slope and local elevation range. Specifically, elevation >2500 metres; elevation 1500–2500 metres and slope >2 degrees; elevation 1000–1500 metres and slope >5 degrees or local elevation range (7 kilometres radius) >300 metres; elevation 300–1000 metres and local elevation range (7 kilometres radius) >300 metres; isolated inner basins and plateaus less than 25 square kilometres extent that are surrounded by mountains.
Demographic		
Population *CIESIN et al (2004)*	Population counts.	1km spatial database indicating the distribution of population based on census data corresponding to administrative and urban extent boundaries (GRUMP model).
Urban extents *CIESIN et al (2004)*	Footprints of urban areas.	1km spatial database indicating urban extents based primarily on National Oceanic Atmospheric Administration (NOAA)'s night-time lights 1994/1995 stable city lights data set.

Sources: Adapted from Millennium Ecosystem Assessment (2005), Chapter 2, Box 2.2, pp54–55; McGranahan et al (2007).

use a highly simplified method. The urban extents data – from the Global Rural–Urban Mapping Project (GRUMP, see CIESIN et al, 2004; Balk et al, 2005) – produce a single estimate for urban footprints, circa 1995, as the extents are largely based on the night-time light's stable city 1994/1995 composite database of the United States National Oceanic and Atmospheric Administration (Elvidge et al, 1997).[3]

The GRUMP model, though it produces estimates of population associated with each urban extent for 1990, 1995 and 2000, is not intended for change analysis. As a result, the base-year data – population estimates for 1995 coupled with the estimates of urban land area for 1995 – are interpolated forwards or backwards to the target years in this database using country-specific urban population estimates from the United Nations' *World Urbanization Prospects* (2006). To gain percentages of the population that are urban, the rural population is analogously estimated. Because the population of urban and rural areas in the base year as estimated by the GRUMP model are not the same as those in the UN database, the total and urban populations are then adjusted to match those of the UN's estimates for 2025.

The main disadvantage of this approach is that it assumes that all urban areas in a given country experience the same growth regardless of their ecosystem zone. Its strength is that, under the limitations of this transparent if oversimplifying assumption, it does reflect changes in settlement in different zones that result from urbanization itself, or from differential national rates of growth. Estimates that allow for changes in the shares of individual countries' rural and urban populations in the different ecological zones require additional data and methods that are not available at the present time. Readers are advised to consider the estimates of urbanization here as analogous to those typically reported for countries and to recognize that the full potential of spatial data integration has yet to be realized. The estimates of population in 2025 by ecosystem should, in particular, be considered a 'steady-state' scenario in which the only variant is national-level urban and rural growth.

Figure 10.1 shows both a classic view of urbanization – the share of the population of each continent that lives in an urban area – and a view from an ecosystem perspective. The upper panel clearly shows that the populations of Europe, Oceania and North and South America were about 70 per cent urban in 1990, whereas Asia and Africa were both less than 35 per cent urban, with increases by 2000 and projections to 2025 indicated. Even by 2025, the population of Asia and Africa is not expected to become as urban as the current population of Europe or the Americas.[4] In contrast, the ecosystem perspective (though it does not produce mutually exclusive groupings, in contrast to that of continents) shows that zones identified by their proximity to surface water have greater shares of population residing in urban areas than any other zone. Coastal systems, including the LECZ, are unambiguously the most urban zones, with the expectation that their populations will be close to 75 per cent urban by 2025 (also see Table 10.2). Mountain zones are the least urban, and, though they show quite a bit of

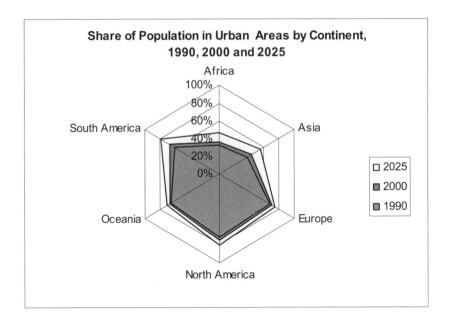

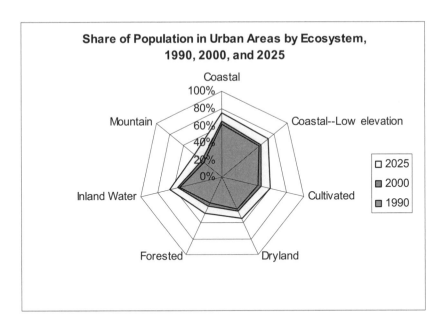

Figure 10.1 *Percentage of the population that is urban, shown by continent and ecological zone, 1990, 2000 and 2025 (projected)*

Sources: Population data are from GRUMP (Balk et al, 2005, CIESIN et al, 2004) and projected to 2025 with data from the UN (2006); ecosystem data are from the Millennium Ecosystem Assessment (described in Table 10.1; see also McGranahan et al, 2005).

Table 10.2 *Share of the population that is urban, 2000 and 2025 (in %)*

| System | 2000 | | | | | | |
	Africa	Asia	Europe	North America	Oceania	South America	World
Coastal	62	59	83	85	87	86	65
Coastal – low elevation	60	56	80	82	79	82	61
Cultivated	38	42	70	75	67	67	48
Dryland	40	40	66	78	49	61	45
Forested	21	28	53	64	36	53	37
Inland water	51	47	78	84	77	71	55
Mountain	21	27	46	50	11	54	32
Continent average	36	42	69	74	66	66	49

| | 2025 | | | | | | |
	Africa	Asia	Europe	North America	Oceania	South America	World
Coastal	73	70	87	89	90	92	74
Coastal – low elevation	71	68	85	86	83	90	71
Cultivated	48	55	75	81	72	80	59
Dryland	51	51	70	84	60	75	55
Forested	31	41	59	72	40	68	47
Inland water	62	58	82	88	80	83	64
Mountain	30	40	53	60	13	67	43
Continent average	47	55	75	80	70	78	59

Sources: Population data are from GRUMP (Balk et al, 2005, CIESIN et al, 2004) and projected to 2025 with data from the UN (2006); ecosystem data are from the Millennium Ecosystem Assessment (described in Table 10.1; see also McGranahan et al, 2005).

growth through to 2025, they remain much less urban than other ecosystems or continental groupings.

Ecological zones, perhaps obviously, are not evenly distributed across continents or smaller political units such as countries or provinces within countries: Africa, for example, contains one-third of the world's dryland, and its land area is about two thirds dryland (not shown). More than half of China (56 per cent) is covered by mountainous terrain, primarily in its central and western provinces, while northern China is predominantly dryland, which covers more than a third of the land area (39 per cent). Cultivated ecosystems in China cover approximately one-third (37 per cent) of the land area of China and are primarily concentrated in the eastern portion of the country, where there is no overlap with the extreme mountainous and dryland conditions.

The unequal distribution of resources among ecosystems and of ecosystems between countries implies that some countries will be constrained more than others in their associated distribution of human settlements.

PATTERNS IN HUMAN SETTLEMENT

In terms of human settlement, there are clear patterns. Coastal zones and inland water and, to a lesser extent, cultivated ecosystems are not only more densely populated, they are also more urban than mountain, forest or dryland ecosystems (McGranahan et al, 2005). Historically, their natural waterways have made them suitable for transportation, agriculture and trade. At a global scale, this is especially apparent for coastal systems. In 2000, close to two-thirds of the coastal population lived in an urban area, with slightly more than half (52 per cent) of those urban-dwellers living in an LECZ (see Table 10.2). Though the physical conditions that make rural livelihoods favourable may be quite different from those favouring urban systems (since urban-dwellers need not be primarily dependent on agriculture or fisheries, for example), it seems that the systems preferred for rural residence are also those where urban settlements develop. An open question for future research is whether this tendency can be expected to change as the production of food becomes increasingly efficient and industrialized and less dependent on in situ human labour (Rees, 2003). If it does change, what does this imply for rural residents of the more densely populated zones – will those rural areas transform into urban ones? Will rural population growth switch to zones where there are natural amenities that have more to do with living conditions than with livelihoods, as appears to be happening in the US (McGranahan, 1999)?

In Asia, by 2025, the urban population of coastal zones alone will equal that of urban coastal dwellers globally today. In Africa, while much of the population resides in relatively 'favourable' ecosystems such as cultivated inland water, or even forested systems, there are nevertheless many dryland urban-dwellers: 40 per cent of the urban population of Africa lived in dryland systems in 2000. Cultivated systems supported similarly large urban populations (134 million residents). By 2025, these populations will have more than doubled if national shares remain the same (Table 10.3). Forested and mountainous systems (which occupy a fairly large land area) did not support large urban populations in 2000, but these populations are expected to more than double by 2025. Inland water in Africa, with about 90 million urban residents in 2000, is expected to have over 200 million urban residents in 2025 – an overall rate of change that is higher than any other system in the continent and perhaps salient given the scarcity of water that is already a problem for agricultural production and livelihoods in many areas. Like other continents, Africa's coastal ecosystem supports the highest percentage of urban-dwellers (Table 10.2): already over 60 per cent and expected to be over 70 per cent by 2025.

Even when looking globally, as in Table 10.3 and Figure 10.2, it is obvious that the greatest number of urban persons live in cultivated zones. But that is a large zone in terms of land area, and it is necessary to focus on the level of urbanization (in other words the share of the population that is urban) in each zone as well. On every continent, coastal systems are more urbanized (see Figure 10.3 and Table

Table 10.3 *Population in urban areas (millions) in 2000 and 2025*

	Coastal	Coastal – low elevation	Cultivated	Dryland	Forest	Inland water	Mountain	Continental total
				2000				
Africa	59	34	134	137	37	91	39	294
Asia	458	276	1233	564	164	463	184	1577
Europe	99	40	405	124	79	116	40	504
North America	93	29	176	80	102	115	47	361
Oceania	11	3	4	1	4	5	0	20
South America	56	19	115	61	32	44	49	226
Total	776	401	2065	967	417	835	359	2982
				2025				
Africa	122	68	281	275	83	207	84	629
Asia	767	464	2057	983	252	788	300	2610
Europe	107	44	425	119	81	119	43	527
North America	125	39	238	109	142	155	72	497
Oceania	15	4	5	1	5	8	1	29
South America	86	30	184	102	53	72	81	366
Total	1223	649	3189	1590	617	1348	582	4656

Sources: Population data are from GRUMP (Balk et al, 2005, CIESIN et al, 2004) and projected to 2025 with data from the UN (2006); ecosystem data are from the Millennium Ecosystem Assessment (described in Table 10.1; see also McGranahan et al, 2005).

10.2). In 2000, both the coastal and LECZ had greater shares of urban population. This pattern persists through to 2025, though inland water systems increase in the urban percentages to come close to the proportions in coastal areas (Table 10.2). While these differences between all other systems and coastal systems now, and including inland water systems in the future, are apparent on all continents, they are most pronounced in Africa and Asia, the two continents expected to experience the greatest future urban growth.

The same disaggregation from continents to ecological zones can be done by country. In China, the world's most populous country, for example, the bulk of the population lives in the tropical and coastal zones in the east and south-east, where most of the large urban centres are also located (see Table 10.4). Over 85 per cent of China's urban land area and urban population is located in cultivated ecosystems. The most striking urban concentrations are in the coastal and LECZ, however.

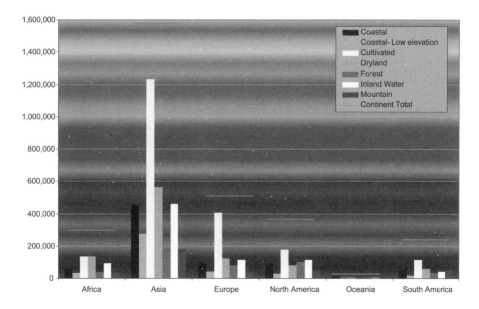

Figure 10.2 *Estimates of urban population (000s) in 2000, by continent and ecological zone*

Sources: Population data are from GRUMP (Balk et al, 2005, CIESIN et al, 2004); ecosystem data are from the Millennium Ecosystem Assessment (described in Table 10.1; see also McGranahan et al, 2005).

Table 10.4 *Percentage of total and urban land area and population in China in 2000*

	Land area		Population, 2000	
	% Total	% Urban	% Total	% Urban
Coastal	2	16	14	23
Cultivated	37	85	83	86
Dryland	39	35	27	31
Forest	21	16	23	14
Inland water	13	21	20	26
Low elevation coastal	2	13	11	18
Mountain	56	22	27	15

Sources: Population data are from GRUMP (Balk et al, 2005, CIESIN et al, 2004); ecosystem data are from the Millennium Ecosystem Assessment (described in Table 10.1; see also McGranahan et al, 2005).

With only about 2 per cent of the land area, the coastal zone contains 23 per cent of the urban population, as compared to 14 per cent of overall population. With even less land, the LECZ contains 18 per cent of the urban population. Moreover, these are comparatively dense urban settlements, as evident from the fact that the urban population shares are considerably higher than the urban land shares.

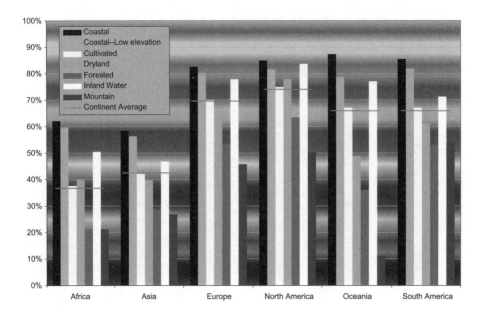

Figure 10.3 *Percentage of urban population in 2000, by continent and ecological zone*

Sources: Population data are from GRUMP (Balk et al, 2005, CIESIN et al, 2004); ecosystem data are from the Millennium Ecosystem Assessment (described in Table 10.1; see also McGranahan et al, 2005).

Urban population densities[5] are generally greatest in the coastal zone – even more so in the LECZs of Africa and Asia – and notably much more dense, on average, in the cities of Asia and Africa, where they exceed averages of more than 1100 persons per square kilometre, than on other continents (see Figure 10.4). Forested and mountainous cities tend to be the least dense everywhere, except in South America, where the densities are largely comparable. Though population concentrations confer benefits of efficiency (Chomitz et al, 2006), higher densities can also lead to congestion and higher exposure to pollutants, particularly if urban locations are not well managed (Montgomery et al, 2003). These concerns are amplified in Africa and the poorer countries of Asia.

Changes in urban population from 1990 to 2000, by ecosystem, are shown in Figure 10.5, with average annual rates given in Table 10.5 for selected intervals. It is evident that the least urban continents – Asia and Africa – experience the most rapid change. Perhaps more obvious than noteworthy, but insofar as Asia and Africa will experience urban growth in all ecosystems, new ways of assisting urban development will be required in all environments, taking into account the attributes unique to each ecosystem. That said, globally mountain ecosystems tend to experience the most rapid rates of change, exceeding that of most others (though

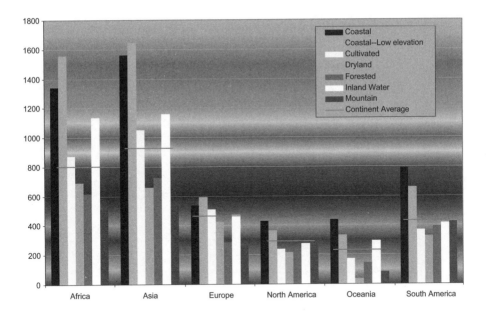

Figure 10.4 *Urban population density (persons per square kilometre) in 1995, by continent and ecological zone*

Sources: Population data are from GRUMP (Balk et al, 2005, CIESIN et al, 2004); ecosystem data are from the Millennium Ecosystem Assessment (described in Table 10.1; see also McGranahan et al, 2005).

only slightly in some instances). In Africa, forested zones appear to experience the most rapid rate of urban growth. Since mountain and forested cities are the least dense, it will be important to plan for growth in environmentally sustainable ways. In particular, Africa's forests are relatively scarce and vulnerable. Development that promotes increases in densities – given the relatively low starting levels – may be environmentally superior to strategies that maintain the relatively low levels of urban population density currently observed.

In higher-income continents, some changes are also noteworthy: when comparing across systems, greater than the average growth is found in the coastal and LECZs of Europe, and mountain systems in North America. One ecological zone, drylands in Europe, experiences urban population decline. The more vulnerable LECZs have a higher rate of annual growth than the coastal zone in general in the more developed, already highly urbanized continents of the Americas, Europe and Oceania, and in Asia. Only in Africa is the LECZ growing somewhat below the average rate of the other ecological zones.

Lastly, when examining urban trends by ecological zone, there is also the question of whether some zones are more likely to support large centres and others more likely to support smaller urban centres. About half of the urban population of

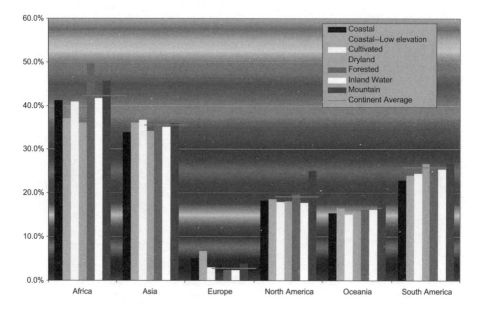

Figure 10.5 *Percentage change in urban population, 1990–2000, by continent and ecological zone*

Sources: Population data are from GRUMP (Balk et al, 2005, CIESIN et al, 2004); ecosystem data are from the Millennium Ecosystem Assessment (described in Table 10.1; see also McGranahan et al, 2005).

the world lives in urban centres of less than 500,000 persons (UN, 2006), but the highest rates of urban growth are expected to take place in these and other smaller cities (of less than one million persons). Urban centres of different sizes are not uniformly distributed, however. Nearly two-thirds of the urban population of the coastal zones live in cities of one million persons or more, and only 10 per cent of their urban-dwellers live in urban settlements of less than 100,000 persons. Urban residents in mountainous and forest ecosystems, on the other hand, are more likely to live in smaller urban centres: close to 60 per cent live in urban centres of less than one million persons. Thus large and very large cities are disproportionately found in coastal and LECZs. This, when combined with growth, may be an important consideration for local and regional planners.

IMPLICATIONS

This chapter has presented estimates of rates of urbanization and urban growth by ecological zone, as well as by continent. Continental, regional and country-level

Table 10.5 *Average annual rate of change of the urban population, 1990–1995 and 1995–2025 (%)*

	Coastal	Coastal – low elevation	Cultivated	1990–1995 Dryland	Forest	Inland Water	Mountain	Continental total
Africa	3.6	3.2	3.6	3.2	4.4	3.6	4.0	3.7
Asia	3.0	3.2	3.2	3.0	3.1	3.1	3.2	3.1
Europe	0.6	0.7	0.4	0.1	0.4	0.4	0.4	0.4
North America	1.7	1.8	1.7	1.7	1.9	1.7	2.3	1.8
Oceania	1.5	1.6	1.6	1.4	1.5	1.6	1.8	1.5
South America	2.1	2.2	2.3	2.5	2.3	2.3	2.6	2.3
Total	2.4	2.7	2.4	2.5	2.2	2.5	2.7	2.4

	Coastal	Coastal – low elevation	Cultivated	1995–2025 Dryland	Forest	Inland Water	Mountain	Continental total
Africa	2.9	2.8	3.0	2.8	3.4	3.3	3.2	3.1
Asia	2.2	2.2	2.2	2.3	1.9	2.3	2.1	2.2
Europe	0.4	0.4	0.2	-0.1	0.1	0.1	0.3	0.2
North America	1.3	1.3	1.3	1.3	1.4	1.3	1.8	1.3
Oceania	1.3	1.4	1.2	1.4	1.4	1.4	1.8	1.4
South America	1.8	1.9	1.9	2.1	2.0	2.0	2.0	2.0
Total	1.9	2.0	1.8	2.0	1.7	2.0	2.0	1.9

Sources: Population data are from GRUMP (Balk et al, 2005, CIESIN et al, 2004) and projected to 2025 with data from the UN (2006); ecosystem data are from the Millennium Ecosystem Assessment (described in Table 10.1; see also McGranahan et al, 2005).

views are significant, but ecological zones are more environmentally relevant. They take on special significance in light of changing environmental conditions and the possibility that urbanization trajectories will come into conflict with these environmental shifts.

Climate change is likely to challenge the suitability of existing settlement patterns and trends, not only because existing urban systems are dependent on fossil-fuel combustion and other processes emitting greenhouse gases, but also because many are ill-located and ill-adapted to alternative climate regimes. Sea-level rise and more severe storms are a particular concern to coastal settlements, and, as indicated above, coastal settlements are not only heavily populated but are highly urbanized. The implications of this are explored in more detail in Chapter 9 and have been explored for major ports in a recent report (Nicholls et al, 2007).

The possibility that some drylands will suffer reduced precipitation raises further concerns. Although the data presented here does not indicate that drylands are particularly densely settled or that their urban centres are growing particularly rapidly, a combination of increasing populations and declining water resources could easily create serious problems, as the total urban population of drylands is nearly one billion. Further research on settlement patterns in drylands is clearly warranted. In relation to both coastal settlements and drylands, however, it should be kept in mind that urbanization itself is unlikely to be the problem. Rather, the problem lies in forms of urbanization that neglect the changing environmental conditions upon which all urban development depends.

Unlike the scenarios presented here, where national urban and rural growth were not allowed to vary by ecosystem, a more refined model would take into account growth trajectories that permit ecosystem services to vary (deFries et al, 2005). Such an analysis might reveal different trends and point to different concerns. A fuller spatial analysis would be able to show the relationship between urban areas in neighbouring environments. It would allow for determining whether coastal cities grow more rapidly than, say, inland water or dryland cities, as well as whether urban networks of cities experience more growth if different environments (such as coastal and forest) are connected and share resources or if they are isolated (and thus perhaps conserve resources).

Further, the initial level of urbanization and city size may also affect the manner in which future urban growth will impact the underlying ecosystem resources. Urbanization in the next few decades will be much more rapid and concentrated in Asia and Africa. This urbanization will occur in many localities with low levels of economic development – little urban infrastructure, inadequate sanitation and water, and a lack of housing for the poor. Many of these urban residents currently face severe local environmental health problems, which have more to do with poverty and access to urban services than to the ecosystem regions where the urban areas are located. Addressing these existing concerns can be expected to become more complicated in the future. Asia, with many large deltaic regions, and Africa, with vast drylands, will face development challenges with very different ecosystem resources and constraints than those already experienced in the rest of the world. Planners and development agencies need to respond to these challenges by taking broader environmental issues seriously, while also addressing the current more localized deficiencies and inequities found within most cities. In short, the challenge is to include broader environmental considerations in urban development, without losing sight of current priorities.

NOTES

1   We thank Karen von Muehldorfer for her assistance with the preparation of the tables and graphs. The underlying data for this report were developed by the Socioeconomic

Data and Applications Center (SEDAC) at the Center for International Earth Science Information Network at Columbia University (contract No NAS5–03117). Deborah Balk received additional support from the National Institute of Child Health and Human Development (grant No 5R21HD054846-02).

2   Polar and island zones are omitted, the former because it is virtually uninhabited, the latter because the 'island' designation used for the Millennium Ecosystem Assessment was guided by treaty affiliation and did not systematically capture both island nations and sub-national island land area.

3   The stable city lights data are available only for 1994/1995. Though other night-lights products have been generated for other time periods (1992/1993 and 2000), they have not been tested for their ability to measure change in urban extent, electrification or built area.

4   North and South America refer to physical rather than social continental groupings. Mexico and the countries of Central America, along with the Caribbean island nations, are grouped with North America.

5   Density calculations are shown for 1995 only, as there is only a single snapshot of the area of the urban extents. Readers are reminded that the urban extents are based on stable city lights rather than built-up area, and that lights and economic activity are highly correlated (Doll et al, 2006). No systematic assessment has been undertaken to access whether the lights are biased such that wealthier urban areas appear larger than poorer ones irrespective of the true size of the urban area.

REFERENCES

Balk, D., Pozzi, F., Yetman, G., Deichmann, U. and Nelson, A. (2005) 'The distribution of people and the dimension of place: Methodologies to improve the global estimation of urban extents', Proceedings of the Urban Remote Sensing Conference, International Society for Photogrammetry and Remote Sensing, Tempe, AZ, 14–16 March

CIESIN, IFPRI, World Bank and CIAT (2004) 'Global Rural–Urban Mapping Project, alpha version (GRUMP alpha): Gridded population of the world, version 3, with urban reallocation (GPW–UR)', Socioeconomic Data and Applications Center (SEDAC), Columbia University, Palisades, NY, http://sedac.ciesin.columbia.edu/gpw, last accessed 10 February 2008

Cohen, M. (1993) 'Mega-cities and the environment', Finance and Development, vol 30, no 2, pp44–48

Chomitz, K. M., Buys, P., de Luca, G., Thomas, T. S. and Wertz-Kanounnikoff, S. (2006) 'At loggerheads? Agricultural expansion, poverty reduction and environment in the tropical forests', World Bank resource report, World Bank, Washington, DC, http://econ.world bank.org/WBSITE/EXTERNAL/EXTDEC/EXTRESEARCH/EXTPRRS/ EXTTROPICALFOREST/0,,contentMDK:21092971~menuPK:3070979~ pagePK:64168098~piPK:64168032~theSitePK:2463874,00.html, last accessed 10 February 2008

deFries, R., Pagiola, S., Adamowicz, W. L., Akçakaya, H., Arcenas, A., Babu, S., Balk, D., Confalonieri, U., Cramer, W., Falconí, F., Fritz, S., Green, R., Gutiérrez-Espeleta, E., Hamilton, K., Kane, R., Latham, J., Matthews, E., Ricketts, T. and Yue, T. X. (2005)

'Analytical approaches for assessing ecosystem condition and human wellbeing', in R. Hassan, R. Scholes and N. Ash (eds) *Ecosystems and Human Wellbeing: Current Status and Trends*, Millennium Ecosystem Assessment, Island Press, Washington, DC

Doll, C. N. H., Muller, J. P. and Morley, J. G. (2006) 'Mapping regional economic activity from night-time light satellite imagery', *Ecological Economics*, vol 57, no 1, pp75–92

Elvidge, C. D., Baugh, K. E., Kihn, E. A., Kroehl, H. W. and Davis, E. R. (1997) 'Mapping city lights with night-time data from the DMSP Operational Linescan System, *Photogrammetric Engineering and Remote Sensing*, vol 63, no 6, pp727–734

Fujita, M. and Thisse, J-F. (2002) *Economics of Agglomeration: Cities, Industrial Location and Regional Growth*, Cambridge University Press, Cambridge, UK

Hassan, R., Scholes, R. and Ash, N. (eds) (2005) *Ecosystems and Human Wellbeing: Current Status and Trends*, Millennium Ecosystem Assessment, Island Press, Washington, DC

Henderson, J. V. and Thisse, J-F. (eds) (2004) *Handbook of Regional and Urban Economics: Volume 4: Cities and Geography*, Elsevier North-Holland, Amsterdam

Kasperson, R., Dow, K., Archer, E., Caceres, D., Downing, T., Elmqvist, T., Eriksen, S., Folke, C., Han, G., Ivengar, K., Vogel, C., Wilson, K. and Zierevogel, G. (2005) 'Vulnerable people and places', in R. Hassan, R. Scholes and N. Ash (eds) *Ecosystems and Human Wellbeing: Current Status and Trends*, Millennium Ecosystem Assessment, Island Press, Washington, DC, pp143–166

Levy, M., Babu, S., Hamilton, K., Rhoe, V., Catenazzi, A., Ma Chen, Reid, W. V., Sengupta, D., Cai Ximing, Balmford, A. and Bond, W. (2005) 'Ecosystem conditions and human wellbeing', in R. Hassan, R. Scholes and N. Ash (eds) *Ecosystems and Human Wellbeing: Current Status and Trends*, Millennium Ecosystem Assessment, Island Press, Washington, DC, pp123–142

McGranahan, D. (1999) 'Natural amenities drive rural population change', Agricultural Economic Report No AER781, Food and Rural Economics Division, Economic Research Service, United States Department of Agriculture, Washington, DC

McGrahanan, G., Marcotullio, P., Bai, X., Balk, D., Braga, T., Douglas, I., Elmqvist, T., Rees, W., Satterthwaite, D., Songsore, J. and Zlotnik, H. (2005) 'Urban systems', in R. Hassan, R. Scholes and N. Ash (eds) *Ecosystems and Human Wellbeing: Current Status and Trends*, Millennium Ecosystem Assessment, Island Press, Washington, DC

McGranahan, G., Balk, D. and Anderson, B. (2007) 'The rising tide: Assessing the risks of climate change and human settlements in low elevation coastal zones', *Environment and Urbanization*, vol 19, no 1, pp17–37

Montgomery, M. R., Stren, R., Cohen, B. and Reed, H. E. (eds) (2003) *Cities Transformed: Demographic Change and its Implications in the Developing World*, Panel on Urban Dynamics, National Research Council, National Academy Press, Washington, DC

Nicholls, R. J., Hanson, S., Herweijer, C., Patmore, N., Hallegatte, S., Corfee-Morlot, J., Chateau, J. and Muir-Wood, R. (2007) 'Ranking port cities with high exposure and vulnerability to climate extremes: Exposure estimates', Environment Working Paper No 1, Organization for Economic Cooperation and Development, Paris

Rees, W. E. (2003) 'Understanding urban ecosystems: An ecological economics perspective', in A. R. Berkowitz, C. H. Nilon and K. S. Hollweg (eds) *Understanding Urban Ecosystems: A New Frontier for Science and Education*, Springer-Verlag, New York, pp115–136

Satterthwaite, D. (2005) 'The scale of urban change worldwide, 1950–2000, and its underpinnings', Human Settlements Discussion Paper, Urban Change, No 1, International Institute for Environment and Development, London

Small, C. and Cohen, J. (2004) 'Continental physiography, climate and the global distribution of human population', *Current Anthropology*, vol 45, no 2, pp269–277

United Nations (2006) *World Urbanization Prospects: The 2005 Revision*, Population Division, United Nations, New York

11

Urban Sprawl: A Challenge for Sustainability

Daniel Joseph Hogan and Ricardo Ojima

INTRODUCTION

Two interrelated facets of contemporary urban growth – population size and physical patterns of expansion – have received unequal attention by urban researchers. Urban expansion spurred by population growth may take different forms, with distinct consequences for quality of life, for the environment and for urban governance (Angel, 2006). What has emerged as a new challenge to the growth of urban areas in the 21st century is not only the pressure of numbers, but also the pressure that comes from the forms of consuming space in a globalized world. These patterns, and how they challenge the sustainable future of cities, are still insufficiently understood. Several forms occur simultaneously in different world regions, some of which are more sustainable than others. One of these forms is *urban sprawl*, a pattern of low-density settlement, widely regarded as undesirable from many perspectives.

This chapter will review the sprawl debate, seeking to differentiate sprawl from other forms of dispersed urbanization. It will also consider a parallel debate on concentration versus decentralization, which has emerged in the wake of the generalized condemnation of urban sprawl. It will summarize the measurement issues and, finally, reflect on the implications of sprawl for urban sustainability.

THE SPRAWL DEBATE: FROM AMERICAN SUBURBIA TO GLOBAL PHENOMENON

Urban sprawl, or the discontinuity between population growth and the physical expansion of urban space, was perceived as a problem in the US as early as the 1960s. The term emerged as a pejorative expression to designate the uncontrolled expansion of American urban agglomerations, especially with the dissemination of suburban growth patterns. Not surprisingly, most of the literature on urban sprawl thus far focuses on the negative effects of suburbanization. This reflects the influence of political groups that have campaigned for the control of sprawl. Such movements promote the values of compact and functional cities and include on their agendas principles related to environmental sustainability, quality of life and consumer awareness. The 'smart growth' movement is a common theme therein, and sprawl is regarded as one of the principal villains of urban environmental problems.

The studies concerned with this uncontrolled expansion of land use emphasize various negative social, economic and environmental impacts. Growing spatial mobility, especially an increase in daily commuting, is closely related to urban sprawl. The relative dependence on individual transportation is a key feature of the lifestyles associated with sprawl. The intense use of cars after World War II considerably increased the living spaces of daily life, separating place of residence from place of work and from access to services. Smaller families and the increase of women's participation in the labour force – processes concurrent with suburbanization – often meant different daily destinations for commuters from the same household. A strategic choice of suburb – no longer a central city location – was often a means to minimize the commuting costs of a household.

The greater the distances there are between different spheres of daily life – such as work, residence, schools and shopping – the greater the demand for automobile transportation. At the same time, the suburban pattern of settlement required new locations for trade and services responding to the new consumption patterns of the post-war era. Shopping centres and high-speed, limited-access highways answered this demand, as both causes and consequences of the new automobile-dependent order.

From this perspective, rather than being a simple empirical phenomenon of decreasing densities observable in the contemporary city, sprawl reflects a social process related to contemporary lifestyles. Essentially, it mirrors the values of modern society and people's expectations in relation to patterns of consumption. For instance, in the 1970s and 1980s, when environment and nature suddenly became more socially relevant in terms of values, an implicit contradiction emerged. On the one hand, people increasingly desired to live in cities; on the other, they desired to live closer to nature. As the global village has become more integrated, these consumption and lifestyle aspirations have become more widespread.

It is precisely this contradiction that has resulted in the major problems that are faced today as urban sprawl spreads throughout the world. Sprawl reflects a combination of changing values as well as an expansion of globalized patterns of consumption. It involves an entire set of new meanings and representations that not only permeate that part of the population with greater purchasing power, but also creates a new lifestyle that spreads across societies. Social status is no longer limited to geographical location but involves the style of life to which American suburbs aspire. New phenomena, such as the environmental movement, communication technology, globalized economic production and consumption expectations, can all impact quickly on residential preferences and, thus, on urban form.

While originally a North American phenomenon, a considerable body of research now points to the importance of sprawl in other regions of the world as well. Even in Europe, where cities have traditionally been associated with compact urban design (Richardson and Chang-Hee, 2004), there are signs that sprawl is increasing. Although there are still problems in identifying and comparing the distinct processes across Europe, there is a certain consensus that, in comparison with countries having an Anglo-Saxon tradition, urban sprawl has a more recent history. In France, the urbanized area increased fivefold between 1969 and 1999, while the population of these areas grew by only 50 per cent (Pumain, 2004). This phenomenon is more recent in Spain, Italy and other countries of Mediterranean Europe (Munoz, 2003; Pumain, 2004; Roca et al, 2004).

But current urban dispersion is not limited to residential patterns or to the growth of American-style suburbs and gated communities. Another process widely discussed in the literature on sprawl is non-contiguous urban development, or 'leapfrog development'. This pattern of development has been associated with land speculation and urban territorial expansion. Strongly related to low densities, non-contiguous development is an important feature in the fragmented form of contemporary urban space. Distances between nodes of urban development within the same region are increased as globalization, together with improvements in transport and communication, allows de-concentrated growth. The growth of urban settlements not adjacent to the built-up urban centre implies different mobility needs for work, study and access to a variety of services. Typically, these developments do not evolve into residential suburbs, but remain urban islands, more or less linked to the central city.

Deliberate strategies of letting land lie vacant while development passes it by, thus increasing its value as urban infrastructure (water, sewerage, electricity, refuse collection, transport lines, paved streets and so on) is put into place, are seen as responsible for increasing the social costs of urban development in the core. This feature of urban development may be more specific to developing countries, where zoning, tax structures, and the lack of profitable and secure investments increase the appeal of investment in land.[1] Measures of sprawl which capture points in time rather than underlying processes may confuse such patterns with suburbanization.

Subsequent 'fill-in' growth, however, may re-establish the contiguity of the urban fabric, reinforcing the importance of the central city.

Especially in Asia and Africa, urban dispersion has been studied as 'peri-urbanization', defined as the urban expansion that occurs in transitional zones between rural and urban areas (Tacoli, 1998). Leaf (2002) identifies the process of globalization of the economy as an important factor in the expansion of the peri-urban areas of China and Viet Nam, pointing to the need for specific policies in developing countries. The term has arisen to describe and analyse urban activities found within traditional rural areas, often at the boundaries of cities. For Leaf, the changes seen in settlement forms within the limits of consolidated urban centres are part of greater economic transformations. In this regard, peri-urbanization occupies a growing segment of the literature on urbanization processes, especially in the developing world. In parallel with these accounts of urban researchers, similar results have been identified by students of agriculture and rural areas, where a 'new rurality' has developed on the basis of non-agricultural activities directly associated to urban demands (Graziano da Silva, 1995).

Globalization processes play an important role in blurring rural–urban distinctions. An urban rationality comes to dominate all social behaviour, even in traditionally rural areas. Globalization, while redefining the economic roles of 'global cities', also transforms the area outside such cities. Its impact is perhaps more evident in regions undergoing early stages of the urban transition, especially in the urban agglomerations of Africa and Asia. Latin America, where much of this transition preceded contemporary globalization, may have a more established urban system that is more resistant to contemporary trends. While peri-urbanization may be present in Latin America, the fact is that this region has a greater diversity of forms and processes of urban transformation occurring simultaneously.

Urban sprawl has been associated with globalization, which implies the generalization of models and patterns of consumption whose origin is remote from local contexts. These models transform space and reveal new urban forms. According to Lefebvre (2003, p18), the late 20th century witnessed the dawn of a truly urban society, a complete urbanization, where the urban fabric encompasses whole territories, dissolves the large city, and gives way to 'questionable excrescences: suburbs, residential estates or industrial complexes, small satellite agglomerations not much different from urbanized cities'.

The linkages examined in the rural–urban literature give greater attention to economic components than does the sprawl literature, which is mostly limited to the analysis of residential land use within large urban agglomerations. The conclusions from a review of the literature on rural–urban linkages emphasized a new situation in which industry and services can be found in rural areas – a process which Costa (2000) has called 'peripheral and fragmented urbanization' – or agricultural activities can be found in or close to towns (Tacoli, 1998). Again, measures of sprawl which take a cross-sectional approach may miss such important distinctions.

MEASURING URBAN SPRAWL

The complex overlay of social values in reference to diverse empirical patterns of land use has made the science of sprawl a difficult enterprise. Despite the use of sophisticated analytical instruments, such as satellite images and geographic information systems (GIS), the studies that seek to characterize sprawl have not yet developed a refined conceptual treatment. Aesthetics, social justice, green space, energy efficiency and climate change are all points of departure for studying sprawl that affect the definition employed, as does the spatial scale being analysed.

A local, regional, national or international focus leads researchers to definitions of sprawl that imply greater or lesser complexity. On the other hand, careful, nuanced local studies are difficult to replicate at larger scales. American studies, which use census definitions of metropolitan areas, greatly increase the geographical scope of analyses but are difficult to translate into international settings. More important, the literature on sprawl often confuses causes and consequences and thus tends to be used in the literature to denominate a diversity of different conditions, which opens the way for distinct and often contradictory interpretations (Galster et al, 2001).

Even in careful, data-based analyses, urban–suburban cut-offs are justified with terms such as 'two hundred persons per square mile *roughly corresponds*' and 'an estimate of density that is *commonly held*' [emphasis added] (Lopez and Hynes, 2003, p333). There is therefore a somewhat arbitrary, subjective dimension in most of this literature. Nevertheless, such exercises reveal wide distributions of sprawl 'scores', which suggest that sprawl is not an inevitable consequence of contemporary urban growth (Lopez and Hynes, 2003, p341). It is also suggested that not all low-density urbanization is negative, a point which will be discussed later in this chapter.

Density and concentration may occur in a number of combinations in specific societies and geographies, implying different *types* of sprawl (Galster et al, 2001) or different forms of urban dispersion. As noted earlier, urban sprawl in North America is a continuation of post-World War II suburban growth, while in Europe, sprawl challenges a historical pattern of more compact cities and has generated more systematic responses. In the developing world, urban dispersion takes on more varied forms.

How, then, considering the variety of scales and data sources used, and especially the difficulty of identifying *process* while examining cross-sectional data, can we assess the extent of sprawl in the world today? What are the gains from – and the limits to – the experience of researchers in measuring sprawl? There are now a wide range of indicators from varied perspectives and instrumental approaches. Density – the ratio of the total population of the urban agglomeration to its urban area – is the most frequent indicator of sprawl. Research that emphasizes the intensity of the sprawl process also shows the gap between urban population growth rates and urban area growth rates. Other indicators of sprawl have been used to complement or qualify the density factor. With the help of satellite images and GIS, more complex indicators of sprawl became possible, and current studies consider a variety of other aspects of urban form that characterize different modes of sprawl:

- *Continuity–discontinuity*: GIS is used to measure the degree of fragmentation of a particular region.
- *Concentration*: Similar densities observed in aggregated analyses of a region may be more or less concentrated, forming two or more urban centres. Measuring how concentration is dispersed may identify important differences between regions with similar densities. Strip development, for example, is a common characteristic of sprawl.
- *Diversity of land use and jobs*: While rarely used in measuring sprawl, the degree of homogeneity of economic activities within an urban area can also affect sprawl. The mix of jobs and land uses, for example, can impact commuting patterns.

The impacts described in case studies show that urban sprawl may be different not only in terms of the increase of the urbanized area relative to population growth, but also in terms of the designs and functions of intra-urban spaces. That is, there will be different impacts on urban form in two regions with similar urban densities depending on whether their urban fabric is more or less disconnected or whether the diversity of urban activities is more or less accentuated.

In spatial terms, the analysis of the modern city has always been identified with the analysis of the monocentric industrial city (Figure 11.1, Diagram 1) or with its successor, which includes a more or less extensive periphery (Diagram 2). This model, marked by centre–periphery and rich–poor dichotomies, is the most common today, and it reinforces the idea of the homogeneity of intra-urban space. If the model of the monocentric city was once the principal model of urban settlement, however, a new scenario is evident today, in which multiple population concentrations occur over the space of a single city, as seen in Diagram 3 (Ojima, 2007).

Studies of sprawl have enriched our understanding of the spatial expansion of modern cities. The indices that have been developed, however, are ambiguous when used as instruments for the development of sustainable urban policies. Urban expansion that swallows up the countryside without regard to the integrity of natural areas is not sustainable. Nor is urban expansion sustainable when it compromises the quality of water resources, when it is driven by the uncoordinated search for affordable and amenable housing, and when it multiplies the number of hours spent in daily commuting between home and work. To distinguish such expansion from other forms of dispersed settlement, however, requires using spatial studies combined with local, in-depth research on specific cities. The difficulty in

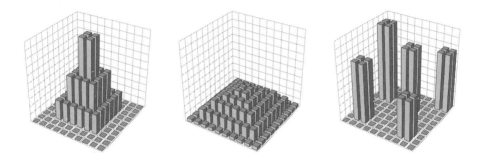

Figure 11.1 *Schematic diagrams of urban form*

Source: Ojima (2007), p106.

distinguishing different forms of urban dispersion when using aggregated data should not lead us to dismiss the negative aspects of sprawl. Comparative and historical research may contribute to constructing typologies of dispersion that permit planners to distinguish among more and less sustainable patterns.

CHALLENGES FOR A SUSTAINABLE FUTURE: DISPERSED VERSUS COMPACT CITIES

The urban planning literature has for some time sustained a lively debate on the advantages and disadvantages of compact versus decentralized cities, a debate not always joined by other disciplines concerned with urban form. This section examines this debate with a view to evaluating the light it may shed on the (un)desirability of sprawl.

The more widely publicized negative consequences of sprawl include:

- *Air pollution*: Ewing et al (2002) report a strong correlation between indices of urban sprawl, as developed in their research, and maximum ozone levels. Among the variables tested for American metropolitan areas, the degree of sprawl was the best predictor of ozone.
- *Water consumption*: Western Resource Advocates (2003) discuss the impacts of the pattern of suburban development as one of the principal factors in explaining recent increases in water use. Consumption patterns associated with increasingly large residential lots lead to greater water use, especially in yards and gardens. Furthermore, a large portion of water wastage is related to losses over the distribution system, such as from leaky pipes and breaks in water mains. Due to the greater extension of the supply network as a result of the growth of the areas to be served, the probability of losses increases and maintenance capacity is compromised.

- *Loss of green space*: In terms of the impacts of urban sprawl on natural resources, this is perhaps the most dramatic. The expansion of the urbanized area, at low densities, occurs at the expense of areas earlier dedicated to agriculture or previously untouched land.
- *Urban flight*: In many parts of the US, people seek to escape heavy traffic, crime and the lack of green space by recreating their 'cities' in areas far from consolidated centres. The irony of this process is the reproduction of the same problems they sought to escape. The suburbs, which served as refuges from problems earlier restricted to older centres, come to reproduce the same problems on a scale made more serious by the absence of urban infrastructure. Indeed, many services, such as adequate public transportation, public security, schools and health services are only viable in more densely settled areas.
- *Health issues*: Among the consequences identified are the increase in fatality rates from motor vehicle accidents (Ewing et al, 2002), weight gain and associated problems from the more sedentary lifestyles associated with sprawl, and a growing incidence of traditionally rural illnesses affecting urban populations.
- *Fragmentation*: Among the more evident impacts of urban sprawl is the fragmentation of the city. In the search for a quality of life closer to nature, the urban fabric is created in fragmented segments, slicing up intermediary spaces with no concern for the necessary contiguousness of natural processes. (One result of this phenomenon is the importance now given to such remedial measures as ecological corridors for the survival and reproduction of wildlife (Jongman and Kamphorst, 2002).) Resulting environmental risks, thus multiplied and widely distributed, are added to the social and health risks mentioned above, and the sought-after quality of life becomes an elusive goal.

The conventional wisdom that sprawl increases these various evils – and that compact cities are therefore to be preferred – is already being questioned, however (Breheny, 1995). Neuman (2005), who titles his article 'The compact city fallacy', reviews the case for identifying compact cities with sustainability and concludes that 'conceiving the city in terms of form is neither necessary nor sufficient to achieve the goals ascribed to the compact city. Instead, conceiving the city in terms of process holds more promise in attaining the elusive goal of a sustainable city' (p11).

What are the implications of this position for the critics of sprawl? The debate is more intense in Europe, perhaps because sprawl is more recent, contradicting a long tradition of compact cities. In The Netherlands and Northern Europe, both urban policy and academic urban planners have focused on measures to reinforce traditional urban forms, often facing challenges to the desirability of defending the status quo. Much of this heated debate reflects values and aesthetics that render empirical evaluations of the success of policy measures ambiguous. In their review of Britain's experience in controlling sprawl, for instance, Cho et al (1997) express major doubts about 'the economic, political and technical dimensions of compaction and particularly the unacceptability of higher densities to many urban residents' (p209).

Empirical evaluations of factors thought to be affected by compact cities have produced mixed results. Burton's (2001) empirical analysis of the components of equity led her to conclude that 'while compactness appears to be positive for some aspects of social equity, it may be negative for others' (p13), and that the impact of compactness may be more straightforward for equality than equity. Power (2001) discusses equity in terms of the social exclusion of the poor: hidden subsidies promote sprawl, while central cities are left to deteriorate. Goodchild (1991), on the other hand, suggests that 'in practice the compact city can intensify competition for housing and involve the displacement of existing low-income residents' (p426). These are perhaps not questions that can be answered by empirical tests, given the methodological difficulties and the political-ideological components which still underlie most positions in this debate.

The discussion often centres on the specific advantages claimed by advocates of compact cities for energy efficiency. Less commuting would mean less use of gasoline and less air pollution (Newman and Kenworthy, 1989). This popular view has, however, been challenged by Gordon and Richardson (1997), who point to job decentralization and the consequent increase of suburb-to-suburb commuting. Longer distance trips, then, would be unrelated to expanding out from central cities. Polycentric cities, they suggest, would be a better answer to sprawl.

These are surely legitimate issues, but the evaluation of specific concerns ignores the question of the overall desirability or undesirability of sprawl, especially in its environmental aspects. Proponents of sustainable development and, by extension, of sustainable cities have never assumed that the issues are limited to their economic, political and technical dimensions. Not only is the environment central to the question, but the ethical aspect has also been highlighted. That is, what is unacceptable to many urban residents today may (must?) become acceptable tomorrow: changes in values are intrinsic to the sustainability debate. Ethics may be economically, politically and technically challenging, but such difficulties do not negate the paramount need for fundamental guiding principles.

What is least present in this debate is the green dimension. Urban planning studies that evaluate the benefits of compactness do not generally address the concern of the environmental movement for the loss of green space. But trade-offs also need to be considered. Burby et al (2001), for example, caution that compact cities 'can lead to increased exposure to natural hazards and higher losses in disasters' (p475) and point to mitigating measures which may be necessary to contain such unintended side-effects of controlling sprawl. Without a consistent, integrated urban policy, which directly treats issues such as social equity and energy consumption, efforts to control decentralization or sprawl will have limited effects.

This discussion, as is the case with the parallel sprawl debate, has also failed to produce a comprehensive view of urban expansion processes. It has added to the complexity of the challenge, however, which can be seen as a step in the right direction.

SPRAWL AND SUSTAINABILITY

What are the new challenges for urban sustainability, given this debate on urban form? In response to ongoing changes in consumption patterns, the dispersed city seems to be where people currently want to live. Market forces alone would be incapable of promoting this model of urbanization if people were not interested in this style of life. However, the structural limitations to choice also have to be factored in when analysing consumer preferences. In the US, for instance, as Chin (2002, p5) points out, the financing, marketing and regulation of development have become standardized over the last half-century, favouring single-family homes in automobile-oriented neighbourhoods. Thus, residential preferences of the past have been incorporated into institutional arrangements and are now critical in determining current choices.

That preference and choice are moulded by the market has long been a basic tenet of consumer studies. The fact that there is disagreement on compact or dispersed cities may be evidence that people can take satisfaction and find quality of life in either situation. If there are environmental and other considerations which make more compact cities or other urban forms necessary, human adaptability may, indeed, be up to the challenge of change.

From the standpoint of those who prefer a large house on a large lot only accessible by car, the compact city may appear an undemocratic way to change desired lifestyles and a limitation on freedom of choice. However, it should be noted that this is the view of those who can choose where to live. For those whose choice is constrained by financial limitations – the great majority of the world's population – reaping the benefits of sprawl is not an option.

Social and environmental considerations point to the limited benefits of unfettered sprawl. In this sense, sprawl can be seen as a classic case of the tragedy of the commons. If all who have the necessary means were to contribute to urban sprawl, everyone would lose. Those left behind in deteriorating cities, in central or run-down peripheral neighbourhoods, are even farther away from the recreation and leisure afforded by the green spaces in outlying urban areas, and resources that could be used to improve urban infrastructure are diverted to building highways and providing services in newly occupied remote areas. The sprawlers themselves commute greater distances (producing more pollution, limiting interaction with their families and reducing options for leisure time), increase the costs of providing infrastructure and services, and ultimately destroy the green space they sought, reducing it to the limits of their (admittedly larger) lots. And the environment itself suffers from loss of biodiversity, from compromising watershed protection and from accelerating climate change (through CO_2 emissions and increasing paved-over or built-up areas).

It seems clear that only regulation will interrupt the sprawl component of urban dispersion; there is no invisible hand to order growth policies according to societal needs or intergenerational concerns. Urban and regional planning, which in many countries was placed on the back burner in the decades of rapid population (and city) growth, and further ostracized by structural adjustment policies, will have to be rehabilitated to meet this challenge. The premises of sustainable development include solidarity with present and future generations, an idea that subordinates freedom of choice to values which promote the wellbeing of the population as a whole. These premises also include the participation of populations in defining their futures: urban planning will have to join technical and environmental considerations to new mechanisms which widen the participation of social groups in designing the future.

The tendencies of urban sprawl suggest that the decision on urban form is being made at the individual level and that the compact city may be a nostalgic option in a modern world which does not recognize this model as a way of satisfying contemporary demands of consumption and of individuality. Reversing these tendencies and promoting acceptable yet sustainable patterns of urban growth require technical prowess, democratic participation in decision-making and better advocacy for values that are adapted to the realities of the 21st century.

Ultimately, the choice may not be between sprawl and compact cities but for urban forms that are designed with an explicit concern for environmental values and the need to ensure sustainability. Some urban dispersion may be a form of postmodern, environmentally friendly growth. The emergence of polynucleated urban systems that maximize suburban comfort while minimizing transportation, for example, may be a sign of the diversity of possible solutions to harmonizing urban growth and environmental integrity. As mentioned earlier, measures of dispersion have not yet permitted us to effectively separate unsustainable sprawl from other more acceptable dispersed residential patterns.

At the root of the resistance to unsustainable sprawl is a rejection of both individual free choice as the first maxim of urban planning and the belief that any form of urban expansion can be harmonized with environmental concerns. While some compact cities continue to provide excellent living conditions, even those cities that have suffered inner-city degradation – sometimes because of urban sprawl – can overcome this to become attractive for residence as well as work, offering a quality of life of the highest standards. However, since quality of life is a notoriously subjective notion, bright lights and bucolic niches will each continue to have their distinct publics.

The challenges of sustainability are often presented as requiring technical or political innovation. This is undeniably true, but, without a basis in social values regarding what constitutes wellbeing, no lasting solution will be possible. It is by no means clear that such change will be forthcoming, although the sustainability literature abounds with encouraging examples. In the case at hand, people must come to see that the wellbeing they seek in outlying green spaces may be found within urban morphologies that preserve this green space.

In the end, this debate requires the consideration not only of how to regulate urban expansion, but of how to provide sustainable and socially agreeable living spaces within denser cities. The sprawl debate must be expanded from the consideration of its negative effects and efforts to control it, to proposals for revitalizing deteriorated urban centres, for providing the new services demanded in the 21st century, for increasing the access of city-dwellers to the green spaces of the hinterlands (which implies increasing the protection of such areas), and for conciliating environmental concerns with other aspects of quality of life (UNFPA, 2007).

Finally, two issues are clear from this review. First, while the forms of urban expansion are changing in ways that appear to be similar in various world regions, different approaches have not yet produced consensus on basic conceptual issues. Observers have identified different aspects of ongoing trends: dispersed cities, compact cities, sprawl, peri-urbanization and the 'new rural'. The challenge that remains for students of contemporary urbanization is to understand whether different languages always reflect different processes, or whether measurement procedures have homogenized and reified certain aspects that are more universal. The need for more comparative research, both historical and geographical, is clear. The dilemma is that choosing historical experience as a guide to the future may induce premature generalization, with negative consequences for both theory and practice. Only continued research will avoid this dilemma.

Second, recent tendencies of the world urbanization process in a context of globalized markets point to a situation in which regions (as opposed to specific localities) emerge as economic and political arenas with greater autonomy of action at national and global levels. City-regions, as identified by Scott et al (2001), among others, constitute nodes that express a new social, economic and political order; instead of losing importance as a result of the globalization process, city-regions thus become increasingly central to modern life. One image of future urbanization is that of a polynucleated city, fragmented, with low densities, over wide-ranging territorial extensions, but, at the same time, increasingly integrated. Such integration may be the basis for new paradigms of urban growth, reconciling a diversity of morphologies with sustainability. Integration may be the mechanism necessary to give priority to solutions that promote common concerns over the individuality expressed in the origins of urban sprawl.

NOTE

1   The leapfrog strategy can backfire, however, as organized land invasions become a marked feature of city life in many countries. In Campinas, Brazil, for example, a large, vacant tract on the edge of a four-lane highway, close to the city centre and surrounded by residential development and associated services, was invaded in 1997 and became a community of 30,000 overnight (Pascoal, 2002). Urban planners in São

Paulo, having concluded that 25 per cent of the city's territory was unoccupied, called for more intense, compact development as a more rational economic strategy, thereby optimizing public investment in the urbanized area (Rolnik et al, 1990, p111).

REFERENCES

Angel, S. (2006) 'Measuring global sprawl: The spatial structure of the planet's urban landscape', unpublished paper

Breheny, M. (1995) 'The compact city and transport energy consumption', *Transactions of the Institute of British Geographers*, vol 20, no 1, pp81–101

Burby, R. J., Nelson, A. C., Parker, D. and Handmer, J. (2001) 'Urban containment policy and exposure to natural hazards: Is there a connection?', *Journal of Environmental Planning and Management*, vol 44, no 4, pp475–490

Burton, E. (2001) 'The compact city and social justice', paper presented to the Housing Studies Association Spring Conference 'Housing, environment and sustainability', University of York, York, UK, 18–19 April

Chin, N. (2002) 'Unearthing the roots of urban sprawl: A critical analysis of form, function and methodology', Working Paper Series No 47, Centre for Advanced Spatial Analysis, University College London, London

Cho, S-A., Hernandez, A., Ochoa, J., Lira-Olivares, J. and Breheny, M. (1997) 'Urban compaction: Feasible and acceptable?', *Cities*, vol 14, no 4, pp209–217

Costa, H. S. M. (2000) 'Indústria, produção do espaço e custos socioambientais: Reflexões a partir do exemplo do Vale do Aço, Minas Gerais', in H. Torres and H. Costa (eds) *População e Meio Ambiente: Debates e Desafios*, Editora Senac, São Paulo, Brazil, pp191–212

Ewing, R., Pendall, R. and Chen, D. (2002) 'Measuring sprawl and its impacts: Smart Growth America, Washington, DC', www.smartgrowthamerica.org/sprawlindex/MeasuringSprawl.PDF, last accessed 3 October 2007

Galster, G., Hanson, R., Ratcliffe, M. R., Wolman, H., Coleman, S. and Freihage, J. (2001) 'Wrestling sprawl to the ground: Defining and measuring an elusive concept', *Housing Policy Debate*, vol 12, no 4, pp681–717

Goodchild, B. (1991) 'Housing and the compact city: Principles and practice in Britain', *Architecture et Comportement/Architecture and Behaviour*, vol 7, no 4, pp423–430

Gordon, P. and Richardson, H. W. (1997) 'Are compact cities a desirable planning goal?', *Journal of the American Planning Association*, vol 63, no 1, pp95–106

Graziano da Silva, J. (1995) 'Urbanização e pobreza no campo', in B. P. Reydon and P. Ramos (eds) (1995) *Agropecuária e Agroindústria no Brasil: Ajuste, Situação Atual e Perspectiva*, ICEA Gráfica e Editora Ltda, Campinas, Brazil

Jongman, R. and Kamphorst, D. (2002) *Ecological Corridors in Land-Use Planning and Development Policies*, Nature and Environment Series No 125, Council of Europe, Strasbourg, France

Leaf, M. (2002) 'A tale of two villages', *Cities*, vol 19, no 1, pp23–31

Lefebvre, H. (2003) *The Urban Revolution*, translated by Robert Bononno, University of Minnesota Press, Minneapolis, MN (originally published in French in 1970)

Lopez, R. and Hynes, H. P. (2003) 'Sprawl in the 1990s: Measurement, distribution and trends', *Urban Affairs Review*, vol 38, no 3, pp325–355

Munoz, F. (2003) 'Lock living: Urban sprawl in Mediterranean cities', *Cities*, vol 20, no 6, pp381–385

Neuman, M. (2005) 'The compact city fallacy', *Journal of Planning Education and Research*, vol 25, no 1, pp11–26

Newman, P. and Kenworthy, J. (1989) *Cities and Automobile Dependence: An International Sourcebook*, Gower, Aldershot, UK

Ojima, R. (2007) 'Análise comparativa da dispersão urbana nas aglomerações urbanas brasileiras: Elementos teóricos e metodológicos para o planejamento urbano e ambiental', doctoral dissertation in demography, State University of Campinas, Campinas, Brazil.

Pascoal, G. (2002) 'Ocupações revelam déficit habitacional', *ComCiência*, www.comciencia.br/reportagens/cidades/cid05.htm, last accessed 3 October 2007

Power, A. (2001) 'Social exclusion and urban sprawl: Is the rescue of cities possible?', *Regional Studies*, vol 35, no 8, pp731–742

Pumain, D. (2004) Urban sprawl: Is there a French case?', in H. W. Richardson and C. B. Chang-Hee (eds) *Urban Sprawl in Western Europe and the United States*, Ashgate, Bodmin, UK, pp137–157

Richardson, H. W. and Chang-Hee C. B. (eds) (2004) *Urban Sprawl in Western Europe and the United States*, Ashgate, Bodmin, UK

Roca, J., Burns, M. C. and Carreras, J. M. (2004) 'Monitoring urban sprawl around Barcelona's Metropolitan Area with the aid of satellite imagery', paper presented at the 20th ISPRS Congress, Istanbul, Turkey, 12–23 July

Rolnik, R., Kowarik, L. and Somekh, N. (eds) (1990) *São Paulo: Crise e Mudança*, Prefeitura de São Paulo/Brasiliense, São Paulo, Brazil

Scott, A. J., Agnew, J., Soja, E. and Storper, M. (2001) 'Global city-regions: An overview', www.lse.ac.uk/collections/geographyAndEnvironment/whosWho/profiles/storper/pdf/GlobalCityRegions.pdf, last accessed 29 October 2007, published in Portuguese as 'Cidades-regiões globais', *Espaço e Debates*, no 41, pp11–25

Tacoli, C. (1998) 'Rural–urban interactions: A guide to the literature', *Environment and Urbanization*, vol 10, no 1, pp147–166

Tacoli, C. (2003) 'The links between urban and rural development', *Environment and Urbanization*, vol 15, no 1, pp3–12

UNFPA (2007) *The State of World Population 2007: Unleashing the Potential of Urban Growth*, UNFPA, New York

Van der Waals, J. F. M. (2000) 'The compact city and the environment: A review', *Tijdschrift voor Economische en Sociale Geografie*, vol 91, no 2, pp111–121

Western Resource Advocates (2003) 'Smart water: A comparative study of urban water use in the Southwest', Western Resource Advocates, Boulder, CO, www.westernresources.org/water/smartwater.php, last accessed 3 October 2007

Part IV

The Changing Face of Urban Demography and its Challenges

INTRODUCTION

The pace and manner of urban growth are closely linked to demographic dynamics. The evolution of demographic processes, in turn, affects the ability of different social groups to benefit from the advantages of urbanization. Rapid changes in rates of population growth, age composition and migration patterns in developing countries create a fast-changing panorama of opportunities and liabilities. This section focuses on how the changing demographic dynamics associated with urban growth impact on different social processes.

In chapter 12, Hakkert examines the influence of urbanization on poverty. Using a model that decomposes national poverty rates into three elements (decline of rural poverty, decline of urban poverty and a component related to the rising proportion of the population living in urban areas, where poverty rates are lower), he finds that rural–urban migration generally contributes to national poverty reduction, though at varying levels, and that upward economic mobility is greater in the cities than in the countryside. The fact that urbanization is so often associated with rising poverty may be because people tend to focus primarily on *urban* poverty – the rate of reduction of which is, indeed, slowed by migration – rather than on national levels. Moreover, the very real positive indirect effects of urbanization on rural poverty are generally overlooked.

Observing that urban growth is increasingly due to natural increase, Hakkert also examines the extent to which this is affected by access to sexual and reproductive health services and to fertility preferences. He suggests that such access has a greater effect on rural areas, where fertility is consistently higher. Given that a rapid pace of urbanization is often seen as undesirable, increased access to reproductive healthcare and family planning still holds the best potential for reducing urban growth through its impact on rural–urban migration flows, even in countries that are well advanced in their demographic transition.

Urban settings provide the main arena for reshaping gender relations, as observed by Mora in Chapter 13. Urban conditions can be more difficult for poor women and children, exposing them to new forms of exploitation, discrimination and violence, in addition to greater environmental risks; however, urban settings can also present new opportunities for gender equality, allowing women to escape the traditional forms of discrimination that prevail in rural areas, encouraging work outside the home, and facilitating access to education, income and health services, as well as participation in public and political life. Mora addresses some of these contradictory trends with respect to several interrelated issues: working outside the home, living conditions, family formation and social participation.

Two broad trends stand out with respect to labour force participation in cities: the feminization of the labour force and the informalization of the labour market – which can be either a boon or a drawback for women. A critical issue is that the most available options for women's work occur in settings that are not compatible with the care of children and dependants. Urban women are also confronted with new forms of vulnerability and discrimination, often linked to housing. Moreover, women and children bear the health burdens of water, sanitation, hygiene and related inadequacies. Nevertheless, urban women generally benefit from better infrastructure than those living in rural areas. Much could be improved with greater attention to women's needs in urban planning, small investments aimed at attending to women's needs, and, above all, a greater reliance on women's and other neighbourhood organizations.

Chapter 14 centres on the youth bulge in developing-country cities and discusses some of the main challenges and opportunities that it poses. An increasing majority of young people will make their transition from childhood to adulthood in urban areas, and the size of this contingent will have huge implications for future development. The concurrence of the demographic and urban transitions will make cities the prime beneficiaries of the much-vaunted 'demographic dividend'. The concern, however, is that employment creation lags far behind the labour supply and young people are twice as likely to be unemployed. Bridging this gap will require investments in education and capacity-building as well as the generation of economic activities.

Slowing the pace of urban growth and improving its consequences will depend to a large extent on investments in young people, especially among the poorest sectors. Urban life can help young women overcome restrictive gender norms and practices, but they need targeted support in education, employment opportunities and social services to live out the urban promise. Young men are most affected by unemployment and violence, but young people are everywhere playing a key role in improving urban communities. Unmet needs for social services are great in slums, where higher fertility rates also contribute to the intergenerational reproduction of slum conditions. Investments in human development that target young people and improved access to reproductive health and other services would help them exercise their sexual and reproductive health rights while also reducing the inertial component of urban growth.

Rapid urbanization in developing countries will inevitably concentrate increasing numbers of older persons in urban areas. In Chapter 15, Guzmán and Saad analyse the implications of this double demographic transformation. Their findings underscore the potential advantages of urbanization in terms of creating an enabling environment for improving the life conditions of older people. Urbanization can indeed be an ally in dealing with population ageing, given the higher income levels of urban localities and their inherent advantages of scale and proximity in the provision of services. Nevertheless, specific policies will be necessary to maximize the development benefits of urbanization for older persons while minimizing its possible negative impacts.

Moreover, increases in the proportion of the rural population composed of older people, due to migration patterns, have raised concerns about their wellbeing.

A specific aspect that is broached by Guzmán and Saad is the often-voiced hypothesis that urbanization provokes a decrease in social-networking and family-support structures. The results in this regard are not yet conclusive and appear to vary considerably by country, but, on the whole, they seem to indicate that strong informal support systems persist. To take advantage of the potential advantages of urban life, older persons need economic security and/or strong social-support systems. They also need access to good transportation and to the use of urban space. Poverty and invisibility in developing-country cities will negate urban advantages unless specific and explicit policies are enacted.

The significance of interactions between urbanization and the AIDS epidemic has not received sufficient attention, Collins argues in Chapter 16. Higher HIV prevalence in urban areas and the observation that certain characteristics of urbanization can potentially increase vulnerability generally lead people to assume that urbanization impacts negatively on the AIDS pandemic. The potential benefits of urbanization in terms of socioeconomic improvements, empowerment of women and children, access to information, advocacy and better services, as well as civil society engagement, have been an overlooked component in the response to the AIDS epidemic. Collins examines this connection in the framework of urban poverty and gender inequality. She also takes a closer look at relative prevalence levels in rural and urban areas and reviews the ways that AIDS interacts with migration, fertility, morbidity and mortality, and age composition.

Collins also notes that, although engaging key populations where risk and vulnerability converge is critical to the AIDS response, few policy declarations note that such groups are predominantly found in urban areas. Many of the impact-mitigation efforts of the AIDS response are particularly well suited to implementation in urban areas. In short, urbanization can provide many critical untapped advantages in dealing with the pandemic, but this potential needs to be recognized and acted upon.

The final chapter in this section (Chapter 17) addresses the issue of how evidence-based urban policy and action can benefit from updated approaches to the generation and utilization of timely and reliable socio-demographic data. Torres makes the point that improvements at the local level are particularly vital, especially in smaller cities, which have accumulated growing responsibilities under worldwide decentralization processes. The obstacles are clear: demographic techniques are less well equipped to deal with small areas, and analyses would require the use of geographic information systems (GIS) that are often unavailable; meanwhile, local administrators are frequently uninterested or unfamiliar with socio-demographic information. These are all aspects that have to be tackled with advocacy and technical assistance.

Torres argues that good information can increase the visibility of the poor and thus help to improve the coverage and quality of social services. Spatial and demographic disaggregation of this information can be useful in locating public equipment where needs are most critical and in identifying the most needy groups. In all cases, improvement of the information base and its flow among policymakers, the media and different social groups can not only support better decision-making but also help to promote accountability.

Taken together, the chapters in this section highlight the complexity and multiplicity of demographic shifts that are taking place simultaneously with rapid urbanization in developing countries. In principle, this dynamism could constitute a powerful force for improving people's lives. In practice, taking advantage of these changes will require a better understanding, to which the various chapters in this section contribute, of the potentialities and exigencies, and improved governance reflected in more effective policies.

12

Notes on Urban–Rural Poverty Projections and the Role of Migration

Ralph Hakkert[1]

INTRODUCTION

Much of the migration literature of the past few decades paints a somewhat bleak picture of the role of rural–urban migration in determining poverty. Two lines of thought in particular stand out: the Harris–Todaro (1970) model of rural–urban migration and employment, and the urban bias thesis popularized by Michael Lipton (1977). Although neither assigns a leading role to migration as a poverty determinant, both see it as part of a larger problem of inefficient resource allocation between urban and rural areas.

The Harris and Todaro thesis – that in a dual urban economy, expected long-term returns to migration may keep migrants coming despite rising unemployment – led to the suggestion that policymakers should avoid modern-sector employment creation and instead seek rural development. More recent extensions of the thesis (for example Fields, 2005) have considered a wider set of welfare implications, including poverty, and in doing so have confirmed that, under the assumptions of the model, rural development would indeed produce better labour market outcomes. However, the assumptions of the Harris–Todaro model are themselves increasingly open to debate. Montgomery et al (2003, Chapter 8) point out that the scope for high, rigid urban wage setting, as stipulated by the model, is now believed to be too narrow and perhaps confined to the public sector. Urban formal-sector wage advantages, to the extent that they ever existed, have now been largely eroded, especially in Africa. The other dubious assumption is that migrants rely on a 'move first, then search' strategy with regard to employment, since there is increasing evidence that migrants often arrange employment prior to their move to the city.

Lipton's urban bias thesis proposed that urban groups in poorer countries use their social and political power to skew public policies in their favour and against rural classes, resulting in a resource allocation that is both inequitable and inefficient. The rural disadvantage would manifest itself in insufficient and inappropriate education, overpricing of rural inputs and underpricing of rural products, all resulting in rural–urban migration. This process would be inefficient in that, at the margin, government investment would earn higher returns in small-scale agriculture or rural off-farm employment creation than in cities or large-scale urban-based industries. More recently, Eastwood and Lipton (2000a) have argued that, overall, within-country inequality has increased significantly since the early 1980s, that this increase has not been offset by declining rural–urban inequality and that this absence of offset, save for a few countries in Latin America, must be accounted for by a rise in urban bias in the distribution of resources at a time of reduced price distortions operating against the countryside.

As in the case of the Harris–Todaro model, the claims of the urban bias perspective have been disputed. For instance, the notion that additional urban workplaces cost far more (in equipment, education and infrastructure) than rural and farm workplaces, and that services have a greater marginal benefit for poorer people in rural areas, may not be correct, as is the suggestion that rural areas contain most of the low-cost sources of potential advance. Investments in small-scale agriculture can be costly, particularly when current rates of fertilizer use are low or where water management or common property usage are inefficient. Many non-primate cities in the developing world have grown not so much because of distorted patterns of political access, but because the urban bias in public expenditure and provision is, in fact, an efficient allocation of resources, due to the economies of scale and the spillover effects that arise from the clustering of innovative economic activities. Many goods and services can be efficiently produced in urban areas and made available to people in rural areas at reasonable cost, particularly when the two sectors are closely linked. Finally, several cities suffer from disproportionate tax burdens compared to GDP and revenue receipts.

Part of the reason why it has been difficult to assess adequately the role of the urban–rural duality and, more particularly, of rural–urban migration in the dynamics of poverty is the scarcity of data. The theoretical importance of the rural–urban migration link is belied by the fact that very few countries can estimate even gross flows between areas of residence, let alone associate them with the characteristics of migrants. Bilsborrow (2002) only came up with 14 countries where data on all four types of flows (i.e. rural–rural, rural–urban, urban–urban and urban–rural) were available, and in only four of them (Thailand, 1980; Ecuador, 1982; Honduras, 1983; and the Republic of Korea, 1995) were census data available on residence at a fixed time in the past. (To these, one should add the 2000 Brazilian census, which also provides this kind of data.) In most other developing countries, rural–urban flows have to be approximated by residue methods, which only provide net flows and do not allow for the socioeconomic characterization of the migrants, or by the analysis of migrations between territorial units that are predominantly rural or urban (under the assumption that the origin of the migrants within those territorial units will be more-or-less in accordance with the rural or urban characteristics of the unit).

Clearly, this is not an ideal starting point for understanding the interaction of migration and poverty reduction. Even in the best of cases (the five countries cited above), only the respondents' (rural or urban) area of origin and destination and their current poverty status are known; their poverty status prior to migration is not usually known. In recent years, however, econometricians have devised estimation methods to infer something about the income changes that accompany migration. One of the first to do so, based on a Heckman two-step procedure, was Tunali (2000) for Turkey. More recently, there have been similar applications in Latin America, for example Laszlo and Santor (2004) for Peru and Golgher (2007) for Brazil. The latter found that 65.9 per cent of all migrants to and from rural areas in the 1995–2000 period improved their income as a consequence of the move, with a higher percentage for unskilled (70.2 per cent) than for skilled migrants (52.7 per cent). In short, even though migration does not bring monetary benefits and poverty reduction to all migrants, it is worth the gamble because in most cases the move will pay off.

NATIONAL POVERTY REDUCTION AND THE DIFFERENTIAL GROWTH OF URBAN AND RURAL POPULATIONS

If rural–urban migration were non-selective and only served to move rural poverty to urban areas, and if no other factors intervened to improve the situation of residents in either area, both rural and national poverty levels would be expected to remain constant and urban poverty to increase with rural–urban migration. If migration were slightly selective of the non-poor, poverty would increase in both rural and urban areas, while national poverty rates would remain constant; this would be due to the fact that an increasing proportion of the population would live in urban areas where poverty rates, though rising, are still lower than in the countryside. In fact, however, despite considerable variation between countries and regions, there are other intervening factors, and poverty rates have mostly been declining in both rural and urban areas, although more so in the former than in the latter.

One illustrative measure to describe these processes is the decomposition of national poverty rates into three components: decline of rural poverty, decline of urban poverty and a component related to the rising proportion of the population living in urban areas, where poverty rates are lower. Results for several developing countries are shown in Table 12.1, with the three aforementioned components given in the last three columns.[2]

In most cases, the data on urban and rural poverty rates assembled by Eastwood and Lipton (2000b) show relatively low or even negative contributions of urbanization. Exceptions include The Philippines (1961–1988: not reproduced in Table 12.1), where urbanization accounted for 22.7 per cent of the total national poverty reduction, Bangladesh (1984–1990, 28.2 per cent) and Colombia (1977–1992, 28.2 per cent). More recent data yield higher percentages in some countries. In Bolivia (1999–2005), urbanization accounted for 28.3 per cent of a small reduction in national poverty, whereas the 5.1 per cent national poverty reduction in Brazil between 1999 and 2004 was 17.0 per cent due to urban growth. The recent publication of regional data by Ravallion et al (2007) also makes it possible to compute a world estimate. Using the formula in Note 2 (p231) on aggregated world data yields an estimated proportion of 13.4 per cent of extreme poverty and 17.3 per cent of general poverty reduction attributable to urbanization between 1993 and 2002.[3]

The table must be approached with caution, however, as it does not singly determine the processes involved. The easiest case to interpret is that of Nicaragua (1998–2001), where urban and rural poverty barely changed, but the national poverty rate nevertheless fell by slightly over 0.5 per cent due to urbanization. China (1995–2001) is more challenging in that, in the context of rapid urbanization, poverty (US$2 per day criterion) fell substantially in both urban and rural areas: from 55.0 per cent to 47.3 per cent nationally between 1995 and 2001, with 44.1 per cent of the change due to the increase in the urban population. In theory, this result could have come about by very different processes, such as:

1   Zero migration of the rural poor to urban areas, equally high upward economic mobility of both the urban and the rural poor, and massive migration of the rural non-poor to the cities; or
2   Very high urban economic mobility combined with much lower rural economic mobility and moderate rural–urban migration of both the poor and the non-poor, some of which is accompanied by simultaneous upward mobility of the poor.

Projecting the population of China, without age or sex detail, for another two periods (12 years) based on the projection matrices describing these two scenarios, identical national poverty levels (35.7 per cent) are found for 2013. However, if the projection matrices are constrained to zero rural–urban migration in order to assess the latter's effect on overall poverty, the results are different for either matrix specification. Under the first scenario, overall poverty remains practically the same as under the unconstrained variant, but under the second scenario, the zero migration variant would substantially raise national poverty (to 42.4 per cent)

Table 12.1 *Breakdown of changes in poverty rates among urban and rural areas*

	Urban 1	Urban 2	Rural 1	Rural 2	Total 1	Total 2	DegUr 1	DegUr 2	Δ Urban	Δ Rural	Δ DegUr
China 1995–2001	9.74	6.48	75.77	70.95	55.04	47.29	31.40	36.70	13.21	42.68	44.11
Indonesia 1984–1990	45.70	26.60	15.90	11.20	23.44	15.91	25.30	30.60	64.20	46.64	–10.84
Malaysia 1973–1989	44.80	14.30	55.30	19.30	51.60	16.85	35.20	49.00	30.89	67.12	1.99
Philippines 1985–1988	56.80	49.50	69.40	62.80	63.98	56.62	43.00	46.50	42.61	51.07	6.32
Bangladesh 1984–1990	40.90	33.60	53.80	52.90	51.75	49.08	15.90	19.80	43.47	28.35	28.19
India 1994–1999	71.68	60.54	92.36	88.41	86.90	80.75	26.40	27.50	47.78	47.24	4.98
Sri Lanka 1985–1990	16.40	18.30	31.70	24.40	28.43	23.10	21.40	21.30	–7.64	107.80	–0.11
Bolivia 1999–2005	51.50	50.98	81.58	80.19	62.65	61.47	62.94	64.08	27.84	43.83	28.33
Brazil, 1999–2004	29.00	25.40	61.40	54.40	35.29	30.16	80.60	83.60	56.57	26.47	16.96
Colombia 1977–1992	12.10	8.00	38.40	31.20	22.36	14.96	61.00	70.00	33.81	37.96	28.23
Guatemala 1989–1993	51.00	55.00	56.10	39.70	54.07	46.05	39.80	41.50	–19.85	123.1	–3.24
Nicaragua 1998–2001	30.07	30.13	67.80	67.80	47.01	46.48	55.10	56.60	–6.21	0.00	106.2
Ghana 1988–1992	27.40	26.50	41.90	33.90	36.81	31.09	35.10	38.00	5.52	90.73	3.75
Kenya 1992–1997	29.29	49.20	46.33	52.93	41.76	51.72	26.80	32.40	53.58	48.51	–2.10
Nigeria 1985–1992	4.90	10.90	16.10	15.40	12.66	13.74	30.70	36.80	170.2	–44.82	–25.36
Zambia 1991–1996	27.20	34.00	79.10	74.90	59.07	60.01	38.60	36.40	277.52	–272.7	95.14

Source: Eastwood and Lipton (2000b), complemented with more recent data by the author.
Note: Poverty rates expressed as percentages. See note 2 to this chapter for explanation of data in columns 10–12.

compared to the variant with migration. The actual outcome may lie somewhere in between, although probably closer to the second scenario than to the first, because the latter implies improbably high migration rates of the rural non-poor. It is likely, therefore, that rural–urban migration in China is indeed contributing to national poverty reduction, but precisely how much is a question that needs additional information to answer.

A Closer Approximation

Despite the missing links evident in the previous paragraphs, upward economic mobility is greater in the cities than in the countryside. At least this seems to be the case in China, with its industrially driven economic boom. Whether it also applies to other developing countries is less evident (Montgomery et al, 2003, pp329–331). Such mobility tends to be reduced somewhat by the fact that the urban poor have higher fertility than the urban non-poor, resulting in a higher natural growth rate, which raises urban poverty. Another factor having a similar influence is that rural–urban migrants are typically poorer than urban residents (except, of course, in the hypothetical and improbable first Chinese scenario of the analysis above).

In the following discussion, the fertility–migration–poverty dynamic will be approximated more closely using age- and sex-specific multi-state projection methods. Unlike the econometric methods referred to earlier, these do not use detailed individual-level information about the migrants, but instead estimate aggregate trends by means of 4×4 annual projection matrices (to account for transitions between urban poor, urban non-poor, rural poor and rural non-poor). However, the exact estimation of these matrices for all age groups in the base period is usually difficult, because of the shortage of information on some of the needed components. As indicated earlier, data on the poverty status of migrants prior to their migration are almost entirely missing in all countries, but some countries at least have approximate data on migration flows between urban and rural areas by age and sex.

One such case is Brazil, which published such data in its 2000 census. The data refer to migration in the strict sense, in other words territorial moves that cross a relevant (in this case municipal) administrative boundary. This leaves out both reclassification of rural areas as urban and migration between the rural and urban areas of the same municipality, which do matter in the present context. In both of these cases, it is likely that changes from rural to urban will predominate over changes in the opposite direction by a large margin. Therefore, to make up for these omitted movements, the projections were prepared under the (admittedly somewhat arbitrary) assumption that the ratio of rural–urban to urban–rural migration in each age/sex group should be twice the ratio found in the 2000 census. If this overestimates the importance of rural–urban relative to urban–rural flows, the projected rate of urbanization will be slightly too fast, as was pointed out several years ago by Andrei Rogers (1985) with respect to the UN urbanization projections.

For the purposes of this exercise, it was also estimated that urban poverty fell from 29.0 per cent in 1999 to 25.4 per cent in 2004, while rural poverty fell from 61.4 per cent to 54.4 per cent.[4] The age- and sex-specific projection matrices should correctly reproduce these changes, as well as the change in the degree of urbanization. Furthermore, it was assumed that migration and economic mobility operate independently, in other words that the probability of experiencing both is the product of the probabilities of each. Finally, any remaining ambiguity was resolved by the assumption of minimum movement, meaning that the preferred matrix is the one that transfers the smallest number of people between residence/ poverty categories.

The first group, of 0–4-year-olds in 2004, consisted of people born during the 1999–2004 period and thus requires special treatment. Suffice it to say that the estimation procedure for this group attributed to individuals the residence-poverty status of their mothers five years earlier and then applied a standardized age pattern of fertility to the various female age groups from 15 to 50, in order to estimate a proportionality factor between the number of women and the number of births. The factor is similar to a general fertility rate, but it implicitly corrects the mortality bias as well, so it is actually a combined fertility/mortality/international migration factor. Implicitly, this procedure assumes that the *age pattern* of fertility is the same in all four categories of migration, which may not be true, but the result is not terribly sensitive to such discrepancies. The more important issue is the difference in fertility *levels* between strata, which *is* being considered.

All in all, these procedures are certainly not beyond dispute, and, consequently, the results are best thought of as plausible scenarios rather than as definite estimates. In the projection, the matrices computed in the data analysis are applied to the last observed population (in this case 2004) and, after each projection step, the populations of each age/sex group are adjusted to the corresponding national totals, as previously projected by the Brazilian census bureau.

Table 12.2 displays the mean annual transition matrix averaged over all ages and both sexes (using the 1999 population weights). Again, some caution has to be exercised in interpreting this matrix, particularly with respect to the components of economic mobility: while net mobility rates are probably reasonable, each separate component (upward and downward) may be underestimated. According to Table 12.2, upward mobility of the poor in urban areas is substantially greater (0.0660) than in rural areas (0.0265), while, predictably, migration of the rural poor to urban areas is much more common (0.0805 + 0.0018 = 0.0823) than the movement of urban poor to rural areas (0.0123 + 0.0008 = 0.0131). Finally, the rural poor migrate much more to the cities (0.0805 + 0.0018 = 0.0823) than do the rural non-poor (0.0002 + 0.0240 = 0.0242). Put differently, as many as 82.9 per cent of the rural–urban migrants during the 1999–2004 period were poor – more than the level of the poor among the rural population in 1999, which was only 61.5 per cent.

Table 12.2 *Estimated mean annual transition matrix, averaged over all sex and age groups for the 1999–2004 period*

	Urban poor	Urban non-poor	Rural poor	Rural non-poor
Urban poor	0.9048	0.0005	0.0805	0.0002
Urban non-poor	0.0660	0.9884	0.0018	0.0240
Rural poor	0.0123	0.0000	0.8717	0.0085
Rural non-poor	0.0008	0.0018	0.0265	0.9541

Table 12.3 *Birth, death, net migration and net mobility rates per 1000 population for the four population strata*[5]

	Urban poor	Urban non-poor	Rural poor	Rural non-poor
Births	37.1	18.8	32.4	16.3
Deaths	8.6	8.6	11.4	16.0
Net migration	18.2	1.9	−48.6	−6.4
Net mobility	−51.8	20.1	−18.0	17.8

A different way to understand the joint poverty–population dynamic in the aggregate is in terms of net flows, as displayed in Table 12.3. It may seem strange that the birth rate of the urban poor should be higher than that of the rural poor, but these are gross figures which are affected by the age structure, and the percentage of women of child-bearing age among the urban poor is higher than among the rural poor. The 2004 population of the urban poor also had more than three million recent rural migrants, who would be particularly prone to starting their families at this moment in their life cycle. The unexpectedly high death rate of the rural non-poor has a similar explanation, in addition to the fact that this rate is based on observed survival ratios which are also affected by international migration.

Projecting by the age- and sex-specific matrices underlying Table 12.2, the resulting population distributions for 2010 and 2015 are as shown in Table 12.4.

Table 12.4 *Recent and projected population distributions averaged over all sex and age groups for the four population strata*

	Urban poor %	Urban non-poor %	Rural poor %	Rural non-poor %
1999	23.68	57.81	11.38	7.14
2004	21.45	63.11	8.41	7.03
2010	18.20	68.65	6.18	6.97
2015	15.80	72.45	5.01	6.74

The 1999–2004 period was characterized by a very substantial reduction in rural poverty. In this projection, this rate of reduction is also applied to the subsequent periods, painting a picture that may be excessively optimistic. One thing that might change is the rhythm of rural–urban migration, and it is logical to ask how this would affect poverty trends in both areas. If it is assumed, for instance, that all rural–urban migration flows will be cut by 50 per cent, the evolution of the population distribution is as shown in Table 12.5.

Table 12.5 *Recent and projected population distributions adjusted to assume rural–urban migration flows reduced by 50%*

	Urban poor %	Urban non-poor %	Rural poor %	Rural non-poor %
1999	23.68	57.81	11.38	7.14
2004	21.45	63.11	8.41	7.03
2010	17.00	67.93	7.61	7.46
2015	14.32	70.96	7.08	7.64

It should be noted that under this second scenario, overall poverty in 2015 increases slightly, from 20.81 per cent to 21.40 per cent. Urban poverty under this reduced migration scenario would still be lower (16.79 per cent instead of 17.90 per cent), but in rural areas it would be higher (48.08 per cent instead of 42.65 per cent). This confirms existing perceptions that rural–urban migration does indeed contribute to *urban* poverty, in addition to burdening urban infrastructure. In the case of Brazil, this effect is more than offset by the positive effect of migration on *rural* poverty, so that the overall rural–urban migration causes a slight poverty reduction at the national level. Although Brazil may, in some ways, not be representative of global trends, these findings are entirely in line with the conclusion drawn by Ravallion (2007, p15):

> We believe that, by facilitating overall economic growth, population urbanization has helped reduce overall poverty – however, the process of urbanization has affected rural poverty more than urban poverty.

UNMET DEMAND FOR REPRODUCTIVE HEALTH SERVICES AND URBAN–RURAL POPULATION GROWTH

Finally, a note on the role of fertility and access to reproductive health services is appropriate. In the previous example of Brazil, 42.4 per cent of urban and 73.4 per cent of rural children born during the 1999–2004 period were poor in 2004, much more than the corresponding figures of 25.4 per cent and 54.4 per cent for the population as a whole. Considering that today in most countries more than 50 per cent of urban growth derives from natural, rather than migratory, increases, and that natural increase in rural areas is a major driving force behind rural–urban migration, it may be asked to what extent natural increase – both urban and rural – is affected by access to sexual and reproductive health services and fertility preferences.

Natural increase may account for a significant portion of urban growth, but the reproductive pattern of the urban population is likely to be closer to its fertility preferences than that of the rural population. Consequently, the promotion of sexual and reproductive health in urban areas may not affect natural increase as much as in rural areas. Two separate scenarios were developed, based on data from the Colombian Demographic and Health Survey (2005).[6] The first presumes that the projected urban and rural fertility rates during the 2005–2025 period will be replaced by the wanted fertility rates reported in the DHS country report. A limitation of this approach is that the concept of 'wanted fertility', as reported by the DHS, excludes from past fertility those births that elevated family sizes above the declared ideal size, but does not include those births that were desired but did not occur.[7] The second scenario, in contrast, includes all desired births that women can accommodate within the 20–39 age interval. It presumes that fertility rates are zero before age 20 and after age 40 and that women have one birth every three years until they reach their desired family size.

Under the first scenario, urban population growth during the 2005–2025 period is reduced from an average of 1.66 per cent per year to 1.21 per cent per year. Under the second scenario, due to the inclusion of desired births that did not occur, the urban growth rate actually increases slightly, to 1.86 per cent per year. In the rural areas, the effect is larger and more consistent. Under the first scenario, the average annual rural growth rate is reduced from –0.20 per cent to –0.83 per cent, under the second scenario to –0.78 per cent. This shows that rural growth and hence rural–urban migration can be further reduced – even in Colombia, which is far along in its fertility transition – by extending the access of rural women to reproductive healthcare and family planning. Whether the same also applies to urban areas is not entirely clear.

FINAL REMARKS

Although the computations presented in this chapter are only approximate and may not be representative of all developing countries, they suggest that, at least in some, rural–urban migration contributes modestly to the reduction of overall national poverty rates. That it is so often associated with rising poverty may be because of the tendency to see its effect primarily on *urban* poverty, which may indeed be adversely affected. This result coincides with that of Ravallion et al (2007), who conclude that urbanization is a generally positive factor in overall poverty reduction and that higher rates of increase in the urban population tend to be associated with steeper rates of overall poverty reduction.

The positive indirect effects, through higher rural living standards, appear to be more important than has generally been thought. Indeed, the evidence suggests that urbanization has done more to reduce rural '$1 a day' poverty than to reduce urban poverty. Rural poverty levels tend to fall more rapidly in countries with higher rates of urbanization. Urbanization appears to be having a compositional effect on the urban population, in that the new urban residents tend to be poorer than the previous urban population. Naturally, this slows the pace of urban poverty reduction, even when poverty is falling in rural areas and for the population as a whole.

Strictly from the viewpoint of poverty reduction, more rapid advances will probably require a faster pace of urbanization, not a slower one – and development policymakers will need to facilitate this process not hinder it (UNFPA, 2007; Ravallion, 2007). If too rapid a pace of urbanization is undesirable because of its other policy implications, increased access to reproductive healthcare and family planning still holds the best potential to reduce rural–urban migration flows, even in countries that are well advanced in their demographic transition.

Notes

1   An earlier version of this chapter was prepared as a background paper for UNFPA's *The State of World Population 2007*.
2   The formula underlying this decomposition is the following: Total2–Total1 = DegUr2 (Urban2–Urban1) + (1–DegUr2) (Rural2–Rural1) + (Urban1–Rural1) (DegUr2–DegUr1), where Urban1, Urban2, Rural1, Rural2, Total1 and Total2 are poverty rates in the respective areas at times 1 and 2, and DegUr is the degree of urbanization. The last three columns, ΔUrban, ΔRural and ΔDegUr, refer to percentage of overall poverty change at the national level (i.e. of Total2–Total1) attributable to each of the three components of this formula. Incidentally, this is the same formula as the exact version of formula (3) used by Ravallion et al (2007). For the purposes of their analysis, however, the first factor of each term is treated as a fixed coefficient to be determined statistically.
3   The authors themselves, who use the formula in its modified form (see note 2), find slightly higher proportions – 18.4 per cent of extreme poverty and 18.8 per cent of general poverty.
4   The data are from the National Household Survey (PNAD), corrected for deviations in the age/sex composition from the official population projections and (in the case of the 1999 survey) for distortions in the rural–urban distribution with respect to the 2000 census. The 1999 PNAD did not cover the rural areas of six states of the Northern Region. In order to maintain comparability, these areas were also removed from the 2004 data and from the projections for 2010 and 2015. Brazil does not have

an official poverty line. The poverty figures are based on the common, but unofficial, criterion of classifying as poor all those households whose per capita income is less than half the national minimum wage in Brazil as of September 2004 (i.e. R$260). For 1999, the same value was used, but corrected for inflation.

5   'Deaths' include persons removed from the population by international migration and exclude infant deaths, which are directly discounted from the birth rate.

6   The rural and urban population projections for Colombia for 2005–2025 are based on CELADE (2002).

7   Whether these should be included is a matter of some dispute. To the extent that this was the result of the woman being unmarried or separated or divorced, it might be argued that these are private matters beyond the sphere of public policy. However, if the births did not occur because women had no access to daycare for their children or because they perceived the cost of providing healthcare and education as beyond their family budgets, there might be a legitimate role for public policy.

REFERENCES

Bilsborrow, R. E. (2002) 'Migration, population change and the rural environment', *Environmental Change Security Project Report No 8*, Woodrow Wilson International Center for Scholars, Washington, DC

CELADE (2002) Demographic Bulletin No 76 (LC/G.2175-P), Centro Latinoamericano de Demografía (CELADE), Santiago

Eastwood, R. and Lipton, M. (2000a) 'Pro-poor growth and pro-growth poverty reduction: Meaning, evidence and policy implications', *Asian Development Review*, vol 18, no 2, pp22–58

Eastwood, R. and Lipton, M.(2000b) 'Rural–urban dimensions of inequality change', *WIDER Working Paper No 200*, World Institute for Development Economics Research, Helsinki

Fields, G. S. (2005) 'A welfare economic analysis of labour market policies in the Harris–Todaro model', *Journal of Development Economics*, vol 76, no 1, pp127–146

Golgher, A. B. (2007) 'Migration strategies and income in Brazil: Implications for rural poverty', unpublished paper, CEDEPLAR/UFMG (Centro de Desenvolvimento e Planejamento Regional/Universidade Federal de Minas Gerais), Brazil

Harris, J. and Todaro, M. (1970) 'Migration, unemployment and development: A two-sector analysis', *American Economic Review*, vol 60, no 1, pp126–142

Laszlo, S. and Santor, E. (2004) 'Internal migration and borrowing constraints: Evidence from Peru', unpublished paper, McGill University, Toronto, Canada

Lipton, M. (1977) *Why Poor People Stay Poor: A Study of Urban Bias in World Development*, Temple Smith, London

Montgomery, M. R., Stren, R., Cohen, B. and Reed, H. E. (eds) (2003) *Cities Transformed: Demographic Change and Its Implications in the Developing World*, National Academies Press, Washington, DC

Ravallion, M. (2007) 'Are poor people gravitating to towns and cities? Yes, but maybe not quickly enough', *Finance and Development*, vol 44, no 3, pp15–17

Ravallion, M., Chen, S. and Sangraula, P. (2007) 'New evidence on the urbanization of global poverty', World Bank Policy Research Working Paper No 4199, World Bank, Washington, DC

Rogers, A. (1985) *Regional Population Projection Models*, Scientific Geography Series vol 4, Sage Publications, Beverly Hills, CA

Tunali, I. (2000) 'Rationality of migration', *International Economic Review*, vol 41, no 4, pp893–920

UNFPA (2007) *The State of the World Population 2007: Unleashing the Potential of Urban Growth*, UNFPA, New York

13

Women's Empowerment and Gender Equality in Urban Settings: New Vulnerabilities and Opportunities

Luis Mora

INTRODUCTION

Urban settings currently provide the main arena for reshaping gender relations. The process of urbanization provides both advantages and disadvantages for gender equality and the empowerment of women. In turn, gender relations are often critical in shaping the urbanization process itself, affecting decisions as to who migrates to cities, as well as how the household unit, family roles and local community organizations will be structured in the urban context.

Urban conditions are frequently more difficult for women and children, especially among the poor, exposing them to new forms of exploitation and discrimination, in addition to greater environmental risks. Urban settings can, however, also present new opportunities for gender equality, allowing women to escape from the traditional forms of discrimination that prevail in rural areas, encouraging work outside the home, and facilitating access to education, income and health services, as well as participation in public and political life. This chapter addresses some of these contradictory trends with respect to several interrelated issues: working outside the home, living conditions, family formation and social participation.

WOMEN IN URBAN LABOUR MARKETS: LIGHTS AND SHADOWS

Working for income outside the home is a key facet of women's empowerment. Paid employment for women can elevate their status and favour transformations in gender roles. Urbanization has undoubtedly presented new opportunities for women in terms of access to employment and income, although this access is still gender-differentiated. Two broad trends prevail: the feminization of the labour force and the informalization of the labour market.

There has been a huge increase in female labour-force participation in non-agricultural wage employment (UNRISD, 2005). This rise is partly due to a growing demand for female labour in industrial activities and partly to changing household survival strategies brought on by urbanization itself. Trade liberalization has created employment opportunities for women, particularly in export-oriented light manufacturing. For instance, in Bangladesh, the export-oriented garment industry provided jobs to 1.8 million workers in 2000; of these new jobs, 1.5 million went to women (Kabeer and Mahmud, 2004).

For many women in developing countries, especially young women, export processing zones (EPZs) have represented a means of escape from oppressive home and community environments. During the 1980s and 1990s, most developing countries attracted foreign investment through the EPZs, particularly in South and East Asia and Central and South America. In 2003, 70 to 90 per cent of the workforce in these economic zones was estimated to be female (World Bank, 2003). This trend undoubtedly led to the greater integration of women into the global economy.

Nevertheless, these opportunities can disappear quickly, as business ventures move from country to country or as labour demands change. Moreover, the same factors that led to women's inclusion in the global economy in the first place – unskilled work, low wages and low productivity – can also exclude them. New strategies to address competitiveness in export markets are leading to a reduction in the proportion of women employed in EPZs, while more men are being recruited into new industries that are more technologically sophisticated and demand higher skill levels (Avirgan et al, 2005; UNRISD, 2005). In Mexico, for instance, the *maquiladoras* (textile and garment sweatshops) have shed almost 200,000 jobs since 2000, and women have consistently been released at a faster rate than men as the composition of the sector has shifted towards electronics and transportation equipment (UNIFEM, 2005).

Moreover, in spite of the positive effects of the EPZs on women's autonomy, working conditions in export-oriented manufacturing are often unfavourable (UNIFEM, 2005). Women remain segregated and concentrated at the margins of the production process and at the lower end of the commodity chain in these female-intensive subsectors. Wages are low, contracts are rarely formalized and social benefits (health insurance, vacations, and maternity or sick leave) are rare.

Indeed, employers express a preference for young women in factory jobs and often terminate employment once a worker gets married or becomes pregnant. In some countries, such as Indonesia, these intolerable working conditions have led women workers to become more bold and militant, and they make up the bulk (80 to 95 per cent) of those involved in class actions, as well as a majority of the entities elected to lead them.

Women in the urban informal economy

The deregulation and informalization of the labour market that accompanied economic restructuring in the developing world has led to an increase in working at home. Women are now a large majority in informal and non-standard employment, especially among own-account workers in non-agricultural employment. For example, own-account workers represent 52 per cent of women's informal employment in El Salvador and 39 per cent in Ghana (Avirgan et al, 2005; UNIFEM, 2005).

The contribution of the informal sector to GDP is being increasingly recognized: estimates indicate that it represents 29 per cent of GDP in Latin America and 41 per cent in Asia (ILO, 2002). It comprises half to three-quarters of non-agricultural employment in developing countries and constitutes a larger source of employment for women than for men: over 60 per cent of female non-agricultural workers in the developing world are in this sector (ILO, 2002). In sub-Saharan Africa, 84 per cent of women non-agricultural workers are informally employed compared to 63 per cent for men; in Latin America, the figures are 58 and 48 per cent respectively. In Asia, on the other hand, the proportion of non-agricultural workers in informal employment is roughly equivalent among women and men (ILO, 2002).

But employment in the informal sector can be either a boon or a drawback for women. While it does offer positive opportunities, such as flexibility of work hours and the convenience of working from home, informal employment often does not provide adequate working conditions. A study of street vendors in Asia found that the income of women was lower than that of men, that women often suffered harassment and that they were not allowed to sit on the pavement (Mitullah, 2004; Bhowmik, 2005). Moreover, the level of unionization was higher among male vendors, affording them better protection than the women. Nevertheless, some trade unions had incorporated a women's wing, as in Bangladesh and India.

WOMEN'S ACCESS TO HOUSING AND BASIC SOCIAL SERVICES

Access to secure and safe housing is critical for exploiting what the city has to offer, especially for women. Yet, according to UN-Habitat (2006), close to a billion people today live in substandard housing. Moreover, it is generally acknowledged that women's priorities tend to be ignored in the design of human settlements, the location of housing and the provision of urban services. Urban planning has been more concerned with issues that are defined in physical and spatial terms and that are linked to men's work patterns: housing projects for the poor, for example, rarely consider the needs and priorities of women in terms of site design and the nature of infrastructure and service provision (Masika et al, 1997).

In addition to suffering the effects of overcrowding, inadequate infrastructure and services, and insecurity of tenure, women and children bear the health burdens of water, sanitation, hygiene and related inadequacies, the most serious of which tend to be concentrated in and around people's homes. The labour burden of these inadequacies falls especially hard on women living in poverty. Other hazards, such as exposure to air pollution from smoky cooking fuels, also predominantly affect women (Songsore and McGranahan, 1998).

These conditions should not, however, overshadow the fact that urban women generally benefit from better infrastructure than those living in rural areas. For instance, urban households are more likely to have flush toilets or piped water either in or near the home. They are also much more likely to have access to public transport and to live near a health centre. However, access to, as well as use of and control over, urban infrastructure facilities and social services is different for men and women: Such disparities are linked to inequalities in household relations, property rights and cultural restrictions (Masika and Baden, 1997). Women tend to be disadvantaged as a result of socio-cultural factors and gender discrimination in urban services. For instance, women are often subject to greater risks in public toilets or showers.

Access to public transport

Mobility is one of the main conditions for social and economic insertion in urban environments, but the relations between gender and transport go unrecognized in city planning (Peters, 1998 and 2001; Vandermissen et al, 2001). Women's travel needs are at least as great as those of men, though often radically different. Poor women, who must balance productive, social and reproductive roles in societies, often have higher demands on their time than do poor men (Peters, 2001).

Both economic and social considerations determine women's choices in modes of transport. The findings of a study in five different developing-country cities indicate that (a) more women than men have no mode of transport available and are thus forced to walk; (b) more women than men depend on public transport; (c) women are less likely than men to have access to motorized means of transport; and (d) women are less likely than men to have access to bicycles or other intermediate means of transport (Peters, 2001).

Even when available, public transport is often inadequate; this has various effects on women, including isolation, physical wear and stress, and health costs.

Where bus frequencies are reduced, the ability of elderly women to reach basic services or to visit relatives is also decreased. Similarly, women's comparatively restricted mobility hinders them in gaining access to health knowledge and health services (World Bank, 1999; OECD, 2004). Gender-responsive infrastructure interventions can free up women's time, thereby increasing the enrolment of girls in school and facilitating women's participation in income-generating and decision-making activities.

Access to childcare services

High rates of urbanization and increasing levels of female participation in the labour force increase the demand for non-parental childcare in cities of developing countries (Hallman et al, 2003; UNFPA and GTZ, 2007). Holding a job and caring for one's children are often separate activities that compete for a mother's time, especially when distances are great and transportation facilities are inadequate. Moreover, rural-to-urban migration often entails moving away from one's extended family, a traditional source of informal childcare.

In short, greater options for women's work often occur in settings that are not compatible with the care of children and other dependants. The decision to participate in the labour market is often influenced by the availability of childcare. The lack of childcare facilities is especially crucial for women without a spouse, who often have to choose informal-sector jobs due to their greater flexibility. Reliable and affordable childcare alternatives are thus becoming increasingly important in urban areas. A study in Accra and Guatemala City indicated that life-cycle and household demographic factors, notably age of children, appear to be significant (Quisumbing et al, 2003). In the case of Guatemala City, a high proportion of working mothers are in the informal sector; they are single, separated, divorced or widowed and tend to be poorer than non-working mothers (IFPRI, 2003).

FAMILY, FERTILITY AND GENDER TRANSFORMATIONS IN URBAN CONTEXTS

Urban living makes the biggest difference in gender relations at the household level. The typologies and characteristics of families and households present important rural–urban differences. The shift from extended to nuclear families is more prevalent in urban areas and has paved the way for several new family forms. The increase in divorce, separation, cohabitation and remarriage rates in urban areas also places different strains on women's and on men's social and economic lives.

Worldwide, some 25 per cent of the world's households have women as their heads. In some urban areas – especially in Latin America and sub-Saharan Africa – that proportion can exceed 50 per cent (UNDP, 2003). This growth in female-headed households is commonly equated with an increase in poverty, but female headship can also have positive effects, particularly in urban settings. Female-headed urban households are less likely to be constrained by patriarchal authority, and women may experience greater levels of self-esteem, freedom and control over their economic resources, as well as less physical and emotional abuse. Female heads are also better able to pursue both their personal interests in education and business, and thus to secure the wellbeing of their dependants (Chant, 2007).

Family, fertility and gender identities

Urbanization is considered one of the major social changes associated with the fertility transition in classic demographic theory (Mason, 1997). However, in developing countries, this has been overshadowed by widely shared assumptions that rapid urban growth is a negative phenomenon (Casterline, 1999). In spite of this perception, urban areas are universally acknowledged to provide powerful incentives, as well as lifestyle constraints, that can serve to change the fertility regime, resulting in lower fertility rates (UNFPA and PRB, 2005; McNicoll, 2006).

Higher levels of education, wage work and other opportunities for women associated with urban living are among the mechanisms underlying lower urban fertility. Women in urban areas are also more exposed to modern values that encourage control of their own reproduction and later marriage, and they are less under the influence of kin who control the timing of marriage and choice of spouse (Singh and Samara, 1996; Mensch et al, 2005). Young women and men living in urban contexts in the developing world are thus much less likely to marry early (Mensch et al, 2005).

Urbanization also increases access to education and life options for girls and women. In Guatemala, for example, primary school completion among urban women is more than double that of rural women (Hallman et al, 2006). However, urban residence appears to benefit young people in the upper two income categories more than the extremely poor. The disparity between secondary school enrolment in urban and rural settings is even more skewed (58 versus 14 per cent).

Violence against women

Urban women are confronted with new forms of vulnerability and discrimination. Violence against women in urban areas is often closely linked to access to housing and shelter. Women subjected to domestic violence may remain in abusive relationships if they are unable to secure rights to land and property except through their husbands. In some contexts, violence between different urban groups is often played out by attacks on women, thereby restricting their access to public life and space.

Transitional cultural contexts present particular problems. For instance, in urban centres in Kenya, human rights organizations have documented numerous cases of in-laws exploiting women when their husbands die: relatives interfere with widows' access to pensions, death benefits, bank accounts and property (Human Rights Watch, 2003).

On the other hand, cities often develop more comprehensive policy responses to gender-based violence. Security, legal and health services for female victims of violence are much more likely to be available in urban areas. Several cities construct partnerships between women's organizations and the city administration to address safety issues for both women and men. Others set up special police forces and tribunals to deal with violence against women. And in others, women's safety audits have become a key strategy in the modification of social structures, politics and institutional procedures.

Access to reproductive health services

Urban areas can provide services and infrastructure at a much lower per capita cost due to their obvious advantages in terms of scale and proximity. Thus urban–rural differences in access to basic public health infrastructure are striking, even in poor countries, where many cities have managed to respond to basic public health needs. In China and India, for instance, government investments in the health sector tend to favour urban areas, while the provision of basic health services in rural areas is still lacking (Fan et al, 2005). Overall expenditures in social services declined in India under the structural adjustment programmes. Moreover, subsidies have been redirected away from rural areas towards urban industrial centres: while the rural sector is home to about 65 per cent of the Indian population, only 20 per cent of the health subsidies are directed towards this sector (Fan et al, 2005).

These overall urban advantages, however, are very unequally shared between poor and non-poor groups. The situation of poor urban populations is often akin to those of the rural poor. A study on the health of urban women and young children in developing countries found that household living standards have a substantial influence on two measures of women's health: unmet need for modern contraception and attendance of a trained provider at childbirth (Montgomery and Hewett, 2004). Taken together, these measures describe a relatively high-risk period in the lives of women.

URBAN SETTINGS AND WOMEN'S ECONOMIC AND SOCIAL EMPOWERMENT

Urban spaces provide many opportunities for women's interaction, association and participation in public life. The ability to join an association and participate in public life is an important resource for women's social, economic and political empowerment in urban settings. Modest neighbourhood groups started by women can be transformed into powerful national and international forces for social change. Among the many prominent examples that could be cited, three will be discussed here.

In India, the world-renowned Self-Employed Women's Association (SEWA) is a trade union with 700,000 members – all poor women working in the informal economy – in six Indian states (SEWA, undated). SEWA was the first trade union of informal workers in the world. Started in 1972 in the State of Gujarat, it is closely linked to the Shri Mahila Sewa Sahakari Bank for poor self-employed women in urban areas. The bank gives poor women control of natural and financial resources, for example by helping them to build their own water-producing facilities. Loan recovery rates are high thanks to mutual trust and an understanding of borrowers' individual circumstances. Members avoid predatory private moneylenders and gain self-confidence as they develop the skills required to deal with formal organizations, thus breaking the vicious circle of indebtedness and dependence on middlemen and traders. This has changed women's bargaining power for the better. Today, SEWA Bank has 200,000 depositors and a working capital of 900 million rupees (US$20.6 million). SEWA also advocates at the national and international levels for policies that benefit informal workers. Among its successes is the National Policy for Street Vendors in India (2004) and lobbying for the adoption of the ILO Convention on Home Work (1996).

In some African countries, poor women in urban centres have also formed groups for economic purposes (so-called 'merry-go-rounds', where members contribute money to lend to an individual) and to provide for their needs (purchases of household items and so on). Group members also assist each other for funerals, weddings and emergency fundraising. In Chad, the Union of Women Fish Vendors was founded in 2002 to protect the vendors' economic interests by increasing the price of fish and improving storage facilities (UNIFEM, 2005). It also seeks to build women's solidarity through education and social activities. These mutual support networks provide ties beyond kinship and have served as vehicles for campaigns against child abuse and wife-beating.

At the global level, StreetNet International, founded in 2002, is an alliance of street vendor organizations. Member-based organizations that directly organize street vendors are entitled to affiliate to StreetNet, which promotes the exchange of information and ideas on critical issues facing the vendors; develops practical organizing and advocacy strategies; and promotes local, national and international solidarity among organizations of street vendors, market vendors and hawkers (who are often in competition). At present, 19 street vendor organizations have affiliated with StreetNet. The alliance has attempted to ensure that men do not dominate its leadership through its constitution, which stipulates that at least 50 per cent of both its international council and its office holders must be women (StreetNet, 2004; UNIFEM, 2005).

In short, various experiences and initiatives are helping to find ways in which urban settings can become spaces for the redefinition of gender roles, and where women can find new ways and life choices through better access to association, public participation and decision-making.

THE WAY AHEAD: LEARNING FROM POSITIVE EXPERIENCES IN ENGENDERING URBAN GOVERNANCE

The foregoing sections highlight both the potentialities and the limitations of urban life for gender equity. Much could be improved with greater attention to women's needs in urban planning, through small investments, and, above all, with a greater reliance on women's and other neighbourhood organizations. Urban governance demands that issues of social equity and political legitimacy be increasingly incorporated to bolster administrative efficiency. Men and women experience and use the urban environment in different ways and have different priorities in terms of services and infrastructure. A gender-sensitive approach to urban governance would increase women's participation in the development of human settlements and improve the performance of cities in taking advantage of the urban potential for social improvement.

REFERENCES

Avirgan, T., Bivens, L. J. and Gammage, S. (eds) (2005) *Good Jobs, Bad Jobs, No Jobs: Labour Market and Informal Works in Egypt, El Salvador, India, Russia and South Africa*, Economic Policy Institute, Global Policy Network, Washington, DC

Bhowmik, S. K. (2005) 'Street vendors in Asia: A review', *Economic and Political Weekly*, vol 40, no 22, pp2256–2264

Casterline, J. (1999) 'The onset and pace of fertility transition: National patterns in the second half of the twentieth century', Population Council Working Paper No 128, The Population Council, New York

Chant, S. (2007) 'How can we make the feminization of poverty more policy-relevant? Towards a "feminization of responsibility and obligation"', in UNFPA and German Technical Cooperation (GTZ) (eds) *Social Cohesion, Reconciliation Policies and Public Budgeting: A Gender View*, UNFPA and GTZ, Mexico City, pp197–226

Fan, S., Chan-Kang, C. and Mukherjee, A. (2005) 'Rural and urban dynamics and poverty: Evidence from China and India', FCND Discussion Paper No 196, Food Consumption and Nutrition Division of the International Food Policy Research Institute, Washington, DC

Hallman, K., Quisumbing, A. R., Ruel, M. T. and de la Brière, B. (2003) 'Childcare and work: Joint decisions among women in poor neighbourhoods in Guatemala City', FCND Discussion Paper No 151, International Food Policy Research Institute, Washington, DC

Hallman, K., Peracca, S., Catino, J. and Ruiz, M. J. (2006) 'Multiple disadvantages of Mayan females: The effects of gender, ethnicity, poverty and residence on education in Guatemala', Policy Research Division Working Paper No 211, The Population Council, New York

Human Rights Watch (2003) *Kenya: Double Standards: Women's Property Rights Violations*, vol 15, no 5(A), Human Rights Watch, New York

IFPRI (2003) 'Guatemala: A focus on working women and childcare', IFPRI City Profiles, International Food Policy Research Institute, Washington, DC

ILO (2002) *Women and Men in the Informal Economy: A Statistical Picture*, ILO, Geneva

Kabeer, N. and Mahmud, S. (2004) 'Globalization, gender and poverty: Bangladeshi women workers in export and local markets', *Journal of International Development*, vol 16, no 1, pp93–109

Masika, R. and Baden, S. (1997) *Infrastructure and Poverty: A Gender Analysis*, BRIDGE Report No 51, BRIDGE, University of Sussex, Brighton, UK

Masika, R, de Haan, A. and Baden, S. (1997) *Urbanization and Urban Poverty: A Gender Analysis*, BRIDGE Report No 54, BRIDGE, University of Sussex, Brighton, UK

Mason, K. O. (1997) 'Explaining fertility transitions', *Demography*, vol 34, no 4, pp443–454

McNicoll, G. (2006) 'Policy lessons of the East Asian demographic transition', Policy Research Division Working Paper No 210, The Population Council, New York

Mensch, B. S., Singh, S. and Casterline, J. B. (2005) 'Trends in the timing of first marriage among men and women in the developing world', Policy Research Division Working Paper No 202, The Population Council, New York

Mitullah, W. V. (2004) 'A review of street trade in Africa', working draft, review commissioned by Women in Informal Employment: Globalizing and Organizing (WIEGO), Harvard University, Cambridge, MA

Montgomery, M. R. and Hewett, P. C. (2004) 'Urban poverty and health in developing countries: Household and neighbourhood effects', Policy Research Division Working Paper No 184, The Population Council, New York

OECD (2004) *Why Gender Matters in Infrastructure*, Development Assistance Committee, Network on Gender Equality, Organisation for Economic Co-operation and Development, Paris

Peters, D. (1998) 'Breadwinners, homemakers and beasts of burden: A gender perspective on transport and mobility', *Habitat Debate*, vol 4, no 2, pp12–15

Peters, D. (2001) 'Gender and transport in LDCs: A background paper in preparation for CSD-9', Expert Workshop on Gender Perspectives for Earth Summit 2002: Energy, Transport for Decision-Making, Berlin, 10–12 January

Quisumbing, A. R., Hallman, K. and Ruel, M. T. (2003) '*Maquiladoras* and market mamas: Women's work and childcare in Guatemala City and Accra', FCND Discussion Paper No 153, International Food Policy Research Institute, Washington, DC

SEWA (Self-Employed Women's Association), undated, www.sewa.org, last accessed 4 December 2007

Singh, S. and Samara, R. (1996) 'Early marriage among women in developing countries', *International Family Planning Perspectives*, vol 22, no 4, pp148–157 and 175

Songsore, J. and McGranahan, G. (1998) 'The political economy of household environmental management: Gender, environment and epidemiology in the Greater Accra Metropolitan Area', *World Development*, vol 26, no 3, pp395–412

StreetNet (2004) www.Streetnet.org.za, last accessed 4 December 2007

UNDP (2003) *Human Development Report 2003: Millennium Development Goals: A Compact among Nations to End Human Poverty*, UNDP, New York

UNFPA and GTZ (eds) (2007) *Social Cohesion, Reconciliation Policies and Public Budgeting: A Gender View*, UNFPA and German Technical Cooperation, Mexico City

UNFPA and PRB (2005) *Country Profiles for Population and Reproductive Health: Policy Developments and Indicators 2005*, UNFPA and Population Reference Bureau, New York and Washington, DC

UN-Habitat (2006) *State of the World's Cities 2006/7: The Millennium Development Goals and Urban Sustainability*, Earthscan, London

UNIFEM (2005) *Progress of the World's Women: Women, Work and Poverty*, UNIFEM, New York

UNRISD (2005) *Gender Equality: Striving for Justice in an Unequal World*, United Nations Research Institute for Social Development, Geneva

Vandermissen, M. H., Villeneuve, P. and Thériault, M. (2001) 'Mobilité et accessibilité: Leurs effets sur l'insertion professionnelle des femmes', *Recherches de Pointe en Francophonie*, no 4, pp289–305

World Bank (1999) *Gender and Transport: A Rationale for Action*, PREMNote No 14, World Bank, Washington, DC

World Bank (2003) *World Development Report 2003: Sustainable Development in a Dynamic World*, Oxford University Press, New York

14

Young People in an Urban World

Rogelio Fernandez Castilla, Laura Laski and Saskia Schellekens

INTRODUCTION

Today, the world has the largest generation of young people ever witnessed in history. Numbering over 1.5 billion, adolescents and youths aged 10 to 24 constitute nearly 30 per cent of the total population in developing countries (Lloyd, 2005). During the next two decades, their proportion will continue to swell as a growing number of developing countries progress in their demographic transition.

Since rapidly growing urban areas already make up more than half of the world's population, and since they generally have larger proportions of young people, an increasing majority of these young people will undergo their transitions from childhood to adulthood in urban localities. Given the dimensions of this youthful contingent, the pathways of these transitions will be critical for the development of future societies.

Life in cities is generally associated with more opportunities and better access to education, health, employment and other services. Cities are also engines of economic growth and centres of innovation and participation. Because of their huge and growing numbers at this particular historical moment, young people represent an enormous untapped potential. However, a context of increasing poverty could spell frustration for this mass of young urbanites, unless economic growth generates more decent employment opportunities and social policies are able to meet the specific needs and rights of poor young people.

Many cities in developing countries have large segments of their population living in overcrowded slums that lack essential services such as water, sanitation and energy and that are threatened by environmental hazards, violence and social exclusion (UNFPA, 2007a). Such slums generally have a higher proportion of young people than the rest of the city. This means that, unless compensatory policies are put into place, a disproportionate number of young people will face the future with multiple disadvantages and the potential opportunities of urban life may not materialize for the majority of this large and growing cohort.

This chapter considers the vital role played by young people living in cities and makes the case that protecting their rights and fostering their wellbeing, economic opportunities and social participation are key priorities for development. It situates the growing youth bulge within the context of the demographic transition and discusses some of the main challenges and opportunities that the resulting configuration poses for the development community at this particular historical moment.

THE DEMOGRAPHIC TRANSITION AND RAPID URBAN GROWTH

The confluence of the demographic transition with urbanization, technological changes and globalization is placing young urban people at the centre of social and economic changes. One of the most important consequences of the demographic transition taking place in the developing world, especially in its cities, is the increasing concentration of population in productive age groups, particularly the 15–24 age cohort. As fertility declines, child dependency ratios[1] also decrease, producing a population composition that has relatively more working-age adults and fewer non-working-age dependants (Bongaarts, 2000).

At this particular historical stage, often referred to as the 'demographic dividend' phase, a window of opportunity opens up, during which the dependency burden on societies and the economy is reduced. If the increased population in active-age groups is effectively employed, the potential for personal savings and investments during this time greatly increases. It is true that development itself tends to prolong the dependency of the younger population, but this extension is essentially positive because it stems from staying in school longer, marrying later and entering the labour force before having children.

Urban settings are at the forefront of the demographic transition because fertility declines earlier and faster in urban areas (UNFPA and PRB, 2005). The effects of reduced fertility on the urban age structure are further enhanced by the in-migration of young people. Consequently, as shown in Figures 14.1 and 14.2, urban areas have much larger proportions of their population in working-age groups than rural areas in all three major developing regions. As the figures show, both child and overall dependency ratios are systematically lower in urban areas.

The historical evolution of dependency differentials is exemplified with regard to Africa in Figure 14.3. As can be seen therein, urban dependency ratios have fallen earlier than those in rural areas, and they are expected to continue to fall at a faster rate. Rural Africa currently carries a high demographic burden, with as many dependants (0–15 and 60+) as people of productive ages (15–59), while urban areas have 10 persons of working age for every 7 dependants. Similar urban

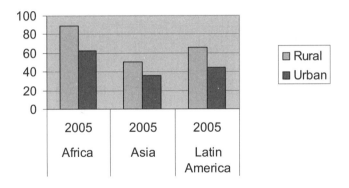

Figure 14.1 *Child dependency ratios in developing regions, 2005*

Source: United Nations (forthcoming).

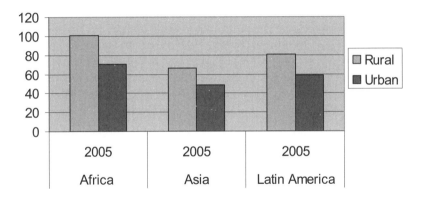

Figure 14.2 *Overall dependency ratios in developing regions, 2005*

Source: United Nations (forthcoming).

advantages can also be observed in the evolution of the age composition in Asia and Latin America over the past 35 years (not shown).

RAPID URBANIZATION, DEPENDENCY RATIOS AND YOUTH EMPLOYMENT

The theoretical advantages that accrue to urban areas in terms of their improved dependency ratios during the demographic transition may, in practice, become a burden if they are not materialized through massive increases in urban job opportunities and supported by adequate social policies. It is estimated that, over

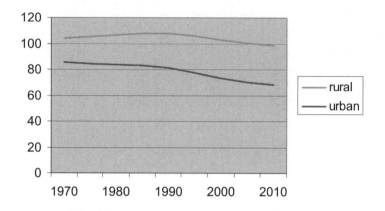

Figure 14.3 *Evolution of overall dependency ratios in Africa, 1970–2010*

Source: United Nations (forthcoming).

the next 10 years, 1.2 billion young women and men will enter the working-age population (United Nations, 2006). A majority of this increment will occur in urban areas. They will make up the best-educated generation ever, constituting an enormous potential force for economic and social development. However, if the employment expectations of young urban people are not satisfied, they will not only be condemned to the same poverty as their parents, but could also constitute huge national and even global social problems.

Accelerated urbanization in the context of globalization has undoubtedly stimulated economic activity and created opportunities for social development. For example, large numbers of young women are employed in globalized industries, especially in the growing garment manufacturing industry and in the service sector (Levine et al, 2008). For the most part, these industries are located in urban areas.

Overall, however, employment creation still lags far behind labour supply and the gap is greatest for young people. Unemployment and underemployment in that age group are disturbingly high, and it is increasingly difficult for youths to break into the labour market. Young people make up 43.7 per cent of the world's unemployed population, and they are more than twice as likely as adults to be unemployed (ILO, 2006). Failing to find productive, decent livelihoods, they often enter into a cycle of poverty, suffering high rates of unemployment across their lifespans.

Employment in the urban informal sector as a percentage of total employment has risen sharply in developing countries during the last decade (UN-Habitat, 2006). Thus it is not surprising that, for the majority of young people in developing countries, the informal sector is their entry point into the labour market. Many young job-seekers resort to 'forced entrepreneurship' and self-employment (United

Nations, 2005). Most young people working in the urban informal sector live in slum areas. Many adolescents are exploited in the job market, often working for low pay under hazardous conditions and with few prospects for improvement. Exploitation, frustration and exhaustion can cause disillusionment and alienation among young workers.

The chances for success for poor young people in the job markets will be affected by policies and programmes that bridge the inequality gap with the non-poor and that empower them to get decent, non-exploitative jobs. Overall increases in education, as well as programmes that can provide them with the right skills to respond to the demands of the labour market – including in the informal sector – and that also allow them to make their best contributions, are thus critical (ILO, 2005). The ability to negotiate decent, equitable working conditions, in terms of both working hours and social protection, is part of that package.

Ultimately, however, the issue will also hinge on the ability of the economic sectors to generate productive activities at a pace that will be able to absorb effectively a rapidly growing army of young people in ways that will motivate and reward them for their labours. The complexities and challenges of generating this economic dynamism are beyond the scope of this chapter, but it is clear that the urban youth bulge is a huge and still insufficiently appreciated part of success or failure in development. The frustrations accompanying long-term unemployment among large populations of young people in urban areas may, in turn, feed political and ideological unrest and provoke increased violence.

RAPID URBAN GROWTH, THE YOUTH BULGE AND FERTILITY DECLINE

Policymakers in rapidly urbanizing nations would generally prefer slower rates of urban growth in order to manage it better, and they sometimes attempt to achieve this through policies to slow down rural–urban migration. As amply demonstrated in various chapters of this book, such measures rarely work. Moreover, natural increase, rather than migration, is generally the main factor in urban growth.

The role of today's young people will be significant in determining the level of future urban growth rates. Slowing the pace of urbanization and of population growth will depend to a large extent on investments in young people. Urban female adolescents, as well as other women of reproductive age, have lower fertility. For example, in countries such as Burkina Faso, Kenya, Mali and Mozambique, fertility rates among 15–19-year-old girls are about twice as high among the rural population as among their urban counterparts (MEASURE DHS, 2007).

Rural residents, including youths, tend to have less access than urban populations to sexual and reproductive health services, including family planning. Furthermore, child marriage is prevalent in rural areas in many parts of the developing world. For example, in sub-Saharan Africa and South Asia, about half of all rural girls are married by age 18, about twice the rate of their urban counterparts (Lloyd, 2005). The fertility rates of girls who marry as children tend to be higher than of those who marry later.

Secondary schools, higher educational institutions and healthcare centres are generally of higher quality and are more available in urban areas. This 'urban advantage' is reflected, for example, in the disparity between the rates of school attendance among urban and rural youth in developing countries: rural boys' and girls' school attendance rates are, respectively, 26 and 38 per cent lower than those of their urban counterparts (Lloyd, 2005). However, these urban benefits are not evenly distributed. For instance, in Mozambique, quintile analysis shows that the poorest 15–29-year-old urban girls are 2.5 times less likely to have completed four or more years of schooling than their richest female counterparts (30 per cent versus 75 per cent); they are also much less likely to have completed four or more years of education than boys of the same age and economic condition (30 per cent versus 59 per cent) (The Population Council, 2001).

Unmet needs for social services, including those in the area of reproductive health, are high in slums. The urban poor have higher fertility rates than other urbanites: poor women have less education and less autonomy, they have less knowledge about sexual and reproductive health services and have little access to them (See Chapter 12). In Niger, the fertility rates of women living in slums are three times higher than those of urban women not living in slums. This differential is a constant in most urban areas in Africa. It results in a faster rate of population growth in slum areas than in the rest of the city, and thus in the intergenerational reproduction of slum conditions.

A significant part of natural increase is inertial, associated with the large proportions of new couples beginning procreation, rather than with high fertility rates per se. Inertial growth, associated with young age structures, is often considered as 'inevitable growth'. Yet investments in human development that target young people serve to effectively delay marriage and procreation, and this, in turn, has a significant impact on reducing the inertial component of demographic growth.

Access to sexual and reproductive health information and services helps all young people to exercise their reproductive rights and make informed choices about their procreation. It helps to delay young people's family formation and to improve human capital through education and access to employment skills. Delayed family formation, and thus delayed financial and other responsibilities for the care of dependent children, helps young people to accumulate personal savings and overcome poverty, and, on an aggregate level, contributes to the country's economic growth.

Finally, it should be noted that urban population growth results not only from the combination of unmet needs, unwanted fertility and inertial growth. Rural migrants to the city bring with them rural fertility patterns that influence overall fertility (UNFPA, 2007a): the rapid integration of these migrants into the opportunities and services available in the city will accelerate the fertility transition.

URBAN CHANGE AND ADOLESCENT PREGNANCY

In addition to quality education and job skills, adolescents and youths also need support as they go through the dramatic transition to becoming autonomous adults. The area of sexual and reproductive health is a critical component in this context. Adolescence is a time of intense changes, many of which are associated with emerging sexuality.

Early fertility thwarts human capital formation, and this disproportionately affects the poor. One-quarter of all girls in developing countries become mothers before the age of 18. Early childbearing is closely correlated with poverty: girls from poor households are three times more likely than non-poor girls to give birth during adolescence, and they bear twice as many children (UNFPA, 2007a). When they have access to services, young women living in slums are more likely to postpone pregnancy and to have smaller and healthier families.

Early childbearing also has negative effects on the economic situation of adolescent mothers and their children, especially among the poor (Buvinic, 1998). A study in Mexico focused on women who had delivered their first child in a major hospital in Mexico City: four years later, it was found that mothers who gave birth before age 18 were six times more likely to live in poverty than women who gave birth for the first time at age 21 or later (Buvinic, 1998). In Santiago, poor women who gave birth at age 19 or younger had significantly lower wages than those who gave birth after age 20 (Buvinic, 1998). Early childbearing thus seems to entrench the poverty of low-income women. Attaining a certain level of schooling and contributing to family income are two positive factors that help women to stem what otherwise could be a vicious cycle of poverty for themselves and their children (Buvinic, 1998).

Thus, for adolescent girls living in slums, the 'urban advantage' also requires access to programmes that provide them with the information, skills and services to exercise their rights in the area of sexual and reproductive health.

URBAN LIFE AND GENDER EQUALITY AMONG YOUTHS

The social pressures that adolescents experience at their stage of life vary from one society to another and differ significantly for boys and for girls. Puberty changes for adolescent girls in some societies may spell isolation, restraint from participation in public life, discrimination and sexual exploitation. Once differentiated gender roles are installed, opportunities for adolescent girls may be further constrained. They may also be subject to sexual violence, child marriage, early pregnancy and unsafe abortion.

Along with better economic opportunities, urban life can help young women to overcome some of the restrictive gender norms and traditional practices commonly found in rural areas and to get a sense of autonomy and control over their lives.

A survey in the slum areas of Addis Ababa found that one in every four female adolescent migrants aged 10–19 had come to the city to escape being forced into marriage (Ethiopia Ministry of Youth, Sports and Culture et al, 2006). Moreover, a study of adolescent girls who had migrated from rural to urban areas in Bangladesh shows that only 31 per cent were married by age 18, compared to 71 per cent of their peers who stayed behind (Lloyd, 2005).

Young women in urban areas marry later because of greater opportunities for education and participation in the labour force, the advantages of which, in turn, allow them to improve their social position. That is, young women who have control over their earnings have more freedom to decide when and whom they marry, as well as to choose the timing, number and spacing of their children. Nevertheless, adolescent girls and young women living in poor urban settings may need targeted support – in, for example, access to education, employment opportunities, and sexual and reproductive health services – to overcome pervasive discrimination and to live out the gender equality promise of urban life.

Differentiated gender roles also condition the trajectories of young boys, who are more likely to engage in violence and participate in gangs. Young people growing up in cities with limited opportunities are regularly reminded of their social inequalities. Exclusion impacts on crime and violence in many cities: violence tends to increase when youthful expectations for a better life are not fulfilled. Rapid urban growth, when combined with economic crises, unemployment and weak institutions, contributes to urban crime and violence (Winton, 2004). Escalating demand and shortages of resources for urban services, law enforcement and violence-prevention programmes often overwhelm urban management.

The 'anti-urban bias' (discussed in Chapters 2 and 21), and its attendant lack of a proactive approach to the needs of the poor, ends up contributing to shelter deprivation, unemployment, crime and violence, aspects closely associated with poor youthful populations. But the increase in crime and violence also contributes to a general feeling of insecurity in the city (Vanderschueren, 2000). In particular, the poor lack the means to defend themselves: vulnerability to urban violence erodes social capital, breaks down socio-cultural bonds and frustrates social mobility, especially for young people (Vanderschueren, 2000). On the plus side, young people living in slums have shown a propensity to engage in a culture of prevention, promoting support for adherence to law and reducing unemployment among at-risk youths (UN-Habitat, 2006).

THE PARTICIPATION OF YOUNG PEOPLE AS CITIZENS OF THEIR OWN COMMUNITIES

Hundreds of millions of urban-dwellers live in crowded homes and neighbourhoods with little or no infrastructure. Such conditions impact directly on young people, who feel excluded from the promise of everything that city life brings to so many others. Large numbers live in miserable conditions, without access to basic social services, merely existing from day to day (see Chapter 2). Poverty also excludes many young people from civic participation and denies them the opportunity to exercise their rights. They have no access to decision-making forums, nor are they acknowledged as partners in the decision-making process.

Opportunities for participation are important both for the development and socialization of individuals and for the political and economic stability of communities and the larger society. Participation ensures the sustainability and strength of democracy. Young people's experience in citizenship and community involvement affects the extent and nature of their civic participation over their lifetimes.

Increasingly, young people are playing a key role in organizing for better living conditions in urban communities. Successful municipal initiatives throughout Latin America, for example, have demonstrated that active consultation with young people helps to develop solutions to their concerns (Cabannes, 2006). Cape Town, Karachi and other cities have involved young slum-dwellers in surveying, documenting and mapping their urban communities, generating essential data and information for city authorities. Such initiatives have helped to build partnerships with official agencies in ways that strengthen and support young people's participation and that have influenced the planning, finance and management of urban infrastructure (Cabannes, 2006).

Cities are spaces for community organization that have young people among their more enthusiastic participants. This lays the foundations for organizations that strengthen democratic institutions. For instance, it helps to create accountability mechanisms to monitor government programmes so that these can better serve the needs of poor urban communities.

WHAT ACTIONS ARE NEEDED FOR URBAN YOUNG PEOPLE?

The condition of young people ripples out to their families, communities and countries and echoes into future generations in special and profound ways. Compelling data show that key future social and economic outcomes depend heavily on the conditions of adolescents and youths today – not only on their access to quality education, which has become a well-accepted, although still unfulfilled, part of the development agenda, but also on their labour skills and on their access to other basic services. Their potential for participation in society is another important asset that young people bring with them, making a dynamic force for change and democratization of their urban territories and societies.

By virtue of their age and social position, young people's opportunities and prospects are fundamentally shaped by those closest to them, particularly family members. But the opportunities provided by urbanization have tremendous potential even for urban young people living in poverty – if they are given a chance.

On the other hand, urbanization may leave young people of poor backgrounds on the margins if policies and resources do not target them more decisively.

It is therefore critical that human capital be developed through investing in young people. Young people need access to quality education which can make them adequately skilled and competitive, as part of an integral strategy of job and employment creation. Social programmes targeting the urban poor should address underlying factors of marginalization, social inequalities and lack of opportunities. Adolescent girls' empowerment should be prioritized, in order to increase their access to education and employment. Young people should be provided with good quality sexual and reproductive health information and services. This will empower them to exercise their reproductive rights in a way that is conducive to delayed procreation and smaller, healthier families.

Only by taking measures that will help meet the needs and ensure the rights of young individuals, and by providing them with equitable opportunities to reap the benefits that urban life has to offer, will societies be able to materialize the potential provided by urbanization and the demographic transition, offset the negative effects of the inertial fertility decline of the poor, and improve their prospects for economic growth.

Population momentum, combined with urban decline in fertility rates, provides a unique chance to spur economic development as the workforce increases and the dependency burden of society decreases. The demographic bonus will have a positive effect on opportunities for savings and economic growth in aggregate terms, provided the economically productive population is effectively employed and enabled to delay procreation until adulthood.

But this momentum is also likely to create adverse effects for young people, who will face greater obstacles in entering an already crowded labour market, especially if they are not equipped with the skills to be competitive. Consequently, there is a need for compensatory, socially equitable public policies to offset the disadvantages that this generation is likely to suffer. In the absence of such policies, the intergenerational cycle of poverty will remain unbroken, social inequalities will be perpetuated, and there is a distinct danger that the so-called 'youth bulge' could translate into a multiplicity of social conflicts.

Economic growth, structural changes, job creation and educational upgrading are a *sine qua non* for all efforts aimed at taking advantage of the demographic dividend and the youth bulge in developing-country cities. City governments will have to take the initiative in attracting investments, generating economic activity and creating jobs in the present globalized and decentralized context. They should also play a critical role in facilitating a favourable regulatory environment, thus improving the prospects for youths to obtain decent work in both the formal and informal economies.

Young people are a dynamic force. If mobilized for social change they will respond in a committed, productive and responsible way so that they can become part of the solution of their own problems. This will have a tremendous impact on poverty reduction, social harmony and human security, and they will look at the future with the optimism that characterizes them.

NOTE

1   The dependency ratio is equal to the number of individuals aged below 15 or above 64 divided by the number of individuals aged between 15 and 64, expressed as a percentage.

REFERENCES

Bongaarts, J. (2000) 'Dependency burdens in the developing world', in N. Birdsall, A. C. Kelley and S. Sinding (eds) *Population Matters: Demographic Change, Economic Growth and Poverty in the Developing World*, Oxford University Press, New York, pp55–64

Buvinic, M. (1998) 'Costs of adolescent childbearing: A review of evidence from Chile, Barbados, Guatemala and Mexico', *Studies in Family Planning*, vol 29, no 2, 'Adolescent Reproductive Behaviour in the Developing World', pp201–209

Cabannes, Y. (2006) 'Children and young people build participatory democracy in Latin American cities', *Environment and Urbanization*, vol 18, no 2, pp195–218

Ethiopia Ministry of Youth, Sports and Culture, UNFPA, and The Population Council (2006) 'Program brief: Berhane Hewan ("light for eve"): A program to support married and unmarried adolescent girls in Rural Ahmara Region, Ethiopia', www.popcouncil. org/pdfs/Ethiopia_BerhaneHewanBrief2006.pdf, last accessed 8 February 2008

ILO (2005) 'Youth: Pathways to decent work: Report VI: Promoting youth employment: Tackling the challenge', International Labour Conference, 93rd Session, ILO, Geneva

ILO (2006) *Global Employment Trends for Youth*, ILO, Geneva

Levine, R., Lloyd, C., Greene, M. and Grown, C. (2008) *Girls Count: A Global Investment and Action Agenda*, Center for Global Development, Washington, DC

Lloyd, C. (ed) (2005) *Growing up Global: The Changing Transitions to Adulthood in Developing Countries*, National Research Council and Institute of Medicine of the National Academies, The National Academies Press, Washington, DC

MEASURE DHS, STAT compiler, www.measuredhs.com, accessed 8 November 2007

The Population Council (2001) *Facts about Adolescents from the Demographic and Health Survey: Statistical Tables for Programme Planning: Mozambique 1997*, The Population Council, New York

UNFPA (2007a) *The State of World Population 2007: Unleashing the Potential of Urban Growth*, UNFPA, New York

UNFPA (2007b) *The State of World Population 2007: Youth Supplement: Growing Up Urban*, UNFPA, New York

UNFPA and PRB (2005) *Country Profiles for Population and Reproductive Health: Policy Developments and Indicators 2005*, UNFPA and the Population Reference Bureau, New York and Washington, DC

UN-Habitat (2006) *The State of the World's Cities 2006–2007: The Millennium Development Goals and Urban Sustainability*, Earthscan, London

United Nations (2005) *World Youth Report 2005: Young People Today and in 2015*, Department of Economic and Social Affairs, United Nations, New York

United Nations (2006) UN Secretary-General Kofi Annan's address to the 4th European Union/Latin America and Caribbean Summit of Heads of State, Vienna, 12 May

United Nations (forthcoming) *The Age Structures of Urban and Rural Populations*, Population Division, United Nations, New York

Vanderschueren, F. (2000) 'The prevention of urban crime', paper presented at the Africities 2000 Summit, Windhoek, South Africa, May

Winton, A. (2004) 'Urban violence: A guide to the literature', *Environment and Urbanization*, vol 16, no 2, pp165–184

15

Urbanization and Ageing in Developing Countries

José Miguel Guzmán and Paulo Saad

AGEING AND URBANIZATION: AN OVERVIEW

Two inexorable demographic trends – urbanization and population ageing – have generated widespread concern in recent years. The projected large increase in urbanites in developing countries has been well documented (see Introduction and Chapter 1). Meanwhile, the later stages of the demographic transition are being marked by huge increases in the population of older persons. This raises many questions concerning the probable quality of life of these growing, older cohorts. Developing countries, characterized by limited access to social services, high incidence of poverty and low coverage of social security, are particularly challenged to meet their needs.

Rapid urbanization in developing countries will inevitably concentrate increasing numbers of older persons in urban areas. What implications will this have? The trends analysed in this chapter underscore the potential advantages of urbanization in terms of creating an enabling environment for improving the life conditions of older people. Overall, urbanization can be seen as a potential ally in efforts to come to grips with population ageing due, *inter alia*, to the relatively higher income levels of urban localities and to their inherent advantages of scale and proximity in the provision of services. Nevertheless, specific policies are necessary to maximize the development benefits of urbanization for older persons while minimizing its possible negative impacts.

PATTERNS OF AGEING IN RURAL AND URBAN AREAS

Population ageing is now almost universal, but where is it occurring at a faster rate? If fertility and mortality patterns were the only factor, urban populations would be much older than rural ones. Lower fertility levels and longer life expectancy in urban areas would translate into lower proportions of children and youths and higher proportions of adults and older persons. However, migration of young people from rural to urban settings, plus return migration to rural areas by older persons, could offset this tendency by depleting younger cohorts and swelling older cohorts in rural areas. Thus rapid urbanization has actually exacerbated rural population ageing in many developing countries (Kreager, 2006; Knodel and Saengtienchai, 2007; Zimmer et al, 2007). As of the 1990 round of censuses, rural areas had a greater proportion of elderly people than urban areas in 53 of the 67 developing countries for which data were available (Stloukal, 2001).

Recently available data at the world and regional levels illustrate how population ageing has progressed in urban and rural areas in a context of rapid urbanization. Table 15.1 shows that, while the world's urban population increased from 36 to 45 per cent between 1970 and the mid-1990s, the proportion of the world's population aged 60 and over grew by two percentage points in urban areas and by one percentage point in rural areas. As was to be expected, the increase in the older age groups of both urban and rural populations was considerably larger in more developed regions, where the percentage aged 60 years and over grew from 15 to 20. There, older people continued to make up a larger proportion of the rural population than of the urban population. Meanwhile, in less developed regions, the over-60 category increased by two percentage points in urban areas and by one percentage point in rural areas. In Asia, Latin America and the Caribbean, the proportion of the 60 and over category grew by two per cent in both rural and urban areas, while in Africa this category increased from four to five per cent in urban areas and remained stable at six per cent in rural areas.

In short, up until the mid-1990s, both out-migration of the young and return migration of older age groups to rural areas were indeed countering what, from fertility and mortality trends alone, would have been faster growth of the ageing population in urban areas. It is also possible that data for the more recent period (post-1995), during which population ageing proceeded at an increasing rate, will show an acceleration in the trend of faster population ageing in the rural areas of developing countries, emulating the tendencies in more developed countries.

Of course, it is important to point out that, given rapid rates of urbanization, older people are concentrated increasingly in urban areas in both developing and developed regions. For instance, estimates for Latin America suggest that the proportion of the regional population aged 60 and over living in cities increased from 60 per cent in 1970 to 80 per cent in 2005 and that it is expected to reach 85 per cent in 2050 (ECLAC, 2007). Unfortunately, similar estimates are

Table 15.1 *Urbanization level and percentage of total, urban and rural populations aged 60 years and over at two points in time, by level of development and major area*[1]

| Major Areas | Urbanization rate | | Percentage aged 60 years or over | | | | | |
	Percentage	Year	Total population	Year	Urban population	Year	Rural population	Year
World	36	1970	8	1970	9	1971	8	1971
	45	1995	10	1995	11	1996	9	1996
More developed regions	65	1970	15	1970	13	1970	16	1970
	73	2000	20	2000	18	2001	21	2001
Less developed regions	25	1970	6	1970	6	1972	7	1972
	38	1995	7	1995	8	1994	8	1994
Africa	25	1975	5	1975	4	1974	6	1974
	32	1990	5	1990	5	1991	6	1991
Asia	23	1970	6	1970	7	1971	7	1971
	37	2000	9	2000	9	2000	9	2000
Latin America and the Caribbean	57	1970	6	1970	7	1971	6	1971
	73	1995	8	1995	9	1993	8	1993
Northern America	74	1970	14	1970	14	1970	14	1970
	79	2000	16	2000	16	2000	18	2000
Europe	63	1970	16	1970	14	1970	17	1970
	72	2000	20	2000	17	2001	21	2001
Oceania	71	1970	11	1970	13	1972	9	1972
	70	1990	13	1990	15	1990	11	1990

Sources: United Nations (2006, 2007a and 2007b).

still unavailable at the world level, but it is obvious that towns and cities will increasingly harbour larger numbers of older people as urbanization progresses. The policy implications of this trend cannot be overstated. In essence, urban areas theoretically offer more opportunities to deal with a changing population composition, but these would have to be materialized, in practice, through better policies on a wide front.

Increases in the proportion of the rural population composed of older people have raised concerns about their wellbeing. On the one hand, rural elders in developing countries tend to be more vulnerable than urban elders because of their higher incidence of poverty, greater transportation problems, and lack of access to social services and infrastructure. On the other, the rural-to-urban migration of young adults can also represent a deteriorating factor in the quality of life of older persons by decreasing younger people's ability to provide material, physical and emotional support for their older relatives still living in rural areas, particularly those in ill health or with disabilities.

The lack of formal support from public welfare systems makes a considerable segment of the older population in developing countries partially or completely dependent on the informal support provided by the family. Therefore, living alone in these countries is generally viewed as a factor that increases the vulnerability of older persons (United Nations, 2001).

However, the effect of urban versus rural residence on the living arrangements of older persons has, so far, been reported to be rather minimal (Bongaarts and Zimmer, 2001; United Nations, 2005). In particular, no consistent difference among countries has been found in terms of the urban–rural differences in the proportions of older persons living alone or living with adult children. In addition, in most countries, the differences that do exist are of little significance. Given the clear potential advantages of urban residence for older people, the factors that have impeded their realization must be considered. Specifically, issues such as co-residence, changing values and the effects of urban poverty must be assessed.

Co-residence with adult children is generally understood as a key determinant of support for older populations. Such a pattern remains very common in developing countries, in both urban and rural areas, despite the increasing levels of population mobility and urbanization in these countries (Hermalin, 2002; Saad, 2003; Chan, 2005; Knodel et al, 2005). In Latin America and the Caribbean, as well as in Africa, the average proportion of older persons living with children is slightly higher in urban than in rural areas, but in Asia, co-residence levels are slightly higher in rural than in urban areas (United Nations, 2005).

Although this situation could be regarded solely as the result of higher past fertility in older populations of developing countries, it could also be due to the fact that the decisions to migrate taken by rural younger adults take into consideration the needs of older adults. In Cambodia and Thailand, for instance, the majority of older persons with only one child in rural areas live either near this child or within the same village (Zimmer et al, 2007).

Although out-migration of adult children inevitably decreases the availability of physical support for older parents remaining in rural areas – a situation that tends to become more critical as the number of children decreases – cases in which older persons are left completely abandoned are rare. In many instances, migration can be seen as part of a household's economic strategy that also brings benefits to older adults through the return flow of capital from geographically distant offspring (Zimmer et al, 2007).

The so-called 'time-for-money hypothesis', in which parents provide household labour and childcare to the families of their adult children in exchange for transfers of money or food, has been often observed in Asian families. Silverstein et al (2007), for instance, show that, in rural areas of China, where dependence on adult children is virtually the only option available to older persons, it is common for grandparents to provide childcare for their grandchildren. This allows adult children the opportunity to migrate and take jobs at better pay in urban locations, enabling them to send larger remittances back to their original rural communities. Likewise, a recent study on the impact of migration on the quality of life of older persons 'left behind' in rural China shows that 'having migrant children improves both the economic wellbeing and housing conditions of the rural elderly in China, although no significant influence is found on the psychological status of the elderly' (Zhuo and Liang, 2006, p16).

Urbanization is expected to result in a decrease in social networking and family support structures. Traditional ties could also be eroded by the difficulties of exchange between family members. Such trends would inevitably have negative consequences on the wellbeing of older persons. Thus an important empirical question is whether, in a context of increasing urbanization, traditional socio-cultural norms, values and traditions will remain strong enough to stimulate families and communities to provide the support needed by the growing population of older persons.

The results in this regard are not yet conclusive. In Asia, a study by ESCAP (2006) shows that, in Japan, the proportion of adult children living with older parents seems to be declining and that in other countries of the region, the informal support systems also seem to be growing weaker. However, as reported in many studies (Knodel et al, 1992; Ofstedal et al, 1999; Hermalin, 2002), family support is still high in this region, even in a context of rapid change. Furthermore, in some countries and territories (Hong Kong, SAR China; Malaysia; the Republic of Korea; Singapore; Taiwan, Province of China; and Thailand), family support systems can be seen as positively adapting to changes: 'Urban youths still expect to live with and support their older parents. Deep-seated social norms concerning the moral obligation of children to support their parents still prevail today' (ESCAP, 2006, p7).

In Latin America, a study carried out in five cities has shown that a strong informal support system continues to prevail, although at variable levels among countries (Saad, 2003). Results based on data from the same survey also showed that, more than the number of children living in co-residence, which is still high in the region, co-residence is what matters for receiving support in daily life (United Nations, 2005).

Although recent findings do not support the notion that modernization, urbanization or population mobility have contributed to the abandonment of older people by their families in the short term, the question still remains whether current transformations in family structure and economy – resulting from population ageing, urbanization and globalized development – will eventually undermine informal, family-based systems of old-age support and security. This concern is greatest in places where formal support is limited.

Urban Facilities versus Urban Poverty

In principle, urban areas offer a more favourable environment for promoting and implementing actions that can contribute to a healthy and successful ageing. Population concentration, with its advantages of scale and proximity, helps increase access to social services, such as better transportation systems, healthcare facilities, home-nursing services and recreational facilities, and creates a more enabling environment for social participation and integration, leisure, and communication with relatives. This is particularly relevant considering the need to strengthen medical and long-term care as the older population increasingly concentrates in the oldest age groups. Additionally, urban settings offer older persons greater access to information and new technologies that can have significant implications for their wellbeing (Cutler and Hendricks, 2001). Finally, urban areas favour the formation of associations for older persons, as well as the development of community-based services intended to give support to older people in need.

However, none of these advantages are guaranteed. Unless older persons have economic security and/or strong social-support systems and access to good transportation, and are not prevented by physical or institutional barriers from using the urban space, they will not fully benefit from the opportunities the city offers (UN-Habitat, 1993). In most cities of the developing world, the potential advantages for older urban people may be undermined by restrictions and barriers stemming from overall conditions of poverty. One-third of the world's urban population live in slums, where access to urban services – in health, education and transport, *inter alia* – tends to be deficient. Such restrictions are likely to be even worse for older people. An additional barrier is invisibility, a situation in which older persons' needs are 'lost' in the midst of the competing needs of other segments of the population.

It could also be argued that the process of development itself will eventually ensure that older persons have access to the best opportunities cities can offer. However, even major cities in the developed world have not yet found a full solution to meeting the needs of a growing ageing population. Results from the World Cities Project (Rodwin and Gusmano, 2002), carried out in London, Paris, New York and Tokyo, have questioned the capacity of big cities in developed countries to accommodate 'this revolutionary demographic change' (p449) and to make all the innovations in health and social policy that will be required to simultaneously serve both old and young citizens. Thus, 'despite the success of public health reformers and urban planners in improving their quality of life over the past century, these world cities still confront onerous health risks' (p449), such as the re-emergence of infectious diseases, the increase in social inequalities – expressed in increasing rates of homelessness and poverty in all four cities[2] – and the barriers that poor and ethnic minorities face in accessing quality medical services.

In conclusion, living in cities can have positive impacts, particularly in terms of the potential for access to services and amenities. However, this is undermined by the conditions of poverty in which a large segment of the older population finds itself and may eventually be countered by increasing changes in values and other factors that affect the strength of traditional social networks. Proactive policies will need to be developed and implemented in order to reduce negative impacts while increasing the comparative advantages of living in cities.

URBAN SEGREGATION OF OLDER PERSONS

In many big cities of the developing world, older persons are more likely to live in specific areas, particularly in older settlements situated in downtown areas, as illustrated by the case of Santiago (see Figure 15.1). This phenomenon occurs because the ageing of people tends to parallel the ageing of their neighbourhoods and because older persons tend to have greater access to health, recreational and service facilities in downtown areas.

Some countries, however, explicitly attempt to populate downtown areas with young families, thus motivating older persons to move to other neighbourhoods. For instance, the Shanghai Municipal Government is encouraging seniors living in rest homes in the city's downtown area to consider moving out to the suburbs, where medical care will be provided for them. Given the overcrowded conditions prevailing in downtown areas, this is expected to improve their quality of life. However, some argue that negative effects on family support could result because living in suburbs can make it more difficult for children and relatives to visit regularly.[3]

CHALLENGES FOR LOCAL AND NATIONAL GOVERNMENTS: NEW ORGANIZATIONAL APPROACHES

The contrast between the potential benefits of urbanization for older people and the realities of their situation reinforces the need for adequate policies, at both the national and local levels, in order to materialize the synergy between the two demographic processes of urbanization and ageing.

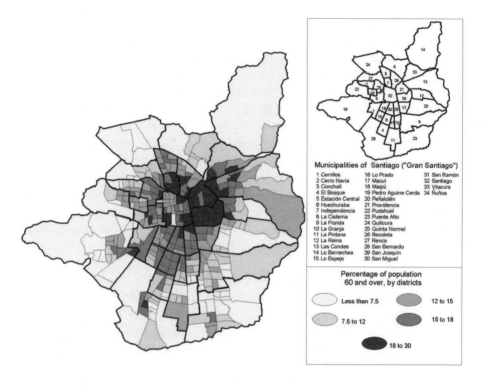

Figure 15.1 *Percentage of older persons by municipalities (communes) in Chile in the 2002 Census*

Sources: REDATAM data processing of census database available at CELADE, www.eclac. cl/celade/noticias/paginas/3/9353/boletin_envejecimiento.PDF, last accessed 17 December 2007; CELADE (2002).

To this end, the Madrid International Plan of Action on Ageing (MIPAA) (United Nations, 2002) includes specific recommendations for implementing policies and programmes that ensure economic security and access to adequate health services while also favouring an enabling environment. One 'priority area' of MIPAA is of the utmost importance in relation to the urbanization process: it specifically recommends the improvement of 'housing and environmental design to promote independent living' (United Nations, 2002, p34), by creating urban spaces free of barriers to mobility and access, by promoting shared and multigenerational co-residence through the design of housing and public space, and by assisting older persons in making their homes free of barriers to mobility. The latter is crucial in view of the widespread trend in developed as well as in developing countries towards more independent forms of living arrangements (United Nations, 2005).

In this plan, countries were also encouraged to increase the 'availability of accessible and affordable transportation for older persons' (United Nations, 2002, p34). In many countries, laws, policies and executive decrees have been issued to ensure the mobility of older persons, through lowering transportation costs, giving special discounts and other measures. However, in most cities of the developing world, older people face enormous difficulties in moving from one place to another, even within the city limits, because of transportation- and security-related issues.

In addressing the ageing process adequately, in accordance with MIPAA recommendations, national and local authorities, urban planners and communities must consider strategies and actions in at least three main areas. The first refers to the reduction of dependency in old age, by helping older persons to preserve their autonomy and independent living. This includes the redesign of urban space to take into account the specific needs of older persons and the disabled – including personal security – making it possible for older persons to interact positively with younger generations. In addition, it requires the design and implementation of an affordable and user-friendly transportation system and support for the creation of community-based associations, clubs, and other means of social integration and participation.

The second area concerns the provision of adequate and easy-to-access health and other social services. In addition, it must also cover long-term care services, including direct support for families, as well as services provided by institutions, such as day-care centres, that allow respite for family caregivers. The need for investments in long-term services is crucial, given the expected increase in the number of older persons becoming dependants. This is a result of the projected ageing of the older population itself, expressed by an increase in the proportion of the population aged 80 years and over, in a context of declining family support networks – a situation of particular concern for the most vulnerable social groups. In particular, the longer-term health needs of older persons during emergencies and disasters must also be foreseen, particularly for those who are more exposed due to their residence in environmentally vulnerable areas.

The third area focuses on ensuring higher levels of economic security through social protection systems for those who are socially and economically vulnerable, in particular those living in extreme poverty. In a context of limited coverage of social protection systems and lack of affordable housing and services, the incidence of poverty in urban areas would increase, thus creating a greater loss of income security and economic independence. This is undoubtedly the most difficult challenge facing policymakers, given the enormous difficulties that poorer people, even the young and healthy, encounter in gaining access to services, even in urban areas.

Lastly, it should be stressed that there is a need for quality and up-to-date data on the issues discussed in this chapter. In this regard, the use of already available information, such as administrative and census data, is recommended to map the situation of older persons in cities, including their social and spatial segregation (as suggested in Chapter 17). This would help planners to define more accurately the most appropriate locations to place specific facilities, to identify clusters of poorer segments of the older population and to define the recreational areas that should be created to respond to the needs of older persons. As aptly stated by Rodwin et al (2006, p4), 'Developing programmes that identify vulnerable older people without violating their civil liberties is a crucial challenge.'

NOTES

1   Using data gathered by population censuses, supplemented in a few cases by information collected by nationally representative surveys, it was possible to obtain the age distribution of the population classified by urban or rural area of residence for at least two points in time for 119 of the 192 countries or areas of the world that had a population of 100,000 or more in 2000. For almost all the countries with data, the first data set refers to a date within the period 1960–1980 and the second to the period 1981–2005. Those periods were selected to make possible an assessment of changes in the age distributions of urban and rural populations from about 1970 to the 1990s. The countries with data available had a combined population of 5.2 billion in 2000; that is to say, they accounted for 85 per cent of the world population at the time. Note that coverage is somewhat better for developed than for developing countries (68 per cent versus 60 per cent of countries have data respectively) and that, in terms of major area, coverage ranges from 50 per cent of countries in Oceania to 68 per cent of those in Europe and North America.

2   In the case of New York, it has been found that 'during a decade of economic expansion and the generation of extraordinary wealth, many older persons in New York City became poorer. The fastest growing segments of the 65-and-over population – racial and ethnic minorities – are among the poorest segments of the population. Growing income inequalities and concentration of poverty in economically deprived neighbourhoods of New York are reflected in the economic circumstances of older persons' (Gusmano et al, 2002, p5).

3   Based on information in the *China Daily*, 30 November 2006.

REFERENCES

Bongaarts, J. and Zimmer, Z. (2001) 'Living arrangements of older adults in the developing world: An analysis of DHS surveys', Policy Research Division Working Paper No 148, The Population Council, New York

CELADE (2002) 'Los adultos mayores en América Latina y el Caribe: Datos e indicadores', *Boletín Informativo*, Edición Especial con ocasión de la II Asamblea Mundial de Naciones Unidas sobre el Envejecimiento, Madrid, 8–12 April

Chan, A. (2005) 'Formal and informal intergenerational support transfers in South-Eastern Asia', Report of the United Nations Expert Group Meeting on Social and Economic Implications of Changing Population Age Structures (ESA/P/WP.201), Mexico City, 31 August–2 September, Population Division, United Nations, New York

Cutler, S. J. and Hendricks, J. (2001) 'Emerging social trends', in R. H. Binstock and L. K. George (eds) *Handbook of Aging and the Social Sciences* (fifth edition), Academic Press, San Diego, CA

ECLAC (2007) *Informe sobre la aplicacion de la estrategia regional de implementacion para America Latina y el Caribe del Plan de Accion Internacional de Madrid sobre el Envejecimiento* (LC/L.2749(CRE-2/3), Naciones Unidas/CEPAL, Santiago

ESCAP (2006) 'Ageing in Asia and the Pacific: Emerging issues and successful practices' (ST/ESCAP/2235), Social Policy Paper No 10, Economic and Social Commission for Asia and the Pacific, Bangkok

Gusmano, M. K., Hodgson, M. G. and Tobier, E. (2002) 'Old and poor in New York City', Issue Brief, International Longevity Center-USA, New York, www.ilcusa.org/_lib/pdf/b20021121a.pdf, last accessed 4 December 2007

Hermalin, A. I. (ed) (2002) *The Wellbeing of the Elderly in Asia: A Four-Country Comparative Study*, University of Michigan Press, Ann Arbor, MI

Knodel, J. and Saengtienchai, C. (2007) 'Rural parents with urban children: Social and economic implications of migration for the rural elderly in Thailand', *Population, Space and Place*, vol 13, no 3, pp193–210

Knodel, J., Chayovan, N. and Siriboon, S. (1992) 'The familial support system of Thai elderly: An overview', *Asia-Pacific Population Journal*, vol 7, no 3, pp105–126

Knodel, J., Kim, K. S., Zimmer, Z. and Puch, S. (2005) *Older Persons in Cambodia: A Profile from the 2004 Survey of Elderly*, Population Studies Center Research Report No 05-576, Institute for Social Research, University of Michigan, Ann Arbor, MI

Kreager, P. (2006) 'Migration, social structure and old-age support networks: A comparison of three Indonesian communities', *Ageing and Society*, vol 26, no 1, pp37–60

Ofstedal, M. B., Knodel, J. and Chayovan, N. (1999) 'Intergenerational support and gender: A comparison of four Asian countries', *Southeast Asian Journal of Social Science*, vol 27, no 2, pp21–42

Rodwin, V. G. and Gusmano, M. K. (2002) 'The World Cities Project: Rationale, organization and design for comparison of mega-city health systems', *Journal of Urban Health: Bulletin of the New York Academy of Medicine*, vol 79, no 4, pp445–453

Rodwin, V. G., Gusmano, M. K. and Butler, R. N. (2006) 'Growing older in world cities: Implications for health and long-term care policy', in V. G. Rodwin and M. K. Gusmano (eds) *Growing Older in World Cities: New York, London, Paris and Tokyo*, Vanderbilt University Press, Nashville, TN

Saad, P. (2003) 'Transferencias informales de apoyo de los adultos mayores en America Latina y el Caribe: Estudio comparativo de las encuestas SABE', *Notas de Población*, no 77, CEPAL, Santiago de Chile

Silverstein, M., Cong, Z. and Li, S. (2007) 'Intergenerational transfers between older people and their migrant children in rural China: Strategic investments, strategic returns', paper presented at the 2007 Population Association of America Annual Meeting, New York, 29–31 March

Stloukal, L. (2001) 'Rural population ageing in poorer countries: Possible implications for rural development', Population Programme Service, Women and Population Division, FAO, Rome, www.fao.org/sd/2001/pe0501a_en.htm, last accessed 11 December 2007

UN-Habitat (1993) *Improving the Quality of Life of Elderly and Disabled People in Human Settlements: Volume 1 – A Resource Book of Policy and Programmes from around the World*, UN-Habitat, Nairobi

United Nations (2001) *Population Bulletin of the United Nations: Living Arrangements of Older Persons*, Special Issue, nos 42/43 (Sales No E.01.XIII.16), United Nations, New York

United Nations (2002) *Report of the Second World Assembly on Ageing: Madrid, 8–12 April 2002* (A/CONF.197/9), United Nations, New York

United Nations (2005) *Living Arrangements of Older Persons around the World* (ST/ESA/STAT/SER.A/240), Population Division, United Nations, New York

United Nations (2006) *World Urbanization Prospects: The 2005 Revision*, CD-ROM Edition, Population Division, United Nations, New York

United Nations (2007a) *World Population Prospects: The 2006 Revision*, CD-ROM Edition, Population Division, United Nations, New York

United Nations (2007b) *The Diversity of Changing Population Age Structures in the World*, Report of the United Nations Expert Group Meeting on Social and Economic Implications of Changing Population Age Structures, Mexico City, 31 August–2 September 2005, Population Division, United Nations, New York

Zhuo, Y. and Liang, Z. (2006) 'Migration and the wellbeing of the elderly in rural China', paper prepared for presentation at the Population Association of America 2006 Annual Meeting, Los Angeles, CA, 30 March–1 April

Zimmer, Z., Korinek, K., Knodel, J. and Chayovan, N. (2007) 'A comparative study of migrant interactions with elderly parents in rural Cambodia and Thailand', paper presented at the 2007 Population Association of America Annual Meeting, New York, 29–31 March

16

Confronting Urbanization and the AIDS Epidemic: A Double-Edged Sword

Lynn Collins

INTRODUCTION

Urbanization and the AIDS epidemic are both growing global phenomena that are changing the landscape of development. Their intersection is complex and has not received sufficient attention either in the literature or in policy directives. While considerable effort has been devoted to understanding how the AIDS epidemic is impacting on national development, there has been less emphasis on learning how urbanization affects the AIDS epidemic. The key policy documents outlining strategies for strengthening the response to AIDS are no exception.[1] This represents a missed opportunity to call global attention to the susceptibility to HIV associated with urbanization and, even more important, to the recognition of the potential benefits that urbanization could provide in AIDS responses.

Higher HIV prevalence in urban areas and the observation that certain characteristics of urbanization can potentially increase vulnerability have led to the assumption that, overall, urbanization impacts negatively on the AIDS pandemic. The potential benefits of urbanization, in terms of socioeconomic improvements, empowerment of women and children, diffusion of information, advocacy, better services, and civil society engagement, have been an overlooked component in the response to the AIDS epidemic.

Given the complexity of the interactions and the absence of hard data on many of these issues, this chapter aims to spark further debate and research rather than provide definitive answers concerning this bidirectional dynamic relationship.

URBAN POVERTY

The reciprocal link between poverty and HIV is well established (UNFPA, 2003). Globally, the AIDS epidemic is severely curtailing development and has been singled out as being the worst threat to development of our time (UNDP, 2005). It worsens morbidity and mortality, depletes the labour force, distorts the age structure, imperils households, increases the number of orphans, burdens health systems, disrupts education systems, interferes with food production, compromises incomes and expenditures, causes psychological distress, and challenges the stability of communities. Poverty contributes to increased vulnerability to HIV and a lessened ability to cope with its consequences because of inadequate access to healthcare services, lack of information and education, forced migration to escape dire conditions, entry into sex work, inability to practise safer sex, prohibitive costs of treatment drugs and poor access to condoms, unsafe injecting drug use, and, ultimately, insufficient disposition to take a long-term view.

Determining how urbanization affects the relationship between HIV and poverty is essential and coloured by the reality that about one-third of the 3.3 billion people living in urban areas reside in slums (Sclar et al, 2005). These impoverished areas are typified by the poor physical and mental health conditions of their inhabitants and by inadequate services. Although some gains have been made on the public health front in urban areas, the benefits are clearly not universal, with urban slums matching some rural mortality and morbidity rates (Sclar et al, 2005).

Insofar as cities can make good on their promise of better socioeconomic conditions, however, they can contribute to a downturn in the epidemic. Today, cities generally account for a much larger share of national economic production and have much greater potential than rural areas for reducing poverty and fulfilling aspirations (UNFPA, 2007). The greater economic dynamism of cities can afford a robust health infrastructure, social services and human resources, and, despite inequities, the overall standard of living is usually significantly higher.

GENDER INEQUALITY

HIV does not impact equally on men and women, and gender inequality is now recognized as one of the driving forces of the epidemic (UNAIDS, 2006a). The greater vulnerability to HIV and its consequences experienced by women, particularly young women, is due to limited economic assets, difficulty negotiating safer sex, physiology, inadequate access to information and services, unpaid work as caregivers, exploitation, including gender-based violence, discriminatory laws and policies, and detrimental cultural practices such as child marriage. Young women usually know less than their male counterparts about how HIV is transmitted and how to prevent it (United Nations, 2006b). Women and girls are especially prone to trafficking to urban areas, resulting in increased vulnerability to HIV. The way in which urbanization influences gender dynamics and women's empowerment, thereby affecting their vulnerability to HIV and its impact, is not straightforward and deserves further enquiry. Taking only a few variables – violence against women, feminization of poverty and unequal gender norms – the scorecard appears to be mixed and complicated by inadequate data.

Violence against women in its many heinous forms is a key marker of gender inequality and is associated with increased transmission of HIV from coerced, unprotected, often physically violent sex, and with instilling fear that prevents women from seeking services and coping with being HIV-positive. Accurate statistics comparing the many manifestations of violence against women in urban and rural areas, however, are scarce and suffer from under-reporting. Unfortunately, violence against women is known to be high in both settings. It is possible that there is less intimate-partner violence in urban settings as a result of an increase in economic and other forms of independence for women. On the other hand, sexual exploitation is known to occur when women take on manual labour in employers' homes, a common practice in urban environments. Security measures can lessen violence against women, and urbanization can contribute favourably depending on the organization of neighbourhoods (lighting, distance travelled, law enforcement, community support and so on). Overall, evidence is mixed as to whether gender-based violence increases in urban areas.

Women and men experience urban poverty differently. The impact on HIV vulnerability is complex and calls for better information on such issues as the relative frequency and socioeconomic significance of female-headed households in urban settings, AIDS-related care, and the level of discrimination experienced by women, especially in the realms of housing, employment and access to social services (Van Donk, 2005). Adolescent girls and young women are particularly vulnerable to HIV: they often land in slums where they are ill-equipped to cope with the new surroundings, are exploited or orphaned, head households, form relationships with older men, and are marginalized from social networks and services (Mabala, 2006).

Fortunately, urbanization can also enhance women's independence and economic opportunities, narrowing the gender inequality gap by fostering more 'enlightened' attitudes and non-discriminatory practices. Urbanization facilitates wage earning outside the home and participation in networks, which can be empowering. Rural areas can be bastions of conservatism, with long-standing cultural practices that often hold women back from attaining their aspirations and exercising their rights. Many of the factors that motivate women to migrate to urban areas – to escape from poverty, conflict, gender-based violence, and limited educational and economic opportunities – are those that contribute to the increasing vulnerability of women to HIV in rural areas.

Urban areas are sometimes characterized as conferring more anonymity, with less tight control over sexual relationships. With this empowerment, women can conceivably have more command over the circumstances of their sexual relationships, resulting in less HIV transmission and better care for those women living with HIV. On the other hand, this 'freer' environment can lead to an increase in coerced and voluntary unprotected sex and an increase in the number of sexual partners. Despite greater access to condoms in urban areas, their use is not yet habitual. By and large, however, urbanization has the potential to decrease vulnerability through increased economic and social autonomy and greater access to services.

HIV PREVALENCE IN URBAN SETTINGS

HIV prevalence tends to be higher in urban than rural settings, and even within rural areas, towns and larger settlements have higher levels of HIV (Dyson, 2003; Van Donk, 2005). There is considerable speculation, data shortcomings aside,[2] about this phenomenon. Population density itself has been offered simplistically as an explanation.

There are, indeed, some commonalities with the historical epidemics of bubonic plague and cholera – people lived in close proximity in overcrowded and impoverished circumstances analogous to today's slum conditions and under rapidly changing social conditions that fostered the spread and sustainability of infection. Urban areas, growing towns and settlements were also crossroads for the introduction of new infections (Morse, 1995). HIV is not, however, transmitted through airborne particles or casual contact, which would be directly associated with population density. Instead, more sophisticated patterns of vulnerability attributable to urban life are responsible, including gender disparities, migratory patterns, sexually transmitted infection levels, sexual violence, overstretched services and poverty. Now established in densely populated urban centres, HIV has firmly taken root and is further transmitted by complex migration patterns.

DEMOGRAPHIC ASPECTS OF HIV AND URBANIZATION

Migration is inextricably linked to the AIDS epidemic through a complex relationship that has been fairly well documented (UNFPA, 2003). Without adequate support services and faced with possible exploitation, physical violence, stigma and discrimination, separation from families, and socioeconomic and political marginalization, migrants are more vulnerable to acquiring and transmitting HIV, and thus tend to have higher rates of infection (May, 2003; UNAIDS, 2004). In urban slums, migrants are also more inclined to start having sex at an earlier age, have a larger number of sexual partners, and are less aware of or likely to practise safer sex (UN-Habitat, 2004).

Many rural inhabitants who migrate to urban areas in search of economic opportunities are obliged to leave partners and family behind, and either or both partners may enter into new sexual relationships that can potentially lead to the spread of HIV (Van Donk, 2005). Some people living with HIV migrate to cities to escape stigma and discrimination and to obtain better treatment and care, including antiretroviral drugs (UNDP, 2006). There is also some evidence that migrants, whether urban–rural or rural–rural, may be less likely to practise safer sex (Brockerhoff and Biddlecom, 1998).

Women are increasingly migrating, many to urban areas, and now account for almost half of all migrants (UNFPA, 2006). They often can only find lower-status, poorer-paying jobs, and some may engage in sex work to survive. And, as noted above, when separated from their rural partners, women may engage in unprotected sex with other partners.

But there is also some emerging evidence of urban-to-rural migration related to HIV in high prevalence areas (Dyson, 2003). Some people living with HIV return to their rural origins to be taken care of by relatives when they fall ill. Also, following AIDS-related deaths to family members in urban areas, surviving partners and children may decide to return to their rural communities (Gregson et al, 2003). Conversely, migration to urban areas can result when family and friends move to take over the caregiving or livelihood functions of people living with HIV. Migration patterns related to the AIDS epidemic and to urbanization may be somewhat convoluted, but they are clearly significant.

There is ambiguity regarding how HIV affects birth rates and, indirectly, the pace of urbanization (Matanyaire, 2005). Where AIDS-related death rates are high, men and women of reproductive age will be lost. Mortality-related loss of reproduction, coupled with possible infertility related to AIDS and decisions concerning childbearing, will affect the rate of natural increase in urban areas (EngenderHealth et al, 2006). There is already some evidence that the pace of urbanization may be slowed due to the AIDS epidemic in some countries, such as Botswana, Mozambique, Namibia and Swaziland (Dyson, 2003).

The morbidity and mortality associated with HIV have notable consequences for individuals and for urban communities. At the macro level, untreated HIV is associated with overstretched health and education services, the collapse of families, more orphans and street children, a shortfall of productive members of society, a slower rate of urbanization, increased vulnerability to HIV, compromised development, changing demographics, and an increased burden of care, especially on women and children.

Age is yet another factor postulated for the increase in urban HIV rates (UNAIDS, 1999), particularly as young unmarried people migrate to urban areas to benefit from the perceived greater economic opportunities and a potentially less restrictive environment governing sexual behaviour (Buvé et al, 2002). Some of these young people start sexual relationships at a relatively early age and may be more likely to have more sexual partners over time. Condom use, while increasing among youths in some urban areas, is not universal. Young people in urban areas are vulnerable to HIV despite having higher knowledge of HIV than their rural peers – partially attributable to less rigid social control (Collins and Rau, 2000). The link between HIV and early marriage, however, has been well established, so the higher marriage age in urban areas may reduce young women's vulnerability (IPPF et al, 2006).

KEY POPULATIONS

Efforts to engage key populations,[3] where risk and vulnerability converge, and to reach out with prevention, treatment and care services are recognized as fundamental to the AIDS response (WHO et al, 2005). Key populations are often concentrated in urban areas, although few AIDS policy declarations make this connection explicitly. While acknowledging that there are other groups who are variously at risk and vulnerable to HIV, such as young women and girls, prisoners, migrants, uniformed services, slum residents, and out-of-school young people, the following sections focus on two of the main key populations in the urban context: sex workers and injecting drug users.

Sex work

The extent of sex work worldwide is not known, although global estimates are as high as tens of millions, with hundreds of millions of clients (UNAIDS, 2006b). Sex work itself is associated with urbanization, and a significant percentage of sex workers are migrants, forced or voluntary (UNAIDS, 2002). The characteristics of urban centres that foster sex work include a large sexually active population, men outnumbering women, clients with disposable income and sex workers in need of economic gain, tourism, locations for sex work, and a degree of social flexibility and anonymity. Among sex workers, who are predominantly but not exclusively young and female, HIV prevalence is usually high (UNAIDS, 2006b).

Paradoxically, many of the critical elements for an effective response are present in the urban setting. For those coerced into sex work, and those being subjected to violence, there may be a greater chance of being reached by sex worker protection programmes. Sexual and reproductive health services, including HIV-related services, are more available, although not always accessible for vulnerable groups. Commodities such as condoms, including female condoms, are more within reach. Although few of the interventions addressing sex work are comprehensive, the urban setting may be more conducive to enabling safer sex work, conferring some degree of protection through social and legal services, and offering income-generating alternatives.

Injecting drug use

Injecting drug use is positively correlated with urbanization (United Nations, 2006a). Despite data limitations, injecting drug use is estimated to be increasing as a mode of HIV transmission in Africa and the Arab States, and accounts for slightly less than one-third of new infections elsewhere (UNAIDS, 2006b). Injecting drug use tends to be higher in urban settings, partly because supplies are easier to obtain and because it often goes hand in hand with sex work. Drug use can be the impetus for engaging in sex work to support a drug habit; some sex workers are coerced into using injecting drugs, while others report using drugs as a means of easing the stress of their work.

Yet urbanization can also be viewed as contributing to the better health of injecting drug users, as many harm-reduction programmes are located in urban settings. Such programmes include drug substitution, clean needles and syringes, counselling, and condom distribution. Most of these commodities and services are more easily accessible in urban settings and have the potential to both reduce HIV transmission and provide supportive services to injecting drug users, including those living with HIV.

STIGMA AND DISCRIMINATION

Stigma and discrimination against people living with HIV and marginalized populations are pervasive. Although not well documented, stigma and discrimination may be lower in urban areas because of better education, more exposure to people living with HIV and aggressive anti-stigma campaigns. Other critical elements include the enactment and enforcement of laws protecting the rights of people living with HIV and of key populations, increased access to treatment, public information campaigns, transformation of societal attitudes, greater involvement of people living with HIV, and workplace programmes (Aggleton and Parker, 2002). The more open stances on traditional norms and the greater presence of key populations in the urban environment may also favour greater tolerance. The closer reach of government authority may also help provide an environment that is less stigmatizing and discriminatory than in rural areas. As a result, people living with HIV, including some key populations, may migrate to cities to gain access to antiretroviral drugs and to escape stigma and discrimination. Altogether, however, more work needs to be done to ascertain and enhance these potential advantages.

POTENTIAL BENEFITS OF URBANIZATION IN THE CONTEXT OF HIV

As mentioned above, health services, including HIV prevention and treatment and sexual and reproductive health programmes, tend to be more available, accessible and comprehensive in urban areas (UNAIDS, 2006b). There are more opportunities to address such health concerns as sexually transmitted infections, which may affect the acquisition and transmission of HIV. Admittedly, however, these advantages are not as apparent in slum areas. Moreover, there is a risk that, in the face of spending cuts and increased demand for HIV- and AIDS-related services, rapidly expanding urban centres will not be able to maintain or increase social-service coverage to their populations.

The donor community has variously contributed to the rural–urban imbalance by targeting major cities or their immediate surroundings to capitalize on existing health infrastructure and proximity. Duplication of efforts, with overlapping activities supported by multiple implementers, is problematic, and not enough stakeholders reach out to underserved rural communities or even to marginalized groups within cities.

Urbanization can exert a positive impact on the epidemic if HIV prevention and treatment efforts are escalated significantly and the drivers of the epidemic are sufficiently addressed. There have, indeed, been some notable downturns already in rates of HIV infection in the urban areas of some countries (United Nations, 2006b). Urban areas have higher education levels, associated with greater awareness of safe sex practices and increased condom use; more outlets for media campaigns; more supplies (such as antiretroviral drugs and condoms); and better treatment opportunities.

The greater access to antiretroviral therapy parallels the concentration of health services in urban areas (UNAIDS, 2006b). In contrast, access to voluntary counselling and testing and treatment for sexually transmitted infections is limited in rural areas, adversely affecting HIV prevention and treatment. One of the entry points for antiretroviral therapy for women is through programmes for the prevention of mother-to-child transmission which have been operating in urban areas for some time.

Many of the impact mitigation efforts of the AIDS response are particularly well suited to implementation in urban areas. Scaling up HIV prevention and treatment programmes simultaneously, which produces a synergistic impact on the epidemic (UNAIDS, 2005), would be easier in urban settings that already have a head start in establishing the full range of related interventions. Impact mitigation, especially targeting the urban poor through social protection programmes, micro-financing, education, workplace-based programmes, and efforts to eliminate stigma and discrimination, can potentially find fertile ground in the urban climate.

Moreover, remittances sent from urban to rural areas contribute to bridging the financial gap and broadening the scope of prevention efforts.

The significant engagement of the private sector in urban areas is increasingly contributing to the response to HIV. This can result in effective interventions such as workplace programmes and the provision of drugs to treat opportunistic infections and AIDS through links with multinational corporations and sponsorship of local community groups addressing HIV prevention and support.

Urban centres can provide a space for AIDS activism to spotlight bottlenecks in implementation, emerging health and rights issues, and the need for policy and programmatic redirection. With the greatest concentrations of organizations (non-governmental, urban poor, people living with HIV, and young people) and many marginalized and vulnerable groups, urban settings offer extensive opportunities to synergize efforts. The dynamism of these organizations working together and their proximity to government and the private sector provide an important opportunity to intensify national responses to the epidemic. Policy changes require the active engagement of such networks in direct lobbying and pressuring parliamentarians and other government officials. Access to the media is also enhanced, which can lead to increased awareness of salient issues and help mobilize further support, including donor support.

CONCLUSION

With about half of the world's population residing in urban areas, it is imperative to understand how urbanization and HIV interact and to use the advantages of urbanization more effectively. Some inroads have been made in unravelling these complex phenomena, but further research is needed. Urban growth and viability is influenced by the AIDS epidemic through demographic dynamics (death and birth rates, migration patterns and age distribution). HIV and AIDS also impact on sustainable urban development and quality of life. Urbanization affects the AIDS epidemic in both favourable and unfavourable ways. Admittedly, urbanization can increase vulnerability to HIV through structural determinants such as urban poverty, gender inequality and marginalization of key populations, but, as pointed out above, urbanization can also provide many critical untapped advantages in dealing with the pandemic, not the least of which is its potential for relieving human poverty and unleashing aspirations. Less stigma and discrimination, better access to quality social services, and greater engagement of civil society are upsides of urban life that should be fostered. Global responses need to understand these potentialities and accentuate them through overdue policy action to help shape the future direction of these intertwined determinants of human development. Let not the double-edged sword become a sword of Damocles.

NOTES

1   See, for instance, UNAIDS (2005); United Nations (2006b).
2   The HIV surveillance systems used to capture data fall short of universal coverage and tend to be biased toward urban areas and larger settlements in rural areas, skewing results. Statistics are further complicated by return migration of those who are ill and may die. Size of 'urban areas' also differs greatly.
3   Key populations in the AIDS epidemic are those where risk and vulnerability converge. They vary depending on the local context but usually include sex workers and their clients, men who have sex with men, and injecting drug users.

REFERENCES

Aggleton, P. and Parker, R. (2002) *A Conceptual Framework and Basis for Action: HIV/ AIDS Stigma and Discrimination*, UNAIDS, Geneva

Brockerhoff, M. and Biddlecom, A. (1998) 'Migration, sexual behaviour and HIV diffusion in Kenya', Policy Research Division Working Paper No 111, The Population Council, New York

Buvé, A., Bishikwabo-Nsarhaza, K. and Mutangadura, G. (2002) 'The spread and effect of HIV-1 infection in sub-Saharan Africa', *The Lancet*, vol 359, no 9322, pp2011–2017

Collins, J. and Rau, B. (2000) 'AIDS in the context of development', UNRISD Programme on Social Policy and Development, Paper No 4, UNRISD and UNAIDS, Geneva

Dyson, T. (2003) 'HIV/AIDS and urbanization', *Population and Development Review*, vol 29, no 3, pp427–442

EngenderHealth, Harvard University, ICW, Ipas and UNFPA (2006) *Sexual and Reproductive Health of HIV Positive Women and Adolescent Girls: A Dialogue on Rights, Policies and Services*, EngenderHealth and UNFPA, New York

Gregson, S., Mushati, P. and Nyamukapa, C. (2003) 'Adult mortality and erosion of household viability in AIDS-afflicted towns, estates and villages in eastern Zimbabwe', paper delivered at the Scientific Meeting on Empirical Evidence for the Demographic and Socioeconomic Impact of AIDS, University of Natal, South Africa, 26–28 March

IPPF, UNFPA, YoungPositives, and Global Coalition on Women and AIDS (2006) *Ending Child Marriage: A Guide for Global Policy Action*, International Planned Parenthood Federation, London

Mabala, R. (2006) 'From HIV prevention to HIV protection: Addressing the vulnerability of girls and young women in urban areas', *Environment and Urbanization*, vol 18, no 2, pp407–432

Matanyaire, S. D. (2005) 'The AIDS transition: Impact of HIV/AIDS on the demographic transition of black African/South Africans', paper presented at the 25th International Population Conference, Tours, France, 18–23 July

May, A. (2003) 'Social and economic impacts of HIV/AIDS in sub-Saharan Africa, with specific reference to aging', Working Paper No PAC2003-0005, Institute of Behavioral Science, Population Aging Center, University of Colorado at Boulder, Boulder, CO

Morse, S. D. (1995) 'Perspectives: Factors in the emergence of infectious diseases', *Emerging Infectious Diseases*, vol 1, no 1, pp7–15

Sclar, E. D., Garau, P. and Carolini, G. (2005) 'The 21st century health challenge of slums and cities', *The Lancet*, vol 365, no 9462, pp901–903

UNAIDS (1999) *Sex and Youth: Contextual Factors Affecting Risk for HIV/AIDS* (UNAIDS/ 99.26E), UNAIDS Best Practice Collection, UNAIDS, Geneva

UNAIDS (2002) *Sex Work and HIV/AIDS: UNAIDS Technical Update*, UNAIDS Best Practice Collection, UNAIDS, Geneva

UNAIDS (2004) *2004 Report on the Global AIDS Epidemic* (UNAIDS/04.16E), UNAIDS, Geneva

UNAIDS (2005) *Intensifying HIV Prevention: UNAIDS Policy Position Paper* (UNAIDS/ 05.18E), UNAIDS, Geneva

UNAIDS (2006a) *Keeping the Promise: An Agenda for Action on Women and AIDS*, UNAIDS, Geneva

UNAIDS (2006b) *2006 Report on the Global AIDS Epidemic* (UNAIDS/06.20E), UNAIDS, Geneva

UNDP (2005) *Human Development Report 2005: International Cooperation at a Crossroads: Aid, Trade and Security in an Unequal World*, UNDP, New York

UNDP (2006) 'You and AIDS: The HIV/AIDS Portal for Asia Pacific: Mobility and Migration', www.youandaids.org/Themes/Migration.asp, last accessed 22 October 2007

UNFPA (2003) *The Impact of HIV/AIDS: A Population and Development Perspective*, Population and Development Strategies Series No 9, UNFPA, New York

UNFPA (2006) *UNFPA Annual Report 2006*, UNFPA, New York

UNFPA (2007) *The State of World Population 2007: Unleashing the Potential of Urban Growth*, UNFPA, New York

UN-Habitat (2004) *The State of the World's Cities 2004/5: Globalization and Urban Culture*, Earthscan, London

United Nations (2006a) 'Preventing the transmission of HIV among drug abusers: A position paper of the United Nations System', United Nations Office on Drugs and Crime, Bangkok, Thailand, www.unodc.un.or.th/factsheet/hiv.pdf, last accessed 22 October 2007

United Nations (2006b) *Declaration of Commitment on HIV/AIDS: Five Years Later: Report of the Secretary-General* (A/60/736), United Nations, New York

Van Donk, M. (2005) '"Positive" urban futures in sub-Saharan Africa: HIV/AIDS and the need for ABC (a broader conceptualization)', Dark Roast Occasional Paper Series No 22, Isandla Institute, Cape Town, South Africa

WHO, UNFPA, UNAIDS and IPPF (2005) *Sexual and Reproductive Health and HIV/ AIDS: A Framework for Priority Linkages*, International Planned Parenthood Federation, London

17

Providing Information for Social Progress in Urban Areas

Haroldo da Gama Torres

INTRODUCTION

There is growing awareness that socioeconomic and demographic information (SDI) is of vital importance to planning in developing countries and to the adoption of an 'evidence-based' policy perspective in public programmes (Solesbury, 2001; Court and Young, 2003). SDI is also seen as critical to the work of civil society organizations. The use of SDI is relatively consolidated at the national level in most countries. Central governments regularly produce and utilize demographic estimates, health indicators and specific SDI analyses to plan their actions. However, in the sub-national and urban areas of developing countries, such data are often unavailable. Even in the face of rapid urbanization, information needed for regional and urban social policies remains a neglected issue.

The problem is particularly critical in smaller cities. Analyses of urban growth patterns throughout the world reveal not only that more than half of all urban growth still occurs in relatively small cities, but that this pattern will continue into the future. Smaller cities present both advantages and disadvantages. They can be more flexible in terms of critical decisions about issues such as land use, spatial expansion, infrastructure and services. Moreover, they are more amenable to popular participation and political oversight. On the downside, such cities tend to be under-resourced and underfinanced. Technical capability and information is less likely to be available for planning, monitoring or evaluation.

Developing countries have undergone significant changes as a result of the decentralization of social policies and fiscal resources. There is currently a 'worldwide movement to decentralize' (World Bank, 2003, p89). In Latin America, a number of countries have experienced such changes – albeit at different rates and with different decentralization models (Finot, 2005). Since the transfer of resources from federal to state or municipal governments tend to be based on demographic and other operational criteria, the demand for SDI at regional and urban levels has increased significantly. These data have been used in different ways: to establish criteria for budget allocation, to monitor the process through indicators of coverage and service quality, and to strengthen public control over service delivery.

Nevertheless, there are various reasons for the inadequate use of SDI at the local level. On the one hand, demographic techniques are less well equipped to deal with small areas. Many of the analyses for such areas require the use of geographic information systems (GIS). These are not always available, either because they have not been constructed or because national statistical agencies do not disseminate compatible data. On the other hand, local administrators are often unfamiliar with SDI and thus do not recognize its potential or else adopt negative stances regarding its usage.

To overcome these problems, different organizations are attempting to produce data and indicators at regional and intra-urban scales. There is a global movement towards the development and use of 'poverty mapping', which would allow better policy targeting and rapid food security initiatives (UNEP, 1998; CIESIN, 2006). At the same time, international organizations and professional groups are promoting various indicators to serve as a basis for regional and urban policies, often without being fully aware of the possibilities and limitations of available data.

This chapter focuses mainly on needs for SDI at the local government level. It is divided into six sections. The first discusses the issue of the invisibility of the poor and its consequences. The second argues that the spatial disaggregation of information is critical in enhancing the use of SDI. The third discusses more broadly the kinds of SDI needed for local social policies, while the fourth covers in more detail the technical and operational dimensions of providing information at the local level. In the fifth section, the main difficulties in implementing local-level projects on SDI are reviewed. Finally, a summary of the main arguments offered here is presented.

THE INVISIBLE CONTINGENT

The invisibility of the poor is a key obstacle to the implementation of social policy. On the one hand, poor people are less able to make their voices heard by public office holders; on the other, public information systems do not accurately register them or their places of residence. In many cases, they live in poor and remote rural, urban or peri-urban areas that are not often visited by high-ranking officials. This lack of visibility has significant consequences for the coverage and quality of social services. Even when they exist, these services are often of inferior quality, which results in badly located schools and clinics, high absentee rates for doctors and teachers, and a significant social distance between providers and their clients (World Bank, 2003, p22).

When effectively available, good information can increase the visibility of the poor for three distinct audiences: the media, poor people themselves and public officials. In order to have a positive role, the media must seek good information on poverty levels and trends and the spatial distribution of service delivery. Together with civil organizations, they can then help pressure governments to reduce the gaps in service provision for different social groups and areas. The information should be straightforward in terms of content and organized around simple indicators that can be easily grasped.

The poor themselves, especially their urban organizations, make up the second audience (D'Cruz and Satterthwaite, 2005). The so-called 'participatory mapping' initiatives – which produce and share mapped information with organizations of the urban poor – can address the challenge of bringing data content to ill-educated groups, thus enhancing their ability to understand their current situation (Mitlin and Thompson, 1995). Such techniques can also provide powerful devices for the discussion of poverty issues in the public arena. Some countries, such as Kenya and Morocco, adopted urban poverty lines that are associated with mapping tools in order to guide social policy and monitor programme accountability (CIESIN, 2006). Different ways of linking poverty-line estimates and mapping tools are also used in South Africa, Malawi, Viet Nam and Mexico (CIESIN, 2006; Székely, 2006). Participatory mapping can also be linked to participatory budget initiatives, thereby improving people's skills in social participation. Here, the nature of the information provided and the formats used to present it must be tailored to specific audiences.

Public officials, the third major audience, often lack adequate information on the size, characteristics and spatial distribution of the population to be covered by a given service. In fast-growing neighbourhoods, this deficiency can lead to important shortfalls in service delivery. Information and data provided to public officials should be more accurate and policy-oriented, and include population estimates and projections for small areas, inasmuch as possible.

Realistically, however, providing information to these three distinct audiences can, in practice, be complicated. In developing nations, there is often a contradiction between information disclosure and type of political regime. In many cases, countries under authoritarian rule have sophisticated information systems not easily accessible by non-government users. Democratic nations, on the other hand, while more open to the idea of disclosing information, tend to have less-organized systems. The politics behind information sharing and control are a critical issue, especially for minority groups and disputed zones, but one that would take us far afield from the focus of this paper, which is on the more operational aspects of information systems for local planning processes.

SPATIAL DISAGGREGATION OF INFORMATION

Demand for SDI has increasingly taken on a more regional and intra-urban character, for at least three major reasons. First, there are substantial intra-urban inequalities, extensively documented in the urban literature (Gugler, 1996; Massey, 1996; Jones and Visaria, 1999). These are reflected in large differentials in social indicators such as infant mortality and teenage pregnancy. Unfortunately, the build-up of intra-urban data and indicators is still incipient in most developing countries, in spite of some progress achieved through the use of GIS techniques.

Negative social indicators are territorially cumulative. It is possible to find people living in areas that can be characterized simultaneously as being environmentally hazardous and lacking basic sanitation, educational facilities and social services. These areas often have high concentrations of children and women as heads of household. Such a scenario challenges the traditional strategies of supplying public services through different administrative branches acting in isolation. Residential segregation may also substantially impact public policies. Segregated areas have high concentrations of poor populations where health risks are greater, access to the job market is worse and school performance is lower (Yienger, 2001; Briggs, 2005).

Second, the high levels of irregularities in land ownership – estimated, for instance, at 80 per cent for the major urban areas of Africa (Lim, 1995) – limit the ability of local governments to obtain sound data on their cities. Policymakers have difficulty gathering information on shanty towns and illegal settlements for different reasons: records from government and utility companies are normally incomplete precisely because of the poor provision of public services, and the areas themselves frequently change shape due to land invasion and evictions. Moreover, the local population sometimes avoids providing information for fear of government sanctions or police actions.

Third, many large cities in developing countries present highly variable intra-urban demographic dynamics, even where growth rates are relatively moderate. Some of them, such as Mexico City and São Paulo, are losing population in central areas while distant suburbs are experiencing strong demographic increases (Torres, 2005). Such urban dynamics are a challenge for policy management. Even if the health services offered are theoretically adequate and compatible with the existing population, imbalances in the intra-urban relationship between supply and demand may lead to underutilized central health outposts and overcrowded ones in fast-growing peripheral areas.

As a consequence of limited SDI, public equipment is not always located in areas where it is needed the most. It is possible to identify, in the same city, schools with vacancies and children without schools (even when the city's rate of coverage approaches 100 per cent). On the one hand, this is partially due to the high cost of social equipment and the refusal of both teachers and doctors to work in very poor – and therefore distant – districts (World Bank, 2003). On the other hand, high transport costs cause the poorer population to seek services closer to their places of residence, even if they could obtain better quality elsewhere. Spatially disaggregated systems allow social policy managers to direct resources to those areas that most need them.

In summary, spatially disaggregated information allows analysts to reflect on the important issue of *where to act*. Disaggregated SDI enables skilled analysts to identify areas with distortions between supply and demand, as well as those that present cumulative negative social indicators. Traditionally, this problem has been addressed through political representatives and/or social movements. Consequently, those areas (and groups) that succeed in having their requests heard sooner and more forcefully become the recipients of public investments. Those less informed or organized usually have fewer chances of expressing their needs and reaching governments.

Some technical issues on disaggregating information

Issues of compatibility between census and other administrative divisions present an additional challenge (Finot, 2005). In the case of urban policies, public managers often request data based on geographic subdivisions that cannot be easily obtained from demographic censuses or are not compatible with those employed by other sources of administrative data, such as school districts, health districts and policy planning units. Although modern GIS systems offer alternative techniques to overcome such problems, information experts have so far devoted little time to discussing them and their analytical consequences for policy analysis. Additionally, few public administrations have such systems available, and fewer still have the capabilities required to use them properly.

It is important to observe that databases, such as civil registers, that have specific location information, can be automatically dealt with by using GIS address-matching tools. This allows analysts to have appropriate data for all desired geographies. However, address-matching requires electronic maps covering all streets, including those in poorer areas. Although the demographic censuses of many developing countries (for example Kenya, Malawi, Mexico and Panama) have made substantial improvements in generating electronic maps for small areas, their street mapping, when available, is usually done by private companies that do not care about irregular settlements. As a result, the address-matching feature may under-record registers in poorer areas. Therefore, using this tool to produce policy indicators requires well-trained users and skilled analysts capable of handling distortion cases – for instance by using spatial statistics to correct inaccurate point distributions derived from incomplete address-recording.

These systems make it possible to perform complex operations that were rather difficult to process with analogue formats, such as working with detailed geographic scales and comparing databases of different origins at detailed scales (for example compatibility between numbers of students in a given school with numbers of children in neighbouring census tracts). Additionally, they allow analysts to introduce new geographical information into a traditional database, for example the average distance between a given census tract and the nearest school. This kind of information may help to build new indicators of access to public services.

These elements indicate the need for national statistical agencies to update existing street maps. Although local maps may be available, they are often in analogue formats and tend not to cover irregular and invaded areas. Theoretically, this updating initiative may be conducted in parallel with the development of digital data for census tract boundaries, which has become the norm in the censuses of developing countries. Besides their obvious usefulness for local administrations, digital street maps can greatly streamline the operations of the censuses themselves and therefore contribute to a better integration between GIS and census mapping (United Nations, 2004).

SOCIAL POLICY INFORMATION SYSTEMS

Social programmes at both national and local scales involve a complex set of dimensions, from the definition of a legal basis for the programme, its goals and its funding sources, to criteria for resource allocation and mechanisms for social participation (Wholey et al, 1994). In this context, all social programmes require the definition of basic demographic parameters in order to operate properly, including the identification of the programme's target audience, which is critical in assessing its scope, as well as its costs and the barriers to its implementation.

Although this definition of parameters will often be ad hoc, it has to be followed by demographic studies that estimate the size of the target population, as well as its relative distribution and growth over time. In almost all cases, age, regional or normative criteria are adopted to outline the universe of users, with important consequences for the programme's effectiveness, cost and distribution.

Policymakers must also estimate the share of the target audience not covered and any potential leakages (Wholey et al, 1994). While such exercises may seem simple from an aggregated-data perspective, they can become rather complex when spatial disaggregation is required. If no census data or samples are available, special surveys must be carried out to estimate the required parameters.

The above discussion clearly illustrates the fact that SDI is the starting point for almost all social programme implementation. This is true for both state and federal programmes: states and cities act as planning units for nationally centralized programmes while also acting as executors for decentralized federal programmes. This new attribute of local governments – that of running a multitude of social programmes in the areas of health, education, sanitation and housing – implies having technical capabilities at the local level that were not previously required. It is possible to identify a large number of situations in local policy implementation that require specific SDI efforts.

Social policy administrators sometimes handle the issue of supply and demand management by organizing user records. Students are enrolled when they start school; families enrol themselves as beneficiaries in income-transfer programmes; and patients are registered when they are admitted to hospitals, with their basic data later cross-referenced with information related to diagnosis and medical procedures. This kind of practice is worth a closer look.

Using such records to capture existing demand may lead to a series of significant distortions in the quality of information, especially that provided by poor families. When recording is performed at different locations, enrolling may imply travel costs for the poorer population. Moreover, the information on where to enrol for a particular programme and the requirements for enrolment may not be available for the poorer strata of the population. This is further complicated if the target audience lives far away or if it has limited access to the information itself. Both instances may imply poor coverage or the exclusion of very needy families from the programme (Torres, 2002).

When records are computerized, data based on information provided by worse-off families tend to be less accurate, rendering the database less reliable. Illiterate people and those with lower levels of education generally provide incomplete information or documentation on variables such as age, identification, income and proof of address. Addresses are particularly inaccurate for people who live in irregular areas, where mail is often redirected to other contact locations such as local 'mom and pop' stores close to their place of residence.

In the case of records for income-transfer programmes, distortions may occur due to the interest of potential users in becoming beneficiaries. A questionnaire for enrolment purposes cannot be mistaken for a census survey; the population quickly learns that it is used as an operational tool and starts providing information strategically in an attempt to meet selection criteria regardless of their actual socioeconomic conditions (González de la Rocha, 2005).

Key strategies to overcome the problem of inaccurate records, such as a request for documents to confirm the information provided, either become a source of additional red tape (leading to an increase in programme costs) or are difficult to implement. For example, it is virtually impossible to obtain reliable income statements from people working in the grey economy, making it difficult to identify those cases in which real income is above the poverty line.

Records of many developing countries have yet to be entered into a computer system. Several schools and hospitals in poor developing countries register information on paper only, thus making it nearly impossible for it to be analysed afterwards. Even in those cases in which electronic records do exist, their quality, the format of databases and the technical characteristics of the information systems may restrict their use. While in some countries, there is a growing trend towards computerizing records, including the use of magnetic cards for income-transfer programmes, the same is not necessarily true for all regions and for all policies. And, as stated above, even electronic recording is not totally free of distortions.

In summary, using administrative records as a primary source to capture existing demand may imply a high level of under-recording. Although administrators count on such records to gauge demand, it is critical to stress the obvious fact that they cannot be used to identify those families not served by a given programme. Even if other distortions are ignored – such as the inclusion of users that theoretically do not belong in the target audience (leakage) – records tend to be a rather limited resource for identifying potential users.

USING INFORMATION SYSTEMS AT THE LOCAL LEVEL

Implementing urban SDI systems to manage social policies meets formidable barriers resulting from both the low technical skills of many public bureaucracies and the relative permeability of the state in developing countries to private interests of different kinds (Evans, 2002). In other words, the decision as to whether such systems should be implemented is related to issues of accountability.

In many developing nations, there is a substantial turnover of technicians at both local and national levels, particularly because the head of the executive power can appoint thousands of technical and managerial personnel for a variety of bureaucratic positions. Local information management groups are often built and then dismantled following changes in government, because of turnovers in human resources. As a consequence, the disappearance of relevant databases during government transitions is not unusual. Some are even taken by private companies that monopolize the information to sell databases on the market.

Having SDI systems is a necessary step to improving service provision, but it does not guarantee its usage for policy implementation (Heeks, 2002). For instance, it is possible to find highly sophisticated projects that require a long maturation period, but that are subsequently discarded by the organization due to their high costs and inability to yield results. A lack of cooperation between different areas of the same administration can also hinder the exchange of relevant information and duplicate work.

Different bureaucracies present different problems. Overall, the administrative structures responsible for taxes are better organized and insulated, thus generating sound information systems. In a number of countries, relatively well-organized bureaucracies are found in some social policy segments – particularly in the areas of health, sanitation and education. Technical capabilities for the use of information nevertheless vary substantially when considered on a more local scale; even large cities can be incapable of operating adequate SDI systems. Other major public policy areas – for example social services, housing and environment – usually have more precarious information systems at their disposal.

Until recently, the area of planning was responsible for managing public information, centralizing data, and serving other public agencies and bodies. In some places, planning departments have been replaced by IT departments. However, it is difficult to imagine today that one single administrative body would be able to manage all the information required by different policy areas, especially in the context of the increase in the information produced and the demand generated by growing decentralization. Centralized information may entail substantial administrative discontinuities, making policy administrators dissatisfied with the timing and quality of the information available for decision-making.

In reality, urban administrators of every social policy must face the key challenge of building stable information units that are capable of gathering, processing and analysing data relevant to their particular policy fields. Unit size largely depends on policy complexity and the number of inhabitants. At least four different aspects need to be considered when discussing the organizational dimensions pertaining to the provision of information for local social policies.

The first step is the consolidation of information units in different public sector bureaux or in associated institutions such as universities or non-governmental organizations. The literature on research and policy links indicates that there are mixed results from using a combination of internal and external groups for information provision (Crewe and Young, 2002; Court and Young, 2003). Unlike a federal statistical bureau, such units would be located close to the agencies responsible for making policy decisions in order to produce information synchronically that matches the timing of the decision process. These units should be able to operate as a network, sharing experiences, exchanging databases for common use and avoiding duplication of efforts.

The second issue refers to IT solutions: to ensure reduced costs, it is important to invest in the development of accessible SDI systems. Consulting and software companies prefer to market complex solutions, which may require the commitment of extensive resources, not only in financial terms (acquisition costs), but also for the implementation, training and maintenance involved. Free software solutions – such as the ones available from the Canadian project JUMP and the Economic Commission for Latin America and the Caribbean's REDATAM Project – are examples of relevant initiatives to solve this problem. However, these systems often need to be further adapted to the problems faced by local administrations and/or formatted to become accessible to the average, not-so-skilled user.

The third fundamental dimension refers to specific training that users need in order to manage SDI systems. Several countries offer courses on government, sociology and demography; however, although these may be comprehensive and important for formative purposes, they often focus on giving scientific and academic training rather than on preparing professionals to analyse information in the actual conditions presented by local public administrations. Few of these courses, for instance, concentrate extensively on the use of GIS and/or on how to estimate the population in intra-urban areas.

Finally, the fundamental importance of fostering a culture of free access to public information should be highlighted. Local social policy administrators frequently face difficulties in obtaining relevant information or databases from other public bodies. Even though the internet has substantially improved access to information, a conscious and continuous effort to stimulate free access is still needed, particularly within less organized and more insulated government agencies.

IMPLEMENTING SDI PROJECTS

Although SDI associated with GIS techniques can substantially impact social policies, there is significant opposition to them in the policy arena. Broadly speaking, 'information is power', and the provision of detailed information to local administrations and the media may challenge traditional power structures (Crewe and Young, 2002; Székely, 2006). Even with funds and political willingness, various obstacles must be overcome if an SDI project is to be properly implemented at the local level.

A project of this kind must address the fact that its results are likely to challenge the prevailing practices for resource distribution. Since it is critical to ensure political support for the project, the group responsible for producing information may obtain such support by associating the initiative with respected institutions, for example universities, professional organizations or local United Nations offices. Implementing a 'community of actors' can help overcome the barriers that information providers may face in developing countries (Evans, 2002). However, sensitive results demand a wise communication strategy in order not to place the future of the project at risk – that is, the project's institutional partners must be careful not to jeopardize the activities of the local core group.

Such initiatives are also subject to a number of internal criticisms – for example on length of implementation, excessive project sophistication, quality of available data, and lack of internal and/or external participation (Crewe and Young, 2002; Székely, 2006). Because SDI projects may take some time to produce relevant results, it is critical not only to keep them as simple as possible but also to render their benefits practical and explicit by producing short-term results. To this effect, useful low-tech and low-cost solutions must be chosen in order to reduce project complexity and the duration of its implementation.

By the same token, while data quality is an unavoidable problem for social policy analyses, this should not be used as an argument for disregarding available information. Different demographic techniques, including population projections and demographic small-area estimates (Ghosh and Rao, 1994), may help update SDI at the local level, together with simpler methods to meet the needs of generating short-term results. To demonstrate the validity of available information of a more geographic nature, good metadata and recognized accuracy standards should be employed.

Regarding lack of participation, it is, of course, important to share information with all key internal stakeholders. Having them as both sources and users of the information system creates ownership and increases benefit awareness, while also developing a small community around the project. In terms of external participation, it should be noted that SDI projects do not necessarily present an obstacle to participation. Theoretically, there should be no contradiction between SDI and participatory processes, although a few problems may arise for various reasons, for example the different professional backgrounds of practitioners in the two fields and related misunderstandings about the nature of their respective practices. A better comprehension of participatory processes and the possible role to be played by information systems may help resolve such issues.

Participation could be associated with social policy information initiatives in at least two important ways. On the one hand, it could enhance data quality and information availability. Particularly in areas with poor data collection, participation could be an important element for analysis and monitoring tasks. Even when data are available, participation could help tackle issues that could not be identified earlier (Bass et al, 1995). Furthermore, data could be presented to the local population in interactive ways – especially through visual techniques such as maps – and this interaction might provide new insights for data interpretation and for producing new information (Sydenstricker-Neto et al, 2004).

On the other hand, information can be used to provide support for ongoing participatory processes. Governments must share information with participants in order to make the process effective. Often, those members of the community that are more involved in participatory initiatives are better informed and/or connected in proactive social networks. This kind of interaction may imply the under-representation of particular individuals, groups or areas. Different mechanisms may address this problem, for example the active recruitment of participants and positive feedback from previous participatory rounds (Abers, 1997). Of course, SDI systems may also bring information on the groups or areas that do not take part in the participatory process, thus enhancing the equity of decisions produced in the participatory arena. In this kind of situation, visual materials and maps may again be of great value.

In brief, the organization of local SDI initiatives can be extremely helpful, but they are not necessarily simple to implement. NGOs and international donors may play a critical role in disseminating knowledge on good practices, as well as in convincing governments of the need for long-term initiatives in this field.

CONCLUSIONS

Although almost every stakeholder recognizes the importance of having information in order to enhance decision-making processes, many experts do not consider SDI systems a real priority. The idea of a rational administration that bases its decisions on good information is seen by many practitioners in developing countries as a kind of luxury for a state strongly pressed by massive demands and lack of resources. Convincing top public administrators that information is essential for social service provision is thus a key priority.

International organizations often include components on SDI and/or programme evaluation activities in their projects with developing countries. Those activities are often proposed under the umbrella of 'capacity-building' initiatives. However, many administrators see this more as a formal obligation (Court and Young, 2003). And since such efforts are not generally perceived as an objective of the projects (which are dedicated to public works, construction and so on), they are neither properly evaluated nor is their discontinuity seen as producing an impact on project performance. Informational activities are therefore easily discontinued.

Activities regarding information systems vary significantly from project to project. There are no general standards, and different international agencies sometimes avoid exchanging resources and information with each other. Technical cooperation activities from developed countries are often associated with the adoption of technical standards, software, satellite images and hardware originating in the donor country. Such technological packages are sometimes not suited for the particular experience of a local group, nor are they well adapted to the specific management problems in place, leading to duplication of data acquisition or database development, and information misuse.

In sum, although the organization of social and SDI systems that could enhance social policies seems to be a key issue for the development agenda, important hurdles remain to socioeconomic data production and delivery, information system structuring, and institutional development. It is hoped that this chapter will help practitioners in developing countries improve the quality of the information underlying social policies, particularly in the context of massive urbanization.

REFERENCES

Abers, R. (1997) 'Learning democratic practice: Distributing government resources through popular participation in Porto Alegre, Brazil', in M. Douglass and J. Friedmann (eds) *Cities for Citizens: Planning and the Rise of Civil Society in a Global Age*, John Wiley and Sons, Chichester, UK, pp39–65

Bass, S., Dalal-Clayton, B. and Pretty, J. (1995) *Participation in Strategies for Sustainable Development*, Environmental Planning Group, International Institute for Environment and Development, London

Briggs, X. S. (2005) 'More pluribus, less unum? The changing geography of race and opportunity', in X. S. Briggs (ed) *The Geography of Opportunity*, Brookings Institution Press, Washington, DC, pp45–80

CIESIN (2006) *Where the Poor Are: An Atlas of Poverty*, Center for International Earth Science Information Network, Columbia University, New York

Court, J. and Young, J. (2003) 'Bridging research and policy: Insights from 50 case studies', ODI Working Paper No 213, Overseas Development Institute, London

Crewe, E. and Young, J. (2002) 'Bridging research and policy: Context, evidence and links', ODI Working Paper No 173, Overseas Development Institute, London

D'Cruz, C. and Satterthwaite, D. (2005) 'Building homes, changing official approaches: The work of urban poor organizations and their federations and their contributions to meeting the Millennium Development Goals in urban areas', Working Paper on Poverty Reduction in Urban Areas No 16, International Institute for Environment and Development, London

Evans, P. (2002) 'Political strategies for more liveable cities: Lessons from six cases of development and political transition', in P. Evans (ed) *Liveable Cities? Urban Struggles for Livelihood and Sustainability*, University of California Press, Berkeley, CA, pp222–246

Finot, I. (2005) 'Descentralización, transferencias territoriales y desarrollo local', *Revista de la CEPAL*, vol 86, pp29–46

Ghosh, M. and Rao, J. N. K. (1994) 'Small area estimation: An appraisal', *Statistical Science*, vol 9, no 1, pp55–76

González de la Rocha, M. (2005) 'Familias y política social en México: El caso de oportunidades', paper presented at 'Reunión de expertos "Política hacia las familias, protección e inclusión socials"', CEPAL, Santiago, 28–29 June

Gugler, J. (1996) *The Urban Transformation of the Developing World*, Oxford University Press, New York

Heeks, R. (2002) 'Failure, success and improvisation of information systems projects in developing countries', Developing Informatics Working Paper Series No 11, Institute for Development Policy and Management, University of Manchester, Manchester, UK

Jones, G. W. and Visaria P. (eds) (1999) *Urbanization in Large Developing Countries: China, Indonesia, Brazil and India*, Oxford University Press, London

JUMP Project (undated), software available for download, www.jump-project.org, last accessed 2 November 2007

Lim, G-C. (1995) 'Housing policies for urban poor in developing countries', in J. M. Stein (ed) *Classic Readings in Urban Planning*, McGraw-Hill, New York, pp521–537

Massey, D. S. (1996) 'The age of extremes: Concentrated affluence and poverty in the 21st century', *Demography*, vol 33, no 4, pp395–412

Mitlin, D. and Thompson, J. (1995) 'Participatory approaches in urban areas: Strengthening civil society or reinforcing the status quo?', *Environment and Urbanization*, vol 7, no 1, pp231–250

REDATAM Project (undated), software available for download, www.eclac.org/redatam/, last accessed 2 November 2007

Solesbury, W. (2001) 'Evidence-based policy: Whence it came and where it's going', ESRC Centre for Evidence Based Policy and Practice Working Paper No 1, ESRC Centre for Evidence Based Policy and Practice, London

Sydenstricker-Neto, J., Parmenter, A. W. and DeGloria, S. D. (2004) 'Participatory reference data collection methods for accuracy assessment of land-cover change maps', in R. S. Lunetta and J. G. Lyon (eds) *Remote Sensing and GIS Accuracy Assessment*, CRC Press, Boca Raton, FL, pp75–90

Székely, M. (2006) 'Income and consumption maps', paper presented at the seminar 'More than a pretty picture: Using poverty maps to design better policies and interventions', World Bank, Washington, DC, 11 May

Torres, H. G. (2002) 'Social policies for the urban poor: The role of population information systems', Working Papers Series No 24, UNFPA Country Support Team for Latin America and Caribbean, Mexico City

Torres, H. G. (2005) 'Información demográfica y políticas públicas en la escala regional y local', paper presented at 'Reunión de expertos sobre población y desarrollo local', CELADE/CEPAL, Santiago, 27–28 October

UNEP (1998) 'Synthesis report on the international workshop on poverty mapping', United Nations Environment Programme/GRID, Arendal, Norway, www.povertymap.net/publications/doc/ottopov.pdf, last accessed 2 October 2007

United Nations (2004) *Integration of GPS, Digital Imagery and GIS with Census Mapping* (ESA/STAT/AC.98/14), Statistical Division, United Nations, New York

Wholey, J. S., Hatry, H. P. and Newcomer, K. E. (eds) (1994) *Handbook of Practical Program Evaluation*, Jossey-Bass, San Francisco, CA

World Bank (2003) *World Development Report 2004: Making Services Work for Poor People*, World Bank and Oxford University Press, Washington, DC

Yienger, J. (2001) 'Housing discrimination and residential segregation as causes of poverty', in S. H. Danziger and R. H. Haverman (eds) *Understanding Poverty*, Russell Sage, New York, pp359–391

Part V

Regional Patterns of Urbanization and Linkages to Development

INTRODUCTION

The world's three main developing regions find themselves at different stages in the urban transition. Levels and patterns of urbanization vary considerably, but policy approaches present remarkable similarities. Latin America has had an early and rapid urban transition, while most countries in Asia and Africa, though currently experiencing massive urban growth, lag far behind. Yet, in all three regions, policymakers have shown considerable aversion to urban growth. This section describes the main processes and reflects on critical issues of urban growth in relation to key regions: sub-Saharan Africa, Asia's two behemoths – India and China – and Latin America.

White, Mberu and Collinson review urbanization trends and their implications for sub-Saharan Africa in Chapter 18. They address a concern that is repeatedly expressed by policymakers and researchers: are the cities of that region unique in that they lack the capacity to serve as engines of growth? In sub-Saharan Africa, urbanization has been alluded to as the source of growing poverty, rather than of economic dynamism. Urban shanty towns attract particular attention because they are such readily visible manifestations of disadvantage. This often triggers anti-urban responses among policymakers.

Discussions of migration and urbanization in sub-Saharan Africa have been hampered by inadequacies in census data. Nevertheless, survey data provide a strong indication that migration is generally positive for migrants, for household wellbeing and for the economy. They also suggest that temporary migration is an effective economic and social mobility strategy rather than a simple back and forth movement of the unemployed.

According to the authors, the purported stagnation of city economies in sub-Saharan Africa, and their declining wellbeing compared to rural areas, may have been overstated. As in other parts of the world, there is a strong overall link between level of urbanization and level of economic development. Despite their obvious problems, cities in the region continue to provide more opportunities for national development and personal realization. Still, this is insufficient to promote the level and kind of economic growth that would hasten the reduction of poverty and the delivery of improvements in wellbeing in the region. Various structural problems and contextual features, rather than the failure of urbanization, have to be blamed for this situation.

India, by contrast, is currently one of the world's fastest-growing economies, but still has relatively low levels of urbanization. Part of this latter feature is methodological, since the definition of rural is broader in the country's official statistics and includes even peri-urban areas. Nevertheless, as shown in Chapter 19 by Chandrasekhar and Mukhopadhyay, urban poverty is on the increase, while rural poverty has decreased significantly, at least in part because of rural–urban migration. The authors argue that Indian policymakers have been slow in attending to urban poverty issues, resulting in a backlog of housing shortages and a variety of accompanying impacts on urban living conditions.

Reviewing figures on the growth of poverty, the authors find that not only do urban areas exhibit considerable heterogeneity, but that there are marked differences within the same city or neighbourhood. Poor urban households are found in areas officially defined as slums as well as in non-slum areas. Community-based organizations and non-governmental organizations have an important role to play in improving access to water supply, drainage, sanitation and electricity, while also reducing the fiscal burden on local governments.

The authors maintain that policies must focus not only on traditional issues, such as increasing coverage of water and sanitation facilities in poor neighbourhoods, but also on the impacts of urban expansion on the semi-urban and peripheral urban areas near the city. The more difficult issue of urban livelihoods for the poor also needs to be tackled, especially in the slums, since the growing service industry is unlikely to absorb the excess manpower.

In Chapter 20, Bai provides a broad overview of the mesmerizing urban transition in China – still the world's most populous country. China is experiencing one of history's most accelerated processes of urbanization and urban population growth, largely as a result of a radical turnaround in economic and migration policy. The number of localities officially defined as 'cities' has jumped from 132 in 1949 to 655 today. One-quarter of these already have more than a million inhabitants. According to the same source, urbanization levels rose from 13 per cent in the early 1950s to 36 per cent in 2000 and are expected to reach 60 to 65 per cent by 2020, which would mean a total urban population of around 900 million. Bai's chapter examines the socioeconomic, environmental and policy implications of this massive transformation.

Gradual relaxation of the traditional household registration system (the *Hukou*), which made it practically impossible for rural people to go to or settle in a city, and changes in rural–urban classification of localities help to explain the demographic change. In turn, such adjustments have to be understood within the Government's increasing acceptance of markets as a force in shaping economic growth and its growing perception of urbanization as an ally of Chinese development efforts. The negative environmental consequences of fast-paced Chinese industrialization and urbanization are noted, as are the huge increases in the 'floating population', housing deficits and unemployment problems. Nevertheless, there are positive signs, such as improved urban leadership, information and environmental consciousness, as well as lessons to be learned from Chinese cities that are committed to sustainability.

The last chapter in this section, by Rodriguez and Martine, provides a description of the more advanced urban transition of the Latin American and Caribbean (LAC) region and a reflection on its possible significance for other regions that are now embarking on their own transitions. Colonial settlement patterns had already produced relatively high levels of urbanization in the LAC region prior to the urban explosion of the last half-century. From this starting point, import-substitution policies, coupled with rapid social change and demographic increase, caused a frenzied escalation in urban growth, especially during the 1950–1990 period. The impetus of this transformation was such that it persisted through political upheavals, changes in economic models and political efforts to reduce urban growth. The result is that, by all accounts, urbanization is now even higher in the LAC region than in Europe.

Viewed in retrospect, the outcomes of this rapid transition have been positive for the economies of the LAC region and for its people. Nevertheless, most policymakers in the region have consistently attempted to retard or even reverse urban growth, albeit to no avail. This resistance, according to the authors, is largely to blame for the main negative consequences of rapid urbanization in the region – large residential areas marked by poverty, inadequate housing, environmental problems, lack of access to services and amenities, and social disorganization. More proactive policies, aimed at attending to the land, housing and service needs of the poor, would have avoided much of this. Thus, the authors conclude, policymakers in Asia and Africa would do well to reflect on the experience of the LAC region and to prepare for inevitable urban growth instead of also trying futilely to prevent it.

The experiences of these different regions no doubt present mixed perspectives on the trajectory and significance of urbanization. As reiterated throughout this book, population and poverty are both increasingly concentrated in urban areas, and policymakers are perplexed about how to deal with this. Yet cities represent our best hope for development and sustainability. Clearly, attempts to prevent or retard urbanization are ineffective. As also highlighted in this book, preparing for inevitable urban growth can unquestionably help to allay shelter poverty, a critical factor in improving the quality of life of the poor and in helping them gain access to what the city has to offer. Proactive approaches can also contribute to more sustainable forms of urban growth and the use of space. As stated at the outset, the challenge of the new global frontier is not to control the rate of urbanization, but to achieve urban development that is beneficial. This will require a greater willingness to review attitudes and processes in order to reap the unquestionable benefits and overcome the inevitable difficulties of massive urban growth.

18

African Urbanization: Recent Trends and Implications

Michael J. White, Blessing U. Mberu and Mark A. Collinson

INTRODUCTION: CONCERNS ABOUT URBANIZATION IN SUB-SAHARAN AFRICA

Urbanization carries important implications for development, poverty, health, environmental quality and social welfare provision. There is considerable concern in sub-Saharan Africa regarding the future of these linkages in the face of large-scale urban growth and stagnant economies.

Now and into the foreseeable future, sub-Saharan Africa (SSA) is expected to have the highest rates of urban growth of any major region. Its cities already have the highest proportion of slum-dwellers. Policymakers are often at a loss for solutions. Doubt has been expressed as to the capacity of cities in SSA to serve as engines of growth. Urbanization has even been alluded to as the source of growing poverty.

Unquestionably, urbanization looms large in the future of SSA. This chapter describes some of the basic trends in urban growth in the region and examines the relationships between poverty and urbanization in that context. It also addresses questions about the uniqueness of the region's urbanization experience and its implications for the future.

PATTERNS OF URBAN GROWTH IN SSA

Despite its status as the world's least urbanized region, SSA already has an urban population as large as that of North America. Moreover, while overall global urban growth rates have fallen below two per cent, those of SSA are projected to continue above three per cent until 2030. Several factors contribute to this distinctive pattern, including low initial levels of urbanization, high rates of overall natural increase and movement from the countryside to cities of relatively modest size (Montgomery et al, 2003). Strong contrasts are found in patterns of urban growth between southern Africa, which has already reached higher levels of urbanization, and east, central and west Africa, where urban growth rates are much higher, as shown in Table 18.1.

How cities grow affects their development trajectories. It is estimated that, in the 1960s and 1970s, rural–urban migration accounted for 40 per cent of African urban growth, most of it directed towards larger cities (Tacoli, 2001). The remainder was mostly attributable to natural increase; the reclassification of rural territory as 'urban' added relatively little. No estimate is readily available for recent periods, but the role of migration inevitably tends to decrease as urbanization rises (UNFPA, 2007). The increasingly dominant role of natural increase in urban growth is a critical factor for policy. Currently, policymakers in SSA often attempt to retard urban growth by discouraging migration, under-appreciating the central contribution made to growth by natural increase.

Mega-cities garner considerable international attention, although they are not the dominant urban form. Large cities do play important economic and political roles in SSA, but only six per cent of the region's urban population lives in cities of five million or more. The majority of urban people in SSA (57 per cent) live in towns or cities with fewer than half a million residents (United Nations, 2006a). This is important because smaller localities generally have less infrastructure and may exhibit levels of human capital, fertility, health and child survival closer to those of the surrounding rural areas (Montgomery et al, 2003). In South Africa, small towns of under 5000 people attract families from rural areas to access public amenities, even if labour market opportunities are not significantly better (Collinson et al, 2000).

Recent studies suggest that the pace of urban growth in SSA tapered off in the 1980s and 1990s, reflecting a decline in both population growth rates and net migration (Bocquier and Traore, 1998; Tabutin and Schoumaker, 2004). Some have argued that this decline is also linked to the deterioration of urban economies, public services and infrastructure that, since the 1990s, has contributed to the increasing urbanization of poverty in the region (Zulu et al, 2002; UN-Habitat, 2003).

Other factors linked to these changes include the spatial decentralization of political power, such as in Nigeria, and of economic investment and planning, such as in Ghana. Moreover, urbanization trends in some parts of the region are strongly influenced by forced movements of people due to drought, famine, ethnic conflicts, civil strife and war (Tacoli, 2001). The overall decline in refugee crises thus could be a factor in reduced urban growth.

Table 18.1 *Urbanization in sub-Saharan Africa's ten most populous countries*

Major SSA Countries	Total mid-2006 population	Percentage urban 2006 estimates
Sub-Saharan Africa	767,000,000	34
Nigeria	134,500,000	44
Ethiopia	74,800,000	15
D. R. Congo	62,700,000	30
South Africa	47,300,000	53
Sudan	41,200,000	36
Tanzania	37,900,000	32
Kenya	34,700,000	36
Ghana	22,600,000	44
Mozambique	19,900,000	32
Côte d'Ivoire	19,700,000	47

Source: Population Reference Bureau (2006).

In the end, however, demographic factors, per se, may explain much of the recent decrease in urban growth. On the one hand, urban growth rates everywhere tend to decline as a function of the larger size of the urban base population on which such rates are calculated. More important, fertility reductions, though still moderate in many countries, have reduced the rates of population growth in most of SSA. Hence, the decline in total population growth rates for SSA between the 1980–1985 and 1995–2000 periods (23 per cent) is larger than the decline in the region's urban growth rate (16 per cent). It is therefore difficult to ascertain whether the urban slowdown in SSA indicates a real change in the factors affecting the preference for urban residence or if it reflects the evolution of other demographic dynamics.

PEOPLE ON THE MOVE IN SSA:
MIGRATION, URBANIZATION AND POVERTY

Discussions of migration and urbanization in SSA have been hampered by inadequacies in data. Many countries lack up-to-date national census data, while few publish data that will allow an estimation of the scale and direction of internal migration. Technical issues, such as long intercensal intervals, delays in processing and releasing census information, and difficulties in data use, all combine with clashing political interests and possible data manipulation to hinder the monitoring of rapid urban growth (Tacoli, 2001). Many censuses do not include specific questions on change of residence, leading researchers to characterize migration data as patchy, inadequate and internationally non-comparable (Oucho, 1998; Tacoli, 2001).

Data that would permit addressing inequalities within urban areas directly are also generally unavailable, as are data that can capture the links between rural and urban areas. With respect to computing urbanization levels, there is considerable variation in what is considered urban by the census bureaus of different countries (Montgomery et al, 2003). Therefore, while census data are the best available option for national comparisons, they fail to provide a full picture (Cohen, 2004).

Closely related to the limitations of censuses is the dearth of national-level surveys on migration in SSA. With very few exceptions, most existing studies on internal migration and urbanization processes in the region are fragmentary, based on case studies done by individual researchers or institutions in a few villages or medium-sized towns, and are variously outdated (Bocquier and Traore, 1998; Oucho, 1998; Mberu, 2005).

Recent debates in the field of urbanization studies have also underlined the limitations of the standard rural–urban dichotomy when analysing the changing pattern of human settlement. In this context, data from demographic surveillance systems (DSSs) provide useful insights.

The databases of the DSS projects in the region can discriminate between different types of migration and assess their relative contribution to urbanization. The Agincourt System, for instance, has followed 70,000 people in 21 rural villages in the north-east of South Africa since 1992 (Kahn et al, 2007). This method involves a rigorous annual update of the demographic status – births and other pregnancy outcomes, deaths, and in-migrations and out-migrations – of every member of the subdistrict population, coupled with an updating of the household roster. This methodology, and the small-scale area covered, enables a sharper discrimination of the types of moves undertaken by people.

As shown in Figure 18.1 (based on data from the Agincourt DSS in South Africa), permanent migration occurs primarily among women aged 15–35 and among children of both sexes. Males are much more prone to be circular or temporary migrants (see Figure 18.2). The vast majority of permanent moves are between the same settlement type, in other words urban to urban or rural to rural. But there is also a two-way flow of people in migration streams between rural and urban settings. People tend to move to closer destinations or to the next level of settlement size, creating a pattern of stepwise migration.

The longitudinal nature of the DSS database enables analysts to sort out the temporal sequences of events such as health changes, migration or other related household change. The main finding is that migration is generally positive for household wellbeing, but negative consequences and vulnerabilities do occur. Structural factors impacting negatively on the rural setting include poverty, gender norms, AIDS, non-communicable disease, environmental deterioration and the rural–urban migration of skilled labour from the community.

Migration selectivity by socioeconomic status is common, but this also varies by type of migration and local context. A study based on the Agincourt DSS data examined changes in the average household asset index between 2003 and 2005

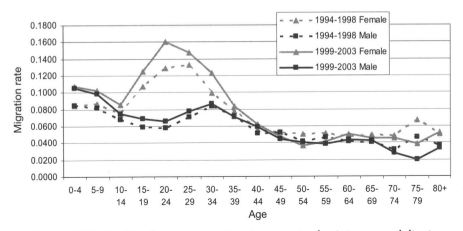

Figure 18.1 *Profile of permanent migration rates in the Agincourt subdistrict*

Source: Collinson et al (2007b).

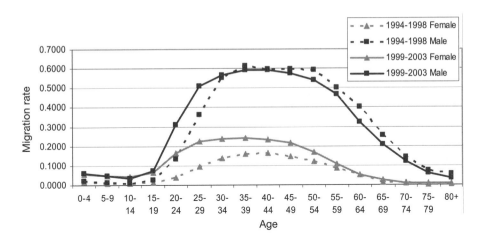

Figure 18.2 *Profile of temporary migration rates in the Agincourt subdistrict*

Source: Collinson et al (2007b).

(Collinson et al, 2006 and 2007a). Positive socioeconomic growth occurred in households having temporary migrants in the city, a finding that buttresses the arguments for the beneficial effects of urbanization in both sending and receiving areas. Notably, however, low levels of temporary migration were associated with poverty in rural sending areas, because migration is required to access livelihoods for rural households. These findings would tend to contradict the common assumption that people move back and forth between rural and urban areas simply because they are unable to find employment and sustenance in cities; on the contrary, temporary migration appears to be an effective economic and social mobility strategy.

On the other hand, according to the Nairobi Urban DSS, childhood mortality in informal settlements remains very high, especially among new migrants. Given the high degree of rural-to-urban migration, the study raises critical public health concerns. Among adults, the healthy migrant hypothesis is supported: due to a combination of age and positive selection, migrants tend to exhibit lower morbidity and mortality than non-migrants (Zulu et al, 2006).

Rural–urban migration interactions are also seen in the 'returning to die' phenomenon (Clark et al, 2007). In South Africa (Agincourt DSS), increasing numbers of circular labour migrants of prime working age who become ill in urban areas come home to be cared for and eventually die in their rural areas of origin. This shifts the healthcare burden to their families and the rural healthcare system, with significant consequences for the distribution and allocation of healthcare resources. In settings highly impacted by HIV, this selectivity may alter the composition-influenced features of urban–rural morbidity and mortality differentials.

In brief, DSS data afford a more fine-grained picture of the patterns of migration in the urban transition. It helps identify some vulnerable subpopulations: a new rural-to-urban migrant, for example, is particularly at risk on arrival in an urban informal settlement. There are also risks associated with a mother's temporary labour migration due to inadequate childcare. Moreover, households in rural areas that are unable to send a temporary migrant can be at risk of extreme poverty. In addition, there are risks of HIV infection associated with the disconnected structure of rural–urban migrant households.

The Agincourt DSS also provides a window on forced migration, another human movement of considerable interest in the African context. As the civil war in Mozambique escalated from 1983, Mozambicans fled to South Africa, dispersed within local settlements and settled on specially allocated land. In 1993, a group-level legal status was obtained, but socioeconomic conditions, including access to water, sanitation and legal rights, remained inadequate for most (Hargreaves et al, 2004). In 1996, the Southern African Development Community offered an amnesty to former Mozambican refugees, encouraging them to apply for permanent South African residency status. While a large number of Mozambicans took advantage of this, outreach to rural areas was limited and the standard of living has remained low in many areas.

Taken as a whole, the DSS findings are consistent with the considerable concern that has been expressed about the implications of urbanization for migrants and cities, ranging from inferior economic outcomes to deteriorating health, social disruption and crime. A cursory glance at rapidly growing cities – and especially informal settlements within them – reinforces this view. Nevertheless, the longitudinal data show that the advantages of migration and urbanization clearly prevail over the disadvantages. The bulk of evidence points to a positive impact on the migrants and on the economy (White and Lindstrom, 2005). This contradicts some of the earlier arguments that emphasized 'over-urbanization'. The fact is that migrants generally express a preference for their current lot over the rural life they left behind, and, over time, migrants do experience upward mobility and gain access to an expanded range of services.

There certainly are cases of deep urban disadvantage or migrant failure. Recent empirical evidence raises the concern that the urban poor (often missed in aggregate rural–urban contrasts) may fare no better than 'ruralites' (Brockerhoff and Brennan, 1998; Montgomery et al, 2003). However, snapshot cross-sectional comparisons often miss the crucial aspects of change over time in migrants' lives. Longitudinal comparisons are central to understanding whether assimilation into the urban environment brings improved health, better jobs and gains in social capital or a downward spiral into long-term disadvantage. Overall, the data reviewed in the DSS, while also highlighting lesser-known aspects of migratory patterns, would seem to provide a somewhat more optimistic scenario of migration and urbanization in SSA.

URBANIZATION, DEVELOPMENT AND POVERTY IN SSA: THE FACES OF EXCEPTIONALISM

Urbanization and socioeconomic change

Scholars increasingly acknowledge urbanization as an intrinsic dimension of economic and social development, reflecting the rational decisions of millions of internal migrants to seek new opportunities in the cities.

In terms of economic output, urban areas represent a much larger share of gross domestic product (GDP) than their share of the population. The very concentration of such activity in cities may lead to more efficient markets and hence promote development, both urban and rural (Kessides, 2006). Similarly, urban centres have been repeatedly identified as privileged sites, hosting the core of modern economic and social functions, with superior amenities and services often stemming from both economic advantages of scale and proximity and political advantages of leverage (Lipton, 1976; Lowry, 1990; Chen et al, 1998). Hence, social indicators usually show urban advantages in public health, associated with improved access to modern health services, safe water and sanitation (Montgomery et al, 2003).

This model of a strong direct association between urbanization, economic growth and social development has prevailed since the Industrial Revolution, but it has recently come under question for SSA. Rural–urban migration and urban natural increase have been linked to the expansion of urban poverty (Mabogunje, 2007). It is estimated that 72 per cent of all urban-dwellers in SSA live in slums (UN-Habitat, 2003). Some urban health and social indicators have either deteriorated appreciably or even reversed in favour of rural areas (Zulu et al,

2002; UN-Habitat 2007). Child mortality rates are higher among the urban poor than among the rural population in several countries (Garenne, 2006).

Urban shanty towns attract particular attention because they are such readily visible manifestations of disadvantage. Mabogunje (2007) argues that the environmental health conditions that many poor urban residents face have undermined the urban advantage in mortality reduction in the region. Physical proximity to social and infrastructure services does not guarantee their actual utilization by, or affordability for, poor urban residents (Kessides, 2006). Both non-monetary and monetary costs of obtaining water or using sanitary facilities can be very significant in urban areas, despite physical proximity to supply points, because the sheer numbers of people overload the existing facilities and services. Large, statistically significant gaps are found between the access of the urban poor and that of the urban non-poor to infrastructure and social services, even though extending services from the better-off to the less-well-off neighbourhoods nearby would cost much less than reaching the same numbers of people in remote settlements.

Doubt has even spread to the capacity of cities to spark economic growth. This was highlighted in the World Bank's *World Development Report 1999/2000*, which stated that African cities are not serving as the engines of growth that cities on other continents have been: 'Instead they are part of the cause and a major symptom of the economic and social crises that have enveloped the continent' (World Bank, 2000, p130). This statement has sparked the notion of 'exceptionalism' in relation to African urbanization: essentially, this suggests the possibility of an African departure from the usual pace, pattern and implications of urbanization.

Other studies appear to corroborate the World Bank's findings. For example, Bouare (2006) found that 71 per cent of the 32 countries he analysed had a negative correlation between GDP and urbanization level over the 1985–2000 period. This would imply that people left rural areas because of poverty, as opposed to being drawn to urban areas by work opportunities. Ezra (2001) similarly linked rural out-migration in northern Ethiopia to push factors related to ecological degradation and poverty in rural areas, rather than a response to pull factors from urban areas. Under these circumstances, the prospect of unprecedented urban growth in a setting of declining economic performance and sprawling shanty towns is obviously threatening (Brockerhoff and Brennan, 1998; World Bank, 2000; APHRC, 2002).

In reviewing the exceptionalism hypothesis, several strands need untangling. Does urbanization increase poverty or simply concentrate larger numbers of the poor? Do the poor have other or better opportunities elsewhere than in cities? Is it true that cities in SSA are unable to generate economic growth? If so, is there anything innate or specific to cities in the region that make them incapable of generating such growth? What other demographic, environmental, historical and political factors affect the capacity of cities in the region to spark economic growth?

The purported stagnation of city economies, and their declining wellbeing compared to rural areas, may be overstated. Recent work at the World Bank has indeed challenged earlier dour assessments, arguing instead that there remains a direct, positive relationship between urbanization and economic growth in the region and that national growth in the 1990s was derived from urban-based sectors of the economy (Kessides, 2006).

According to this analysis, the urbanization-without-growth disconnect is inaccurate. Kessides asserts that in SSA, as in other parts of the world, there is a strong overall link between level of urbanization and level of economic development. She sees the positive roles of urbanization in diversifying incomes, expanding options for more affordable service delivery, and widening horizons for innovation and skill acquisition. Finally, Kessides argues that, for SSA, there again emerges a positive linear relationship between economic growth in the 1990s and increased urbanization over that time.

Contemporary migration theory does suggest that urbanward migration is generally rational. Cities grow faster because people perceive, correctly, that, despite their problems, these localities commonly provide more opportunities for the realization of their aspirations (UNFPA, 2007). Plotting country-level estimates, Ravallion et al (2007) indeed found a strong negative correlation between level of poverty and the urban population share: 'In addition to the direct gains to migrants (some of whom can escape poverty in the process), there can be indirect gains to the (non-migrant) rural poor' (Ravallion et al, 2007, p5). Both urban-to-rural remittances and the tightening of rural labour markets could serve to improve rural conditions.

Overall, then, urbanization benefits both migrants and the economy (White and Lindstrom, 2005). Policymakers in the region have been increasingly inclined to accept the explanation of 'over-urbanization' as a cause of poverty. But urbanization and urban growth, per se, cannot be blamed for African poverty; on the contrary, despite their obvious problems, cities continue to provide more opportunities for national development and personal realization.

What remains of exceptionalism? Implications for poverty

Although cities, per se, cannot be blamed for poverty, some aspects of exceptionalism cannot be discarded altogether. Cities in SSA are not generating development at the same rate as in other regions; meanwhile, the stark realities of growing poverty in the region's cities cannot be ignored. However, the roots of these problems are complex and cannot be attributed simply to changes in population distribution.

A first component of exceptionalism comes from the history of urban settlements in SSA. The region has appreciably lower densities than in some other world regions. The lack of a tradition of town and city settlement, and the historical predominance of agro-pastoral economies, would suggest that Africa is intrinsically different. By contrast, China, for instance, has a long history of dense settlement. Even in 'rural' areas, settlements there can be substantial in aggregate size. Moreover, a long-standing administrative system exists for organizing population and economic activity. Similarly, in Latin America, colonial development spread outwards from vigorous coastal cities: later development models, especially in the 20th century, accelerated that region's urbanization to exceptionally high levels.

Second, although the rate of urban growth in SSA is not much different from that of other regions during their urban transition, the *scale* of current urban growth in SSA is certainly greater than in previous transitions (Montgomery et al, 2003). In contrast to other currently developing regions, fertility decline has been slower; hence rapid urban growth today is fed, in many countries of SSA, by still-high rates of natural increase in both rural and urban areas.

Another element is the long-standing tradition of circular and seasonal population movement in SSA. The findings from DSS surveys cited above indicate high levels of temporary labour migration. This offers an additional twist to the interpretation of the increasing proportion of poverty found in cities: Some migrants may live modestly in the city in order to remit funds back to rural households. Meanwhile, from the rural perspective, positively selected urban labour migrants are key household breadwinners, as shown earlier.

The pattern of temporary movement is frequent in other settings as well. What may be unique in the African setting is the pervasiveness of this mobility regime. As a result, rural–urban lines are arguably more blurred in SSA than elsewhere. Commonly, the region's residents live in both urban and rural places and engage in patterns of migration that link together rural and urban areas in more complex ways. These links are important for resource flows, such as cash or non-monetary remittances, information, and behavioural norms, and they expand the influence of urban living way beyond city and town boundaries.

Urban and rural activities can be interlinked in ways that fundamentally alter the socioeconomic contours of African societies (Montgomery et al, 2003). Examples include the increasing practice of non-agricultural activities in rural areas and of agricultural activities in urban areas, as well as increasing levels of circular rural–urban migration and high levels of social connection between rural and urban households (Gugler, 2002; Simon et al, 2004).

Urban migrants frequently make investments in rural housing or support rural households (Chukwuezi, 2001). Remittances of cash and non-monetary items flow outwards from cities, while rural produce may be used to sustain family members living in the cities. Thus households have been described as 'stretched', spanning rural and urban geographies and employing the different advantages of each place (Ross, 1996; Townsend et al, 2002).

These multiple links between rural and urban populations imply that poverty does not have a distinctly rural or urban character (Montgomery et al, 2003). Urban poverty impacts directly on rural poverty and may reduce remittances or increase the counter-urbanization flows, while rural poverty can increase rural-to-urban migration as households strive to diversify incomes (Montgomery et al,

2003). Conversely, development in one area generally benefits development in the other (UNFPA, 2007).

These dynamic links between rural and urban areas in SSA are lost in the dichotomous data and projections of rural and urban populations. They also colour the discussion of urban pauperization. The links of people and ideas across space are common throughout the developing world, but are particularly strong in SSA, because of the social and political history of the region (Andersson, 2001; Gugler, 2002). Urbanization, being at least partially de-linked from economic development, may foment stronger rural–urban linkages.

Finally, and most consequentially, the inability of cities to promote the level and kind of economic growth that would hasten the reduction of poverty in SSA is generally recognized. Economic and human development in SSA has not kept pace with the rest of the developing world. Even Kessides, in her strong defence of urbanization in the region, admits that 9 of her 24 cases are ones of 'disconnect', with stagnation or economic decline accompanying increasing urbanization (Kessides, 2006). The inability of national economies to deliver improvements in wellbeing appears to be deeply rooted in the socioeconomic and political structures of several countries. While in past decades the UN-based human development index (HDI) has continued to rise in all other world regions, it has flattened in SSA.

Various structural problems, including high levels of national debt and consequent structural adjustment policies, have placed uneven economic burdens on urban populations (Roberts, 2006). Other contextual features in SSA include exposure to broader pressures of global competition, limited outlets for external migration, and loss of the productive workforce and of family security due to HIV/AIDS (Kessides, 2006). Moreover, issues of governance inevitably have to be invoked in the context of SSA. Part of the discrepancy between the urban promise and concrete reality stems from a lack of vision, foresight and a participatory approach to planning that involves the poor in the solution of their problems (Kessides, 2006; UNFPA, 2007).

URBANIZATION AND ENVIRONMENTAL CHANGE IN SSA

The relationship between urbanization and environmental quality has received less attention in SSA than in other regions. Governments and people in this poorest region of the world are being asked to shoulder the burden of preserving their remaining pristine and salvageable ecosystems. While the current environmental rhetoric includes the notion that efforts to fight poverty and to save ecosystems are not intrinsically opposed, there is at least a short-term trade-off between economic growth and resource preservation. This is especially true in the SSA region, since resource extraction – ore, wood, agriculture and fisheries – is such an important component of the region's efforts to compete in the global economy.

Urbanization is frequently seen as problematic in this preservation–exploitation scenario. Cities are often depicted as sprawling absorbers of land and vegetative cover, as well as the prime source of air and water pollution (Cincotta and Engleman, 2000). While cities may be unjustly charged, the pressure to redirect urban growth is part of the negativity prevailing in the governments of SSA. In a recent UN report, in 37 of 46 SSA countries (for which data are available), policymakers would prefer to lower rates of urban growth, while 9 feel that no intervention is warranted (United Nations, 2006b).

The roles cities play in environmental change is undoubtedly complex. Urban density in itself favours conservation by reducing the further invasion of rural ecosystems, but urban production and consumption patterns are at the root of the gravest environmental problems. On the other hand, if urbanization in SSA were better linked to economic growth, urban development could help improve livelihoods and, even more, help create the preconditions for environmental amelioration, in accordance with the desire of urban residents for cleaner natural settings and resource preservation. At the same time, successful urbanization would shift the health exposure regime – accelerating the health transition and making urban illnesses more prevalent (respiratory problems from outdoor air pollution, water-borne disease and the chronic illnesses that appear with lifestyle shifts) – even as traditional rural illnesses wane.

CONCLUSIONS

Africa will continue to urbanize: what path that urbanization will take and how city development will affect overall wellbeing remains to be seen. The historical experience and a reading of the current record would suggest that urbanization is likely to be positive for national growth and for the urban residents themselves. Despite continuing concern and some policy aversion to urban growth, it is likely that migration and urbanization are generally *beneficial* for the migrants and for economies. Migrants are probably making rational decisions in light of the resources, constraints and opportunities in front of them.

This finding does not deny that sprawling slums, the growth in the relative size of the young population and the declining economic performance of many African countries have raised the spectre of a new face of poverty. Impoverished urban neighbourhoods are characterized by underemployment, crime, risky reproductive behaviour, adverse environmental conditions and poor health outcomes (Brockerhoff and Brennan, 1998; APHRC, 2002; Lloyd, 2005).

The urbanization of poverty grows in policy visibility. Large concentrations of urban slum-dwellers will continue to constitute policy challenges in urban Africa during coming years. The policy response, however, should not focus on reducing urbanward migration, but rather on meeting the needs of urban-dwellers for housing, infrastructure and services. This requires a shift in orientation and a proactive urban approach (UNFPA, 2007). Despite negative policy sentiment about cities and city growth, urban-based economic development holds greater promise for both city and countryside (Montgomery et al, 2003; Cohen, 2004; Kessides, 2006; Ravallion et al, 2007). Environmental concerns also loom large for SSA. It is likely that these will play out in an urban dimension. As likely as not – despite some opinions to the contrary – African urbanization may play a key role in environmental amelioration.

The issue of African 'exceptionalism' is not totally resolved. Certain features of migration and urbanization in SSA – comparatively low density, high prevalence of circular migration and the link to HIV incidence in the 21st century – are unique to the contemporary African experience. In addition, deep-seated and structural causes, rather than population distribution patterns, account for the departure of the SSA region from the historical experience of other geographic regions. The longer view suggests that cities may still play the same beneficial role in SSA for both their residents and for national economies that they played in other regions and times.

A final message relates to the need for better information in SSA. Apparent from this work is the sense that the database from which one could better track urban trends, and, more important, analyse their policy implications, has not kept pace with the pace of urban expansion itself.

REFERENCES

Andersson, J. A. (2001) 'Mobile workers, urban employment and "rural" identities: Rural–urban networks of Buhera migrants, Zimbabwe', in M. de Bruijn, R. Van Dijk and D. Foeken (eds) *Mobile Africa: Changing Patterns of Movement in Africa and Beyond*, Brill, Leiden, The Netherlands, pp89–106

APHRC (2002) *Population and Health Dynamics in Nairobi Informal Settlements*, African Population and Health Research Center, Nairobi

Bocquier, P. and Traore, S. (1998) 'Migration and urbanization in West Africa: Methodological issues in data collection and inference', in R. E. Bilsborrow (ed) *Migration, Urbanization and Development: New Directions and Issues*, UNFPA and Kluwer Academic Publishers, New York

Bouare, O. (2006) 'Levels of urbanization in Anglophone, Lusophone and Francophone African countries', in C. Cross, D. Gelderblom, N. Roux and J. Mafukidze (eds) *Views on Migration in Sub-Saharan Africa: Proceedings of an African Migration Alliance Workshop*, HSRC Press, Cape Town

Brockerhoff, M. and Brennan, E. (1998) 'The poverty of cities in developing countries', *Population and Development Review*, vol 24, no 1, pp75–114

Chen, N., Valente, P. and Zlotnik, H. (1998) 'What do we know about recent trends in urbanization?', in R. E. Bilsborrow (ed) *Migration, Urbanization and Development: New Directions and Issues*, UNFPA/Kluwer Academic Publishers, New York

Chukwuezi, B. (2001) 'Through thick and thin: Igbo rural–urban circularity, identity and investment', *Journal of Contemporary African Studies*, vol 19, no 1, pp55–66

Cincotta, R. and Engleman, R. (2000) *Nature's Place*, Population Action International, Washington, DC

Clark, S. J., Collinson, M. A., Kahn, K., Drullinger, K. and Tollman, S. M. (2007) 'Returning home to die: Urban to rural migration and mortality in rural South Africa', *Scandinavian Journal of Public Health*, vol 35, supplement 69, pp35–44

Cohen, B. (2004) 'Urban growth in developing countries: A review of current trends and a caution regarding existing forecasts', *World Development*, vol 32, pp23–51

Collinson, M. A., Garenne, M., Tollman, S. M., Kahn, K. and Mokoena, O. (2000) 'Moving to Mkhuhlu: Emerging patterns of migration in the new South Africa', AHPU Working Paper Series, Agincourt Health and Population Unit, School of Public Health, University of the Witwatersrand, Johannesburg, South Africa

Collinson, M. A., Tollman, S. M., Kahn, K., Clark, S. J. and Garenne, M. (2006) 'Highly prevalent circular migration: Households, mobility and economic status in rural South Africa', in S. E. Findley, E. Preston-Whyte, M. Tienda and S. M. Tollman (eds) *Africa on the Move: Migration in Comparative Perspective*, Wits University Press, Johannesburg, South Africa

Collinson, M. A., Clark, S. J., Tollman, S. M., Kahn, K., White, M. J., Clark, B. D., Eaton, J., Gómez-Olivé, F. X. and Shabangu, M. (2007a) 'Measuring change in absolute socioeconomic status and linking it to contemporary migration patterns in the rural northeast of South Africa', AHPU Working Paper Series, School of Public Health, University of the Witwatersrand, Johannesburg, South Africa

Collinson, M. A., Tollman, S. M. and Kahn, K. (2007b) 'Migration, settlement change and health in post-apartheid South Africa: Triangulating Agincourt Demographic Surveillance with national census data', *Scandinavian Journal of Public Health*, vol 35, supplement 69, pp77–84

Ezra, M. (2001) 'Ecological degradation, rural poverty and migration in Ethiopia: A contextual analysis', Population Council Working Paper No 149, Policy Research Division, The Population Council, New York

Garenne, M. (2006) 'Migration, urbanization and child health: An African perspective', in S. E. Findley, E. Preston-Whyte, M. Tienda and S. M. Tollman (eds) *Africa on the Move: Migration in Comparative Perspective*, Wits University Press, Johannesburg, South Africa

Gugler, J. (2002). 'The son of a hawk does not remain abroad: The urban–rural connection in Africa', *African Studies Review*, vol 45, no 1, pp21–41

Hargreaves, J., Collinson, M., Kahn, K., Clark, S. and Tollman, S. (2004) 'Childhood mortality among former Mozambican refugees and their hosts in rural South Africa', *International Journal of Epidemiology*, vol 33, no 6, pp1271–1278

Kahn, K., Tollman, S. M., Collinson, M. A., Clark, S. J., Twine, R., Clark, B. D., Shabangu, M., Gómez-Olivé, F. X., Mokoena, O. and Garenne, M. (2007) 'Research into health, population and social transitions in rural South Africa: Data and methods of the Agincourt Health and Demographic Surveillance System', *Scandinavian Journal of Public Health*, vol 35, supplement 69, pp8–20

Kessides, C. (2006) *The Urban Transition in Sub-Saharan Africa*, Cities Alliance and World Bank, Washington, DC

Lipton, M. (1976) *Why Poor People Stay Poor: Urban Bias in World Development*, Harvard University Press, Cambridge, MA

Lloyd, C. B. (ed) (2005) *Growing up Global: The Changing Transitions to Adulthood in Developing Countries*, National Research Council and Institute of Medicine, National Academies Press, Washington, DC

Lowry, I. (1990) 'World urbanization in perspective', in K. Davis and M. S. Bernstam (eds) 'Population, resources and environment: Present knowledge, future options', *Population and Development Review*, vol 16, supplement, pp148–176

Mabogunje, A. L. (2007) 'Global urban poverty research: The African case', *Urban Update*, no 10, Woodrow Wilson International Center for Scholars, Washington, DC

Mberu, B. U. (2005) 'Who moves to rural or urban areas? Who stays? The case of rural out-migration in Nigeria', *Journal of Population Research*, vol 22, no 2, pp141–161

Montgomery, M., Stren, R., Cohen, B. and Reed, R. (eds) (2003) *Cities Transformed: Demographic Change and Its Implications in the Developing World*, National Academy Press, Washington, DC

Oucho, J. O. (1998) 'Recent internal migration processes in sub-Saharan Africa: Determinants, consequences and data adequacy issues', in R. E. Bilsborrow (ed) *Migration, Urbanization and Development: New Directions and Issues*, UNFPA and Kluwer Academic Publishers, New York

Population Reference Bureau (2006) 'World population data sheet', Population Reference Bureau, Washington, DC

Ravallion, M., Chen, S. and Sangraula, P. (2007) 'New evidence on the urbanization of global poverty', manuscript, World Bank, Washington, DC

Roberts, B. R. (2006) 'Comparative urban systems: An overview', in S. E. Findley, E. Preston-Whyte, M. Tienda and S. M. Tollman (eds) *Africa on the Move: Migration in Comparative Perspective*, Wits University Press, Johannesburg, South Africa

Ross, F. C. (1996) 'Diffusing domesticity: Domestic fluidity in *Die Bos*', *Social Dynamics*, vol 22, no 1, pp55–71

Simon, D., McGregor, D. and Nsiah-Gyabaah, K. (2004) 'The changing urban–rural interface of African cities: Definitional issues and an application to Kumasi, Ghana', *Environment and Urbanization*, vol 16, no 2, pp235–247

Tabutin, D. and Schoumaker, B. (2004) 'The demography of sub-Saharan Africa from the 1950s to the 2000s: A survey of changes and a statistical assessment', *Population*, vol 59, nos 3–4, pp457–556

Tacoli, C. (2001) 'Urbanization and migration in sub-Saharan Africa: Changing patterns and trends', in M. de Bruijn, R. Van Dijk and D. Foeken (eds) *Forms of Mobility and Mobility of Forms: Changing Patterns of Movement in Africa and Beyond*, Africa Studies Centre, Leiden, The Netherlands

Townsend, N., Madhavan, S., Tollman, S., Garenne, M. and Kahn, K. (2002) 'Children's residence patterns and educational attainment in rural South Africa, 1997', *Population Studies*, vol 56, no 2, pp215–225

UNFPA (2007) *The State of World Population 2007: Unleashing the Potential of Urban Growth*, UNFPA, New York

UN-Habitat (2003) *The Challenge of Slums: Global Report on Human Settlements*, Earthscan, London and Sterling, UK

UN-Habitat (2007) *State of World's Cities Report 2006/7: The Millennium Development Goals and Urban Sustainability*, Earthscan, London

United Nations (2006a) *World Urbanization Prospects: The 2005 Revision*, Population Division, United Nations, New York

United Nations (2006b) *World Population Policies 2005*, Population Division, United Nations, New York

White, M. J. and Lindstrom, D. P. (2005) 'Internal migration', in D. Poston and M. Micklin (eds) *Handbook of Population*, Springer, New York

World Bank (2000) *Entering the 21st Century: World Development Report 1999/2000*, Oxford University Press, New York

Zulu, E. M., Dodoo, F. N-A. and Chika-Ezeh, A. (2002) 'Sexual risk-taking in the slums of Nairobi, Kenya, 1993–1998', *Population Studies*, vol 56, no 3, pp311–323

Zulu, E. M., Konseiga, A., Darteh, E. and Mberu, B. (2006) 'Migration and the urbanization of poverty in sub-Saharan Africa: The case of Nairobi City, Kenya', working paper of the African Population and Health Research Center, Nairobi

19

Socioeconomic Heterogeneity in Urban India

S. Chandrasekhar and Abhiroop Mukhopadhyay

INTRODUCTION

India ranked third among the fastest-growing economies in the world over the period 1990–2004 (Ahmed, 2007). The avowed objective of Indian planners is to sustain the current growth rate of 8 per cent per annum and increase it to 10 per cent by the beginning of the next decade (Government of India, 2006). Although high growth rates have been generally applauded, concerns about the distribution of the benefits have emerged on many fronts. It is now widely acknowledged that economic growth has not been inclusive and has bypassed sections of society. Higher rates of growth have not translated into reductions in unemployment or in faster rates in the reduction of poverty.[1]

The Indian economy embarked on economic reform in the early 1990s. Subsequently, the male unemployment rate in urban areas (as measured by daily status) increased from 6.7 per cent in 1993–1994 to 7.5 per cent in 2004–2005, while the female unemployment rate increased from 10.4 per cent to 11.6 per cent (NSSO, 1996 and 2006). There is evidence to suggest that the annual rate of the reduction in poverty was higher during 1983-1993, the pre-reform era, than during 1994–2005, the era of reforms (Himanshu, 2007; Mahendra Dev and Ravi, 2007).

During the more recent period, the urbanization of poverty also became apparent in India. In 1983, for example, 45.7 per cent of rural Indians were poor, while by 2004–2005 this figure had declined to 28.3 per cent. Urban poverty also declined, from 40.79 per cent to 25.7 per cent over the same period. However, in absolute terms, the total number of urban poor increased by 9.86 million, while the

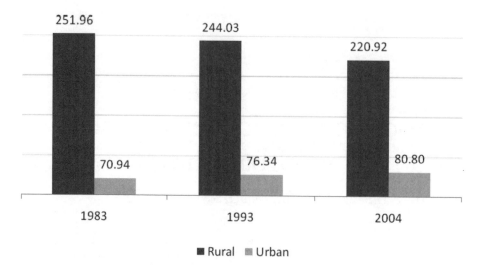

Figure 19.1 *Estimate of number of people living below poverty line (million)*

Source: Government of India (2002c and 2007).

total number of rural poor fell by 31.03 million (Government of India, 2002c and 2007). Given that over 38 per cent of India is expected to be urban by 2026 – an increase of nearly 87 per cent from the base level of 286 million in 2001 (Office of the Registrar General, 2006) – it is reasonable to assume that the total number of urban poor will increase concomitantly.

In light of the increase in the number of the urban poor, what is now needed is a change in the mindset of Indian policymakers, who have in the past exhibited a bias against urbanization. This bias can be traced to the demands that urbanization places on municipal corporations, which are responsible for meeting the increased demand for services, such as water supply, sewerage, solid waste management and related urban infrastructure (for example, housing, transport and roads). It was not until India's eighth five-year plan (1992–1997) that key urban issues were explicitly recognized: the unabated growth of the urban population exacerbating the accumulated backlog of housing shortages, resulting in a proliferation of slums and squatter settlements and the decay of city environments.

In recent years, the Government of India has introduced specific programmes to meet some of these urban needs. These have included the Mega City Project for five selected cities, the Integrated Development of Small and Medium Towns (IDSMT) and the Accelerated Urban Water Supply Programme (AUWSP). However, the country's tenth five-year plan pointed out that a significant number of cities receive no assistance from the central Government since they are not covered under either the IDSMT or the Mega City Project (Government of India, 2002b).

To address this, in 2005–2006, the Government of India launched the Jawaharlal Nehru National Urban Renewal Mission (JNNURM), a programme with a planned duration of seven years. The JNNURM has two sub-missions: Urban Infrastructure and Governance, and Basic Services to Urban Poor (BSUP). However, the BSUP sub-mission does not address an issue that is clearly of central importance to the rural poor who migrate to urban areas – the issue of livelihoods. In light of the projected increase in the number of urban dwellers, the time has come for urban policy to explicitly address rural–urban linkages and the livelihood issues of the vast number of poor rural immigrants.

In this chapter, the emerging issues of urban India are discussed. First, it is established that urban areas exhibit considerable heterogeneity in standards of living. It is also shown that poor urban households live not only in areas defined as slums, but also in non-slum areas and that this heterogeneity can be expected to increase over time. Intra-urban differentials in the characteristics of households living in both areas are described. It is then argued that a three-pronged approach is needed to face the urbanization of poverty. The first is to improve living conditions in the slums and, in particular, to increase coverage of water and sanitation facilities. A beginning has been made in this regard. Second, the focus of existing programmes should be expanded to take into account the impact of city growth on the semi-urban and peripheral urban areas in the proximity of the city. Third, it is imperative to formulate a comprehensive policy addressing urban livelihoods, recognizing that the urban poor live not only in slums but also in non-slum areas. The final section is devoted to a discussion of the challenges ahead.

HETEROGENEITY IN URBAN AREAS: SLUMS, PERI-URBAN AREAS AND PROVISION OF BASIC SERVICES

Estimates of the slum population

In 2004, every seventh urban-dweller in India lived in areas defined as 'slums' (NSSO, 2004). The Government of India's National Sample Survey Organization (NSSO) defines a slum as a 'compact settlement with a collection of poorly built tenements, mostly of a temporary nature, crowded together usually with inadequate sanitary and drinking water facilities in unhygienic conditions' (NSSO, 2003, p6). This definition is similar in spirit to that of UN-Habitat (2003, p12). However, in India, there are two types of slums: notified and non-notified. In the case of notified slums, a notification has been issued by the respective municipalities, corporations, local bodies or development authorities, which imposes some obligations upon the issuer for the provision of services.

During the period 1981–2001, there was a 45 per cent increase in the total number of slum-dwellers, which rose from 28 million to 40.6 million. Midway in this period, however – in 1991 – the number of slum-dwellers was estimated to be

45.7 million. The apparent decline in numbers from 1991 to 2001 is surprising and may be due to an underestimation[2] of the number of slum-dwellers in 2001.

Slums and the growth of peri-urban areas are an outcome of an imbalance in urban growth resulting from regional disparities and an over-concentration of economic resources in a few urban agglomerations such as Mumbai, Kolkata, Chennai, Delhi and Bangalore. In 2001, the urban agglomerations of Mumbai, Delhi, Kolkata and Chennai accounted for 29 per cent of India's slum-dwellers. Some 6.48 million people lived in the slums within the Greater Mumbai Municipal Corporation, 1.85 million within the Delhi Municipal Corporation, 1.49 million within the Kolkata Municipal Corporation and 0.82 million within the Chennai Municipal Corporation (Census of India, 2001). Despite the growth of slums and overcrowding in the urban agglomerations, no systematic efforts have yet been made to disperse industrial growth to medium- and small-sized towns and nodal villages.

Differences in slums and non-slums

Not only do urban areas exhibit considerable heterogeneity, but there are also marked differences within the same city. Two variables, in particular, have implications for the livelihoods of slum-dwellers: literacy and workforce participation rate (WPR).

According to census data for 2001 (Census of India, 2001), the overall literacy rate in the slums was 69.4 per cent, while, in the non-slum urban areas, it was 79.8 per cent. In contrast to the literacy rate, the difference in the WPR was not substantial. The overall WPR was 37.60 per cent in the slums and 35.66 per cent in the non-slums. However, gender-specific differences in participation are evident. The average female WPR in the slums (15.19 per cent) was higher than in the non-slums (12.33 per cent). Across the slums of India, the female WPR varied from 0.74 to 59.33 per cent, while the male WPR varied from 34.16 to 78.95 per cent. In contrast, in non-slum urban India, the female WPR varied from 2.81 to 46.53 per cent, while the male WPR varied from 42.12 to 75.93 per cent.

As mentioned earlier, the urban agglomerations of Chennai, Delhi, Kolkata and Mumbai account for sizeable numbers of slum-dwellers. However, narrowing the focus from urban agglomeration to the level of a municipal corporation exposes the less highlighted fact that there are large variations in the characteristics of the slum population within the wards of a municipal corporation. This is true whether we consider Chennai, Delhi, Kolkata or Mumbai (Figures 19.2 and 19.3).

There appears to be hardly any literature examining the differences in WPR within urban areas and across slums and non-slum urban areas. This is an important avenue for future research since differences in levels of literacy and WPR have implications for the levels of poverty in slums and non-slums.

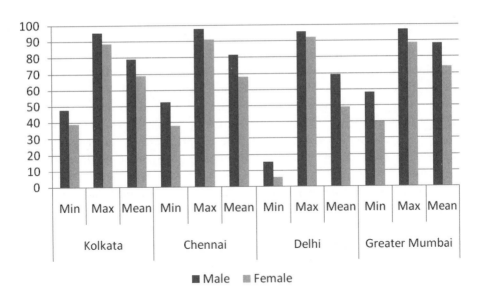

Figure 19.2 *Male and female literacy rates in slum populations residing in different wards of the same municipal corporation*

Source: Census of India (2001).

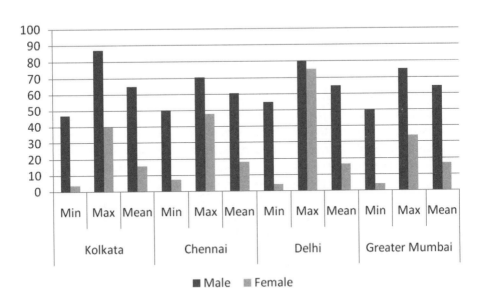

Figure 19.3 *Male and female workforce participation rates in slum populations residing in different wards of the same municipal corporation*

Source: Census of India (2001).

Peri-urban areas

In addition to focusing on the differential outcomes in slums and non-slums, attention also needs to be paid to the relationship between cities and their peripheral areas. There is considerable interest among social scientists and geographers in contrasting the outcomes in the urban centre and the periphery. Two issues emerge in this context. The first is more in the nature of taxonomy on what features characterize a peri-urban area. The second relates to understanding the rate at which socioeconomic indicators deteriorate as distance from the city centre increases.

In India, the dichotomous classification of regions into rural and urban areas does not allow for a transitional category. Dupont (2005) notes that peri-urban zones are classified as rural, and, thus, the growth of population in these peri-urban zones is not reflected in the level of urbanization. Haub and Sharma (2006) point out that, because of this definition, a significant portion of the 16 per cent of Indians living in places with a population of 5000 to 19,999 are classified as rural.

Kundu et al (2002) established that individuals in the peri-urban areas are worse off than those in the urban centre and arrived at three important findings. First, they found a steep decline in per capita income in the immediate vicinity of the urban centre. Second, there was a systematic decline in wage rates for both men and women as distance from the urban centre increased. Third, also as the distance from the urban centre increased, there was a sharp increase in infant and child mortality rates. In a similar vein, Oliveau established that the level of modernization of villages 'decreases rapidly in the first few kilometres, at a pace that is close to an exponential decrease, only to become much more linear after the 5th kilometre' (Oliveau, 2005, p51).

Livelihood issues aside, policymakers have recognized that the level and quality of civic services provided in peri-urban areas leave much to be desired. Deficiencies in service delivery are at least partly attributable to the rural classification of these areas, since often they are not viewed as the responsibility of the municipalities. This has, in fact, been recognized in some of the development plans prepared by cities covered under the JNNURM. For instance, the city development plan for Asansol, in the State of West Bengal, clearly states that 'Most peri-urban slums areas are not legally part of the cities they encircle and thus not commonly viewed as the responsibilities of municipal officials. Many of these areas are totally lacking in infrastructure for water supply, sanitation and solid waste disposal' (Asansol Durgapur Development Authority, 2006, p159). The lack of services deprives peri-urban residents of the benefit of the urban health dividend. The city development plan for Asansol acknowledges that people in the peri-urban areas suffer from the highest rates of mortality and morbidity. The city planners in Raipur, in the State of Chhattisgarh, and Vijayawada, in the State of Andhra Pradesh, have recognized that poor people living in peri-urban areas and the villages have to travel far, often to the city centre, in order to avail themselves of health facilities. However, while the problems of peri-urban dwellers are now being recognized, there are as yet few initiatives to address them.

Access to basic services

Recognizing the fact that slum-dwellers are deprived along multiple dimensions, one of the UN Millennium Development Goals (Goal 7, Target 11) aims at improving the lives of at least 100 million slum-dwellers by 2020 (UN Millennium Project, 2005). If this target is to be achieved, then significant progress will have to be made in improving the livelihoods of slum-dwellers in South Asia and, in particular, in India.

Two facts emerge from Table 19.1. The first is obvious: households residing in slums and squatter settlements are deprived of access to basic services. Only 17.6 per cent of these households have exclusive access to their drinking water source, while 65 per cent of these households use water sources that are open to the entire community. Similarly, 32.4 per cent of households do not have a latrine, and 27.8 per cent do not have drainage facilities. The fact that slum and squatter households are subject to multiple forms of deprivation is borne out by this statistic: 11 per cent lack electricity, latrine facilities and drinking water within their premises.

The second fact – that many non-slum-dwellers are also deprived in access to water and sanitation – has not been given adequate attention. While the averages clearly show that the situation in non-slum areas is better than in slums, there are nevertheless households in non-slums that are also deprived along one or more dimensions. Over 16 per cent of these households do not have a latrine, and over 17 per cent do not have any drainage. 4 per cent of households in non-slums do not have electricity, latrine facilities or drinking water within their premises.

Table 19.1 *Proportion of households having access to basic services*

	Non-slum urban	Slums and squatter settlements
Water source		
Exclusive use	46.9	17.6
Common use of households in building	26.3	17.4
Community use	26.8	65.0
No latrine	16.1	32.4
No drainage	17.4	27.8
Electricity, latrine and drinking water within premises		
Have all three facilities	63.0	15.0
Have none of these facilities	4.0	11.0

Source: NSSO (2004).

Table 19.2 *Distribution (%) of slums by change in condition of services*

	Notified slums			Non-notified slums		
	Improved	No change	Deteriorated	Improved	No change	Deteriorated
Road within slum	52.7	44.8	2.5	21.1	65.7	13.2
Approach road to the slum	51.1	46.3	2.6	40.1	56.7	3.3
Water supply	47.9	48.1	4.0	31.6	62.5	5.9
Electricity	34.5	64.4	0.1	27.1	70.4	2.5
Street lighting	39.4	59.8	0.8	22.7	77.4	2.8
Latrine	49.6	47.8	2.7	33.1	62.4	4.5
Drainage	46.6	50.1	3.3	22.5	66.3	11.2
Sewerage	23.8	71.3	4.9	41.4	54.7	4.0
Refuse disposal	5.7	88.0	6.4	15.4	76.6	7.5

Source: NSSO (2003).

Inadequate access to water and sanitation[3] implies that people living in slums and non-slum urban areas are probably missing out on the urban dividend (i.e. the benefit of improved livelihoods and health outcomes). Compared with residents of non-slum areas, slum-dwellers are more disadvantaged in terms of access to health services[4] and health outcomes.[5]

Table 19.2 gives the distribution of slums in 2002 according to whether the condition of the slum has improved, remained unchanged or deteriorated over the five preceding years. What is apparent from this table is that, except in the case of sewerage and refuse disposal facilities, the proportion of notified slums reporting improvement in services is higher than that of non-notified slums. It is widely acknowledged that the act of notification leads to improved provision of public goods, including water and sanitation.

Although the proportion of slums reporting a deterioration of facilities is not very high, there is still cause for concern about drainage, sewerage and refuse disposal facilities in both notified and non-notified slums and the condition of roads within the non-notified slums. What is of serious concern is that 94.4 per cent of notified slums have not seen improvements in refuse disposal services.

There were improvements, however, in sanitation facilities during the five years preceding the 2002 survey. Nearly 50 per cent of slums reported improvements in latrines, 47 per cent in drainage facilities and 24 per cent in sewerage. To put these numbers into perspective, the findings of an NSSO survey undertaken in 1993 (NSSO, 1997) revealed that, in the five years preceding the survey, 20 per cent of slums reported upgrading of latrine facilities and 30 per cent reported improvements in drainage, but only 10 per cent reported improvements in sewerage facilities. A comparison of results of the 1993 survey and the 2002 survey would suggest that the pace of improvement in living conditions in slums has quickened since 1993. However, it is also true that the number of slums and slum-dwellers has increased. Hence, substantial room remains for improvement.

In both the notified and non-notified slums, the Government has been the leading player in the improvement of facilities. It has initiated improvements in roads, water supply and electricity, while non-governmental organizations (NGOs) have been significant players in improving latrine, drainage and refuse disposal facilities. In notified slums, NGOs were responsible for undertaking improvements in latrine facilities in 9 per cent of slums, while residents were responsible in over 14 per cent of the slums. In non-notified slums, the residents were more active in effecting improvements compared to NGOs. With regard to the upgrading of drainage and sewerage, the residents were responsible for improvements in nearly 21 per cent of notified slums and 27 per cent of non-notified slums. The residents and NGOs were both active in improving the access and availability of electricity in the slums.

These numbers suggest that the stance adopted in the 2001 draft National Slum Policy (Government of India, 2001) of encouraging communities, community-based organizations and NGOs to undertake projects in improving access to water supply, drainage, sanitation and electricity might succeed. A community-driven approach under the appropriate supervision of local urban bodies will, over time, reduce the fiscal burden on local governments. Already, services are being contracted out to NGOs, which have led the way in maintaining pay-and-use toilets, for example.

Less than 35 per cent of notified slums have an association for improving conditions. In the case of non-notified slums, this number is much lower, at 14 per cent. There is a need to make the establishment of resident associations mandatory. A first step has been taken in the National Slum Policy, which stipulates that the formation of a residents' association or society is a prerequisite for granting land tenure. The local urban body would, in turn, recognize this association.

URBAN LIVELIHOODS

The economic growth experience of a large number of developing countries has been characterized by rising urbanization and falling poverty levels (Ravallion et al, 2007), and India has been no exception to the trend. There has been a fall in rural poverty, but it is plausible that this is in part the result of rural–urban migration. This geographical relocation of the poor implies that poverty alleviation needs to be addressed explicitly by urban planners. While the demand for labour from a growing service industry can absorb some of the migrant labour force, it might not be adequate to meet the needs. This is consistent with the slowing down in the reduction of urban poverty, and raises the need to address the issue of providing livelihoods to a growing number of the urban poor. Targeting slum populations may be the most obvious place to start, since slums are visual manifestations of poverty. However, it is not true that all slum-dwellers are poor. A survey of nine slums in Howrah, in the State of West Bengal, revealed that almost two-thirds of the total population was above the poverty line (Sengupta, 1999). A policy aimed only at slum-dwellers would thus bypass the mass of the poor living in non-slum urban areas.

Distributional analysis of outcomes in slums and non-slum urban areas

Using a nationwide survey conducted in 2002 by the NSSO,[6] Chandrasekhar and Mukhopadhyay (2007) compared outcomes in slum and non-slum households by examining the univariate distribution of monthly per capita expenditure (MPCE) and per capita area of dwelling, and also the joint distribution of public goods (rights to water source and type of drainage) and private goods (MPCE and per capita area of dwelling). They established that, if living standards are defined only with respect to public goods such as water and sanitation, then residents in non-slum urban areas are unambiguously better off than slum-dwellers. But does the same result hold for private goods?

Univariate analysis

Figures 19.4 and 19.5 plot, for slum and non-slum areas, an individual's MPCE and per capita area (PCA) of dwelling, respectively, ordered by his or her rank in the distribution.[7] As can be seen, the MPCE plots for the three locations overlap at the bottom (Figure 19.4). A statistical test of distributional dominance reveals that if the poverty line were chosen at a very low level of MPCE – much lower than the current poverty line – the poverty head count would be much larger for non-slum areas than for slum areas (Chandrasekhar and Mukhopadhyay, 2007). However, for higher MPCE levels, the slums have a larger head-count ratio.[8] Thus, where consumption expenditures are concerned, one cannot conclude that non-slum households are unequivocally better off than households living in slums.

Similar to the distribution of MPCE, the plots of per capita area for the three locations overlap at the bottom (Figure 19.5). Thus, a result similar to that of MPCE is obtained when dominance of distribution of per capita area is tested. The similarity of results of these correlated measures of consumption of private goods suggests the presence of an appreciable mass of poor people in non-slum areas. Further analysis reveals that they are distributed across both large and small cities.

Multidimensional analysis

An individual's wellbeing depends on the consumption of both private and public goods and services. Poor households suffer from multiple deficiencies, and these may or may not be correlated. An individual's access to water and sanitation may not only be a function of the economic condition of the household but may also

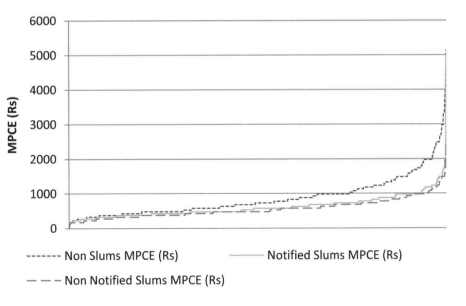

Figure 19.4 *Distribution of households by monthly per capita expenditure class (rupees)*

Source: Chandrasekhar and Mukhopadhyay (2007).

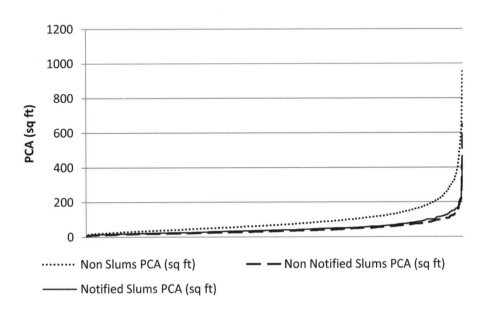

Figure 19.5 *Distribution of households by per capita area (square feet)*

Source: Chandrasekhar and Mukhopadhyay (2007).

depend more crucially upon where he or she lives. A household might not be poor along the income dimension but might live in poor quality housing. Alternatively, rich households may suffer from poor access to water, since it may not be adequately provided by municipal authorities in some urban areas. Or, a household might be poor along the income dimension and yet may have adequate access to water and sanitation.

Since an examination of univariate distributions ignores possible correlations between dimensions, Chandrasekhar and Mukhopadhyay (2007) analysed the joint distribution of different dimensions of urban poverty. In order to do this, for each location they plotted the distribution of MPCE for every type of right to a water facility: community use, common use of households in the building, and a household's exclusive use. This exercise showed that when the all-India urban poverty line is fixed at 496 rupees per month, all six scenarios are found: both poor and non-poor households access water sources which are exclusive to the household, or shared among a set of households or open to the whole community. Also, among non-slum urban areas, the distribution of MPCE of households with exclusive rights to a water source clearly lies below the distribution of MPCE of households without exclusive rights to a water source. Hence, one can infer that the cumulative density function of MPCE of individuals with exclusive rights to water source dominates that of individuals living without exclusive rights to their water source. Such a finding, however, is not true for individuals living in notified and non-notified slums. One interpretation of this is that MPCE is correlated with rights to a water source in non-slum urban areas but the strength of the correlation could be weaker in the slums compared to the non-slums.

Similarly, for each location, the distribution of MPCE for every given level of drainage (no drainage, open *katcha*,[9] open *pucca*, covered *pucca* and underground drainage) can be examined. A similar finding emerges. Once again, MPCE is correlated with type of drainage in the non-slum urban areas, but the strength of correlation is weaker in the slums. These findings (not shown) reflect the importance of analysing not only income or consumption levels but also the access to public services for households across different income or consumption classes.

LOOKING AHEAD

The need to make progress towards attaining the Millennium Development Goals has helped in articulating the size of the urban problem and estimating the resources needed in this regard. In order to meet the Millennium Development Goal of halving the population without access to water supply and sanitation in India by 2015, investments in the order of 96 billion rupees will be needed for the supply of water and 208 billion rupees for sanitation in urban areas. If the objective of providing coverage to India's entire population by 2025 is to be achieved, investments to the tune of 258 billion rupees will be needed for the urban water supply and 539 billion rupees for urban sanitation (Government of India, 2002a).

Allocation of funds aside, there are formidable logistical problems in implementing urban policy initiatives. Under the Constitution of India, issues relating to housing and urban development are assigned to the state governments. More recently, following the 74th Constitutional Amendment Act (Government of India, 1992), many issues relating to housing and urban development have been delegated to local urban bodies. Yet, to date, there has not been any systematic demarcation of the responsibilities of the various levels of government, including municipal bodies, state governments and independent agencies. What compounds the problem further is the lack of a database on municipal finances and a management information system. This hampers the ability to implement bottom–up planning starting at the ward level. More important, decisions on the assignment of the functions of each of these entities are taken independently of their revenue-raising abilities.

The heterogeneity within each city highlights the problem of using the approach of geographical targeting for any programme in urban areas. Poor people live in both the slums and the non-slums. For instance, consider the predicament of city planners in the cities of Kohima, Vadodara and Vijayawada. As mentioned earlier, the JNNURM, the flagship urban development programme, has a sub-mission aimed at providing BSUP. If the BSUP covered only slum households, then in the city of Kohima, 65.1 per cent of the population living below the poverty line would not benefit from such initiatives; in Vadodara, 16 per cent of poor people would not be covered; and, in Vijayawada, nearly 10 per cent of poor people would be bypassed (Dhar et al, 2006). However, not all cities have undertaken such an exercise. It therefore should be made mandatory for city development plans to explicitly address the issue of such exclusion errors.

Improvements in civic infrastructure will probably be easier to achieve than effecting improvements in urban livelihoods. As noted, the BSUP mission does not address the issue of livelihoods. The Government of India, however, has launched the National Rural Employment Guarantee Scheme, an ambitious programme aimed at improving rural livelihoods. The National Rural Employment Guarantee Act (Government of India, 2005) 'provides at least one hundred days of guaranteed wage employment in every financial year to every household whose adult members volunteer to do unskilled manual work'. Given that the programme has only recently been launched, it is too early to quantify its impact. In the future, a systematic evaluation would help quantify the extent to which the programme has helped to improve rural livelihoods and to reduce distress migration. Once the benefits are well understood, it might be opportune to consider whether such a programme can be launched to address the needs of the urban poor.

Given that the programme focuses on unskilled manual work, such an initiative might not work in the cities and towns where average educational attainment is higher than in rural areas.[10] But educational attainment in smaller towns is comparable to those in rural areas. Hence, a good starting point for ushering in livelihood programmes would be in these towns, and the scope of the projects could be widened to include improving rural–urban linkages. However, there is no clear-cut view on what kind of livelihood programmes could be initiated in the larger cities.

NOTES

1   Radhakrishna and Chandrasekhar (2008) have pointed to the weakening of the relationship between growth and poverty during the last decade. Their conjecture is that, since poor households lack assets such as land, capital and skills, their ability to participate and benefit from the growth process is constrained.
2   The latest census data also reflect the problems inherent in not having an accepted definition of slums and the absence of a proper listing of slum settlements in the urban offices concerned with slum improvement and civic amenities. The practice of notifying slums under relevant laws is not being followed, especially where the land involved belongs to the Government or any of its agencies. As a result of these lacunae, these data are not definitive, because towns with a population of less than 50,000 and slum clusters, which are not formally or informally recognized if the population was less than 300, are excluded.
3   Government of India, 2002a, pp45–46:

> *Water-borne diseases are caused by contamination of water with viruses (viral hepatitis, poliomyelitis), bacteria (cholera, typhoid fever, bacillary, dysentery, etc.), parasites (amoebiasis, giardiasis, worm infestation, guinea worm, etc.), or chemicals. India still loses between 0.4 to 0.5 million children under age five each year due to diarrhoea. Community studies from two urban communities have revealed that the incidence (of viral hepatitis) may be around 100 per 100,000 population.*

4   The city development plan for Raipur recognizes that in all the slums, health centres are not adequately equipped with medicines, and households have to procure them from the open market.
5   A large proportion of women in the slums did not opt for any antenatal care or had not sought the requisite three or more antenatal check-ups (Matthews et al, 2005). The higher level of unmet need for contraception in slums translates into higher total fertility rates in slums. In India, the annual growth rate of population in the large cities is 4 per cent, while it is 5–6 per cent in the slums.
6   The NSSO survey covered a total of 41,916 households from urban areas (NSSO, 2004). This data set is unique in that, unlike standard data sets that have information on rural and urban households, it identifies whether a household lives in the slum or in the non-slum urban area. This permits analysis of intra-urban differences.
7   Such comparisons require the population across the two areas to be the same size. Thus, the figure is based on a simulation of 10,000 draws from the actual distribution.
8   If a fixed poverty line for 2002 is used, then the head count ratio of poverty is lower, at 20.66 per cent in the non-slums compared to 34.23 per cent in the notified slums

and 40.62 per cent in the non-notified slums. Note, however, that more people live in non-slum urban areas than in the slums.

9   *Katcha* implies a non-concrete structure and *pucca* implies a concrete structure more permanent in nature.

10 See Kundu and Sarangi (2005) for a detailed discussion of this issue, contrasting the educational attainment of the unemployed across city size class and rural areas.

REFERENCES

Ahmed, S. (2007) *India's Long-term Growth Experience: Lessons and Prospects*, Sage Publications, Los Angeles, CA

Asansol Durgapur Development Authority (2006) 'Asansol urban area: City development plan', Asansol Durgapur Development Authority, Asansol, India

Census of India (2001) 'Metadata and Brief Highlights on Slum Population', www.censusindia.gov.in/, last accessed 11 December 2007

Chandrasekhar, S. and Mukhopadhyay, A. (2007) 'Multidimensions of urban poverty: Evidence from India', unpublished paper, Indira Gandhi Institute of Development Research, Mumbai, India

Dhar, V. K., Sen, R. and Kumar, N. (2006) 'Urban poverty alleviation Initiatives and the JNNURM: A critical assessment', NIUA Working Paper No WP 06-09, National Institute of Urban Affairs, New Delhi, India

Dupont, V. (ed) (2005) 'Peri-urban dynamics: Population, habitat and environment on the peripheries of large Indian metropolises', CSH Occasional Paper No 14, Centre de Sciences Humaines, New Delhi

Government of India (1992) *The Constitution (74th Amendment) Act*, Ministry of Law and Justice, Government of India, New Delhi

Government of India (2001) *Draft National Slum Policy*, October 2001, Ministry of Urban Development, Government of India, New Delhi

Government of India (2002a) *India: Assessment 2002: Water Supply and Sanitation*, Planning Commission, Government of India, New Delhi

Government of India (2002b) 'Urban development', in *Tenth Five Year Plan (2002–2007)*, Volume 2: *Sectoral Policies and Programmes*, Planning Commission, Government of India, New Delhi, chapter 6.1

Government of India (2002c) *National Human Development Report 2001*, Planning Commission, Government of India, New Delhi

Government of India (2005) *National Rural Employment Guarantee Act*, Ministry of Law and Justice, Government of India, New Delhi

Government of India (2006) *Towards Faster and More Inclusive Growth: An Approach to the 11th Five Year Plan (2007–2012)*, Planning Commission, Government of India, New Delhi

Government of India (2007) 'Poverty estimates for 2004–05', Press Information Bureau, Planning Commission, Government of India, New Delhi, www.planningcommission.gov.in/news/prmar07.pdf, last accessed 7 February 2008

Haub, C. and Sharma, O. P. (2006) 'India's population reality: Reconciling change and tradition', *Population Bulletin*, vol 61, no 3

Himanshu (2007) 'Recent trends in poverty and inequality: Some preliminary results', *Economic and Political Weekly*, vol 42, no 6, pp509–521

Kundu, A. and Sarangi, N. (2005) 'Issue of urban exclusion', *Economic and Political Weekly*, vol 40, no 33, pp3642–3646

Kundu, A., Pradhan, B. K. and Subramanian, A. (2002) 'Dichotomy or continuum: Analysis of impact of urban centres on their periphery', *Economic and Political Weekly*, vol 37, no. 50, pp5039–5046

Mahendra Dev, S. and Ravi, C. (2007): 'Poverty and inequality: All-India and states, 1983–2005', *Economic and Political Weekly*, vol 42, no 6, pp497–508

Matthews, Z., Brookes, M., Stones, R. W. and Hossain, M. B. (2005) 'Village in the city: Autonomy and maternal health-seeking among slum populations of Mumbai', in S. Kishor (ed) *A Focus on Gender: Collected Papers on Gender Using DHS Data*, ORC Macro, Calverton, MD, pp69–92, www.measuredhs.com/pubs/pdf/OD32/5.pdf, accessed 10 December 2007

NSSO (National Sample Survey Organization) (1996) *Key Results on Employment and Unemployment*, Report No 406, National Sample Survey Organization, Department of Statistics, Government of India, New Delhi

NSSO (1997) *Slums in India*, Report No 417, National Sample Survey Organization, Ministry of Statistics and Programme Implementation, Government of India, New Delhi

NSSO (2003) *Condition of Urban Slums, 2002: Salient Features*, Report No 486, National Sample Survey Organization, Ministry of Statistics and Programme Implementation, Government of India, New Delhi

NSSO (2004) *Housing Condition in India, 2002: Housing and Constructions*, Report No 488, National Sample Survey Organization, Ministry of Statistics and Programme Implementation, Government of India, New Delhi

NSSO (2006) *Employment and Unemployment Situation in India 2004–2005 (Part I)*, Report No 515, National Sample Survey Organization, Ministry of Statistics and Programme Implementation, Government of India, New Delhi

Office of the Registrar General (2006) *Population Projections for India and States 2001–2026*, Report of the Technical Group on Population Projections Constituted by the National Commission on Population, Office of the Registrar General and Census Commissioner, New Delhi, India

Oliveau, S. (2005) *Peri-Urbanisation in Tamil Nadu: A Quantitative Approach*, CHS Occasional Paper No 15, Centre de Sciences Humaines, New Delhi

Radhakrishna, R. and Chandrasekhar, S. (2008) 'Overview: Growth: Achievements and distress', in R. Radhakrishna (ed) *India Development Report 2008*, Oxford University Press, Oxford, UK, in press

Ravallion, J., Chen, S. and Sangraula, P. (2007) *New Evidence on the Urbanization of Global Poverty*, Policy Research Working Paper No 4199, World Bank, Washington, DC

Sengupta, C. (1999) 'Dynamics of community environmental management in Howrah slums', *Economic and Political Weekly*, vol 34, no 21, pp1292–1296

UN-Habitat (2003) *The Challenge of Slums: Global Report on Human Settlements 2003*, Earthscan, London and Sterling, VA

UN Millennium Project (2005) *Investing in Development: A Practical Plan to Achieve the Millennium Development Goals*, Report to the UN Secretary-General, Earthscan, London and Sterling, VA

20

The Urban Transition in China: Trends, Consequences and Policy Implications

Xuemei Bai

INTRODUCTION

In China, living in cities was long the privilege of a relatively small minority. As of 1980, the country had only 223 cities and an urbanization level of 20 per cent, according to official data. Living in cities meant food security, better sanitation, regularly paid employment, and access to healthcare and education systems. However, conditions have changed, and it is forecast that, in little more than a decade, more than half of China's population will be urban-dwellers. While urban–rural economic disparities may widen in some cases, living in cities no longer brings automatic benefits. This chapter examines the urban transition in China, its socioeconomic significance and its environmental consequences. It concludes with a discussion of the policy implications of urbanization for sustainability.

OVERVIEW OF URBANIZATION TRENDS IN CHINA

China has been undergoing an accelerated process of urbanization, manifested by urban population growth, expansion of existing cities and the rapid emergence of new city centres. As shown in Figure 20.1, China had 132 cities in 1949; it now has 655, according to official data. 12 of these cities have populations of over 4 million, 24 have 2–4 million, 141 have 1–2 million and 275 have populations of 0.5–1 million (National Bureau of Statistics of China, 2005a). This abrupt increase

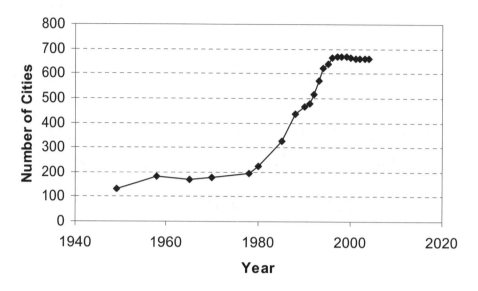

Figure 20.1 *Number of cities in China*

Sources: Data for 1949–1998 from Urban Social Economic Survey Team (1999); data for 1999–2004 from National Bureau of Statistics of China (2001b, 2002b, 2003, 2004 and 2005b).

in the number of cities – the combined product of changing classifications of urban localities and the rapid growth of population in those localities – is one of the most distinctive features of Chinese urbanization. Figure 20.2 shows the evolution of urbanization levels (the proportion of urban population to total population) in China; these have gone from 13 per cent in the early 1950s to 36.1 per cent in 2000, when the urban population reached 456 million.[1] The Chinese Government projects this level to reach 60–65 per cent by 2020, which would mean some 400 million additional urban-dwellers and a total urban population of around 900 million. If new cities were to be built to accommodate this urban population growth, about 40 new Beijings or 80 new Nanjings would be needed.

Population growth in urban China is mainly the result of rural–urban migration and the reclassification of rural towns to urban status. Table 20.1 shows the components of urban population growth in Beijing, Shanghai, Tianjin and Chongqing – the four largest cities in China. It can be seen that while the rate of natural increase is typically around 1 per cent (or even in the negative, such as in Shanghai), the migration growth rate can be as high as 13.5 per cent annually.

Historical trends

Explicit government policy on population distribution, together with economic growth efforts – promoted both by various government policies and, in more

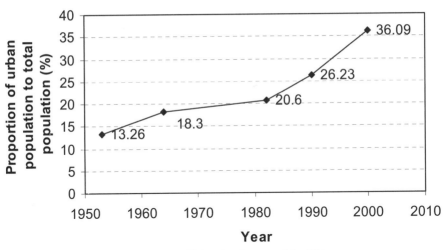

Figure 20.2 *Urbanization trend in China*

Source: Population Census Office under the State Council (2001).

Table 20.1 *Rates of natural increase in, and migration to, the four largest Chinese cities (2004)[2]*

City	Total population	Natural increase (%)	Migration (%)
Beijing	10,576,719	1.19	13.49
Shanghai	12,836,769	−1.08	8.64
Tianjin	7,664,421	0.72	5.04
Chongqing	14,811,305	0.53	2.13

Source: Institute of Population and Labor Economics (2005).

recent times, by market forces – have made important contributions to China's rate and scale of urban growth in recent decades. The interplay between these two forces, however, has varied considerably over time and can be classified into several distinctive periods.

Phase I (1949–1980)

From the time that the People's Republic of China was founded, in 1949, until 1980, the size of urban populations was strictly controlled. The new Government and the Communist Party were wary of the negative influence of Western-lifestyle cities (especially the large former treaty ports), which were perceived as corrupted. Moreover, the low level of urbanization compared to the relatively high level of industrialization, even before the 1980s, has been attributed to Mao's rural bias (Zhang and Zhao, 1999).

The most effective tool in controlling the population inflows to cities during this period was the *Hukou*, or household registration system. Under the socialist regime, urban residents needed to be registered in an urban area in order to receive government support for food, health insurance, education, housing and all other social welfare infrastructure. This system made it practically impossible for rural people to go to or settle in a city, as all essential elements of survival required the presentation of an urban *Hukou*. Since only a limited number of new registrations were issued each year, the system was effective in tying rural people to the land until 1980.

Phase II (1980–2000)

This phase was characterized by the promotion of urban development, especially in small- to mid-scale urban centres. Under this policy, small towns in coastal areas thrived and became the most dynamic elements in national development and urbanization during the post-reform era, with small-scale factories being the primary provider of employment (Lin and Ma, 1994). This was also a period in which China experienced rapid industrialization and maintained a phenomenal economic growth rate. Behind this urbanization policy was the concept of '*Li Tu Bu Li Xiang*' – meaning, leave the soil but not the village. During this period, the rapid growth of township and village enterprises (TVEs) was encouraged in order to absorb the rural surplus of labour. This rural urbanization process has been referred to as 'in situ urbanization' (Zhu, 2000). The promotion of in situ urbanization was also part of the Government's land-use policy, aimed at the reduction of low-efficiency land-use patterns by concentrating dispersed residential clusters into one town or small city. This period thus witnessed a large increase in the number of cities via the upgrading of rapidly growing towns to city status. As shown in Figure 20.2, the urbanization level in China almost doubled during this period, reaching 36 per cent by 2000, and the number of cities grew from about 200 to 660.

Phase III (2000–present)

The State Development and Planning Committee identified urbanization as one of the overarching policy issues for China's Tenth Five-Year Plan, for the period 2001–2005. Perhaps the biggest change was that the Government now clearly perceived urbanization itself as a formidable ally in economic development efforts. Consequently, it started to link urbanization policy more explicitly to its overall economic policy. The bias against large cities gradually weakened as it became apparent that, while local small cities and TVE developments were effective in absorbing local surplus labour, they lacked agglomeration and economies of scale, adequate infrastructure, and access to domestic and international markets, and they also generated negative environmental impacts. Thus a new strategy was adopted, characterized by further relaxation of the household registration system. By the end of 2005, the urbanization level had reached 43 per cent, and the total urban population had reached 561.6 million (National Bureau of Statistics of China, 2006).

Overview of government policy on urbanization

In short, explicit population distribution policies by the Chinese Government played a dominant role in guiding China's urbanization until the late 1970s. Since the 1980s, urbanization has been more closely linked to the country's increasing use of markets to help shape its economic growth (McGranahan and Tacoli, 2006). However, the role of government policy in steering the urbanization process, through various explicit and implicit policy measures, has undoubtedly remained important (Liang et al, 2002; Zhang, 2002; Guang, 2005; Zhu, 2007).

One influential aspect of government policy is the fact that, in China, the upgrading of towns to city status does not simply involve a statistical regrouping of rural populations into 'urban' localities. The transition affects the locality's social status and also entails economic, physical, socio-cultural and political shifts, as well as changes in the locality's administrative system, its infrastructure development and the Government's responsibility towards its residents in terms of service provision (Friedmann, 2005).

In the future, explicit governmental policy on population distribution is likely to play a less significant role, given the increasing emphasis on market-oriented economic polices and the relaxation of the *Hukou* system.

Economic significance of urbanization

As indicated earlier, urbanization in China has been closely linked to industrialization and economic growth, especially since the economic reforms of 1980. One of the rationales for the Government's policy was the understanding that a higher level of urbanization would maintain or even further accelerate its economic development. This rationale finds support in the figures for the urban share of GDP in China: about 85 per cent of the country's economic production is generated in cities (Roberts and Kanaley, 2006). It is widely believed that urbanization in China will accelerate economic growth through the service sectors. For example, experts identify urbanization as the driving force in economic development in the Yangtze River Delta, which had an urbanization level of 40 per cent in 2002. The delta, which accounts for only 1 per cent of China's total area, boasts a gross industrial output equivalent to 21 per cent of the country's total (*People's Daily*, 2002). The level of urbanization in China is seen as lagging behind that of industrialization, and the Government wants to bring a better balance between the two. To quote a high-ranking government official: 'Urbanization and industrialization are two inseparable wheels that carry the vehicle of economic growth' (Zhang, 2004).

Another rationale is that urbanization will create jobs, especially in the service sectors, and will relieve the pressure of rural labour surpluses. China is rapidly becoming a world centre for materials processing and manufacturing (see, for example, Xinhua News Agency, 2005), and almost all of this activity is carried out in factories located in or near cities. Many cities have experienced rapid income growth, far exceeding national averages, and both the labour-intensive materials processing and manufacturing sector and the urban services sector have become major forces in economic growth.

Spatial distribution

The majority of cities and urban populations in China are concentrated on the east coast. According to official data (National Bureau of Statistics, 2001a), 276 of the 662 major cities are in eastern China, 227 are in mid-China and 159 are in western China. There are three distinct urban agglomerations in eastern China: Shanghai–Nanjing–Hangzhou in the Yangtze River Delta; Beijing–Tianjin–Tangshan; and Guangzhou–Hongkong–Macao in the Pearl River Delta. Each of these agglomerations plays a pivotal role in the nation's economic growth.

ENVIRONMENTAL AND SOCIAL SIGNIFICANCE OF URBANIZATION

Environmental aspects

What does rapid urban growth mean in terms of the environment and sustainability in China? In addition to the traditional environmental issues, such as sanitation and industrial pollution, faced by developing countries that experience rapid urban growth (see, for example, Hardoy et al, 2001), Chinese cities also have to address high-consumption-related environmental issues with a lower level of per capita income than cities in industrialized countries (Bai and Imura, 2000; Bai, 2003). Often, the construction of basic infrastructure, such as wastewater treatment plants, cannot keep pace with urban population growth, resulting in large volumes of untreated wastewater discharged into rivers. Also, in some cities, municipal solid waste is not properly treated and disposed of, but is simply dumped on the outskirts of the city. In addition, high-consumption-related issues such as automobile pollution are adding to the already significant air pollution problems.

The amount of solid waste in China has increased significantly over the past two decades. In Beijing, the total volume of solid waste increased by 58 per cent during the 1990–2003 period, and this was closely linked to income levels (Xiao et al, 2007). There were also significant changes in solid waste composition, with higher levels of paper and other recyclables entering the solid waste stream. Before the 1980s, nationwide recycling campaigns were carried out. Each urban district or small city had at least one recycling station where citizens could deposit their glass, clothes, metals and rubber in exchange for a small amount of money. Encouraged by the Government, this campaign also brought additional income to households and schools that conducted recycling programmes.

However, with rising income levels and diluted support from central Government, recycling in Chinese cities has lost its impetus and has become an informal, ad hoc process. This is especially true among younger generations, who have little economic incentive to recycle or 'long-standing conservation habits' (Li, 2003). As a consequence, the transient population and the urban poor, who collect recyclables such as bottles, cans and newspapers door-to-door or pick them up in streets and public parks, have become the major force in informal recycling activities in Chinese cities.

Chinese cities have relatively high levels of access to such amenities as tap water, but not to other infrastructure such as wastewater treatment systems. Many cities are discharging a significant proportion of their municipal wastewater into surrounding water bodies such as rivers or lakes. The Government decreed that, by the end of the Tenth Five-Year Plan in 2005, all cities with populations of over 500,000 should have at least 60 per cent of their wastewater treated. To date, there is no official record as to whether this target was met, but preliminary evidence from different regions suggests that it has not been achieved, as investment in facilities and the ratio of functioning facilities have both fallen. Wastewater discharge from cities makes up an increasing proportion of large-scale river water pollution.

In the case of the Huaihe – one of the most polluted rivers in China – urban sewage discharge has replaced industrial wastewater discharge as the principal contributor to water pollution (Bai and Shi, 2006). Chongqing, the largest city in China, with a population of 35 million within its administrative boundary, discharges nearly one billion tons of untreated wastewater annually, most of which ends up in the downstream reservoir of the Three Gorges Dam, the world's largest hydroelectric dam (Hodum, 2007). To solve this problem, some 150 new wastewater treatment plants are to be developed along the Yangtze River by 2009; however, at the time of writing, less than half that number have been built.

Industrial pollution is an unavoidable aspect of urban life in China, and Chinese cities are often ranked as the world's most polluted. While the concentration of industries is not the sole reason for the poor urban environmental performance of Chinese cities, industries often top the list of polluters. Industrial pollution control has therefore become the focus of urban environmental management (He et al, 2002; Tu and Shi, 2006). Table 20.2 shows the industrial share of major air pollutants in China. It can be seen that around 80 per cent of total SO_2 and total suspended particulates (TSP) are discharged by industries. Recognizing the industrial share in pollution, many cities have adopted the strategy of relocating polluting industries away from the city centre. However, this relocation strategy

Table 20.2 *Major air pollutants by source (unit: 10,000 tons)*

Year	SO$_2$			Smoke dust			Total industrial dust
	Total	Industry	Municipal	Total	Industry	Municipal	
2000	1995.1	1612.5	382.6	1165.4	953.3	212.1	1092.0
2001	1947.8	1566.6	381.2	1069.8	851.9	217.9	990.6
2002	1926.6	1562.0	364.6	1012.7	804.2	208.5	941.0
2003	2158.7	1791.4	367.3	1048.7	846.2	202.5	1021.0
2004	2254.9	1891.4	363.5	1095.0	886.5	208.5	904.8
% Annual change, 2003–2004	4.5	5.6	−1.0	4.4	4.8	2.9	−11.4

Source: Ministry of Environmental Protection (2004).

does not necessarily bring about an environmental gain, since surrounding ecosystems may be even more fragile and environmental management capacity lower than in central districts (Bai, 2002).

The boom in TVEs in peri-urban areas has contributed to the worsening of urban environmental quality. Although it is well known that TVEs often operate with outmoded technology that is low in efficiency and generates significant amounts of pollution, the fact that TVEs are often small and privately owned means that they are rarely included in local environmental regulations and management systems, such as pollution levy schemes.

People move to cities in search of jobs and a better lifestyle, but while industrialization has provided jobs for newly arrived urban-dwellers, high degrees of pollution are taking their toll. For example, the incidence of respiratory diseases in cities is high, and in larger cities such as Beijing, Shanghai, Nanjing, Wuhan and Harbin, pulmonary cancer, attributed by health experts to poor air quality, has become the top cause of death (Xinhua Net, 2003; Yang, 2005). Experts also warn that the urban air pollution problem in China will continue for a long time before it is finally resolved (He et al, 2002), due to both the rapidly expanding industrial sector and the associated growing energy demands and the rapid increase in automobile use in the country (Zhao, 2006).

In addition to worsening inner-city environmental quality, rapid urbanization has also caused increasing negative impacts at both the regional and global levels. The consumption of materials and energy use have risen sharply, in close correlation with rising urbanization, and it has been predicted that China will face a long-term shortage of resources if rapid urbanization continues with the same levels of resource consumption (Shen et al, 2005). Urban sections of water in the Pearl River Delta are often more polluted than the rural sections, and thus the pollution levels seem to be strongly correlated with the level of urbanization (Ouyang et al,

2006). Although the global impacts of Chinese cities are increasing rapidly (for example, the total amount of carbon emissions from solid waste management in Beijing increased from 29.8Gg in 1990 to 84.5Gg in 2003, according to Xiao et al, 2007), integrating measures to counteract these impacts into urban management systems remains a challenge (Bai, 2007a).

Among the regional and global impacts of rapid urban development, the decrease in available arable land has particular significance for China, as urban growth converts surrounding agricultural land to paved urban use. In addition, the dumping of solid waste on the outskirts of cities has also consumed a significant amount of arable land (Chen, 2007). The central Government has established a yearly quota of four million *Mu* (one *Mu* = 0.0667ha) for the conversion of arable land to urban land use, but the actual figure from bottom–up accounts is 12 million *Mu*. This is critical because the lands surrounding cities are often the most fertile in China, and therefore this land-use change represents a greater loss in agricultural productivity than the number of hectares would indicate. As mentioned previously, Chinese cities are concentrated in the south-eastern coastal region, an area which is critical for the country's grain production.

According to the *2006 China Environmental Status Bulletin* (SEPA, 2006), 361,600 hectares of arable land disappeared in 2005, of which urban construction accounted for 138,700 hectares. Over the past five years, a total of 2.19 million hectares of existing or potential farmlands have been converted to urban developments, accounting for about half of the country's total construction area (Liu, 2006). In 2006, the estimated arable land per capita in China was less than 1.4 *Mu*, which is considered the 'redline' (Yu, 2006). There is widespread concern both inside and outside China that this might jeopardize self-sufficiency in the country's food supply and, consequently, become a new national security issue (Gardner, 1996; Liu et al, 2005). The loss of arable land has alarmed the central Government, which has decided to tighten control and reclaim authority over land development decisions from local and provincial governments.

Social aspects

Temporary residents

Part of the rapid urban population growth in China is attributed to transient populations who come to cities seeking jobs. This group of urban residents is sometimes called the 'floating population', as these individuals often do not have a formal or permanent address in the city (Liang and Ma, 2004; Li, 2006). In 2002, the floating population was estimated to be 120 million (National Bureau of Statistics of China, 2002a). Although their income levels are affected by regional disparities, the employment they find in cities is most likely to be in low-income jobs, in, for example, the construction industry and low-ranked manufacturing positions, or as maids and nannies.

Approximately two-thirds of these people live close to their place of employment, either in dormitory-style accommodations provided by their employer or in rented housing. Only 2.5 per cent of them purchase their own houses (Wang, G., 2006). They generally live in informal – and sometimes illegal – constructions, which are commonly concentrated on the boundaries between city and rural areas, lacking water supply and other public services, and more vulnerable to fire and epidemic diseases (Yang, 2006).

Child education within the floating population has become a major social issue in China. Schools often charge higher, unaffordable fees for children whose parents do not have permanent residence in the city. According to a survey conducted by the Office for the Women and Children's Work Committee of the State Council (2003), the sanitation, health and education levels of the floating population's children are significantly lower than the city averages.

Although floating populations are taking on most of the jobs that permanent urban residents are unwilling to do – and are increasingly becoming an integral part of cities – they are more likely to be perceived as a source of problems and a potential threat to urban life. Thus city governments are prone to establish regulations and fines for any misconduct associated with floating populations (Yu, 2001). There is also official discrimination in terms of employment, as many cities restrict the types of occupations that can be assumed by the floating population. They are also vulnerable to infringement of their legal rights and, as a consequence, often have their wages delayed or denied by employers (Duan and Yin, 2002).

Housing

Under the socialist system, housing was provided by the Government to those urban residents possessing a formal *Hukou*. Since the launch of the 1978 reform policy, this system has undergone a process of gradual but significant change from being welfare-based to being market-based. The Government has stopped providing housing and has sold the houses it owned, mostly to the previous tenants. Currently, the most common way of acquiring a house is by purchasing it from a commercial property developer. These developers have put a large number of new houses onto the market, but this has resulted in emerging clusters of 'different standards for different social groups' in Chinese cities. Moreover, the floating population is practically ignored in terms of housing provision (Wang, 2000).

In the case of residential redevelopment in a central area of a city, current tenants are typically given the choice of buying the new apartments, usually at considerable cost, or relocating to a remote suburb. This scenario often presents a dilemma for the less advantaged, who may be fully entrenched in the inner-city lifestyle and surrounded by all their social networks, but who often find it impossible to raise the necessary funds to secure a place in the new development.

Unemployment and urban poverty

Urban-dwellers in China are no longer guaranteed the same levels of social and economic security they once enjoyed. With economic restructuring and the reform of large state-owned enterprises, the urban unemployment rate has been growing since the mid-1990s. Official statistics show an unemployment rate of around 4.5 per cent, but experts estimate it to be closer to 10 per cent (Ng, 2003; Xue and Zhong, 2003; Liu and Wu, 2006). Cities in northern China, which served as the nation's heavy-industry base, and therefore had many large-scale state-owned enterprises, have been the hardest hit by the reforms. Workers in their forties or fifties have been laid off, many with very little or no compensation. Some cities, such as Guangzhou and Shanghai, have succeeded in creating new jobs by developing a private-sector economy, which absorbs 60–65 per cent of those who were previously unemployed (China Labour Bulletin, 2004).

FUTURE TRENDS AND POLICY IMPLICATIONS

China is experiencing urban growth on an unprecedented scale. According to the Vice-Minister of the Ministry of Construction, each year about 18 million people become new urban residents, and each year about one billion square metres of new construction takes place in cities. This rural–urban transition, which is likely to accelerate even further under current central Government policy, encompasses a number of environmental and social issues. Careful navigation through this unprecedented process is vital, as it will largely determine overall sustainability. For example, the urban forms that emerge from this enormous amount of redevelopment and new construction will impact greatly on the energy future of the country (Chou, 2004).

Judging from the evidence associated with this transformation, current trends do not appear to be on the pathway to sustainability. However, urbanization in China is inevitable. It is therefore critical to try to nudge the process closer to a sustainable path, regardless of where the current trajectory is located in the sustainability spectrum.

In this regard, there are many important questions that need resolution. For example: how will cities and their environments change over time? How will the decisions made now by cities influence their environmental trajectories and those of other regions? To what extent will policy interventions be possible and effective? These types of questions are not a matter of mere curiosity, but are being asked by practitioners seeking more theoretical guidance from the academic world.

In addition to the important task of improving urban environments and the wellbeing of city residents, it is vital that cities are encouraged to minimize external environmental impacts in their pursuit of economic growth and to promote better environmental quality beyond their boundaries. As noted, in order to enhance inner-city environmental quality, many cities are relocating their most polluting industries outside their boundaries. Although these cities are subsequently praised by the central Government for their improved inner-city environmental quality, often the only real change is that the offending industries and their associated pollution are simply moved to neighbouring cities or to surrounding rural areas. It is therefore important to evaluate whether any overall environmental improvement is being achieved and, if not, to clarify what measures need to be taken to effectively accomplish much-needed environmental progress (Bai, 2002).

It is critical to adopt an ecosystems approach in urban environmental management. Understanding that city boundaries do not represent the boundaries of their environmental impacts or decisions, and to reflect this understanding in practical terms, requires a paradigm shift in both concept and practice (Bai, 2002).

Sound mechanisms need to be developed to give environmental concerns a higher priority, especially at the city government level; otherwise the results will be unsustainable urbanization and development. For instance, the failure of the decade-long effort to control pollution in the Huai River Basin was partly due to the lack of full commitment from local authorities, including city government officials (Bai and Shi, 2006). However, in a small but positive step, environmental performance indicators have recently been included in the criteria for promotion of local officials.

Much can be learned from cities in China that have embraced the journey towards sustainability. For example, in Rizhao, a small city in Shandong Province, 99 per cent of households in the central districts use solar water heating, and the streets and parks are illuminated by solar energy (Bai, 2007b). Chongqing City has its innovative 'One-Yuan Sunshine Apartment' system, which provides cheap but quality housing for temporary workers (Wang, S., 2006). Nearly 13 billion yuan (US$1.7 billion) was invested in improving overall transportation infrastructure in Beijing during 2006. There, private automobile ownership is forecast to reach 3.8 million by 2010, but there has also been a 1.3 billion yuan (US$166 million) investment to subsidize public transportation. The system was due to start in 2007 and will reduce fares to only one yuan (US$0.13) or less per ride (Xinhua News Agency, 2007; Li, 2007).

Although many different factors can contribute to sustainable urbanization, three deserve highlighting here: leadership, information and citizen awareness. First, although unthinkable a couple of decades ago, it is not uncommon now for cities to have urban leaders who are young, who hold advanced (some even doctoral) university degrees, and who are equipped with strong environmental awareness and vision, innovative thinking, and a strong political will.

Second, the role of the media and greater information disclosure are becoming increasingly important. For example, the people of Shijiazhuang City, a city close to Beijing, were shocked to learn through the media that their city was ranked the worst in China in terms of air quality. The citizens subsequently put tremendous pressure on the mayor to take action. The mayor eventually publicly pledged significant investment and drastic actions to reduce air pollution in the city (Shijiazhuang City Government, undated).

Third, although still emergent, the rising levels of social consciousness in Chinese society, regarding both the right to a better environment and the responsibility of individual actions, will bring positive dynamics to urban sustainability. For example, in the Huaihe River Basin, one of the most polluted river basins in China, some citizens voluntarily take samples and collect evidence of illegal wastewater discharge by industry (Bai and Shi, 2006). In 2006, China awarded ten individuals with the Earth Award, one of the most prominent environmental awards in China. Among the winners was Chen Fei, a farmer from Zhejiang Province, who was fed up with the so-called 'white pollution' of discarded plastic shopping bags. At his own expense, Chen travelled to 11 cities in his province, as well as to larger cities such as Shanghai, Guangzhou and Nanjing, to present citizens with woven bamboo baskets to be used instead of plastic bags when shopping. He has also visited schools, factories and communities to deliver environment-related seminars to enhance public awareness of the issues. His initiative attracted wide media coverage and had profound impacts, including the elimination of 'white pollution' in his hometown.

NOTES

1   The level of urbanization and the total number of the urban population vary depending on the definitions of urban location and urban residence. In this chapter, the definitions and data from contemporary Chinese population censuses are used whenever possible. For further information on the varying definitions and treatment of temporary populations in statistics, see, for example, Ma and Cui (1987).
2   All data are based on city population and exclude prefecture population.

REFERENCES

Bai, X. (2002) 'Industrial relocation in Asia: A sound environmental management strategy?', *Environment*, vol 44, no 5, pp8–21

Bai, X. (2003) 'The process and mechanism of urban environmental change: An evolutionary view', *International Journal of Environment and Pollution*, vol 19, no 5, pp528–541

Bai, X. (2007a) 'Integrating global concerns into urban management: The scale argument and readiness arguments', *Journal of Industrial Ecology*, vol 11, no 2, pp1–15

Bai, X. (2007b) 'City profile: Rizhao, solar powered city', in Worldwatch Institute, *State of the World 2007: An Urbanizing World*, Worldwatch Institute, Washington, DC, pp108–109

Bai, X. and Imura, H. (2000) 'A comparative study of urban environment in East Asia: Stage model of urban environmental evolution', *International Review for Global Environmental Strategies*, vol 1, no 1, pp35–158

Bai, X. and Shi, P. (2006) 'Pollution control in China's Huai Basin: What lessons for sustainability?', *Environment*, vol 48, no 7, pp22–38

Chen, J. (2007) 'Rapid urbanization in China: A real challenge to soil protection and food security', *CATENA*, vol 69, no 1, pp1–15

China Labour Bulletin (2004) 'An overview of unemployment in China', July, www.china-labour.org.hk/public/contents/article?revision_id=18549&item_id=3700, last accessed 30 September 2007

Chou, B. (2004) 'Energy saving starts from selecting urban form', *China Economic Information*, vol 4, pp6–7

Duan, Y. and Yin, J. (2002) 'Urban floating population: Weak social group that needs more attention in social transformation era in China', *Tribune of Social Sciences in Xinjiang*, vol 6, pp38–40 and 46

Friedmann, J. (2005) *China's Urban Transition*, The University of Minnesota Press, Minneapolis, MN

Gardner, G. (1996) 'Asia is losing ground', *World Watch*, November/December, pp19–27

Guang, L. (2005) 'The state connection in China's rural–urban migration', *International Migration Review*, vol 39, no 2, pp354–380

Hardoy, J. E., Mitlin, D. and Satterthwaite, D. (2001) *Environmental Problems in an Urbanizing World*, Earthscan, London

He, K., Huo, H. and Zhang, Q. (2002) 'Urban air pollution in China: Current status, characteristics and progress', *Annual Review of Energy and Environment*, vol 27, pp397–431

Hodum, R. (2007) 'China's need for wastewater treatment, clean energy grows', Worldwatch Institute, Washington, DC, www.worldwatch.org/node/4889, accessed 8 February 2007

Institute of Population and Labor Economics (2005) *Almanac of China's Population 2005*, Institute of Population and Labor Economics, Chinese Academy of Social Sciences, Almanac of China's Population Magazine Press, Beijing

Li, B. (2006) 'Floating population or urban citizens? Status, social provision and circumstances of rural–urban migrants in China', *Social Policy and Administration*, vol 40, no 2, pp174–195

Li, L. (2007) 'Beijing gives priority to public transportation', Worldwatch Institute, Washington, DC, www.worldwatch.org/node/4895, accessed 8 February 2007

Li, S. (2003) 'Recycling behaviour under China's social and economic transition: The case of metropolitan Wuhan', *Environment and Behavior*, vol 35, no 6, pp784–801

Liang, Z. and Ma, Z. (2004) 'China's floating population: New evidence from the 2000 census', *Population and Development Review*, vol 30, no 3, pp467–488

Liang, Z., Chen, Y. P. and Gu, Y. (2002) 'Rural industrialization and internal migration in China', *Urban Studies*, vol 39, no 12, pp2175–2187

Lin, G. C. S. and Ma, L. J. C. (1994) 'The role of towns in Chinese regional development: The case of Guandong Province', *International Regional Science Review*, vol 17, no 1, pp75–97

Liu, J., Zhan, J. and Deng, X. (2005) 'Spatio-temporal patterns and driving forces of urban land expansion in China during the economic reform era', *Ambio*, vol 34, no 6, pp450–455

Liu, Y. (2006) 'Shrinking arable lands jeopardizing China's food security', Worldwatch Institute, Washington, DC, www.worldwatch.org/node/3912/print, accessed 15 February 2007

Liu, Y. and Wu, F. (2006) 'The state, institutional transition and the creation of new urban poverty in China', *Social Policy and Administration*, vol 40, no 2, pp121–137

Ma, L. J. C. and Cui, G. (1987) 'Administrative changes and urban population in China', *Annals of the Association of American Geographers*, vol 77, no 3, pp373–395

McGranahan, G. and Tacoli, C. (2006) 'Rural–urban migration in China: Policy options for economic growth, environmental sustainability and equity', Working Paper Series on Rural–Urban Interactions and Livelihood Strategies No 12, International Institute for Environment and Development, London

Ministry of Environmental Protection (2004) *China Environmental Status Report 2004*, Ministry of Environmental Protection of the People's Republic of China, available at www.sepa.gov.cn/plan/zkgb/04zkgb/ (in Chinese)

National Bureau of Statistics of China (2001a) *China Urban Statistics Yearbook 2001*, Urban Social and Economic Survey Team, National Bureau of Statistics, Beijing

National Bureau of Statistics of China (2001b) *City Statistical Yearbook 2000*, China Statistics Press, Beijing

National Bureau of Statistics of China (2002a) *China Population Statistics Yearbook 2002*, China Statistics Press, Beijing

National Bureau of Statistics of China (2002b) *City Statistical Yearbook 2001*, China Statistics Press, Beijing

National Bureau of Statistics of China (2003) *City Statistical Yearbook 2002*, China Statistics Press, Beijing

National Bureau of Statistics of China (2004) *City Statistical Yearbook 2003*, China Statistics Press, Beijing

National Bureau of Statistics of China (2005a) *China Population Statistics Yearbook 2005*, China Statistics Press, Beijing

National Bureau of Statistics of China (2005b) *City Statistical Yearbook 2004*, China Statistics Press, Beijing

National Bureau of Statistics of China (2006) *China Statistical Yearbook 2006*, China Statistics Press, Beijing

Ng, S. (2003) 'China's paradox: Growth and unemployment', *Asia Times Online*, www.atimes.com/atimes/China/EJ17Ad01.html, last accessed 30 September 2007

Office for the Women and Children's Work Committee of the State Council (2003) *Survey Report on Young Temporary Residents in Nine Chinese Cities*, Office for the Women and Children's Work Committee of the State Council, Beijing

Ouyang, T., Zhu, Z. and Kuang, Y. (2006) 'Assessing impact of urbanization on river water quality in the Pearl River Delta Economic Zone, China', *Environmental Monitoring and Assessment*, vol 120, nos 1–3, pp313–325

People's Daily (2002) 'Urbanization boosts China's local economies', 20 October, http://english.peopledaily.com.cn/200210/20/eng20021020_105382.shtml#, accessed 22 May 2007

Population Census Office under the State Council (2001) *Major Figures on 2000 Population Census of China*, China Statistics Press, Beijing

Roberts, B. and Kanaley, T. (eds) (2006) *Urbanization and Sustainability in Asia: Good Practice Approaches in Urban Region Development*, Asian Development Bank, Manila

SEPA (2006) *2006 China Environmental Status Bulletin*, State Environmental Protection Administration, Beijing.

Shen, L., Cheng, S., Gunson, A. J. and Wan, H. (2005) 'Urbanization, sustainability and the utilization of energy and mineral resources in China', *Cities*, vol 22, no 4, pp287–302

Shijiazhuang City Government (undated) www.sjzxc.gov.cn/reusable/News.aspx?id=1251&type=Newss, last accessed 7 November 2007 (in Chinese)

Tu, W. and Shi, C. (2006) 'Urban environmental management in Shanghai: Achievements, problems and prospects', *Environmental Management*, vol 37, no 3, pp307–321

Urban Social Economic Survey Team, National Bureau of Statistics of China (1999) *City Development in 50 Years of New China*, Xin Hua Press, Beijing

Wang, G. (2006) 'The characteristics and living status of floating population in China', Guang Ming Guan Cha, www.china.com.cn/chinese/renkou/1130362.htm, accessed 22 May 2007 (in Chinese)

Wang, S. (2006) 'Sunshine apartment that only charges one yuan per night for temporary workers in Chongqing', Xinhua News Net, http://news.xinhuanet.com/society/2006-06/13/content_4687563.htm, accessed 21 January 2007 (in Chinese)

Wang, Y. (2000) 'Housing reform and its impacts on the urban poor in China', *Housing Studies*, vol 15, no 6, pp845–864

Xiao, Y., Bai, X., Ouyang, Z. and Zheng, H. (2007) 'The composition, trends and environmental impacts of urban solid waste in Beijing', special issue on Monitoring Quality and Characteristics of Municipal Solid Waste in Developing Countries, *Environmental Monitoring and Assessment*, vol 135, pp21–30

Xinhua Net (2003) 'Air-quality decline: Pulmonary cancer becomes the top killer among malignant diseases in Nanjing', http://health.sohu.com/14/99/article213619914.shtml, accessed 10 October 2006 (in Chinese)

Xinhua News Agency (2005) 'China to be world's biggest auto making center', www.chinadaily.com.cn/english/doc/2005-03/20/content_426560.htm, accessed 25 January 2007

Xinhua News Agency (2007) 'Million dollar subsidy to boost Beijing public transit', 11 January, www.chinadaily.com.cn/bizchina/2007-01/11/content_780940.htm, accessed 20 January 2007

Xue, J. and Zhong, W. (2003) 'Unemployment, poverty and income disparity in urban China', *Asian Economic Journal*, vol 17, no 4, pp383–405

Yang, D. (2006) 'Urban marginalized population living in vicious conditions: 100 million peasant workers can't settle in', *China Youth Daily*, 3 April, www.cpirc.org.cn/news/rkxw_gn_detail.asp?id=6626, accessed 1 August 2006 (in Chinese)

Yang, R. (2005) 'Why large cities have higher pulmonary cancer incidence: Experts' comments on the reasons', *People's Daily*, 21 April, http://society.people.com.cn/GB/1062/3337873.html, accessed 20 October, 2006 (in Chinese)

Yu, D. (2001) 'Problems with current urban non-native population registration system and possible solutions', *Ren Kou Xue Kan* (*Population Journal*), vol 1, pp18–23

Yu, M. (2006) 'Nearly 100 million mu arable land disappeared in five years: Total area close to "redline"', *People's Daily*, 12 April

Zhang, B. (2004) 'Wang Min: Industrialization and urbanization should keep pace with each other', China Urbanization Website, operated by the China Development and Reform Committee Macroeconomic Research Institute, www.curb.com.cn/pageshow. asp?id_forum=003799, accessed 1 August 2006 (in Chinese)

Zhang, K. H. (2002) 'What explains China's rising urbanization in the Reform Era?', *Urban Studies*, vol 39, no 12, pp2301–2315

Zhang, L. and Zhao, S. X. B. (1999) 'Reconsidering the current interpretation of China's urbanization under Mao: A review on Western literature', in G. Chapman, A. Dutt and R. Bradnock (eds) *Urban Growth and Development in Asia*, vol 1, Ashgate Publishing Ltd, London, pp19–33

Zhao, J. (2006) 'Whither the car? China's automobile industry and cleaner vehicle technologies, *Development and Change*, vol 37, no 1, pp121–144

Zhu, Y. (2000) '*In situ* urbanization in rural China: Case studies from Fujian Province', *Development and Change*, vol 31, no 2, pp413–434

Zhu, Y. (2007) 'China's floating population and their settlement intention in the cities: Beyond the Hukou Reform', *Habitat International*, vol 31, no 1, pp65–76

21

Urbanization in Latin America and the Caribbean: Experiences and Lessons Learned

Jorge Rodriguez and George Martine

INTRODUCTION

In recent years, there has been considerable debate on the merits and drawbacks of urbanization. Four issues have received the most attention: To what extent is urbanization inexorable? What is the relationship between urbanization and development? What is the future of cities, particularly the large metropolitan ones? To what extent can public policy retard or reverse urban growth and urbanization? This chapter attempts to throw some light on these questions by reviewing the Latin American and Caribbean experience.

Most of the countries in the region have already gone through their urban transition. Their experience should have much to tell us about the probable trajectory of the urban transition in Asia and Africa, as well as about policies that could be applied or avoided in dealing with their urban growth processes in coming years. To this end, some of the more salient traits of urbanization in the Latin American and Caribbean (LAC) region, as well as the different attempts to deal with it, are analysed here. The last section summarizes some of the key lessons learned.

THE URBAN TRANSITION IN THE LAC REGION

Occupation of the LAC region[1] by Iberian colonists was systematically carried out from strong coastal city bases. This pattern helps explain why, in 1950, the LAC region already had a higher percentage of its population in urban areas than Asia and Africa have today. Yet the subsequent 50 years were still marked by a vigorous urban transition: the urban percentage of the LAC region practically doubled. Now, 8 out of every 10 persons in that region live in an urban area (see Table 21.1). Thus, compared to the experience of other developing regions, the LAC urbanization process happened early and rapidly (see Figure I.1 in the Introduction to this book). The continuity of LAC urbanization over the last half-century has contrasted sharply with the instability of other major processes that have marked the region, namely macroeconomic volatility, political instability and institutional fragility. Even the adoption of a neo-liberal model from the 1980s onwards did not affect urbanization's trajectory.[2]

While the validity of comparisons across regions is often questioned, due to the variable nature of 'urban' definitions over time and space (see, for example, Cohen, 2006), the evidence of high urbanization levels in the LAC region is irrefutable: 63 per cent of Latin America's population lives in cities of 20,000 or more inhabitants, a larger proportion than in Western Europe. Moreover, the share of urban inhabitants living in large cities is also very high.[3]

Approximately two-thirds of urban growth in the LAC region is currently attributable to natural increase, despite the rapid decline in fertility in most of the region, and especially in urban areas (United Nations, 2001; ECLAC, 2004). However, given that fertility is lower in urban than in rural areas, whatever increases are observed in the urban percentage of the total population (urbanization) are due to net rural–urban migration and reclassification of urban limits. Thus, policies aimed at affecting the process of urbanization have to look primarily at rural–urban migration; meanwhile, those attempting to limit urban growth have to deal primarily with natural increase.

Urban growth processes vary greatly between countries, depending on their stage of urbanization. In countries that are more advanced in the urban transition (with the exception of Cuba), cities are little affected by net transfers from rural

Table 21.1 *Growth of the urban and rural populations and evolution of urbanization levels: Latin America and the Caribbean, 1950–2030*

Year	1950	1960	1970	1980	1990	2000	2005	2010	2020	2030
Total	167,321	218,577	285,196	362,210	443,747	522,929	561,346	598,771	666,955	722,377
Rural	97,084	111,062	122,178	126,522	129,007	128,717	126,914	125,210	120,613	113,409
Urban	70,237	107,515	163,018	235,688	314,739	394,212	434,432	473,561	546,342	608,968
% Urban	42.0	49.2	57.2	65.1	70.9	75.4	77.4	79.1	81.9	84.3

Source: United Nations (2006) Tables A.2–A.5.

areas; natural increase accounts for most of the urban growth. At the other end of the spectrum, countries such as Costa Rica, Guatemala, Honduras, Panama and Paraguay owe more than 45 per cent of their growth to net rural–urban migration. Without delving at length into such national differences, it is clear that policies aimed at influencing the urbanization process must consider local specificities, components of urban growth and stages in the transition process.

The structure of urban networks in the LAC region shows the uncommon importance of large cities. In 2005, 4 of the 14 largest metropolitan areas in the world were found there, all of them having more than 10 million inhabitants. One out of every three residents in the region lives in a city of more than a million inhabitants, while cities of 500,000 or more hold 4 out of every 10 persons. This metropolitan character is associated with the high level of primacy (that is, the concentration of a country's urban population in one or two cities) in several countries of the region. Overall, however, intermediate-sized cities show faster rates of growth and account for an increasing proportion of the total urban population.

In short, the region's future will unquestionably be decided in cities. Of course, regional patterns conceal considerable diversity. These are clearly reflected in Figure 21.1, wherein the different urbanization levels of the 20 Latin American countries are classified into four categories. Most of the region, including its two largest countries, Mexico and Brazil, now has more than three-quarters of its population living in urban areas. Three Southern Cone countries (Argentina, Chile and Uruguay), along with Venezuela, have urbanization levels of around 90 per cent and 74 per cent or more of urbanites living in cities of 20,000 or more inhabitants. At the other extreme, poorer countries (Guatemala, Guyana, Haiti and Honduras) are still characterized by lower urbanization and higher demographic growth. Bolivia, Colombia, Ecuador, Paraguay and Peru are among those with between half and three-quarters of their population in urban areas.

Altogether, despite national differences, it is clear that urbanization has been rapid and generalized in the LAC region. Advances have not been significantly affected by economic, social, political or institutional volatility, nor by the switch in recent decades to a development model that has implied greater dependence on primary exports. Thus, urbanization in this region has proved to be ineluctable, resulting in a steadily growing proportion of the total population in settlements that can categorically be described as urban.

THE RELATIONSHIP BETWEEN URBANIZATION AND DEVELOPMENT

The majority of experts systematically reaffirm a close and positive relationship between urbanization and development. This section briefly summarizes some of the prevailing evidence and arguments.

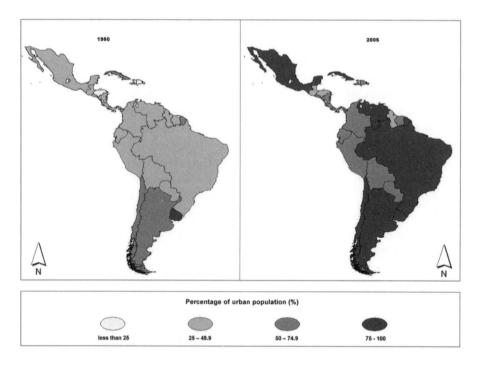

Figure 21.1 *Percentage urban of the total population in Latin American countries, 1950 and 2005*

Source: United Nations (2006).

From a disciplinary perspective, most economists find historical and practical reasons to value urbanization; they would generally support the statement that 'urbanization and economic development go hand-in-hand as a country moves from a rural agricultural base to an urban industrial base' (Davis and Henderson, 2003, p98). Sociologists tend to emphasize the association of urbanization with modernity: in ideas (such as progress, secularization, rationality, citizenship and participation), institutions (such as science, education, smaller families, democracy, meritocracy and markets), values (such as diversity, tolerance and civility) and the superior average living conditions that almost always prevail in cities. Political scientists find that better (more liberal, just and efficient) forms of exercising power tend to be associated with the physical conditions (density) and the cultural conditions (diversity, openness) found in cities. Environmentalists are increasingly discovering reasons to believe that demographic concentration can help reduce the occupation and destruction of natural ecosystems and favour the development of technological and political solutions to the environmental damage that urbanization causes (Cohen, 2006).

The foregoing does not, of course, mean that these various disciplines show undivided support for urbanization. On the contrary, all of them have particular reservations about cities. Many of these, however, are not derived from population concentration or urban density as such, but are rather associated with a particular model of society or a particular economic model.

From an empirical perspective, it is undeniable that urbanization and development are closely associated (Tannerfeldt and Ljung, 2006, p29). However, this does not necessarily reflect causality or the direction that such causality might take. Moreover, new production modalities, as well as technological advances that favour connectivity, allowing greater work autonomy and permitting people to live an urban life in a rural context, are already leading to a minor inversion of urbanization, especially in industrialized countries. Overall, however, the historical concomitance between development and urbanization is a powerful counter-argument to the many critics who have decried rapid urbanization in the LAC region.

URBANIZATION AND DEVELOPMENT: EXPERIENCES AND DOUBTS IN THE LAC REGION

Urbanization is both a consequence of and a prerequisite for economic development, which, in turn, is a requirement for reducing poverty and improving people's lives (Tannerfeldt and Ljung, 2006, pp12–13). Despite its strong correlation with development in the LAC region, however, urbanization is frequently viewed by politicians and the general public there as inimical to development. Specifically, it is argued that conditions underlying the high level of urbanization are different in the LAC region from those prevailing in industrialized countries. Several scholars have even suggested that the LAC region is 'over-urbanized' (Gugler, 1997).

No one would question that cities in the LAC region are marked by greater poverty, precariousness, insecurity and informality than is observed in industrialized countries. This, of course, reflects the peculiarities and frailties of the development process in the region, as well as its social inequalities, labour market segmentation, institutional debility and macroeconomic instability. Yet such flaws undoubtedly affect rural areas even more; hence, despite such shortcomings, cities consistently provide their populations with better living conditions on average. The real question is not whether urbanization is 'precarious' or whether the country is 'over-urbanized', but whether anything would be gained by having a less concentrated population distribution. Persistent urbanization, in spite of all the cities' problems, evidently reflects an even greater lack of opportunities in rural areas. Significant export-oriented and technology-intensive agricultural development in recent years has only accentuated this process.

URBAN CONCENTRATION, CITY SIZE AND THE FUTURE

In the LAC region, urban concentration has historically generated some concern, particularly in view of the region's traditionally high levels of primacy. The fact that these levels are observed in countries that are currently in different stages of the urban transition, as well as at different levels of development, confirms the erratic character of the relationship between levels of population concentration, urbanization and development (ECLAC, 2004).

Historically, there have been changes and inversions in patterns of concentration without reductions in the rhythm of urbanization. The literature recognizes both the overall impact of development and globalization and the role of public policies and programmes (da Cunha, 2002). Different market instruments can also affect concentration in the nodes of a system. Attempts to curb urbanization have historically been associated with authoritarian governments that attempted massive displacements – such as colonization programmes – or that violated the right to free circulation within a country.

Accelerated urbanization over the last 50 years has had its own impact on the structure of urban systems in the LAC region. Different rates of growth, expansion of urban perimeters and the multiplication of urban nodes have all contributed to this. Concentration of the overall population in the largest cities has declined since 1980. Part of this can be attributed to the 'lost decade' of the 1980s, when several megalopolises were particularly affected by the prolonged economic crisis, as well as by changes in the prevailing economic model (Guzmán et al, 2006).

Intermediate-sized cities (between 50,000 and 500,000 inhabitants) have been the most dynamic in the region, capturing a growing proportion of the urban population. This category is composed of a large and highly diversified group of cities whose source of dynamism is difficult to codify. They include border cities – such as several along the northern border of Mexico – agricultural frontier cities, cities affected by tourism, cities benefiting from the expansion of agricultural exports and others that, for diverse reasons, become nodes in a re-articulation of national city systems. Moreover, several cities have benefited from the de-concentration of economic activities from large metropolitan areas. Still others have taken advantage of the greater autonomy that the process of political and financial decentralization has given them in promoting their comparative and locational advantages within the context of globalized economic competition.

THE ANTI-URBAN BIAS AND DE-CONCENTRATION POLICIES IN LATIN AMERICA

Previous sections have demonstrated that urbanization and urban growth in the LAC region have been precocious by comparison with other developing regions and that they are enduring and largely positive. Nevertheless, both policymakers and the public have consistently decried these trends; this has led to various and generally unsuccessful attempts to halt urban growth. This section examines the anti-urban bias that has prevailed during much of Latin America's urban transition, as well as the policies that were idealized – and sometimes implemented – with the intent of reducing the growth of larger cities and of channelling urban expansion into lesser centres. It will serve as a basis for a reflection on approaches to urban growth policy in other developing regions.

The review of public or private discourse on urbanization in Latin America over the past few decades has consistently revealed a concern with rural–urban migration (da Cunha, 1980, pp11–13; Peek and Standing, 1982, pp1–2; CELADE, 1984, pp81–82; Rodriguez, 1997, p12). Now that the urban transition is nearing completion in most countries of the LAC region, does this concern with city growth appear to have been justified? On what basis? What have we learned from the region's experience about policies to retard concentration or to generally influence population redistribution? What can be applied from this experience to ongoing urban transitions in Asia and Africa?

Changing perceptions of urban growth

Undoubtedly, the prevailing patterns of migration in Latin America during the initial stages of its urban transition were rural to urban. It is interesting that, up until the 1960s, such migrations were generally viewed as favouring the economic growth of larger cities and of the countries themselves. In that framework, urbanward migration was perceived as a logical response to structural disparities between different regions, as well as a vehicle for necessary social and economic modernization in general (see literature cited in CELADE, 1994, p13).

This positive appreciation, however, soon gave way, in the 1960s, to the perception that urban growth was occurring at a pace that made it impossible for urban economies to generate enough jobs to keep up with the demand. The already significant role of natural increase in urban growth was slow to be recognized. Thus rural–urban migration, especially to the larger cities, was widely alleged to be the primary factor in overly rapid urban growth, as well as the cause of unemployment, informal occupation, growing marginality and the rapid expansion of slums (see references in CELADE, 1994). The threat of political unrest, which is harder to control when the unemployed and the poor are concentrated in urban areas, was at the root of this concern (Peek and Standing, 1982, p28). Be that as it may, blaming migration for a variety of urban ills became commonplace and, in many instances, persists to this day.

Attempts to stem the flow in Latin America

The prevailing view thus became that urbanization was advancing too quickly. This anti-urban outlook was shared by development institutions such as the World Bank, which, at the time, saw urban problems as major causative factors in economic underdevelopment (Angotti, 1987, p134). In accordance with such perceptions, politicians and policymakers in the region frequently attempted to stem the flow of migrants to cities. A variety of explicit measures, from roadblocks to integrated migration policies, have been tried at different times for this purpose.

The impacts of such efforts have rarely been significant, however, particularly since other policies substantially contributed to greater concentration and since policymakers were not particularly effective in generating alternative destinations for the productive absorption of migrants. Although the story has been repeated in many countries, it can best be illustrated with respect to Brazil, a continent-sized country that, over several decades, attempted a variety of measures to counteract urbanward migration and urban concentration.[4]

Explicit Brazilian Government efforts to intervene in population redistribution began in the 1930s, when the Government promoted the expansion of the Paraná agricultural frontier. In the late 1950s, a new capital city (Brasilia) was built with the intention of occupying the interior, changing the focus of the country's export-based economy and favouring the de-concentration of population from coastal cities. Meanwhile, however, the main thrust of government policies, aimed at industrialization and the substitution of imports, clearly favoured rural–urban migration and concentration from surrounding areas around the hubs of the new industrialization process – the cities of Rio de Janeiro and São Paulo in the south-east. Enormous migration flows from the drought-stricken north-eastern region were also directed towards these cities.

Determined attempts to reduce regional disparities were undertaken in the 1950s with the creation of Superintendencia do Desenvolvimento do Nordeste (SUDENE), a planning agency for the north-eastern region. Regional planning was further expanded under the military regime that came to power in Brazil in 1964. The reduction of migratory movements to the main cities of the south-east was a primary objective of such efforts. Despite such initiatives, however, migration to these large urban centres continued to increase, in both absolute and relative terms.

While efforts to reduce regional disparities and urban concentration were underway, the Brazilian military government also instituted a series of measures aimed at the adoption of new farming technologies and practices in the mid-1960s. Concentration of land resulted, largely from the repartition of subsidized agricultural credit among larger and titled landholders. Small farmers, who had previously constituted the large majority of producers, were pushed off the land in droves. Meanwhile, the demand for temporary labour in rural areas was heightened, while the overall stability of agricultural employment declined. A massive rural exodus resulted from these measures: between 1960 and 1980, more than 30 million people left the rural areas for the cities.

In 1970, as part of the efforts to absorb this mass of small farmers and rural workers who were being pushed off the land, the Government initiated a massive colonization programme in the heretofore sparsely occupied Amazon region. This was to be the most important explicit effort ever made by Brazilian governments to influence population redistribution. These ambitious plans, however, were soon scrapped in light of the practical problems encountered, thus failing to attain the objective of diverting migration streams away from urban areas and from the south-east region. Given the amount of direct and indirect federal investments, however, the Amazon region as a whole attracted a larger proportion of national migration flows than before, but this was still largely insignificant by comparison to the size of the flows directed to the south-eastern cities. Ironically, a major proportion of migrants to the Amazon region also ended up in cities, mostly in state capitals. Finally, rural development efforts soon opened the gates for the massive deforestation that was subsequently witnessed in the Amazon region.

Failing to stem the tide of urbanward migration, the Government turned its attention to controlling urban growth. The new military regime had created, in 1964, two national urban agencies – Servico Federal de habitacao e Urbanismo (SERFHAU) and Banco Nacional de Habitacao (BNH) – to deal, respectively, with urban infrastructure and lower-income housing. However, SERFHAU was soon found incapable of formulating and implementing an overall urban policy, while BNH was, in effect, largely appropriated by powerful construction companies catering to the upper and middle classes. A national commission for urban policy (the CNPU) was then created in 1974 within the powerful Ministry of Planning. The commission aimed at the coordination of an integrated planning system for the nine metropolitan areas and the promotion of growth in medium-sized cities. Results were again limited and dominated by powerful interest groups.

An attempt in the late 1970s to strengthen medium-sized urban centres in order to reduce both the proliferation of small cities and the expansion of south-eastern metropolitan cities was short-lived and ineffectual. Originally, some 130 cities were to be selected for programme grants, but budget constraints during the early 1980s soon narrowed them down to 26 (Gilbert, 1993, pp11–12). Half of these sites were included in the project's first phase; however, the programme's meagre results precluded its expansion to the other 13. Few of the goals were met in the first 13 cities: economic expansion was not effectively promoted and only a small number of jobs were created. Hence the cities did not distinguish themselves as new poles of attraction, and the goal of altering the spatial distribution of population was not realized (CELADE, 1984; Gilbert, 1993, p11–12).

An even more ambitious attempt to control population distribution was made by an inter-ministerial task force that, between 1973 and 1979, worked on the design of a comprehensive internal migration policy for the country. Federal attention to the migration problem had been spurred by pressures from state and municipal authorities in the region most affected by massive in-migration, namely the south-east, particularly the city of São Paulo. The gist of the complaints was that migrations, particularly from the north-east, made it impossible for local administrations to provide their people with minimum services and infrastructure. Even police barricades erected to control flows on roads leading to São Paulo and Rio de Janeiro were to no avail. Violence and crime rates in large cities were on the increase, supposedly as a result of uncontrolled urban migration, and the Federal Government was called upon to take action.

An elaborate research programme was drawn up to generate inputs for a national migration policy. This provided a comprehensive overview of Brazilian migration patterns, their causes, characteristics and consequences. Nevertheless, the results only served to highlight the complexity of the problem. The largest difficulty encountered by the task force lay in identifying the exact nature of the problem that supposedly required the formulation of a national migration policy. Issues tended to be diffuse, offering little by way of clear-cut policy alternatives. In addition, the research made it clear that migrants were acting 'rationally' in the sense that they were moving from the most depressed areas to those that offered the greatest possibility for jobs and improved wages. Moreover, it was found that migrants in large cities tended to be economically active, and that those migrants who remained in large cities for 10 or more years ended up having a superior socioeconomic status, on average, than that of native-born residents (Martine, 1979).

Such findings evidently did not favour, per se, attempts to curtail migratory movements. The principal government intervention proposed by the national migration policy involved something called 'the rationalization of the spatial distribution of population' (MINTER, 1980). This phrase was intended to indicate the need for an overall strategy for population distribution and, within this, to orient the spatial allocation of public and private investments in such a way as to expand employment and improve income levels. Ultimately, all government investments were to be screened with respect to their spatial and employment effects. Within this process, it was understood that the de-concentration of population from the southern region, and especially from their metropolitan areas, was the main priority.

This attempt to formulate an internal migration policy was one of the most comprehensive ever carried out in a non-socialist country. Despite formal approval of the policy at the highest government levels, however, it ended up having little practical effect. Several factors could be adduced for this failure, but, in hindsight, two main reasons stand out. The first was the inability to define with clarity the nature of the migration problem, or to explain what was meant by a 'better' or more 'rational' distribution of population: evidently, the nebulous nature of the problem made it difficult to propose clear solutions.

The second main reason for the failure was that the explicit policy largely ignored the importance of 'implicit' policies on population distribution. Most decisions that affect the transfer or allocation of resources end up having an impact on the spatial allocation of economic activities and, therefore, on job opportunities. Migrants, in turn, are generally looking to improve their conditions and thus respond to perceived differences in employment and income opportunities. Their decisions are what ultimately determine changes in the distribution of population over space.

The overwhelming thrust of implicit Brazilian policies, from 1950 to 1980, favoured concentration in cities. Policies aimed at import-substituting industrialization and at the modernization of agriculture had enormous impacts on the redistribution of economic activity and on population concentration. By themselves, they explain much of Brazil's rapid transition from a rural, agrarian nation to an urban, industrial one. City growth, moreover, was further catalysed by the fact that such policies were enacted at a time when population growth rates were at their highest. The various futile attempts by different government programmes to counteract such overpowering forces by technocratic decree appear, in retrospect, as somewhat quixotic.

The irony is that, while technocrats were trying to formulate a migration policy aimed at de-concentration, many industries had already started moving out of the metropolitan region of São Paulo of their own volition. The reasons for these spontaneous relocations included, *inter alia*, the need to get away from highly organized unions, as well as from increasing environmental controls and growing infrastructure problems in the capital city, and changes in technological profiles, in production and transportation technology, and in market demands. However, the demographic results of this movement were only perceived when the 1990 census results became available. That is, the time lag between the economic decisions of the private sector and their impacts on demographic processes delayed recognition by analysts of an important trend towards de-concentration (Martine and Diniz Campolina, 1997).

Consequences of the anti-urban bias

Anti-urban biases and lack of realism concerning inevitable city growth in the LAC region can be identified as primary factors in the failure to plan for, and to deal more effectively with, urban expansion. In turn, this failure has been partly responsible for the serious social and environmental problems associated with uncontrolled urban expansion in the region. The following discussion of some of these negative consequences suggests that a more positive and proactive approach would help deal more effectively with foreseeable city growth in the developing world, particularly in Asia and Africa.

In demographic terms, urban growth in developing countries is attributable, in large part, to increases in the number of poor people – through migration, natural increase among migrants after their arrival and natural increase among the native urban population (see Chapter 12). Much of the drama of urban growth in developing countries can be traced to the powerlessness of the poor to fend for themselves in land and housing markets (see Chapter 4). Much of the squalor and misery of the new urban populations stem from the fact that they are forced to live in unsuitable areas and have little opportunity to improve their conditions. This is directly attributable to the failure to recognize that the bulk of city growth will be composed of poor people, to the unwillingness to accept inevitable urban growth and, thus, to the failure to plan ahead realistically for the needs of the poor.

In Latin America, as elsewhere, millions of poor people have only been able to obtain access to land and housing through invasion and other informal settlements, particularly on steep hillsides, along riverbanks, on hazardous lands, in protected areas, or in other locales that either are not highly valued by land markets or are being held for speculation. Such squatter settlements are often illegal and precarious, but present the only option that is open to poor people, whether they are incoming migrants or expanding native families.

These informal settlements are rarely provided with water, sanitation, transport, electricity or basic social services. Normally, the resulting pattern of occupation is haphazard and asymmetrical. Thus, when slum-dwellers try to improve their conditions, or when local governments finally try to provide them with minimal services and reduce negative ecological impacts, the economic costs of doing so become astronomical. Just putting in a road for public transportation, or providing channels for water or sewerage, requires tearing down existing constructions (Hardoy et al, 1992, p34). The lack of planning and access roads, inadequate location of housing and the sheer accumulation of miserable conditions make it practically impossible to provide services or redress the accumulated ecological damage *a posteriori*.

Improving access to land and housing for the growing contingents of the urban poor would require a proactive attitude that is rarely found in practice. The traditional negative stance towards urban growth has prevented an effective approach to dealing with the needs of the poor. The failure to plan ahead for the accommodation of poor people has also contributed to the ecological degradation of the cities themselves. In the future, moreover, such conditions are sure to become much worse, since many options previously available to low-income urban populations are disappearing. That is, overall urban growth and mounting land prices serve to further diminish residential options for new urbanites.

CONCLUSION: LESSONS FOR ONGOING URBAN TRANSITIONS IN ASIA AND AFRICA

The previous sections have indicated that the urban transition in the LAC region has, on the whole, been both inevitable and positive for development. They have also shown that the ineluctable urbanization process in the region has resisted both the vagaries of social, political and economic upheavals and the efforts of governments to retard or reverse them. These findings would appear to have considerable significance for Asia and Africa, which still have a large majority of their populations in rural areas and where many policymakers still tend to view urbanization as a negative force, despite its probable inevitability under globalized economic competition. The following lessons learned from the LAC region's experience appear relevant in this context:

- Influencing the distribution of population over space may be justifiable for economic, environmental or social reasons. However, this requires a clear, consensual and justifiable definition of existing problems and of the intended 'better' distribution of population over space in a given country or region. Instinctive anti-urban or anti-concentration sentiments are a poor basis for such initiatives. What constitutes an 'optimal' or 'excessive' concentration is, at best, time-bound and country-specific.
- The impacts of implicit policies currently affecting population distribution and concentration have to be taken into consideration before explicit policies are launched. Implicit policies tend to reflect the overall thrust of development efforts and greatly influence the location of economic activities and population.
- Explicit redistribution policies are only effective if they do not run counter to economic logic. Thus, Brasilia was constructed in the late 1950s at an enormous cost to the country, but it only began to have a noticeable impact on population redistribution more than a decade later, when economic expansion into the vast interior hinterland became economically viable (Martine, 1992, pp209–210).
- Although urban concentration greatly increases the visibility and political volatility of poverty, it has clear-cut advantages over dispersion. Cities are better able to take advantage of the opportunities offered by the global market, thus generating jobs and income for a larger number of people. They are also better able to provide social services and amenities to a larger proportion of the population, because of the advantages of scale and proximity. Cities help accelerate fertility decline and can potentially be a powerful ally to sustainability.
- The very notion that urbanward migration and urban growth can be stopped or significantly slowed is untenable in light of the historical experience. Under globalization, the anti-urban bias, per se, is even more futile.
- It is critical to understand that a large proportion of the people who will contribute to future urban growth – whether through migration or natural increase – are poor. Many of the social problems associated with cities could be reduced through more proactive planning for the needs of the poor, particularly as concerns minimally serviced land, and better urban governance.
- Planning for the land needs of the poor is critical, but it is only one aspect of the broader and critical issue of land use. Left to its own devices, urban expansion, especially in Asia and Africa, will sprawl over lands rich in biodiversity or

agricultural soils, degrade water sources, deforest hinterlands, contaminate soils, and saturate local capacities for absorbing solid waste.

Overall, an effective approach to inevitable urban growth is a proactive one, steeped in the realities of economic growth efforts. Rather than attempting to impede or retard the growth of cities, a proactive stance should be taken in order to minimize the negative consequences and to enhance the positive aspects. This requires vision and a permanent concern with both poverty reduction and environmental sustainability.

NOTES

1   In this chapter, the denomination 'Latin America and the Caribbean' refers to the 42 states and countries located on the American continent (excluding the US and Canada) and in the Caribbean. 'Latin America', in turn, refers to the 20 countries that ECLAC has identified as belonging to that subregion. For further details, see www. cepal.org/celade.
2   Many people predicted, wrongly, that the erosion of urban industrial activities and the resurgence of the primary sector would stagnate or reverse urbanization under this model (see Rodriguez, 2004).
3   For more information, see www.eclac.cl/celade/depualc, last accessed 12 October 2007.
4   The following analysis of Brazilian population redistribution policies is based on Martine (1992 and 1993).

REFERENCES

Angotti, T. (1987) 'Urbanization in Latin America: Towards a theoretical synthesis', *Latin American Perspectives*, vol 14, no 2, pp134–156

CELADE (1984) 'Políticas de redistribución de la población en América Latina', *Notas de Población*, año 12, no 34, pp79–114

CELADE (1994) 'Dinamica de la población de las grandes ciudades en América Latina y el Caribe', in *Grandes Ciudades de America Latina: Dos Capítulos*, CELADE, Santiago de Chile

Cohen, B. (2006) 'Urbanization in developing countries: Current trends, future projections and key challenges for sustainability', *Technologies in Society*, vol 28, no 2, pp63–80

da Cunha, J. M. P. (1980) *Redistribución Espacial de la Población en América Latina*, Serie Población y Desarrollo No 30, CELADE, Santiago

da Cunha, J. M. P. (2002) *Urbanización, Territorio y Cambios Socioeconómicos Estructurales en América Latina y el Caribe*, Serie Población y Desarrollo No 30, CELADE, Santiago de Chile

Davis, J. C. and Henderson, J. V. (2003) 'Evidence on the political economy of the urbanization process', *Journal of Urban Economics*, vol 53, no 1, pp98–125

ECLAC (2004) *Panorama Social de América Latina 2004*, United Nations Publication No LC/G.2259-P, Economic Commission for Latin America and the Caribbean, Santiago

Gilbert, J. (1993) 'Middle-sized cities, basic sanitation and quality of life: Planning for Brazil's growing population centres', Working Paper No 28, Instituto Sociedade População e Natureza, Brasília

Gugler, J. (1997) 'Over-urbanization reconsidered', in J. Gugler (ed) *Cities in the Developing World: Issues, Theory and Policy*, Oxford University Press, New York, pp114–123

Guzmán, J. M., Rodriguez, J., Martínez, J., Contreras, J. M. and González, D. (2006) 'La démographie de l'Amerique Latine et de la Caraïbe depuis 1950', *Population-F*, vol 61, nos 5–6, pp621–733

Hardoy, J., Mitlin, D. and Satterthwaite, D. (eds) (1992) *Environmental Problems in Third World Cities*, Earthscan, London

Henderson, V. (2000) 'How urban concentration affects economic growth', Policy Research Working Paper No 2326, World Bank, Washington, DC

Martine, G. (1979) 'Adaptation of migrants or survival of the fittest? A Brazilian case', *The Journal of Developing Areas*, vol 14, no 1, pp23–41

Martine, G. (1992) 'Population redistribution and state policies: A Brazilian perspective', in C. Goldscheider (ed) *Migration, Population Structure and Redistribution Policies*, Westview Press, Boulder, CO, pp207–228

Martine, G. (1993) 'The phases of agricultural modernization in Brazil', in G. D. Ness, W. D. Drake and S. R. Brechin (eds) *Population–Environment Dynamics: Ideas and Observations*, The University of Michigan Press, Ann Arbor, MI, pp167–186

Martine, G. and Diniz Campolina, C. (1997) 'Economic and demographic concentration in Brazil: Recent inversion of historical patterns', in G. W. Jones and P. Visaria (eds) *Urbanization in Large Developing Countries: China, Indonesia, Brazil and India*, Clarendon Press, Oxford, UK, pp205–227

MINTER (1980) 'Programa Nacional de Apoio às Migrações Internas', Ministério do Interior, Brasília

Peek, P. and Standing, G. (eds) (1982) *State Policies and Migration: Studies in Latin America and the Caribbean*, Croom Helm, London

Rodriguez, J. (1997) 'Migracion hacia las ciudades', paper prepared for the 'Municipalities and overcoming urban poverty in Latin America and the Caribbean' seminar, Quito, October

Rodriguez, J. (2004) *Migración Interna en América Latina y el Caribe: Estudio Regional del Período 1980–2000*, Serie Población y Desarrollo No 50, CELADE, Santiago de Chile

Tannerfeldt, G. and Ljung, P. (2006) *More Urban, Less Poor: An Introduction to Urban Development and Management*, Swedish International Development Cooperation Agency and Earthscan, London

United Nations (2001) *The Components of Urban Growth in Developing Countries* (ESA/P/WP.169), Population Division, United Nations, New York

United Nations (2006) *World Urbanization Prospects: The 2005 Revision*, Population Division, New York

Index

Page numbers in *italic* refer to Boxes, Figures and Tables. Ranges of page numbers in *italic* signify that one or more illustrations appears on each page in the range, inclusive.